An Introduction to the History of Christianity

From the Early Church to the Enlightenment

GEORGE HERRING

continuum
LONDON • NEW YORK

Continuum International Publishing Group

The Tower Building, 11 York Road, London SE1 7NX

80 Maiden Lane, Suite 704, New York NY 10038

www.continuumbooks.com

First published 2006

British Library Cataloguing-in-Publication Data
A catalogue record for this book is available from the British Library.

ISBN: 0–8264–6737–7

Typeset by Kenneth Burnley, Wirral, Cheshire
Printed and bound in Great Britain by MPG Books Ltd, Bodmin

CONTENTS

Preface   xi
Acknowledgements   xv

Introduction: Making All Things New   1

Part One   Christ and Caesar: Christianity *c*. 300–*c*. 500

1 Imperial Christianity   47
2 City and Desert   67
3 The Great Debate   86
4 The African Pilgrim   106

**Part Two   Expansion and Order: Latin Christendom
c. 1050–*c*. 1250**

5 Roads to Canossa   129
6 Keepers of the Keys   150
7 The Enthusiasts   178

**Part Three   Grace and Authority: Western Christianity
c. 1450–*c*. 1650**

8 Reformations   225
9 Diversity Becomes Division   251
10 Divine Winds and Interest Rates   295

Epilogue: Loss and Gain   311

Appendix: Documents   319
Notes   335
Index   355

For Catherine

Cor ad cor loquitur

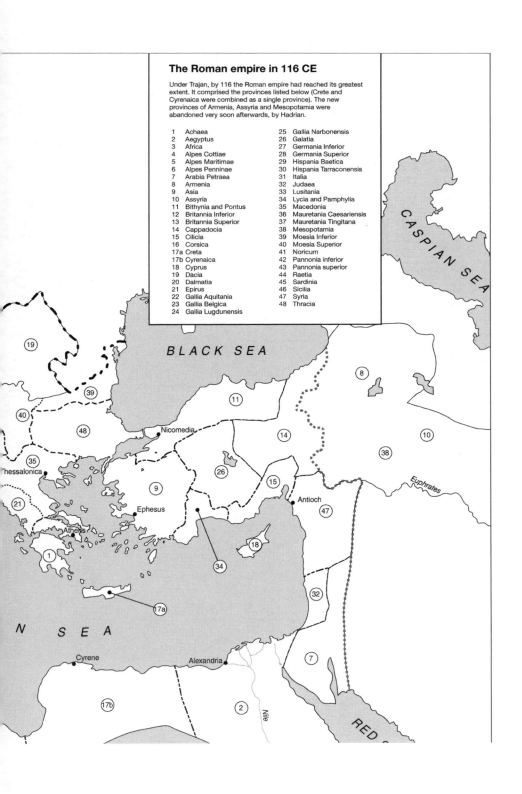

The Roman empire in 116 CE

Under Trajan, by 116 the Roman empire had reached its greatest extent. It comprised the provinces listed below (Crete and Cyrenaica were combined as a single province). The new provinces of Armenia, Assyria and Mesopotamia were abandoned very soon afterwards, by Hadrian.

1	Achaea	25	Gallia Narbonensis
2	Aegyptus	26	Galatia
3	Africa	27	Germania Inferior
4	Alpes Cottiae	28	Germania Superior
5	Alpes Maritimae	29	Hispania Baetica
6	Alpes Penninae	30	Hispania Tarraconensis
7	Arabia Petraea	31	Italia
8	Armenia	32	Judaea
9	Asia	33	Lusitania
10	Assyria	34	Lycia and Pamphylia
11	Bithynia and Pontus	35	Macedonia
12	Britannia Inferior	36	Mauretana Caesariensis
13	Britannia Superior	37	Mauretana Tingitana
14	Cappadocia	38	Mesopotamia
15	Cilicia	39	Moesia Inferior
16	Corsica	40	Moesia Superior
17a	Creta	41	Noricum
17b	Cyrenaica	42	Pannonia inferior
18	Cyprus	43	Pannonia superior
19	Dacia	44	Raetia
20	Dalmatia	45	Sardinia
21	Epirus	46	Sicilia
22	Gallia Aquitania	47	Syria
23	Gallia Belgica	48	Thracia
24	Gallia Lugdunensis		

CASPIAN SEA

BLACK SEA

Nicomedia

Thessalonica

Ephesus

Athens

Antioch

Euphrates

Cyrene

Alexandria

Nile

N   S E A

RED

Europe at the time of the Reformation

The distribution of Reformation churches is indicated by shading:

Anglican

Lutheran

Calvinist

A mixture of Catholic, Lutheran and Calvinist

The area of the Roman Catholic Church is left unshaded.
Many of the Reformers were, of course active in more than one place; for the sake of simplicity a main scene of their activity has been chosen.

1   Amsterdam: (Jacobus Arminius ♟)
2   Augsburg: Diet of Augsburg 1530 receives Augsburg Confession; Peace of Augsburg 1555 recognizes Lutheranism
3   Basle: (Erasmus♟; John Oecolampadius)
4   Cambridge: (Martin Bucer ♟)
5   Canterbury: (Thomas Cranmer♟)
6   Cracow: Socinians (Fausto Sozzini 1538–1604)
7   Edinburgh: (John Knox♟)
8   Frankenhausen: Peasants war ends with death of Thomas Müntzer ♟
9   Geneva: (William Farel 1489–1566; John Calvin♟; Theodore Beza 1519–1605; Michael Servetus burnt at stake 1553
10 London: Henry VIII becomes head of the Church of England 1534 (Nicholas Ridley ♟, Richard Hooker ♟)
11 Magdeburg: Magdeburg Centuriators, Lutheran authors of a church history to 1400, covered by centuries, written 1559–74
12 Marburg: seat of Philipp, Landgrave of Hesse, a vigorous defender of Protestantism; Colloquy of Marburg 1529 seeks to achieve union between Lutherans and Zwinglians
13 Münster: 'Kingdom of David' proclaimed by Anabaptists 1534–5
14 Nantes: Edict of Nantes 1598 grants rights to the Huguenots
15 Naples: (Juan Valdes 1500–41, Catholic reformer)
16 Paris: Robert Estienne prints Bibles; later moves to Geneva and becomes a Calvinist
17 Regensburg (Ratisbon): Reunion conference of Protestant and Catholic theologians 1541; this failed because of the opposition of Luther
18 Rome: (Julius II, Leo X, Paul III, Pius IV the most important popes in Reformation and Counter-Reformation)
19 Seville: Spanish Inquisition (Tomas Torquemada♟)
20 Siena: (Bernardino Ochino 1487–1564, Franciscan turned Protestant reformer)
21 Speyer: Diet of Speyer 1526 suspends Edict of Worms
22 Strassburg: (Martin Bucer ♟)
23 Toledo: (Francisco Ximénez de Cisneros♟)
24 Trent: Council 1545–63
25 Warsaw: Warsaw Confederation 1573 marks the beginning of religious freedom in Poland
26 Wittenberg: (Martin Luther ♟, Philipp Melanchthon ♟)
27 Worcester: (Hugh Latimer 1485–1555, John Hooper c.1495–1555, bishops, English reformers)
28 Worms: Edict of Worms 1521 condemns Lutheranism
29 Zurich: (Huldrych Zwingli ♟, Heinrich Bullinger ♟)
30 Zwickau: The Zwickau Prophets, an early Anabaptist group
31 Denmark-Norway (at the time the two were one kingdom): Reformation introduced 1536 (Johann Bugenhagen 1485–1558)
32 Finland: Reformation introduced 1540s (Michael Agricola)
33 Sweden: Reformation introduced 1527 (Olavus Petri 1493–1552 and his brother Laws 1499–1573)
34 Moravia: Hutterites (Jacob Hutter ♟)
35 Netherlands: Mennonites (Menno Simons ♟)

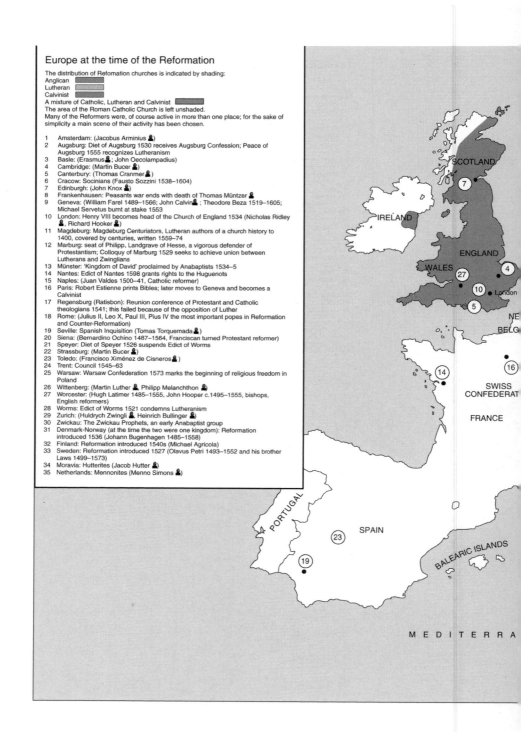

PREFACE

This book is very much the fruit of a quarter of a century of teaching. However, it is intended to be rather more than just an undergraduate textbook. While I hope that those studying history or theology at universities will find it useful as an introduction to some key periods and aspects of Church history, I also hope that it will be appreciated by a much wider readership. With that in mind, and because I know from personal experience that many people approaching the history of Christianity for the first time will come with little knowledge of the beliefs or practices of the faith, I have assumed only the most basic of understanding on the part of the reader opening this book.

At the same time, it approaches Christian history in ways that are perhaps unfamiliar to undergraduates. First of all, whatever else it is, this book is certainly not a comprehensive history of the religion. It is intended to be no more than an introduction. As such it looks in detail at three 200-year periods, preceded by an Introduction; this examines the first three centuries of Christianity, as I believe that at least a basic understanding of the origins and first generations of the religion are fundamental to appreciating its later periods. So much of what was to prove crucial in Church history is there, at least implicitly, in this formative period.

With that in mind, the other difference from standard textbooks is the questions that I examine here. Obviously the book will analyse the developing beliefs, practices, organization and propagation of the faith; but beyond that it explores what Christians have meant when they have used words like 'authority', 'tradition', 'reform' or 'hierarchy'. The Christian understanding of these words is not always the same as the conventional, secular meanings. And that raises the further question of how Christianity relates to the various cultures it has found itself in over the past two millennia.

Christianity, as it has often been said, is an historical religion. It believes that God himself entered time and space in the form of a human being. Divinity has become enmeshed in the processes of human history, and accepted their limitations. But that also implies that this is a religion to which history, in the meaning of the academic discipline, can legitimately be applied in order to achieve greater understanding of how those limitations have affected the faith. Christians have a unique relationship with their own past; it is, for them, as much a spiritual as an intellectual experience. So, for instance, 'tradition' does not mean for Christians what it can mean for others, the dead weight of the past holding them back in the present, but rather a huge resource for both the present and the future. Their past is a treasure store of potential inspiration and hence innovation for Christians, and so leads into that other key word: 'reform'. Christianity exists to change people, and through them the world which they inhabit. It will become clear from reading this book that my view of the Christian faith is that it is dynamic, and that that dynamism is exemplified in its history.

Christianity sees itself as having a prophetic role. But does that mean that Christians should insulate themselves from the world around them, or go out and embrace it? This was a dilemma faced by those first generations in the faith. Generally speaking, most mainstream forms of Christianity have taken the latter view on the assumption that humanity and creation are essentially good as they come from God, and that despite their obvious imperfections, limitations and frustrations they retain a basic predisposition to goodness. Thus ideas, philosophies and other concepts developed by non-Christian societies may contain truths that can legitimately be assimilated by the Christian faith, in the belief that everything that is true has its points of origin and culmination in God. Many early Christians were to argue that the cultures of ancient Greece and Rome found their own true ends in Christianity. Thus Christianity should not only challenge the world in which it finds itself at any given point in time, but it should also grow with it. This religion has been at its most fruitful when it has been able to hold these two seemingly contradictory positions in a positive tension.

Christians, however, are no more morally nor intellectually perfect than any other human beings. As we shall discover, even canonized saints fall short in those regards. And here we find another characteristic of Christian history that will be explored in this book. Nobody has put it more succinctly than St Paul in the passage quoted at the beginning of this book. God is believed by Christians to have revealed the greatest of all treasures, the true knowledge of himself as shown in his Son; but that treasure has been entrusted to 'earthen vessels'. This is the consequence of the limitations accepted willingly by divinity in working through his own fallible creatures. Individual Christians, the institutions they create or the language they use to try to understand this heavenly treasure, all share common weaknesses, vulnerabilities and imperfections. Because human beings are seen to be fallible creatures, marred by what theologians call original sin, neither they nor their own creations will ever be perfect. Christians are always going to have to live with an imperfect faith that is necessarily part of an imperfect world.

In all of this, however, there lies a trap for the unwary. Some Christians may find it tempting to try to escape from the frustrations of the present by retreating into what they might incorrectly see as a more comfortable 'golden age' located somewhere in the past. The problem with this is that for Christians Christianity's 'golden age' is always in the future; it will arrive only when Jesus himself returns. History is for Christians not there to escape into, but rather to be used as a resource to revivify the present and energize the future. For Christianity, re-formation is a continuous individual and institutional process. So, in my view, groups that may appear at first sight to be at opposite ends of the Christian spectrum in terms of their beliefs and practices may, on closer inspection, have much more in common with each other in that they both share this mistaken view. Some Evangelical Protestants who seek a literal realization of the New Testament in the contemporary world, or some Roman Catholics who regard the Tridentine Mass of 1570 as the epitome and high-water mark of eucharistic worship, both misunderstand Christian tradition. Christianity is never static, and Christianity as a faith tradition is not positioned to rest in some imagined time of perfection or purity from which later ages have declined. It looks backwards in order to move forwards.

From what I have said already it should be clear why this is a book intended for a wider audience than just undergraduates. It is also written for those outside of academia interested in Christianity as a historical religion, whether they are religious themselves or not. If your reading about Christian history has so far been limited to the fictions of *The Da Vinci Code*, then it is my firm belief that you will find the reality infinitely more interesting.

Following the Introduction I have organized this book into three main chronological periods. Then within each of these the various chapters examine a specific aspect of the historical experience of Christianity, whether that is achieved through looking at institutions, theological ideas or particular individuals. All the chapters are themselves further divided by a number of headings. It is designed to be read progressively from the beginning; so even if your main interest is the Reformation of the sixteenth century you will find that reading the earlier chapters first will illuminate the later period. It is also intended to build knowledge in a cumulative way. Old problems have a habit of recurring in new forms, so I have assumed that readers have understood the explanation of the original guise in which such a problem, idea or technical term first appeared and will therefore not require subsequent explanation. Each chapter also has a 'Suggested Further Reading' section at the end. I decided to adopt this method rather than just put an alphabetical bibliography at the end of the book as I think it will be of more help to readers who wish to pursue a particular period or aspect of Christian history in more depth. I have made some comments about some of the books which I hope will also be useful, and in some cases have suggested an order in which I think they should be read. Towards the end of the book is an Epilogue which makes some observations on Christianity in the modern world. There is also a short collection of Documents as an Appendix. Like the main part of the book, these are not intended to be in any sense comprehensive, or even representative. They are passages that can either illustrate a point I have made in the main text, or include a piece of writing that I discuss there but which would be too long to place at that point.

In selecting this method of approach I am aware of what has been left out. At the same time I am also conscious of a certain element of self-indulgence on my part; I have generally written about things which particularly interest me, in the hope that they will also interest the reader. There has been an inevitable compromise between covering enough in sufficient detail, without trying to cover everything in the same detail, in order to keep this book within manageable limits. I fear that some readers will think it too short, while others will consider it far too long. I just hope that most will think I have got it about right.

ACKNOWLEDGEMENTS

In writing this book I have incurred many debts of gratitude. Perhaps the first is to those many students who have over the years listened to me, discussed and sometimes challenged what I have had to say when attempting to teach Church history. If any of my former students should happen to read this book they may well notice some familiar phrases or ideas. But in keeping with the intended audience for this book I must also thank those many people I have also taught outside the sphere of higher education. This must include all those groups of parishioners from a variety of churches and denominations who have invited me to come to talk to them over the years. More recently others, such as the Pickering branch of the Workers' Educational Association (WEA) who have been kind enough to allow me to try out, as it were, some sections of this book on them. All of these experiences have, I hope, been synthesized into the final product.

I also owe a debt of gratitude to a number of former colleagues and friends. Here I would like to express my especial thanks to Dr Robert Whiting with whom I shared the teaching of Church history in the years when I taught in what is now York St John College. I have lost count of the conversations over innumerable lunches or cups of tea that I have had with Bob, turning over with him some issue or other of Christian history, let alone the hours we have spent together in the classroom. They were always a pleasure, unfailingly illuminating, and a living proof that individuals who come from what might appear to be quite opposed Christian backgrounds can actually co-operate, if not always agree, much to their mutual advantage. Although no longer colleagues, I am pleased to say that we remain friends.

Among my many clerical friends who have been kind enough to help me in so many ways, both academically and spiritually, I would like to mention first the Rt Revd Dr Geoffrey Rowell, my former supervisor at Keble, and now the Bishop of Gibraltar in Europe. Despite his hectic schedule caring for the 250 or so Anglican Chaplaincies spread across Europe, he was able to find the time to read and comment on some of the earlier sections of this book. So too did the Revd John Bailey who read theology at Keble at the same time that I was doing my doctoral research there and is now an Archdeacon in Canada; Revd Daniel O'Leary, the former parish priest of Ripon and a well-known and much respected spiritual writer; and Revd Eamon McGeough, currently a school chaplain in North Yorkshire. I would like to thank all of them for their time and helpful comments. At a greater distance now in my own personal history, Timothy Ware, then the Archimandrite Kallistos, delivered a truly inspirational series of lectures on early christology which I was privileged to attend at Oxford in the 1970s. It was one of my first encounters with the early Church, and one that I shall always treasure. More recently, Professor Averil Cameron, the present Warden of Keble, gave me the benefit of her enormous expertise in that same field of early Church history during an extensive and fascinating conversation. Needless to say, however, I remain responsible for all of the opinions and interpretations presented in this book.

I think it goes without saying that no single individual could possibly have anything that remotely approaches a level of expertise in all the periods and aspects of Church history that I have covered in this book. My own period of research is nineteenth-century English Church history, as my previous book on the Oxford Movement would indicate. I thus owe a further debt of gratitude to all the many scholars whose own books I have read over the years. One of my intentions in writing this book was to make known to a wider audience the vast wealth of modern scholarship on Church history. Where appropriate, therefore, I have discussed contemporary revisions of past concepts during the course of the book.

As I no longer have a permanent attachment to a particular university, I have borrowed considerable numbers of books through the inter-library loan service provided by the Ripon branch of the North Yorkshire County Library Service for the research for this book. I have renewed acquaintance with some old friends, and made a number of new ones, in the form of the books I have borrowed in this way. I would like to thank the staff for their unfailing efficiency and courtesy. At my publishers, Continuum, Robin Baird-Smith and Ben Hayes have been both extremely patient in waiting for this book to be delivered, and also most helpful in matters such as style and presentation.

I would like to thank my family for their patience and encouragement. The dedication of the book to my wife, Catherine, herself both a history graduate and a teacher of Religious Studies, will, I hope, indicate the much more than mere gratitude that I owe to her in this as in all things. My children, Eleanor and Edward, have shown great understanding and forbearance during the writing of this book.

And finally, I would like to thank an unknown lady. About twenty years ago I turned on the radio to wait for the news a few minutes before it was due to be broadcast, and while I waited I listened to her as she recounted part of the story of her recent trip to Asia. She was obviously an intelligent, well-educated and articulate young woman who told her interviewer that she had gone in search of the mysticism of the East. My jaw fell, however, when she solemnly informed the interviewer and listeners that she had been forced to make this long journey of discovery as no mystical tradition of any kind existed in the West. I don't know which surprised me more: her assertion or the interviewer's failure to challenge it. If this book has a precise if distant point of origin it was then. I can only hope that she may come across this book in a shop or library, read it, and finally learn that Christianity possesses one of the richest mystical and spiritual traditions of any religion anywhere in the world. It was always there, waiting to be discovered, and it still is.

The author and publishers would like to thank the following copyright holders for permission to reproduce material:

Oxford University Press for extracts from: *Documents of the Christian Church*, selected and edited by Henry Bettenson and Chris Maunder, third edition, 1999, pp. 72–3; *Eusebius; Life of Constantine*, translated by Averil Cameron and Stuart Hall, 1999, pp. 80–1; *St Augustine: Confessions*, translated by Henry Chadwick, 1991, pp. 72–3; *Pope Gregory VII 1073–1085* by H. E. J. Cowdrey, pp. 140–1.

Penguin Books for extracts from: *Eusebius: The History of the Church from Christ to Constantine*, translated by G. A. Williamson and revised and edited by Andrew Louth, 1989, p. 237; *Early Christian Writings: The Apostolic Fathers*, translated by Maxwell Staniforth with new editorial material by Andrew Louth, 1987, pp. 62, 72, 74, 80, 93, 94, 103; *Augustine: Concerning the City of God Against the Pagans*, translated by Henry Bettenson, 1972, pp. 593–4; *The Cistercian World: Monastic Writings of the Twelfth Century*, 1993, pp. 69–71; *Thomas Aquinas: Selected Writings*, translated by Ralph McInery, pp. 619–20.

Taylor & Francis for an extract from: *Constantine and the Christian Empire* by Charles Matson Odahl, 2004, p. 198.

SPCK for an extract from: *Life of Antony and the Letter to Marcellinus*, translated by Robert C. Gregg, 1980, pp. 30–2.

A. R. Mowbray for an extract from: *St Athanasius on the Incarnation*, translated by A Religious of CSMV, 1953, pp. 92–3.

The University of Tennessee Press for an extract from: *Fulcher of Chartres: A History of the Expedition to Jerusalem 1095–1127*, translated by Frances Rita Ryan, a Sister of St Joseph, 1969, pp. 65–7.

The Liturgical Press for an extract from: *The Rule of St Benedict in English*, edited by Timothy Fry, 1982, pp. 29–31.

New City Press for an extract from: *Francis of Assisi: Early Documents Vol. I The Saint*, edited by Regis J. Armstrong OFM Cap, J. A. Wayne Hellmann OFM Conv, William J. Short OFM, 1999, pp. 279–81.

Burns and Oates for an extract from: *History of the Church Vol. V Reformation and Counter Reformation*, edited by Hubert Jedin and John Dolan, 1980, pp. 35–6.

The Fortress Press for an extract from: *Three Treatises: Martin Luther; The Freedom of a Christian*, translated by W. A. Lambert, revised by Harold J. Grimm, 1957, pp. 279–80.

Harper & Row for an extract from: *The Autobiography of St Ignatius Loyola*, translated by Joseph F. O'Callaghan, edited by John C. Olin, 1974, pp. 39–40.

For what we preach is not ourselves, but Jesus Christ as Lord,
with ourselves as your servants for Jesus' sake.
For it is the God who said, 'Let light shine out of darkness,'
who has shone in our hearts to give the light of the knowledge
of the glory of God in the face of Christ.
But we have this treasure in earthen vessels,
to show that the transcendent power belongs to God and not to us.

(2 Corinthians 4:5–7)

INTRODUCTION

Making All Things New

And the one who was seated on the throne said, 'See, I am making all things new.' (Rev. 21:5)

At the heart of the faith of early Christianity was the idea of change. This began at its most fundamental level with the individual and the establishment of a new relationship to God through Christ; as Paul wrote: 'if anyone is in Christ. there is a new creation' (2 Cor. 5:17). This idea of a re-forming of humanity permeates the Pauline writings, the earliest in the New Testament collection.[1] This new creation was not just a return of humanity to its pristine condition at the moment of the original creation described in Genesis, when God created human beings in his own image and likeness (Gen. 1:26). This was, so the early Christians came to believe, something infinitely greater, a knowledge of *the* image of God himself revealed at last in the person of Jesus. Such knowledge would release humanity from its bondage to sin and death, and reopen the gates of paradise, a state experienced in a mystical anticipation by Paul himself (2 Cor. 12:1–4). But it would also have more earthly implications. For one thing, it involved the formation of a new type of community which would administer and supervise both entry into this new relationship to God, and the subsequent faithful journey through life. And this would in its turn bring Christians face to face with the problems and hazards of relating their community to the Judaism they were slowly separating from, and the world they were moving into dominated by the Roman Empire and the Hellenistic culture of the eastern Mediterranean. And as Christianity grew in size sufficient to bring it to the attention of the Roman authorities, how would they react? Would they tolerate this strange new cult as they did many others; or would they perceive it as an irredeemably alien force threatening the traditions of their world? For a few Christians there was eventually a price to pay for the spectacular success of their faith: suffering and death. But the very existence of these martyrs was itself a sign that Christianity was succeeding against all the odds, expanding from thousands to millions in the space of three centuries, to the point where it eventually brought down upon itself the wrath of Emperors bewildered by what they saw as a growing menace. Why and how did this obscure Jewish sect increase to such an extent that it became the object of imperial persecution?

Moving from its external relations to its internal structures, other questions arise. As Christianity persisted and grew over time, how did its geographically scattered groups of small communities organize and relate to each other? In particular, how were they to be led? In its early years of existence it was understandable for the leadership of the community to come from the followers of Jesus who had accompanied him during his ministry. But as time passed and this first generation began to die, what qualifications would be required for new leaders, and how would they be chosen? At the same time, questions about the beliefs of these communities would be raised. Did they all believe the same things about the significance of Jesus, and if not, what degree of diversity was legitimate within this new faith, and who was qualified to judge? Also, what relationship should Christianity have with the various polytheistic cults, and the schools of philosophy, found all over the Mediterranean world? Were Christians to be an inward-looking group secure in the knowledge of their purity in a hostile world; or should they open their faith to the intellectual culture of Hellenism and assimilate its learning, and speak to the educated in a language they would understand?

A New Community

In the New Testament, Jesus is recorded using the word *abba*, 'father', as a form of address to God on many occasions. Significantly, this word meant something more intimate, personal and informal than is usually conveyed by the term 'father', if, perhaps, not quite 'daddy'. At his baptism the Spirit descended upon Jesus in the form of a dove, and at Pentecost it is an outpouring of God's Spirit that fills his followers and enables them to speak in a variety of tongues. The first Christians thus envisaged God himself as a form of community, Father, Son and Holy Spirit, united by the power of eternal love, a love which had reached out to his fallen creatures as he gave the life of his Son to make them his new creations. Becoming a Christian, therefore, meant joining a community that linked heaven and earth together.[2]

But what should this new type of community be called? There were already a number of Greek words that could be utilized to describe what it was like to belong to this new form of relationship. One of these was *koinonia*, meaning to have certain things in common, joint undertakings in everything from politics and war, to marriage, friendships or clubs. It conveyed a sense of community or togetherness. Paul used the concept frequently in his letters, and it has normally been translated as 'fellowship'. 'God is faithful,' wrote Paul, 'by him you were called into the fellowship of his Son, Jesus Christ our Lord' (1 Cor. 1:9). However, the word that came to be most frequently applied to the Christian community, used over 100 times in the New Testament, was *ekklesia*, originally meaning an assembly, usually in a political sense of a gathering of the citizens of a city, and eventually emerging as the English word 'Church'. Jesus had announced the arrival of this new community (e.g. Matt. 16:18) and on the day of Pentecost the first Christians believed that it had become a reality. Paul described it as the body of Christ, made up of different parts just as the human body is, each with a particular function (1 Cor. 12:12–31).

Entry into the full life of this Church had, from the beginnings of Christianity, been through the ritual washing of baptism, a practice derived from Judaism, and confirmed by Jesus as the method by which all the nations would be made his followers, exploiting a common theme in the ancient world of the sacred power of water in which death by drowning could be experienced (Matt. 28:19; Rom. 6:3–4). In the first generations of Christianity little preparation or instruction was required, and any sources of water, such as rivers or springs, were employed. As time passed, however, baptism became a more formal rite. A number of accounts of how it was performed in the early centuries of Christianity have survived, one of the fullest being by Hippolytus (*c.* 170–*c.* 236), a cleric of the Church in Rome, and probably dating from the early third century. Baptism was now performed in a designated space inside the building where the Christian assembly gathered, and it was usually preceded by two or three years of preparation in the catechumenate, where those, all adults, desiring admission to the Church were instructed in its beliefs. Baptism was usually performed during the night of the Saturday before Easter Sunday; and in the weeks leading up to this, the period which later became known as Lent, the candidates fasted, abstained from sexual intercourse, and regularly attended the Liturgy of the Word, or first part of the Eucharist.

Various exorcisms were also normally performed during this period to drive out any demons from the candidates. Finally, at the ceremony itself, which was conducted behind curtains, after a formal declaration of faith, they removed all their clothes and walked naked down steps into a pool up to ten feet long, six feet wide, and three feet deep, where they were totally immersed in the water and baptized in the name of the Holy Trinity. Symbolically they had entered into the grave and emerged as a new creation resurrected with

Christ. Having been dried, their bodies were then anointed with olive oil and clothed in white garments. In the ancient world, in the absence of soap, olive oil was the usual astringent used for bodily cleansing, and was also the fuel used in lamps. Thus it had a double symbolism of washing and of light. They then rejoined the assembly and for the first time were allowed to be present at the consecrating of the bread and wine of the Eucharist, and to partake of the sacred elements.[3]

Early Christians, then, did not believe in making entry into their faith easy. It was a deliberately long and testing preparation through which catechumens had to pass to ensure the depth and seriousness of their new convictions. But once they had symbolically passed through death to the new life of the risen Christ, their reward awaited them.

What was this Eucharist that these Christians guarded so carefully? Essentially it was a repetition of the words and actions of Jesus at the Last Supper on the evening before his crucifixion, the details of which had been passed down to later generations of Christians. By the middle of the second century the broad outline of the structure of this *eucharistia*, or 'thanksgiving' for the life and death of Jesus, had been established, but with many local variations in detail and with, as yet, no fixed set of words to recite.

It was divided into two parts. The first was the Liturgy of the Word, in which readings from the Bible culminated in a sermon which took these texts as its subject. Then, after the faithful in the assembly had exchanged a kiss of peace, the catechumens withdrew, leaving only the baptized to witness the bringing of bread and wine. Over these elements the Holy Spirit was then called down in an invocation or *epiklesis*, and the words of Jesus, instructing his followers to do this to remember him, were repeated, and his death, resurrection, and ascension recalled. But this was no memorial or *anamnesis* of the dead. It was not 'remembrance' in the sense of the modern Remembrance Day for the fallen of two world wars. It was, rather, a making present again in the midst of his people the reality of a risen and living *kyrios*, Lord. It encapsulated in words and signs the essential beliefs of the Christian community, and presented a foretaste of the heavenly banquet to come. And when they ate and drank the consecrated bread and wine they truly became what they received: the body of Christ. This mystical food was, in the words of Ignatius of Antioch (*c.* 35–*c.* 107), martyred in the first decade of the second century, 'the medicine of immortality, and the sovereign remedy by which we escape death and live in Jesus Christ for evermore'.[4]

The importance of the Eucharist for the early Christians thus cannot be over-emphasized, as has been recognized by modern historians; Henry Chadwick, for instance, has described it as the central act of the early Christian community whose continual observance week by week was an essential factor in ensuring the Church's continuity, while for Philip Rousseau it was the means by which Christians 'acquired their special identity' and was their unique hallmark. Yet it also brought them controversy and criticism. To those outside their community, the secret nature of Christian worship aroused suspicions of everything from black magic to immorality or even cannibalism. It was originally to counter such accusations that Justin Martyr (*c.* 100–*c.* 165) addressed his *Apology* to the Emperor, in a document that has survived as a record of the hidden life of a worshipping community (Documents 1 and 2).[5]

But Christianity was more than just that. As Justin implied, worship and *koinonia* went hand in hand. Entry to this new type of community also involved a new way of living. Paul had already emphasized in his writings that fellowship meant a sharing of material possessions in order to support the poorer members of the community (Rom. 15:26; Phil. 4:14–20). As in Justin's time, so a century later the Church in Rome was supporting over 1,500 widows and other distressed persons.[6] This mutual support in its turn stemmed from the unusually egalitarian nature of the community: 'There is no longer Jew or Greek, there is no longer slave or free, there is no longer male and female; for all of you are one in Christ Jesus' (Gal. 3:28). In early Christianity it was at least theoretically possible for the senator and the slave to stand side by side in the assembly, and all new members shared the egalitarian nakedness of baptism. Many in the Mediterranean world would have sympathized with the Jews of Thessalonica who claimed before that city's authorities that the Christians were 'people who have been turning the world upside down' (Acts 17:6). This was as true for what Christianity did not permit as for what it positively encouraged, especially in the realm of sexual ethics. In the second and third centuries 'accepted sexual practice in the Roman Empire had a range and variety which it has never attained since', and to turn from the writings of Roman authors to their Christian contemporaries 'is to enter a different world'.[7] Christians followed Jews in condemning a range of practices casually accepted as perfectly moral in the Greco–Roman world, ranging from adultery and fornication, to abortion and infanticide, the latter normally carried out by the practice of exposure of newborn babies. To this list Christianity also added brother–sister marriages common in Egypt, homosexual practices, and performance in, or attendance at, theatres and games. Even going to the public baths was frowned upon as placing Christians in the vicinity of temptation.

Perhaps no group was more affected by Christian morality than women, and nowhere more so than in the Christian teaching about re-marriage and divorce, originating from the recorded sayings of Jesus himself (Mark 10:2–12). While formal marriage was normally only for those with sufficient wealth to make it legally advisable, the Church clearly looked to monogamy among its members.[8] Beyond that, early Christianity strongly advised widows against re-marriage, and saw the state of widowhood as a higher vocation encouraging women to depend on God rather than another husband. In addition Christianity also discouraged early marriage. In Roman law a girl could be formally married from the age of twelve; but among Christians, marriage at this tender age seems to have been far less prevalent. Exposure was also a far more common fate for baby daughters than it was for sons, and its prohibition among Christians was clearly to the benefit of girls. Whatever Greek philosophers might have advocated about equality before God, concern for fellow human beings, contempt for wealth, and the power of temperance, or Jews in the realm of sexual ethics, Christians went beyond both in their moral teachings. It has recently been argued, indeed, that where Romans venerated their families and cities, Christians extended this virtue to the whole of society, and effectively democratized the elevated ethics of a philosophical élite.[9]

Human nature, even newly created in the waters of baptism and fed with the Eucharistic bread and wine, still remained morally flawed, however; Christians were as capable of moral lapses as their polytheistic neighbours. From the time of the first generation of Christians this had been a problem; when faced with a man living with his father's wife, Paul had been clear that the offender should be removed from the assembly (1 Cor. 5:1–5).

But Christianity also taught the necessity of repentance and forgiveness. This was originally enunciated in the teachings of Jesus, in the Lord's Prayer (Matt. 6:12) as well as at other points in the Gospels (e.g. Luke 6:36–7; 17:1–4). The early Christians were also sure that the authority to forgive as well as to condemn had been entrusted by Jesus to his followers (John 20:22–3). By the second century, alongside the developing rites of baptism and Eucharist, there was now emerging a rite of penance. Sins such as theft, adultery and murder required a public confession of guilt before the whole assembly, to be followed by varying periods of fasting, prayer and exclusion from receiving the consecrated bread and wine, the length dependent on the gravity of the sin. By the fourth century the eminent theologian, Basil of Caesarea (c. 330–79) was suggesting twenty years for murder, fifteen for adultery, and one or two years for theft. But for all Christians, whether their sins were as spectacular as these, or depressingly mundane, repentance and an unconditional call to holiness were regarded as obligatory. Baptism was only the beginning of the life of faith.[10]

Christianity and the Roman World

So far we have emphasized the newness, strangeness and difference of Christianity in contrast to the Greco–Roman world in which it was expanding. However, if Christianity had been so totally alien to this world, it is difficult to see how so many Romans would have joined it. There must have been some points of contact and familiarity to attract them, even if interpreted in novel ways. The reasons for the survival and growth of this new religion were, therefore, a complex interplay between the old and the new, the conventional and the revolutionary. Age-old problems were being reassessed and explained in unfamiliar ways, and at the same time the learning of this civilization could potentially be utilized by the new religion in the struggle to formulate its own understanding of itself. It was very much a two-way process.

The Roman Empire was remarkably large geographically, but sparsely populated by modern standards. Although its frontiers were often very fluid and border territories could be lost and regained over time, the Roman Empire was something in the order of two-thirds the size of the modern United States, or perhaps a dozen times the size of France. The population of this Empire is, however, much more difficult to estimate, partly because it was not stable, but rather experienced violent periods of contraction, as in the devastating epidemic of 165–80, which possibly killed from a quarter to a third of its people, followed by subsequent periods of relative recovery and growth. In 110 it possibly contained 60–70 million people; at its peak it may have held as many as 95 million people, but by 400 was possibly as low as 45 million. At any point perhaps 80 per cent to 90 per cent were rural. There was only a handful of comparatively large cities, the biggest being Rome itself with a population peaking at about one million. Next in size was the great port of Alexandria in Egypt with up to half the population of Rome, and several more cities, all in the eastern half of the Empire, with over 100,000 people each. Altogether the Empire may have had about 2,000 cities and large towns, although many of them would now be considered very small. About 10 per cent to 20 per cent of adult males had some form of basic literacy, but only about 2 per cent could be regarded as fluent and sophisticated literates capable of reading and understanding the great works of Greek and Latin literature, again with more in the east than in the west. This latter group also generally formed the governing élite of the Empire, some of whom owned vast estates and were fabulously wealthy. Below them in the social hierarchy were perhaps another 8 per cent who were merchants, lawyers, teachers or others who we would now call 'professionals'. The population of the Empire was thus, by modern Western standards, thin in extent and predominantly living a precarious hand-to-mouth existence, with a tiny minority of urban and disproportionately wealthy rulers.[11]

This Roman world was also intensely religious. In the words of one of its greatest philosophers and statesmen, Cicero, religion was 'the foundation of our state'.[12] And in these words lies an important clue to how the ancients viewed their religion; civic life and religious observance were two sides of the same coin. A citizen was as much born a member of his city as he was his religion. Wealthy citizens gave gifts of statues of gods, built temples to them, or paid for games in their honour in the same way that they could also contribute to the building of public baths or theatres. Such acts not only honoured the gods and the city, but also reflected well upon the benefactor; and the greater the family, the more lavish its gifts in order to compete with rivals.

For the gods of the Roman Empire were neither distant nor passive. People believed that they could intervene directly in the lives of citizens, and thus needed placating and humouring through the correct performance of prayers and animal sacrifices. Some form of uniformity was achieved across the vast geographical and cultural extent of this Empire by the practice of mutating one set of deities to correspond with the local variety. These gods, however, ultimately cared nothing for the fate of humanity, but still looked to these lesser beings to show them the approved worship and honour. The great families thus vied with each other for the further honour of being elected for specific terms to serve as the priests and oracles of the gods, thus helping to reinforce both the distinctions and cohesion of the social order.

And above all was the officially sanctioned worship of the Emperor as a living god, with his predecessors celebrated by their own statues in the temples. Thus the Empire was more than just a political entity. It was the final end of human history, the culmination of divine purpose over which the divine Emperor himself ruled, linking the individual citizens of this vast geographical entity with the realm of the gods. Since 212 all its free inhabitants had been full citizens, and on 21 April 248, Rome celebrated the millennium of its foundation. This world seemed to be eternal, divinely guided and universal in the benefits it bestowed. Christianity questioned all of these assumptions and presented the Empire with a potentially lethal challenge in the extent of its reinterpretation of what it meant to be religious. But in the face of the might of Rome and the sheer numbers ranged against it, the prospect of overturning the religious preconceptions of this world seemed distant indeed.

Nor was the religion of the Roman world a hollow formality; rather it was a living reality for all but a minority of its people. Atheism, as we now understand the word, hardly existed apart from the speculations of a few Epicurean philosophers. The only real 'atheists' in the sense in which the word was then used, meaning deniers of the gods, existed uniquely among minority groups, notably the Jews, and eventually the Christians. In recent decades scholars have come to appreciate the full wealth, diversity and reality of Roman religion, not only through literary sources, but also from the discovery of vast numbers of inscriptions. These form the background to books such as *Pagans and Christians* by Robin Lane Fox, which have demonstrated that the religious practices of the Roman Empire reflected an energizing faith which penetrated the lives of the majority of its inhabitants in a variety of crucial ways. The vast processions to and from temples, some carrying statues venerated for centuries as true images of gods, the music and chanting which accompanied them, and the practice of making offerings to the gods in the form of everything from incense to whole herds of cattle sacrificed and then fed to the crowds, all confirm the picture of a religion widely believed and practised among the peoples of the Empire.

In addition, the reality of the divine was felt in everyday life. The presence of the gods was experienced in a number of ways, through signs and portents, in the vicinity of a statue that could become the living image of the god, or in the sensing of a divine presence by the especially pious. Gods were sighted during battles and sieges, in a variety of disguises, or in dreams; to experience the latter, large numbers of people could spend nights sleeping on the floors of temples in the belief that this was a particularly propitious venue for a divine encounter. These temples could, in addition, have a series of mechanical or optical devices that would make statues move or give the appearance of an approaching divinity.

Finally, oracles could be consulted, such as the one dedicated to Apollo at the temple of Didyma outside Miletus in Asia Minor. Here the female oracle sat in sacred water and breathed in its vapours to 'receive' the god. And the oracle of Apollo at Delphi had been the one who had called Socrates the 'wisest of men'. Such was the veneration in which these shrines were held that it was quite possible for one citizen to have visited them twenty or thirty times, starting as a choirboy accompanying civic delegations.

Encounters with gods were thus taken for granted and called *epiphaneia*, or epiphanies. It was therefore not surprising that early Christian missionaries and miracle workers could be confused with gods come to earth; at Lystra when Paul cured a man unable to walk, the crowds proclaimed that '"The gods have come down to us in human form!" Barnabas they called Zeus, and Paul they called Hermes, because he was the chief speaker' (Acts 14:11–12). Paul and Barnabas had to restrain them from offering sacrifices of oxen to these gods made manifest. Similarly, when Jesus told his followers to have no fear when he appeared to them in his resurrected body, Romans would have heard echoes of similar words uttered by Apollo in similar circumstances; 'That God could visit man was the least novel feature of Christian teaching' in the eyes of the Romans.[13]

Other points of contact also existed between the traditional religion of the Roman world and the new faith of Christianity. As one modern scholar has noted, Christians 'shared many of the values . . . and even more . . . habits of thought and behaviour' of their fellow inhabitants of the Mediterranean world.[14] This was also obvious in a distinct movement among the philosophies and the highly educated minority of this culture; and that was a discernible shift away from polytheism towards monotheism. This is observable in works such as Xenophon's *Memorablia* or Cicero's *De Natura Decorum*.[15] And this is again the background to another early Christian account, that of Paul in Athens sighting an altar dedicated to an unknown god: 'What therefore you worship as unknown, this I proclaim to you' says Paul to the crowd (Acts 17:23–4). A few Romans were coming to what is more technically known as Henotheism: belief in one supreme god, but with subordinate gods who represented certain aspects of him. It was clearly no major intellectual feat to move from that concept to the radical monotheism of Jews and Christians.

And that in its turn raises the whole question of the relationship between the philosophical thought of the ancient world and the developing faith of Christianity. By the time that this new faith had appeared there was already a variety of philosophical schools of thought, ranging from the frugal and austere Cynics searching for a way to live a better life, through the Sceptics who had a critical view of existing dogmas, Stoics who sought a virtuous life through the self-mastery of thought and actions, to the various interpreters of Platonism reflecting on the transcendent nature of God. Was there a way of reconciling these, and other, philosophical schools with the God of the Christians?

Early Christianity had already experienced a not-dissimilar problem when it came to its relationship with the parent from whom it had been born, that great monotheistic religion of the Mediterranean world, Judaism. Clearly the writers of the New Testament had been at great pains to demonstrate that Jesus and his movement represented the fulfilment rather than the destruction of Judaism. Jesus was the culmination of Jewish history and prophesy. To that end the New Testament contains hundreds of quotations from the Jewish scriptures, with a further multitude of allusions and echoes.[16] Later Christian writers then took up this theme and, starting with Origen (*c.* 185–*c.* 254), introduced further linkages between Jewish scripture and Christian concepts, based on typology, an imaginative patterning of God's providential action, pointing beyond the Old Testament to fulfilment in Christ. Certain individuals or events recorded in Jewish history were now interpreted as 'types' of later Christian ideas. Abraham's willingness to sacrifice his son, Isaac, was seen as a type of God the Father sending his Son into the world as a sacrifice to redeem humanity; the passage of Israel through the Red Sea was a type of Christian baptism; manna in the desert became a type of the eucharistic bread; and Noah's Ark was seen as a type of the Church in which the faithful find salvation.[17] Thus Christianity began the process of assimilating and transforming Judaism.

Mainstream Judaism, however, did not accept this view. For Jews, Christianity was but one of a number of deviant sects within Judaism, and before his conversion Paul had been employed in the effort to stamp it out. A major turning point in the relationship between the parent faith and its disobedient offspring came when the Jewish people launched a series of revolts against their Roman overlords. Three times, in 66 to 73, 115 to 117, and 132 to 135, the Jews were overcome by the military might of Rome, and in 70 had their temple in Jerusalem destroyed. The refusal of the much smaller Christian communities to rise alongside their Jewish brethren, especially noted during the first revolt, angered many Jews and marked an important stage in the gradual separation of the two faiths. Over time it was the differences rather than the similarities which came to be emphasized.

But alongside this ongoing assimilation of Judaism, some early Christians thought there were also ways to reconcile Hellenism. One of the first of these was Justin Martyr (*c.* 100–*c.* 165), writing in the middle decades of the second century. Justin had spent his youth searching for an understanding of the truth and meaning of human existence. His quest had taken him on a long intellectual journey through the Stoic, Peripatetic, Pythagorean and Platonist schools of philosophy, but without finding any final or satisfying answers. Only through his encounters first with Jewish and then Christian writings did he find what he sought. For the mature Justin, Christianity was the final goal and home of all philosophies. In defence of this, Justin promulgated his theory of the *logos spermatikos*; in this conception the *logos* stands for both the Word, Jesus, and human reason. In a sense, argued Justin, God had sown fragmentary knowledge of himself among both the Jews and the Greeks, among prophets and philosophers. Seeds of truth are implanted in human hearts and minds, formative principles of correct belief and living, and these are grasped in part by the schools of philosophy. But as Justin's own personal journey culminated in conversion to Christianity, so he saw the final end of human reason as lying there too. Justin's example and arguments were to become powerful tools in the hands of other Christian writers, and his own spiritual journey was to be taken by many others in the ancient world.[18]

For it followed that if a knowledge of God, if only imperfectly or in part, could be found in the reasoning and writing of the Greeks, then their methods, language and ideas could be utilized by Christian thinkers in defence of their own faith. It was largely in Alexandria, one of the main centres of intellectual life in the ancient Mediterranean, that these concepts came to their first maturity in thinkers like Clement (*c.* 150–*c.* 215) and Origen in the third century. 'Philosophy was the schoolmaster to bring the Greek mind to Christ' wrote Clement.[19] For as he had found, he could not tell his educated catechumens to ignore or abandon all the learning of their youth; instead they should bring it with them into their new Christian life. Reason could thus be assimilated into the true faith of the God of reason and be used in his service. As one modern commentator on early Christianity has written: 'If it were to be intelligible it had to be set forth in the universal language of reason.' Or as Origen had put it, the teachings of Christianity were 'in complete accord with the universal notions'.[20] Thus for Origen, Greek thought was providential, part of God's plan for human destiny. Such ideas were to have a profound effect on Christian thinking about its relationship to the world in which it found itself. A century after Origen the Church historian, Eusebius (c. 260–c. 340) would take this as his model for interpreting the history of the Roman Empire itself as equally providential, and equally capable of being assimilated and transformed as a vehicle for Christian use. But at the same time Christianity also reinterpreted the historical process itself, from the common ancient view of repeating cycles, to a linear approach: 'The time is fulfilled, and the kingdom of God has come near' as Jesus himself had told his followers (Mark 1:15).

However, alongside this tradition of a positive engagement with the world of ancient learning, there ran another, diametrically opposed to it, and often centred in the north African city of Carthage. Here the contemporary of Origen and Clement, the Latin writer Tertullian, (c. 160–c. 225) saw a profound danger to the purity of the Christian message. For him the philosophers were false thinkers, the fathers of all perverted views of Christianity. 'What is there in common between Athens and Jerusalem?' thundered Tertullian: 'What between the Academy and the Church? . . . Away with all projects for a "Stoic", a "Platonic" or a "dialectic" Christianity! After Christ Jesus we desire no subtle theories, no acute inquiries after the gospel.'[21] This presented early Christianity with two contrasting models: a faith open to the world beyond itself and the learning that world had acquired; or a closed body of believers preserving their religion from the contamination of a fallen creation. Although the former generally prevailed, the latter was to remain latent within Christianity, and to reappear in new forms and guises down the centuries.

But whatever the potential points of contact between early Christianity and the Roman world, what often appeared most notable were their differences. Christianity offered genuinely new ways of believing and behaving. While some of these have been covered already, there were also others, some profound, some more subtle, in which Christianity presented the Romans with an alternative and, potentially, a challenge to their basic assumptions about the nature of humanity and divinity. However, it would be wrong to assume that the differences between Christian ideas and those conventionally held in the ancient Mediterranean lands appeared overnight. Christians only gradually came to see the implications of their new teachings. This is a point that has been emphasized in relation to Christianity and Judaism, where Christians experienced only a 'gradual dawning' of the discontinuities between the two religions; the same was also true of the relationship between the new faith and Hellenistic society.[22] One such area was in the understanding of creation. For Greeks, a fundamental text was the *Timaeus* of Plato, in which the great philosopher had described God as the *demiurgos* or 'fashioner' of already existing matter, bringing order out of chaos, forming matter as the potter turns clay into objects of utility and beauty, using his reason to create an intelligible universe. This was to become a central point of Greek thinking. As Aristotle put it in his *Physics*: 'nothing can come out of what does not exist'.

The account of creation in Genesis, however, presented a radically different view. For Greeks, the creator was, as it were, *inside* nature, only creating from something that already existed. The implication of Genesis was that the creator was *outside* nature, creating something out of nothing, a view later captured in the Latin formula *creatio ex nihilo*. But it was only in the second century that Christian thinkers began to explore this idea, to the horror of many Greeks.[23]

The bewilderment of Greeks when faced with the new ideas of Christianity extended further from creation to incarnation, crucifixion and resurrection as well. Christians believed that in Jesus, God himself had become a man who willingly accepted death for the sake of his creatures, and had then risen in a real bodily form to give them the promise of eternity with himself. That God could appear on earth in human guise was in itself not impossible for Hellenistic concepts. But for Greeks, divine beings were not subject to change; they were immutable. A *suffering* God was 'stretching accepted ideas to breaking point'; and a God who died the shameful death of a criminal was literally offensive as an idea.[24] Thus Christianity appeared to present conventional thought with the impossible paradox of a God who allowed himself to suffer in the form of his own son. However, to complicate matters further, the concept of gods having sons was in itself common in the ancient world, and many heroes like Hercules had divine fathers, while earthly kings could regularly be given the title 'son of god'; and among the Jews the idea of God as the father of their nation was also well known. But to give such a title to a crucified criminal was 'bordering on the sacrilegious' to the Romans, and the idea that God had only *one* son was an innovation 'offensive to Jews'. The Christian solution to this conundrum was the resurrection, which combined 'a sense of destiny with an acceptance of failure' and was without precedent in the ancient world in this Christian understanding.[25] Here was the original source of Paul's discussion of true strength lying in weakness (e.g. 1 Cor. 1:25). But this then raised the further question: why had God done this? The Christian answer was again bewilderingly original in the face of conventional Greek and Roman ideas. Philosophy saw concepts like pity or compassion as defects of character; the idea that a person in a weaker or subservient position deserved help seemed contrary to justice. Help had to be earned. Yet the Christian God had willingly given himself as a sacrifice for his fallen creatures. But why? For Christians the divine motivation was explained as *agape*, self-giving love. 'God is love, and those who abide in love abide in God, and God abides in them' (1 John 4:16). And Paul had emphasized that love, like God, is eternal (1 Cor. 13:8). Further, in Luke's Gospel Jesus had agreed with the lawyer who had seen love of neighbour as the corollary of love of God, and then illustrated what he meant in the parable of the good Samaritan (Luke 10:25–37). Here again lay the origin of that new type of community the Christians were trying to create, based on mutual love and *koinonia*.[26]

And while Greeks were familiar with the concepts of divine visions, sometimes unrecognized because the god chose to come in disguise, the resurrection appearances of Jesus were again both like and unlike the Greek experience. Jesus, like Greek divinities, was not always immediately recognized by his followers, as in the case of his sudden appearance on a beach at the break of day (John 21:4). Yet at the same time the risen Lord was concerned to demonstrate his physical reality, perhaps most notably when 'doubting' Thomas was invited to examine the wounds of the crucifixion (John 20:24–9). No greater contrast could be found than between this Christian account of resurrection, and the ghostly and insubstantial appearance of the dead Patroclus to the living Achilles in Homer's *Iliad*. As Robin Lane Fox has commented: 'no god had been concerned to prove his bodily reality' before the God of the Christians. As with Thomas, the appearances of Jesus were followed by conversion and declaration of belief: 'My Lord and my God!' exclaimed the overwhelmed apostle (John 20:28).[27] And here was yet again a fundamental difference between Christianity and the so-called Mystery Cults which flourished in antiquity and which, in some other respects, it superficially resembled. Followers of Mithras or Isis could offer no proofs or witnesses in the way that the Christians could. This was one reason why Paul had gone into such detail about the people the risen Jesus had appeared to, including some 500 at one time, most of them still living at the time of writing (1 Cor. 15:6); and why the Gospel writers were at pains to point out that he was no 'spirit' but rather a real, physical person (Luke 24:37).

Perhaps it was the sheer extent of such differences between them that led many Romans to the conclusion that Christianity was not a real or serious religion at all. Certainly the Christians did not have the accepted hallmarks of religion in the ancient world. Where were their temples, their statues, their altars for animal sacrifice performed by duly appointed priests? Even the Jews had these. And the Jews were undeniably an ancient nation with their own religious practices stretching back to a far distant time. Christianity was new, and its very newness disturbed the Romans. Ancient societies venerated the ancient and the traditional; in the 360s the Emperor Julian, who had abandoned Christianity for traditional polytheism, was to use its very modernity as an argument against the claims of Christianity. All the Christians could boast of were small private houses used as meeting places for their assemblies. One of these 'house churches' at Dura Europos on the Euphrates was excavated by archaeologists in the 1930s. Probably dating from the 240s, it had two rooms knocked together, but invisible from the street, in which a few dozen Christians could meet in assembly, and a smaller room for catechumens linked to another for baptisms. All very small and remarkably unimpressive to Romans used to vast and elaborate temple complexes.[28]

So, given the obvious and clear differences between Christianity and the Roman world, and the new faith's radical reinterpretation of what it meant to be religious, the next question that arises is why did Romans join this new movement, and in what numbers?

The Growth of Christianity

There are few things that can be claimed about the demography of early Christianity without fear of contradiction; and they can easily be summarized in the three propositions that early Christians were growing in number, predominantly urban, and mainly found in the eastern half of the Empire. Beyond that, all is largely educated guesswork. Yet this has not prevented historians from speculating about the size of early Christianity. The Christian sources themselves often give the impression that relatively large numbers of converts were being added regularly to the Church, such as the 3,000 who joined on the day of Pentecost after listening to the apostle Peter's explanation of the events they had just witnessed (Acts 2:41). However, modern scholars are rather more circumspect in their claims; but at the same time certain numbers, or percentages, tend to be repeated in a range of modern textbooks, including the figure of about 50,000 Christians in AD 100, and the claim that 10 per cent of the population of the Empire was Christian by 300.[29] On the other hand, there are some historians who have questioned these assumptions; Robin Lane Fox, for instance, guesses at 2 per cent of the Empire Christian in 250, and only 4 per cent to 5 per cent by the early fourth century.[30] And what must always be remembered is that whatever the exact figure, during its first three centuries of existence Christianity was always significantly smaller than Judaism, which consistently numbered several million adherents, most of whom were scattered across the Empire in the Diaspora. Christians were so few indeed that even their existence was barely noticed by the vast majority of Romans for at least the first century of their history. The historian Herodian writing in the early third century did not even mention them in his work, so insignificant were they.

Recently, however, there have been attempts to measure the size and growth rate of Christianity during its early centuries with a greater degree of precision. One of the most influential, but also controversial, of these is the work of the distinguished American sociologist Rodney Stark. For him it is solely a matter of arithmetic. If we can assume a population of about 1,000 Christians in AD 40 shortly after the death of Jesus, argues Stark, then an annual growth rate of 3.42 per cent, or 40 per cent a decade, will give figures of 7,530 Christians in AD 100, 217,795 in 200, and 6,299,832 or 10.5 per cent of the total imperial population of 60 million in AD 300. Stark argues that growth rates significantly higher or lower would grossly distort the final outcome in AD 300. Of course the progress of Christian demography cannot have been quite so smooth, consistent or precise as these figures imply. For one thing, as we have already observed, the population of the Empire rose and fell dramatically during these centuries, largely as a result of epidemics. And given that Christians were disproportionately urban, they would surely have suffered even more catastrophic declines than the population as a whole as infections spread more rapidly in the grossly overcrowded cities.[31]

Yet the fact remains that if we accept that Christianity grew along an exponential curve, then over a long period of time a small number can multiply dramatically, in the same way that compound interest can turn small bank accounts into fortunes, if only we could all live long enough. The historian Keith Hopkins has taken Stark's calculations and explored some of their implications. Using the evidence provided by Adolph von Harnack at the beginning of the twentieth century, there seem to have been 50 known Christian communities in AD 100, and 100 in AD 180. But clearly this must be an underestimate given the 2,000 cities and towns in the Empire; the reason for this is that only a fraction of the documentary evidence to demonstrate the existence of such tiny groups has in fact survived. If, however, we accept for the sake of argument that figure of 50 communities in AD 100, then taking Stark's calculations, that would give each an average membership of 140 or so. But if that figure of 50 is a significant underestimate, then the average size of each community would have been much smaller, presumably to the point at which the capacity to support a number of clergy would have been impossible for many of them. Yet given that we do know of the existence of considerable numbers of Christian clergy in the second century, would that not seem to imply that Stark's base figure of 1,000 Christians in AD 40, and the subsequent one of about 7,500 in AD 100, are too low?[32]

Whatever the exact figures, and it must be emphasized again that calculations are based on no more than educated guesses, all scholars are agreed, however, about one central assumption: Christianity grew significantly in size in its first three centuries, perhaps at a faster rate than any other religious group in the Empire. So why did it grow so significantly? Since at least the time of the historian, Edward Gibbon, in the late eighteenth century, scholars have offered a variety of explanations for this phenomenon. For instance, it is clear that the third century in particular saw a dramatic increase in Christian numbers. Stark estimates an approximately five-fold increase in the first half of the century, and a six-fold increase in its second half, or a thirty-fold increase over the century as a whole. One conventional explanation that has often been used to explain this is the great crisis that the Empire experienced, especially in the middle decades of the century. This affected the whole life of the Empire – political, economic, social and military. In the space of 70 years Rome had no fewer than 27 different Emperors, only three of whom managed a reign of more than five years, and only four dying from natural causes.

It is then further argued that this political instability itself reflected a deeper malaise witnessed by a range of problems from high and sustained inflation to famine, earthquakes and plagues. On its eastern frontier the Empire was also engaged in periodic but large-scale warfare with a revived Persia; and one Emperor, Valerian, was not only defeated but also became the only Roman sovereign to have been captured in battle.[33] Some historians have seen all of this as evidence that the imperial edifice was crumbling, and thus as an explanation for the corresponding rise in the number of Christians. Prominent among them is W. H. C. Frend. As he put this in 1965: 'Loyalty to the gods was shaken, and the ultimate gainer from the insecurity and bewilderment of the times was the Christian Church.' In this thesis traditional polytheism did not seem to have any answers to the chaos of these decades, and as Frend wrote again in 1984 of Egypt: 'The heart had been knocked out of the old national religions.' People turned instead to Christianity, a religion with both an explanation for secular failure and the promise of better things after death.[34]

More recently, however, other scholars have begun to question this direct link between imperial instability and Christian success. Averil Cameron has pointed out that however bad things were in the mid-third century, it does not seem to have appeared to have been quite so catastrophic to contemporaries as to some later historians. There were, by contrast, many compensating features to a weakening of central authority, such as thriving local cultures. And the idea that Christianity filled a vacuum left by a declining traditional polytheism no longer stands up to the scrutiny of more recent investigation.[35] There is now a mass of evidence, notably from inscriptions, that points to a

very different picture of third-century Roman religious life. Far from seeing a
'decline in the popular religion' of Asia Minor as Frend had argued, Robin
Lane Fox now sees traditional religion in the region as very much alive and
prospering.[36] He further points out that in all previous crises the common
reaction of Romans had not been to turn away from their gods, but rather to
step up the attempts to appease them. Why should this crisis in the third
century have been any different? By the end of that century: 'The gods still
commanded a very large majority and the Christians had certainly not won
the arguments'.[37] And as Henry Chadwick has noted, the problems of the
third century were actually often blamed on the Christians for their neglect of
the traditional gods, provoking the latter to vent their anger in such spectacular ways.[38]

Such arguments also have relevance for part of the thesis expounded by
Rodney Stark, namely that new religious cults tend to flourish where large
numbers have ceased to believe in or practise traditional religious rites. 'It is
obvious that people do not embrace a new faith if they are content with an
older one', writes Stark, adding that new religions 'must always make their
way in the market openings left them by weaknesses in the conventional
religion(s) of a society'.[39] Part of the reason for him fixing upon a rate of
growth of 40 per cent per decade for early Christianity is that that is very
nearly the same as the 43 per cent that the Mormons had sustained through
the decades of the twentieth century. Indeed, Stark uses the Mormons,
Moonies and other recent groups who have reinterpreted Christianity as
models for constructing his thesis about early Christian growth. While this can
produce some fascinating insights, as we shall see below, there are clearly
dangers of anachronism in making such comparisons. The twentieth century
saw significant and unrelenting declines in more conventional Christian belief
and practice across much of the Western world. Problems arise, however,
when trying to demonstrate a comparable collapse in popular religion in the
ancient world. Stark does offer some pieces of evidence for disillusionment
with polytheism in the first centuries of Christianity; but in the face of the
wealth of counter evidence for a flourishing and popular religious tradition,
we have to ask how convincing they are. Thus, to argue that the growth of
Christianity was a function of the decline of traditional religions in the ancient
world would appear to be no longer supportable from the available evidence.[40]

If we cannot ascribe the demographic advance of early Christianity to
weaknesses in other religions in the Roman world, what other explanations
are available? One of those often cited, and based on the claims of early Christians themselves, is the phenomenon of martyrdom, in its original Greek root
meaning to give witness, testimony or proof. In his *Apology* of about AD 200,
Tertullian described the Christians who gave their lives for their faith as the

seed of the Church, their blood fertilizing the field of conversion.[41] We must be careful, however, to distinguish between early Christian rhetoric and the actual historical reality. For one thing, the number of Christians who actually met their deaths in this way was very small indeed. In the largest and most sustained of all the persecutions, that initiated by the Emperor Diocletian in the first decade of the fourth century, one reliable estimate is that perhaps between 2,500 and 3,000 Christians died in the eastern half of the Empire, and about 500 in the west, out of a total Christian population of several million, or well below 1 per cent of the Christians then alive. Clearly this was no holocaust. Indeed, the Roman state neither intended it to be, nor had the logistical means to attempt it; what it wanted was Christians willing to offer sacrifice to the Emperor and the gods and thus put aside their religious and civic deviance and become good citizens again. All the evidence suggests that they were relatively successful, as the numbers who did abandon Christianity seem to have significantly exceeded those willing to die for the new faith. In any case, Empire-wide, state-sponsored persecution was itself a relatively rare phenomenon, first appearing only in the 250s with the much briefer persecutions of the Emperors Decius and Valerian. Before 250 persecution and martyrdom was spasmodic and highly localized, resulting in the deaths of only single individuals or small groups.[42]

So what effect did martyrdom have on Christian demography? As an explanation for the rapid growth of the faith, modern scholarship is clear that the evidence will not support Tertullian's assertion; martyrdom was responsible for very few conversions. It seems to have been more a consequence of the growth of Christianity rather than a reason for that growth. On the other hand, it did have some important functions for the new faith. Literary accounts of martyrdom, for instance, probably had more impact on already-converted Christians than on non-Christians, acting as bonds holding their community together in periods of strain, and confounding more deviant Christian groups by demonstrating the lengths to which more mainstream Christians would go in order to defend the truth of their faith. At best, martyrdom should be seen as an alternative form of apologetics rather than a device to convert non-Christians; at its worst, as we shall discover, it was actually harmful to the progress of Christianity in that its aftermath fostered some profound divisions within the community.[43]

Another early Christian explanation for the rapid growth of their faith was missions and miracles, two phenomena that often accompanied each other. The classic text describing these was the Acts of the Apostles, where Paul and his fellow missionaries were portrayed as travelling huge distances, meeting numerous potential converts, and performing 'many signs and wonders', so that 'more than ever believers were added to the Lord, great numbers of both men and women' (Acts 5:12–14). This tradition of mass conversion as a result of miraculous happenings was to continue in the early Church, and one of the best examples was that of Gregory, the so-called 'wonder-worker' (c. 213– c. 270). Converted himself by Origen, he became the leader of the Christians in his native city of Neocaesarea in Pontus, in Asia Minor. Here he undoubt-edly had much success in his efforts to convert the polytheistic population of his city; he was undoubtedly a man of great character and popularity. But as a result a wealth of legendary accounts of his exorcisms and spectacular miracles grew up to explain his success. However, two points have to be made about this. The first is that whatever view one may take of miracles, in this respect Gregory stands out as most untypical of third-century missionary work. And the second point is that after the time of Paul and his immediate successors, organized evangelism tapered off very quickly. Individual examples of mis-sionary endeavour can be found, but they alone could not possibly have accounted for the huge increase in Christian numbers, especially in the third century.[44]

So if these traditional explanations fail to live up to the test of modern scrutiny, can any more plausible alternatives be suggested? The answer is that that there are quite a number, but they all tend to be far less spectacular and much more mundane than martyrdom, Empire-wide crisis or miraculous interventions. Here the work of Rodney Stark on modern movements such as the Mormons or the Moonies can provide a number of potential clues. Despite their infamous missionary activity, new groups such as these receive the bulk of their converts through ordinary family and friendship networks: 'conversion tends to proceed along social networks formed by interpersonal attachments'. The key to success lies in keeping these networks permanently open and ever expanding; most new religious groups fail because they quickly close themselves off from the surrounding society. Here the early Christian adoption of the open rather than closed model of the faith as advocated by Tertullian may have been crucial in its demographic success. Stark argues that both the contemporary success of the Mormons and the ancient advances by Christianity have this social openness in common. Roman cities with their massively overcrowded populations of often rootless individuals and families proved excellent recruiting grounds for the new faith. With population den-sities often far worse than those of the worst modern cities like Calcutta, Christians in the cities of the ancient Mediterranean could hardly have remained anonymous to their neighbours or fellow workmen. It was this, rather than organized missionary activity, that was probably the primary source of converts to Christianity, just as it has been for the Mormons.[45]

The next question centres on the particular types or groups most likely to have been attracted to the new religion. Clearly the origins of Christianity were embedded in Judaism, and Jesus only selected Jews as his first followers. But if all the early Christian leaders had kept exclusively to this choice then Christianity would have remained no more than one of a number of deviant sects within the ancient faith. The decision to open Christianity to Gentiles was essential if it was to become a world religion (Acts 15). And among those Gentiles was one specific group we know as the 'God-fearers'; these were people attracted by this monotheistic religion, who attended the synagogue, but who were reluctant to take the painful step of full membership conferred by circumcision, at least so far as male converts were concerned. For some God-fearers Christianity offered a solution, a monotheistic Jewish sect which did not require painful rituals of initiation. Among the early followers of Jesus was also another specific group: women (Luke 8:1–3). From its earliest days women were to be notable converts to the new faith; in one list of Christians Paul mentioned some 28 names, of whom no fewer than nine were women (Rom. 16). Given what was said above about the radically different attitude of early Christians towards women within the Empire, it is perhaps not surprising that modern scholars have identified them as one of the main sources of converts, by the third century perhaps even outnumbering men in the assemblies. Through them husbands, brothers and sons could be induced to view Christianity more favourably, perhaps ultimately converting themselves.[46]

Indeed, it may well have been the radically different social attitudes of early Christians when compared to the world in which they lived that may have attracted those with only a minimal stake in Roman civic society to join this alternative community, 'a drastic experiment in social living' based on fellowship and love. Neither social class, ethnic origin nor educational attainment were necessary controlling factors in seeking admission to this new and comparatively egalitarian faith.[47] And Christians not only proclaimed their love for God's world in a theoretical sense; they also made it into an everyday practical reality. During epidemics, whether local or Empire-wide, for instance, Christians were notable in their caring for, and nursing of, the sick and the dying, as well as for their extreme care of the dead in their burial rites, in contrast to what would now be seen as the callous attitude of most in society. In his Easter letter of about 260, Dionysius of Alexandria saw the Christians as offering explanation and comfort in the crisis of a major epidemic, a calamity sent as 'a schooling and testing as valuable as all our earlier trials'. Many people would have literally owed their lives to the Christians and it is thus possible to speculate that this must have had some impact on the rate of conversion (Document 3).[48]

So, Christianity grew by attraction, creating radically different ways of believing and behaving based on love and fellowship, often at odds with the harsh, cruel and indifferent world of late antiquity. More and more people saw this new faith in action among their relatives and friends in the confines of the urban setting, and were intrigued and then impressed by it. But that practical concern for their fellows came ultimately from what Christians believed. Citizens of the Empire were as much born into their religion as they were their city; presenting them with this choice of potential conversion to a new religion was a novel experience in itself. What was so special and different, then, about these Christian beliefs?

Authorities

The survival and expansion of dozens of tiny Christian communities, like small islands isolated from one another in a vast sea of suspicious and sometimes hostile neighbours, separated by huge geographical distances, was clearly imperilled if they could not achieve at least a basic sense of unity in their beliefs, practices and organizations. Whatever the strength of the external threats they faced, the potential for internal divisions clearly presented nascent Christianity with major challenges. This was compounded by the total lack of any written commands from their founder, Jesus, to which they could appeal for definitive guidance; early Christianity had no guide-book to follow. In addition, the expectation held by the first generation of his followers that his return or *parousia* was imminent meant that there appeared to be no urgent need to prepare for a future when instead the end of all things seemed to be at hand. As time passed, however, and the *parousia* failed to materialize, priorities began to change. Organization implied the need for a universally accepted form of leadership; belief required a system of regulation; and both were necessary to ensure correct practices. But these would inevitably take time to establish, and delay invited the emergence of variant models. It is therefore not surprising that early Christianity is characterized as much by discord as it is by harmony. Even by the beginning of the fourth century in some vital respects Christians were still in open and violent disagreement with each other. At the heart of early Christianity, therefore, was the search for authority.

As the first generation of Christians waited for the return of their Lord, however, this hardly seemed to be a problem at all. 'For salvation is nearer to us now than when we became believers; the night is far gone, the day is near' (Rom. 13:11–12). Time itself seemed to be shrinking in front of them. All that was required was devotion 'to the apostles' teaching and fellowship, to the breaking of bread and the prayers' and some patience (Acts 2:42). But as those apostles, both the original ones called by Jesus and new ones like Matthias elected by the assembly, or Paul called by Jesus in a blinding vision, began to die, complications finally arrived (Acts 1:26, 9:3–9, 22:5–16, 26:4–18). Authoritative leadership was essential to hold together a new and fragile organization dispersed in a widely separated collection of minuscule communities facing a now uncertain future. But who could provide it? Paul had written of the Church as a body composed of many parts: apostles, prophets and teachers; then miracle-workers, healers, helpers, administrators and those endowed with the gift of speaking in tongues (1 Cor. 12:27). Could the prophets, miracle-workers or speakers in tongues provide the new leadership? The problem was that their authority did not originate in the assembly but rather as a direct gift, or *charism*, from the Spirit; it was thus unpredictable, effectively self-appointed, and beyond the regulation of the assembly. As the Church grew in size such a system of leadership seemed increasingly impractical; too individualistic and potentially idiosyncratic in its nature (2 Pet. 1:20–21; 1 Cor. 14:2, 9).

But alongside this charismatic model of leadership, uniquely vertical in its direct origin downwards from divine sources, there emerged another model which originated in the more horizontal choice of the assembly, but still confirmed by the vertical appeal upwards through consecrating prayer. The arrival of this hierarchical model of leadership can be traced through the New Testament writings as they themselves progress through time. The most important of these offices was that of the *episkopos* (plural *episkopoi*), an overseer, supervisor or instructor, followed by a *diakonos* or servant, and a *presbuteros* or elder. By the time we reach the second generation of Christians in the second half of the first century, it was these offices, especially that of the *episkopos*, which were increasingly emerging as the potentially authoritative leadership around whom the unity of the Church could be built (1 Tim. 3, 5:17–22).

This episcopal model of leadership, headed by what in English came to be called bishops, differed markedly, however, in a number of ways from concepts of hierarchy prevalent in late antiquity. For one thing, *episcopoi* were appointed for life. In the civic and religious worlds of Roman cities, with the notable exception of Egypt, the priests, priestesses and oracles were chosen, as we have seen, for fixed terms of office. In contrast to that, a Christian bishop was elected by the assembly, and then had his election recognized by neighbouring bishops, who travelled to the new bishop's city to lay their hands on his head and invoke the Holy Spirit to descend upon him to grant him the *charism* of his office. Once consecrated, this gift could never be taken away; he was a bishop for life. But even more radical was the nature of this new Christian hierarchy. In most societies a hierarchy exists, normally based on status, wealth and power, and can usually be expressed diagrammatically as a pyramid or triangle, with an Emperor, king or other supreme authority at the apex, below whom would be some form of aristocracy in a number of descending ranks, and so forth until the base of the pyramid is reached, in the Roman world normally consisting of the vast army of slaves. The traditional civic priesthood fitted well into this pattern, appointment to high religious office seen as analogous to high rank in the social hierarchy, and often as confirmation of the attainment of social distinction.

The Christian concept of hierarchy, however, turned this model upside down. The Gospels repeatedly stressed the point that the origin of this new conception lay with Jesus himself. At one point in Matthew's Gospel, for instance, the mother of two of the apostles asked Jesus to let her sons sit on his right and left hand in his kingdom, reflecting the conventional view of hierarchy. But Jesus had a totally different conception and announced his reinterpretation to his apostles:

> You know that the rulers of the Gentiles lord it over them, and their great ones are tyrants over them. It will not be so among you; but whoever wishes to be great among you must be your servant, and whoever wishes to be first among you must be your slave; just as the Son of Man came not to be served but to serve, and to give his life a ransom for many. (Matt. 20:25–8; see also parallel text in Mark 10:42–5; also Luke 22:25–7)

He then later reinforced this crucial distinction at the Last Supper. In the heat, dust and sand of the ancient Mediterranean lands, the washing of a guest's feet was more than just a social convention, and this unpleasant task was often reserved for the lowliest slave or servant in the household. Hence the indignant surprise of Peter as Jesus prepared to carry out this lowly office before the apostles ate their last meal with him. But as Jesus explained to them, if he, their Lord and Teacher, could do this, then so should they in imitation of him (John 13:1–20). In his letters Paul took up this theme and described himself and his fellow missionaries as servants and slaves on numerous occasions, again seeing Jesus as the divine model who had 'emptied himself, taking the form of a slave, being born in human likeness' (Phil. 2:7). Thus in the Christian theory of hierarchy the apex and the base of the pyramid were reversed; this was a hierarchy of service, *diakonia*, not of status, power or wealth, in which the great were the slaves and the servants. Leadership was at the service of the *ekklesia*, just as the latter existed to serve the world as a sign of God's love for his creation, and both taking as their model their *kyrios*, Lord, Jesus the Son of God himself. Here again was something quite new in the religious life of the Mediterranean world.

And it was these *episkopoi* who saw themselves as the direct and unique inheritors of this new concept of authority entrusted by Jesus to his apostles, and confirmed at Pentecost by the descent of the Holy Spirit on them in the form of tongues of fire (Acts 2). In Christian writings not included in the New

Testament, but broadly contemporary with the later phases of its composition, there is an unambiguous assertion that the office of the bishop is of apostolic foundation and intended as the living continuation of apostolic authority and teaching, perhaps most crucially in the monopoly of presiding at the Eucharist and repeating the words of Jesus over the bread and wine, and in the granting of penance. In the document we know as the First Letter of Clement, for instance, written in Rome in the mid-90s and directed to the *ekklesia* in Corinth, the line of descent is clear; there is a description of how the apostles 'went through the territories and townships preaching', and 'appointed their first converts – after testing them by the Spirit – to be bishops and deacons for the believers of the future' (1 Clem. 42).[49] About a decade later Ignatius, Bishop of Antioch, an office he claimed to hold as third in direct succession from Peter, wrote a series of seven letters to various churches during his journey to martyrdom in Rome. Here, there are numerous passages which describe and exalt the office of the *episkopoi* as the contemporary successors of the apostles. But it must be remembered that the Ignatian model of hierarchy, the single or 'monarchical' bishop in a city, was not necessarily the universally accepted one at that time. Larger cities, with a number of house churches, could easily have a similar plurality of *episkopoi* existing in a more collegiate model of leadership. And the evidence of the letters also demonstrates that the *episkopoi* had not yet obtained that monopoly of Eucharistic leadership either (Document 4).

Then later in the century, probably between 180 and 185, Irenaeus, Bishop of Lyons, (*c.* 130–*c.* 200) wrote his treatise *Against the Heresies* and again asserted that 'the tradition of the apostles, manifest in the whole world, is present in every church to be perceived by all who wish to see the truth. We can enumerate those who were appointed by the apostles as bishops in the churches as their successors even to our own time', and then lists all the bishops in order whom he considers to have succeeded Peter and Paul at Rome, down to the current Bishop, Eleutherus, the twelfth to claim succession in line from the apostles. But yet again it was, of course, very much in the interest of an episcopal writer to emphasize the unique continuity and descent of his office from the apostles.[50]

However, it should also be remembered that the descent of the Holy Spirit on the apostles at Pentecost was not the only example of similarly direct divine intervention recorded in Acts. The Spirit was to descend four more times during the course of the events recounted in that book. First, the Spirit came down again on the Jerusalem church and 'the place in which they were gathered together was shaken; and they were all filled with the Holy Spirit and spoke the word of God with boldness' (Acts 4:31). This was then repeated with the invocation of the Spirit on the outcast Samaritans (Acts 8:14–17); then in the house of the God-fearing centurion, Cornelius, the Spirit descended on Gentiles (Acts 10:44–8); then finally in Ephesus, twelve of John the Baptist's followers received the Spirit and spoke with tongues and prophesied (Acts 19:1–7). Clearly the gifts of the Holy Spirit were not the unique possession either of the original apostles nor their immediate episcopal successors.

Alongside the hierarchical model of leadership there still persisted an unregulated and unpredictable charismatic type. As we have seen, visions were regarded as a common form of divine inspiration and intervention in most religions of the ancient world; Paul's conversion had come in a, literally, blinding vision, and on the island of Patmos John had been inspired to write his Apocalypse by another visionary experience (Rev, 1:10–11). Here was a further alternative source of authority, and potentially outside the control of apostles, bishops or other agents of the Church. Paul was perhaps the first example of an individual, the origin of whose authority was charismatic, who nevertheless placed his ministry under the authority of the other apostles and the wider Church: 'I laid before them . . . the gospel that I proclaim among the Gentiles, in order to make sure that I was not running, or had not run, in vain' (Gal. 2:2). Clearly, between Paul and his apostolic brethren there was a fruitful tension rather than a destructive one.

But there was no guarantee that all charisms and visions would be in harmony with the views of all Christian leaders. One of the most serious of these breakdowns would occur with a group known as Montanists. They were named after their founder, Montanus, who, partly inspired by John's visionary revelations, began to prophesy in the province of Phrygia in Asia Minor either in 157 or 172, depending on which source is accepted. What made Montanus and his early followers, notably the women Prisca and Maximilla, different was first their claim that the Spirit actually used their vocal cords to deliver a series of oracles, and second their belief that the apocalypse was near and would begin in the small town of Pepuza in Phrygia. This 'New Prophecy' spread rapidly among the Christian assemblies of the Empire, and by about 200 was already known as far away as north Africa, where it soon won its most notable convert, the great Latin Christian writer Tertullian, who labelled adherents of the movement *pneumatici* or 'spirit filled'. Unlike Paul, however, what marked off the Montanists was both their extreme moral rigour and their total intolerance of other Christians who refused to follow them. Tertullian saw them as a powerful movement of reform and revival whose views on fasting and the sinfulness of flight during persecution dovetailed with his own concept of a 'gathered church' of the pure; those who opposed them he called *psychici* or 'animal people' not truly endowed with the Spirit. Thus was revealed the potential danger of a movement where 'authority depended on the vertical gift of the Paraclete [Spirit] not upon the

horizontal transmission of authority from pastor to pastor in apostolic continuity', a danger of division within that very body of Christ, the Church.[51] It had
been in part to prevent or reconcile such potential sources of tension and
division between the hierarchic and the charismatic that an unknown Christian author had penned the work we know as the *Didache* or *Teaching of the
Twelve Apostles* perhaps as much as a century before the Montanists. Clearly
such tensions had arrived early in the history of Christianity and were deeply
enmeshed into its makeup.

But challenges to episcopal authority could also originate within far less
exotic groups than the Montanists. Persecution and martyrdom not only gave
the Church an army of new heroes but also another potential source of alternative authority to that of the *episkopoi*. It has been noted that the charismatic
sources of authority were often at their most pronounced during periods of
tension or crisis in the history of early Christianity, which may partly help to
explain the emergence of Montanism in Phrygia, a province prone to social
turbulence, plagues and warfare. The crisis of persecution leading to potential
martyrdom was thus another fruitful time for the growth of such alternatives.
Bishops and other Christian clergy were clearly prime targets for Roman state
persecution because of their visibility within Christian communities, and on
many occasions they quite sensibly fled and went into hiding at the first whiff
of trouble, a policy with clear biblical authority (Matt. 10:23). The problem
with that tactic, however, was that it immediately created a vacuum in the
leadership of the assembly at a time of particular crisis. Without their bishop to
lead and guide them, who should Christians turn to? It was normally the
practice of the imperial authorities to imprison suspected Christians in the
hope of pressuring them into submission. Christians thus detained in appalling
conditions, awaiting trial and possible death or slavery in the mines, with the
prospects of little nourishment but abundant disease or even torture, acquired
great prestige and came to be known as 'confessors', those who had suffered
greatly for their faith if not quite to the point of death.

It was to these men and women who had proven their holiness through the
charism of fortitude in adversity that many Christians now turned. Those who
had not been so courageous and had abandoned their faith in the face of
threatened arrest and trial could now turn to the confessors for absolution
from the sin of apostasy; during the Decian persecution of 249–51 in Carthage
many such certificates of pardon were issued. And during the Diocletian persecution in the first decade of the fourth century, confessors met in groups in
prison and decided to take this even further by condemning the clergy for
willingly surrendering the books of the scriptures to the authorities, effectively
cutting bishops off from full communion with the Church. Such extreme
actions clearly represented 'an attack on the existing hierarchical system'.

The case of Cyprian, Bishop of Carthage, is a good example. A fine scholar, converted to Christianity in 246 and elected as Bishop just two years later, he fled during the Decian persecution, returning to find his church in turmoil, with many having apostasized, and confessors who had pardoned them on remarkably lenient terms. Cyprian convened a series of local Councils of north African bishops in an effort to reassert episcopal authority based on a more rigorous discipline of penance, and wrote a treatise on Church unity containing the memorable comment: 'He cannot have God for his Father who has not the Church for his Mother.' Cyprian was determined that Christianity was going to be an exclusively hierarchically governed organization. And with the return of persecution he finally put the seal on his own authority by submitting himself to a martyr's death by public beheading in the arena in Carthage in 258.

But other martyrs, however, could remain as critics of the clergy from the safety of the grave. The female north African martyr, Perpetua, who died in 203, left a famous prison diary in which she recorded her extraordinary visions and admonitions to the clergy as she awaited death. Such privileged revelations, combined with her eventual martyrdom, represented 'potentially dangerous encroachments upon authority'. Thus bishops might have become normative centres of authority, but certainly not exclusive ones; they were never to be free from alternative *charisms* of leadership.[52]

If a lifelong hierarchical leadership based on service was an innovation in the ancient world, then so too were the Christian concepts of orthodoxy and heresy. Christianity was quite different from conventional Mediterranean religions in attempting to enunciate its beliefs in a systematic and clearly defined way. This too represented a development from the imperative of unity. As early Christians sought to bring all their scattered communities into one unified body, this sense of emerging social integrity expressed through *koinonia*, *ekklesia*, baptism and Eucharist, led on to a need to bring potential diversity of belief into a similarly integrated system. Thus was born the concept of orthodoxy, right or correct belief, and its opposite, heresy, coming from the Greek *hairesis* or 'choice'. Was the Christian faith a loose set of ideas onto which individuals or groups could impose their own particular interpretations; or was it, rather, itself a unity derived from divinely appointed authority and transmitted through a recognizable tradition?

As early as the 50s, Paul was at pains to stress in his letters the point that his teachings were not his own particular speculations but based on certain fundamental beliefs which had been taught to him: 'For I handed on to you as of first importance what I in turn had received: that Christ died for our sins in accordance with the scriptures, and that he was buried, and that he was raised on the third day in accordance with the scriptures' and then appeared to a number of his followers (1 Cor. 15:3–4). Guarding this basic deposit of faith was a further theme of the Pastoral Letters (1 Tim. 6:20; 2 Tim. 1:13–14), for the danger of deviation from this faith was already clearly present during the decades in which the New Testament writings were composed (Rom. 16:17; 1 Cor. 11:18–19; Gal. 1:6–9; Titus 3:10; 1 John 2:13; 2 John 9). This was very far, however, from a defined notion of orthodoxy threatened by heretical teachings. Modern scholarship sees such ideas as developing slowly over generations out of a variety of possible interpretations of Christian faith, 'a kaleidoscope of varied traditions, beliefs and hopes centred on the single figure of Jesus Christ'.[53]

This raises the further question: what did early Christians mean by this emerging concept of 'tradition'? Today, after decades of criticism, the word 'tradition' has come to be seen in peculiarly negative terms; a dead weight from the past holding back innovation, to be swept aside to allow new ideas to flourish. The Christian view of the concept is, however, more complex, subtle and positive in its understanding. One definition of this begins to open out these ideas and demonstrate the differences with the conventional view: 'Tradition is the living faith of the dead; traditionalism is the dead faith of the living.' This contrasting Christian idea that tradition embodies something which is very much alive is reinforced by another modern comment on the early Christian concept: 'Tradition was organic, a living link between past and present.'[54] Tradition understood in this sense is as much about the future as it is the past, and stands out not only from the conventional modern view, but also from the ancient world in which the old was venerated merely because it was old. Just as the individual Christian was on a journey to re-form himself in the image of Christ, so the whole Christian community was in a similar process of continual renewal. For tradition was not the same thing as custom, as an early Council at Carthage in 256 made clear: 'In the Gospel the Lord said "I am truth". He did not say "I am custom".'[55] Like our fir trees at Christmas, customs may spring up and give the appearance of having been there from the beginning, while in fact they are relatively novel developments that have little to do with essential truths. Tradition in this contrasting Christian sense is the vehicle through which these essential truths are both transmitted through time and space, and also constitute a huge resource for the future.

For Christian tradition is not a static thing, but rather a dynamic force that can be used to rejuvenate the present and future. This point was made in the second century by the Christian writer Hermas in his book *The Shepherd*. In it he used a metaphor, portraying the Church as an elderly woman present with God at creation, but who got progressively younger as time passed, and who will be with Christians into the future.[56] To use another, this time musical metaphor, an original theme can generate almost endless variations introducing new keys, fresh orchestrations, and even new rhythms, but yet remain essentially 'true' to the original underlying musical pattern. As we shall discover as our journey of exploration progresses, Christian history is interspersed with many movements of renewal and reform which have attempted to rediscover the original theme underlying the evolving harmony, and have consequently developed their own fresh variation from it. The problem, however, is to distinguish between a true variation and a completely new theme which introduces an element of discord into the music. And this problem was first encountered in the early centuries of Christianity.

Gnosticism was a case in point. Until fairly recently, most of what was known about this movement came through the writings of its opponents like Irenaeus, Justin, Tertullian and Hippolytus; a classic example of history being written by, or through the works of, the victors. But then in 1945 at a place called Nag Hammadi in Egypt, historical understanding of Gnosticism was transformed by the chance discovery of a sealed jar in the desert sands near an ancient Christian monastic site. The jar contained thirteen codices, or books with bound leaves instead of scrolls, constituting over 50 tractates, of which 40 were previously unknown. They were written in Coptic, the ancient language of Egypt, and dated from the late third or fourth centuries, and were mainly translations of earlier sources. This find ranks alongside the better-known Dead Sea Scrolls as one of the most significant for our understanding of early Christianity. Gnosticism can now be seen as both far more complex in its origins and teachings than previously supposed, and at the same time far more mainstream in its Christianity than its contemporary opponents would have had us believe. These works can only be understood as a contribution to debates within a broader concept of Christianity. No longer can Gnosticism be interpreted as a parasite or a 'fifth column' within the Christian body. They demonstrate that second- and third-century Christianity was notable for the degree of diversity within it; Gnosticism inhabited but one part of a wide spectrum of interpretations.

These particular texts debate a series of issues that were at the heart of early Christian thinking: how could the all-powerful and perfect God have created such a flawed thing as the cosmos, and such an imperfect creature as humankind? How could he be so jealous and wrathful as the God of the Jewish scriptures caring only for one nation among the many on earth? In a series of amazing creation myths the writers of these texts looked beyond Judaism to Greek philosophy and a range of other Middle-Eastern faiths for answers.

Gnosticism was itself a far from homogeneous system, having within it almost as many schools as Greek philosophy; but broadly their answer was that creation was the work of a lesser God, and that the way back to the true but unknown God was by a secret knowledge or insight, *gnosis*, found in the works of enlightened teachers, part of which was a dualism between inferior matter and a superior spiritual reason. All of this had Christian relevance, for Jesus was seen as a great teacher of *gnosis*; but at the same time it raised questions about his precise relationship to the true God, and, at its most extreme, about his physical reality, as the material world of which he had been a part was a fallen one, and thus also about the nature of his presence in the equally material bread and wine of the Eucharist. At this far extreme of the spectrum of Christian beliefs was a tendency that became known as Docetism, from the Greek *dokesis*, a semblance. God could not possibly have taken so base a thing as material existence, and thus Jesus only *seemed* to have a physical reality. Only after extensive and lengthy debate over several generations did the influence of many of these Gnostic ideas wane in Christianity. But in a different context some of the language and concepts remained within the broader centre of the Christian spectrum. Clement of Alexandria used the term *gnosis* and saw Jesus as a teacher of insight and understanding, while rejecting any non-physical theories about his reality.

For here was perhaps the central problem faced by the Christianity of the first three centuries: it possessed no mechanism by which the concepts of orthodoxy and heresy could be distinguished from each other in a universally accepted way. Ideas could be debated, learnèd teachers could write treatises, bishops could preach sermons, write letters and even meet together in localized Councils, but ultimately there was no way of reaching a consensus throughout the scattered but growing Christian communities. Orthodoxy, at best, was in the process of emerging, but was certainly not yet anything like a fixed body of agreements. It remained more of an ideal than an actuality, and too often a retrospective gloss has been put over the wide diversity of the early Christian spectrum of belief. Even the most prestigious of bishops could legitimately disagree with each other. In the 250s, for instance, in order to regularize the chaotic state of the Church in north Africa following the Decian persecution, Cyprian of Carthage argued for the re-baptism of apostates. When he proposed this to Stephen in Rome, however, the latter firmly asserted the principle that baptism was unrepeatable. In their own time the issue was to remain unresolved.

If bishops, however eminent, could not finally settle issues of orthodoxy and achieve unity on matters of belief and practice, was there anywhere else that Christians could look for the necessary authority? Amid the vast and growing body of Christian literature, for instance, were there any specific texts which stood out for their authoritative teaching and which could be utilized to settle issues of orthodoxy and unity? Hence we must now turn to examine how and why what we call the canon of the New Testament emerged as another source of authority in early Christianity. However, certain basic points about the New Testament need to be made clear before we can proceed with a discussion of how it became Christian canonical scripture.

First of all, the language in which all the books of the New Testament were originally written was Greek. For several centuries before the arrival of Christianity, Greek had been the language of the educated throughout the eastern Mediterranean lands. Indeed, one of the problems for some of these highly educated people had been that not only was the central figure of Christianity a condemned criminal, but also that the Greek in which the significance of his life was recounted was clearly crude and inferior to that of the great classics. How could such a divinity be taken seriously by educated people if his followers could not even write in an elevated style? The Greek language, however, had first arrived in the region with the settlers who founded the first Greek colonies. But the crucial events were the conquests of Alexander the Great and the subsequent dynasties established by his generals. Just as English became the language of the educated in the Indian sub-continent as a result of the Raj, so Greek now emerged in the eastern Mediterranean, if not as a direct consequence of deliberate policy by the ruling power, as in India.

Second, the division of the books of the New Testament into chapters and verses is a much later development. The chapter division was first devised by Stephen Langton, a future Archbishop of Canterbury, while teaching at the University of Paris in the early thirteenth century. The further breakdown into verses is even later, originating in mid-sixteenth-century Geneva, with the first English Bible to copy this dating from 1560. And third, many of the titles by which we now know and identify particular books of the New Testament were not original; the common ascription of the four canonical Gospels to named individuals dated only from the second century, in some cases several generations after their composition. For originally 'gospel' meant not a piece of writing but the oral proclamation of the 'good news'. On top of that, none of the authors of these books consciously set out to write 'scripture' at all. As one modern scholar has commented:

> It is not uncommon to meet Christians who think that God told Luke, for example, to take a pen and some papyrus, find a desk and then sit down and write at the dictation of some heavenly voice. It just did not happen that way! . . . What God did, however, was to subject his written word to the same historical process as he did with his incarnate word, Jesus.[57]

Then the next point to remember is that the present collection of texts in the New Testament represents only *some* of the Christian writings of the first and second centuries; there are many more Gospels, Acts, and Apocalypses than those now found in the standard 27 books of Christian scriptures. This was implicitly acknowledged by Luke at the opening of his Gospel when he wrote: 'many have undertaken to set down an orderly account of the events that have been fulfilled among us' and goes on to describe his task as one of composing an ordered and accurate account (Luke 1:1). In addition, we do not possess any of the original, or autograph, manuscripts. It is impossible to reconstruct the original form of these books much before AD 200, although there are some fragments of texts somewhat earlier than this. The nearest we can get is about two generations from the original writings. Because of scribal errors in the process of copying, for instance, this has also led to a host of variations in the extant early texts, although the bulk of them are of only minor concern. This in itself, however, is far from unusual in the study of ancient literature. Many of the works of such eminent writers as Plato, Herodotus, Thucyddides, Livy and Tacitus only exist in copies made centuries after their authors' deaths, while our knowledge of the love poems of Catullus derives from a single Latin manuscript made some 1,500 years after their composition. Similar problems arise when modern scholars attempt to reconstruct the lives of even the most prominent individuals of antiquity. Take Alexander the Great himself. As one modern scholar has commented:

> More than twenty contemporaries wrote books on Alexander and not one of them survives. They are known by quotations from later authors, not one of whom preserved the original wording: these later authors are themselves only known from the manuscripts of even later copyists and in the four main sources these manuscripts are not complete. The most detailed history goes back to only one manuscript, whose text cannot be checked; another, much used, has often been copied illegibly.[58]

Thus at one level the New Testament shares many of the same problems of textual analysis as any other writings from the ancient world, but is all the more remarkable for having preserved so much from so near the time of a minor itinerant Jewish teacher who died the death of a common criminal in an obscure backwater of the Empire.

And the final point to remember is the time-span over which the books of the New Testament were composed. This is reflected in the changing perceptions of the writers who are themselves reflecting developments inside the community; as we have seen, Christianity was never a static religion.

So how did the 27 books of the New Testament emerge as authoritative Christian scripture? Perhaps not surprisingly, the process was both complex and protracted. For the first generation of Christians the necessity to record events in the life of Jesus, or to begin a theological reflection on their meaning, would have seemed pointless as his *parousia* was regarded as imminent. There is thus a passage of time between these events and the first Christian writings, probably in the order of fifteen years or so. Then Paul began composing a series of letters to various Christian communities, possibly covering the period from about 50 to the early 60s. The first Gospel, generally accepted by modern scholars to be that of Mark, was probably composed between 65 and 75; this was followed by those of Matthew and Luke in the 80s; these three together called 'Synoptic', or deriving from a common view. Indeed, some modern scholars have speculated that the similarities in some passages of Matthew and Luke were the result of a further, but unidentified, common 'source' or *quelle* in German, and hence called Q. Whatever the truth of this, the fourth Gospel, John, is later, dating sometime between 80 and 110, and in a number of ways quite different in approach and style to the Synoptics. The Acts of the Apostles is by the same author as Luke's Gospel and continues the narrative into the history of the first years of Christianity and especially the missionary journeys of Paul. Other letters, to specific individuals or to the infant Church at large, and the Apocalypse, meaning an 'unveiling', complete the collection, the latest date for the final works possibly as late as 150.

Thus the New Testament represented a collection of writings by a variety of authors over at least two or three generations and possibly even longer. All of this, in addition to the textual problems raised above, has led to a marked divergence in interpretations in modern times, ranging from those who regard the whole of Christianity as based on fiction and fable, to so-called fundamentalists who see the New Testament as literal and historical in every detail. However, most scholars tend to divide along the interpretive pathways of invention or discovery. The former, while not doubting the historical person of Jesus, would argue that the length of time between the events and the writings, combined with the possible creative editing of texts, let alone scribal error, led to an increasingly imaginative and fabricated view of Jesus; his teachings and his significance becoming hopelessly distorted in the effort to justify the later beliefs of the Christian community. The latter, by contrast, while not rejecting the concept of change evident within the writings themselves, would argue that this was a natural process of increasing understanding of who Jesus was, and his theological significance, as much generated by prayerful meditation and Christian living as intellectual manipulation.[59]

Whatever the truth of the matter, it must be assumed that Christians began to write and record for similar reasons to those that led them to organize, namely a growing realization that the *parousia* was not about to happen, combined with the deaths of the apostles and others who had known Jesus personally gradually robbing Christians who had not so known him of that direct contact. The threads linking the next generation back to their Lord were snapping and the necessity of preserving contact in some way gradually became more urgent. So just as the first generation passed much on by word of mouth, the second generation would have needed to have this oral transmission supplemented by writing. In the case of the Gospels, the good news was originally encapsulated in a large number of 'sayings' of Jesus, which then formed the raw material for the books. These sayings were selected, and a composition produced which integrated them into a narrative of the events of his life, sometimes with great artistry. Obviously the few hours that it would take to read aloud the sayings in the four canonical Gospels cannot possibly be a comprehensive collection covering all that Jesus said in a ministry of three years, as the author of the fourth Gospel acknowledged (John 21:25). The non-canonical Gospel of Thomas, heavily influenced by Gnosticism, contained a collection of 114 sayings of Jesus, and probably originated in the mid-second century. Interestingly, about two dozen of these sayings parallel those in the Synoptic Gospels, and some scholars argue that a few of the others do probably represent genuine sayings. In any case, whatever else the Gospels may be, what they are not is biographies; they are essentially selective theological reflections on the life and teachings of Jesus.

What criteria, then, were used to discriminate between canonical and apocryphal (meaning to hide from general use) writings, and when did this process begin and end? The word 'canon' itself is derived from another Greek word, *kanon*, meaning a straight rod, a tool often used by a craftsman as a level or plumbline, or as a scribe's ruler. Broadly speaking in the context of scripture, it provided a criterion or standard by which to measure the truth, but was not used of the authoritative collection of Christian writings in that way before about 350.[60] That in itself begins to give a clue as to how long this process took. Today, if asked for criteria to justify the authority or canonicity of the New Testament, many Christians would first use the word 'inspired', in the sense of divine origin. Early Christians, however, would not have affirmed this as the major reason. While not denying that the Bible was inspired, they would not have seen it as the ground of its uniqueness; inspiration was a far broader activity than just biblical, and involved other writings, as well as sermons, decrees of Councils and a variety of other activities. The often-quoted verse about all scripture being inspired (2 Tim. 3:16) referred exclusively to the Jewish scriptures, as the writer of the letter had neither a sense of composing scripture himself, nor any concept at that date of specifically Christian scripture. In short, inspiration was not the reason that certain writings were authoritative: 'A writing is not canonical because the author was inspired, but rather an author is considered to be inspired because what he has written is recognized as canonical, that is, is recognised as authoritative in the Church.'[61]

Any writer could claim divine inspiration for his work; what was required was an external and more objective judgement to affirm or deny this. The problem was that just as early Christians had no universal mechanism for discerning orthodoxy from heresy, so they had no recognized system for declaring certain texts canonical, and therefore inspired. Thus if one examines what prominent individual Christians, or groups of Christians, regarded as authoritative writings in these early centuries, one will find both surprising inclusions and omissions. So, for instance, a number of the Christian writings mentioned above but not now included in the New Testament were regarded as scripture by many influential early Christians. The *Didache* was so regarded by Origen and Clement of Alexandria, and *The Shepherd* of Hermas was used as scripture by Irenaeus, Tertullian, Clement and Origen. At the same time, many of these early Christian writings quote from what is now regarded as canonical scripture, but in such a way that makes it clear that their authors did not consider it so. For instance, the author of the First Letter of Clement quotes from several Pauline letters, but in a way that makes it clear that he did not see them as scripture; the same is true for Ignatius of Antioch, Hermas and other second-century writers.

Even by the early fourth century the Church historian, Eusebius, was still unsure whether or not a number of books should be counted as scriptural. He lists 22 books which he regards as unquestionably scriptural, and all of them are in our New Testament, but then sees a number of others where his evidence is divided about their exact status, including the letters of James, Jude, 2 Peter, and 2 & 3 John. He is also rather ambivalent about the exact status of Revelation, shown by the fact that he places it in both his list of canonical books and his list of spurious ones. Thus even after three centuries it was still not precisely clear to the most educated and informed of Christians what was, or was not, canonical scripture.[62] It was not, in fact, until 367 that we find the first occasion in which a list of canonical New Testament writings contains exactly the 27 books of our version without additions or subtractions, included in one of his Easter letters by Athanasius, Bishop of Alexandria (*c.* 296–373). However, that should not be taken to mean that the issue was settled; this was only the personal opinion of one bishop. A contemporary of Athanasius, Gregory of Nazianzus (330–90) still omitted Revelation from his list, and in Armenia and Georgia Revelation was not added to their New Testaments until several centuries after that.[63]

But by about 300 it was generally accepted that there was a core of about twenty books which were more or less universally recognized as authoritative, including the four Gospels, Acts of the Apostles and Pauline letters. Around the periphery of this large core group there were a number of other writings added or subtracted, containing both the modern canonical books and apocryphal writings, the precise mix of which depended on the particular individual or geographical region concerned. In coming to this conclusion of whether or not a particular text was scripture, the date of its composition was not a major factor, however; for instance, the First Letter of Clement, written in the mid-90s was contemporary with many books now in the canon, and indeed somewhat earlier than several others, but has not been considered as scripture itself for over seventeen centuries. Age in itself was not good enough. There were three main criteria that did emerge, however, as the crucial ones for determining canonicity; these can be classified as orthodoxy, apostolicity and consensus.

First of all a book had to be considered orthodox, or teach right belief, in its entirety. One reason why the Gospel of Thomas was suspect was that some of its listed sayings of Jesus were clearly influenced by Gnosticism. Thus it did not pass the test of truth handed down by tradition. The second test was apostolicity. That did not necessarily mean that the text had to be personally written by an apostle, but it did mean that its basic teaching and narrative of events had to derive ultimately from an apostolic source. Thus the Gospel of Mark was considered to have been derived from Peter, and Luke was a personal associate of Paul, thus guaranteeing his authority. The third test was consensus. Had a particular book been accepted and used, in the sense of read in the liturgy and used for teaching, by a large number of local churches over a long enough period of time? Was there a wide enough consensus, in other words, that a book was both orthodox and apostolical? Writing in 414 about the disputed authorship of the letter to the Hebrews (was it really by Paul?), the great biblical scholar Jerome, (*c.* 345–420) argued that precise authorship was not the crucial issue, but rather that a book had been constantly read in the churches.[64] By about 300, then, it was these three criteria together that were now consistently applied to determine canonicity.

Yet this was still largely a matter of convention; there were no written guidelines that stated that these three were to be followed exclusively. And in coming to these conclusions it had sometimes been the influence of both internal and external forces that had been crucial. Gnosticism had produced its own gospels which sometimes utilized, but distorted, material from the four canonical ones, thus perhaps helping to oblige other Christians to define more clearly which texts and which ideas were orthodox, and accelerating the movement from an oral to a written tradition. Then in the 140s a Christian called Marcion, believing that the Church was already in need of reformation, especially in the sense of purging of its Jewish influences, and in pursuit of this goal, effectively produced his own canon of scripture containing one Gospel, Luke, and ten of the Pauline letters, all with their Jewish influences edited out.

Did this force other Christians to begin thinking in terms of a canon of their own? The utterances of the prophets of Montanism were regarded as scripture by their followers, rather like the Book of Mormon in the nineteenth century, which may have acted negatively to cast doubts over other apocalyptic writings and encouraged a greater emphasis on the apostolic origins of texts. And as ever, Christianity was not immune to secular forces outside itself. During periods of persecution one of the consistent demands of the imperial authorities was for Christians to surrender their sacred books; this in its turn may have helped to make Christians decide which books could or could not be given up with a clear conscience.[65] But however these three criteria were applied, and whatever influences brought them to prominence in the second century, there still remained no final and unquestionable authority that could determine canonicity. In the course of the fourth and fifth centuries, as we shall see in the following chapters, many Councils of bishops were to meet to try to determine issues of faith and practice in the Church. Yet not one of them drew up a list of canonical books. In fact it was not until the Council of Florence (1439–43) that the Western Church finally issued a definitive list of 27 canonical books of the New Testament.[66]

By the close of the third century Christians thus had a number of evolving authorities to which they could appeal for guidance. They had a hierarchical clergy, an emerging concept of orthodoxy, and a basic core of scriptural writings. But as yet none of these was finalized or clear cut; bishops faced challenges from more charismatic individuals and groups, there was no mechanism for establishing a universal definition of orthodoxy on a range of disputed interpretations, and the final form of the biblical canon was still unclear. And which of these three took precedence? From Carthage, Tertullian had argued that scripture could not be the sole source of authority, while in third-century Alexandria bishops forbade laymen from expounding on the scriptures in church, seeing it as an exclusively episcopal function, and later in Caesarea in the fourth century Basil was to argue that the Bible could only be the starting point in an understanding of the faith. Yet at the same time it could also be asserted that: 'In Scripture, a greater voice spoke, to which the bishop, too, was subordinate.' Tensions between these fluctuating centres of authority already existed, and were to be rehearsed frequently in the coming centuries. In some ways, then, while Christianity had on the one hand survived the opposition of Judaism, Hellenism and Roman imperialism, and had grown spectacularly in numbers, on the other hand it still remained in a state of comparative infancy and vulnerability.[67]

Conclusion

Early Christians believed that a great religious treasure had been entrusted to them, the knowledge of a God who had given himself to the world as a sacrifice for the sins of humankind, and the means to become new creations and enter into a living relationship with him. But that treasure had been entrusted to some very fragile earthen vessels. Just as God had made himself vulnerable by entrusting his incarnate Son, Jesus, to the processes of human history, so also his written word, his human followers and the organizations they had created were equally part of that historical process, and equally vulnerable and fragile. Human history is seldom neat and tidy; more often it is positively messy. But for the history of Christianity that was the consequence of incarnation. What we have been examining was a process, or, if you prefer, a journey through time and space that reveals how untidy Christian history could be.

But it also included another process, that of a developing relationship. Just as each individual Christian believed that he or she was on a journey of spiritual self-discovery through a relationship with a risen and living Lord, so the whole Christian community was also travelling on a parallel collective journey. Both were processes; neither was a completion. The incarnation, crucifixion and resurrection represented both a fulfilment and a commencement, rather like Americans use the word of their university degree ceremonies. Completion would only come with the *parousia* and the end of time and space themselves. Until then Christ's body, his *ekklesia*, was also vulnerable in a fallen world. But it was to that world that this new faith presented new challenges: as the Jews of Thessalonica had found, these Christians were turning the world upside down. Religion for them was a matter of personal choice not birth, led by a totally new type of hierarchy based on service not status, where tradition had become a living and ever-new force, not just the veneration of a dead past. These at least were the ideals. The great question for the unfolding history of Christianity was how far it could remain true to these ideals, and how far the flawed nature of the world would compromise them. Would tradition become traditionalism, a dead faith? Similarly, would authority lapse into authoritarianism, domination rather than service?

As Christianity moved into its fourth century, it had survived imperial persecution, battered but still intact, if fragile and vulnerable like its divine founder. What did the future hold for it? Would its weakness be its strength? As Christians contemplated that future, in 312 a Roman general was marching with his legions to seize the imperial throne in Rome, in itself an event that had already been repeated many times in the history of the Empire. But this general was about to experience his own encounter with divinity, his own epiphany, in a vision and a dream, both like and unlike that which many Romans had experienced before him. No one could have predicted it, but its outcome would represent one of the pivotal moments in the history of both Christianity and the Empire, and its effects would reverberate down the centuries to come.

Suggested Further Reading

There are many general histories of Christianity, but among those published in recent years I would perhaps begin with Christopher Catherwood, *Crash Course on Church History* (Hodder and Stoughton, 1998). This covers all two millennia in under 200 pages, and is very well done. Owen Chadwick, *A History of Christianity* (Weidenfeld and Nicolson, 1995) is somewhat more substantial and also illustrated. *The Oxford Illustrated History of Christianity* (Oxford University Press, 1990), edited by John McManners, is a collection of essays by different authors, but is heavily weighted to the post-1800 period. Adrian Hastings (ed.), *A World History of Christianity* (Cassell, 1999) is also a collection of pieces by a variety of scholars, and this time weighted towards the non-European experience of Christianity. At the more 'popular' end of the market Brian Moynahan, *The Faith: A History of Christianity* (Pimlico, 2003) shares both the strengths and weaknesses of this approach, being an easy read and well illustrated. But its use of original sources is too often rather uncritical, and the bibliography and footnotes reveal some crucial gaps in the secondary literature reflected in the main text. Perhaps the book that achieves the best balance of being scholarly, readable and comprehensive is David L. Edwards, *Christianity: The First Two Thousand Years* (Cassell, 1997). But be warned, it is a very substantial book.

Among document collections, Henry Bettenson and Chris Maunder, *Documents of the Christian Church* (Oxford University Press, third edition, 1999) is excellent. For general reference books it would be hard to beat *The Oxford Dictionary of the Christian Church* (Oxford University Press, third edition, 2005) edited by F. L. Cross and E. A. Livingstone. It is 1,800 pages long and very expensive, but it has established itself as perhaps the best single-volume reference work. For a collection of maps, supplemented by pictures and text, *Atlas of the Christian Church*, edited by Henry Chadwick and G. R. Evans, and published by Time-Life Books in 1988, is excellent.

Among the shorter general introductions to the history of the early Church, which cover not only the first 300 years but also the areas that we shall be dealing with in the following chapters, a good starting point is provided by Joseph F. Kelly, *The World of the Early Christians* (The Liturgical Press, Collegeville, Minnesota, 1997). This makes few assumptions about the reader's existing knowledge, is written in a straightforward style, but by an acknowledged scholar in the field. Outwardly a little more sophisticated in approach is Gerard Vallée, *The Shaping of Christianity: The History and Literature of Its Formative Centuries (100–800)* (Paulist Press, 1999), but which would also make an excellent initial read. Other relatively short modern introductions include Norbert Brox, *A History of the Early Church* (SCM Press, 1994), while Ian Hazlett has edited a collection of essays, *Early Christianity: Origins and Evolution to 600* (SPCK, 1991) which, like many such collections, has some essays which would interest particular readers more than others. And for a long time Henry Chadwick's *The Early Church* (Penguin, 1967) has rightly been regarded as an essential introduction.

Two more substantial books stand out. The first is W. H. C. Frend, *The Rise of Christianity* (Fortress Press, Philadelphia, 1984). It is detailed and scholarly, but is perhaps now beginning to date a little, especially in some of its interpretations and generally rather 'triumphalist' approach to the growth of Christianity. The other is by Henry Chadwick. *The Church in Ancient Society: From Galilee to Gregory the Great* (Oxford University Press, 2001) is obviously more recent, and the fruit of a long and distinguished career; however, despite the wealth of detail and learning, some readers might find it a little disappointing, and this is largely due to its structure. It has over 60 short chapters, further divided by numerous sub-headings, many of which are based around a particular individual, and all of which can tend to break up the flow of ideas.

However, once a good general understanding of early Christianity has been acquired, then Philip Rousseau, *The Early Christian Centuries* (Longman, 2002) becomes an enlightening read. Original and sophisticated in approach, definitely not a starting point, but a book that will reward perseverance, and cannot be too highly recommended. It also includes extensive modern bibliographies.

To move on to more specific topics discussed in this chapter, then on baptism and the Eucharist perhaps a classic work is Gregory Dix, *The Shape of the Liturgy* (Dacre Press, 1945). More recent is *The Study of Liturgy* (Oxford University Press, revised edition, 1992), edited by Cheslyn Jones and others, which covers the whole history of Christian liturgy from the New Testament down to the present day. There is a good collection of documents, *Life and Practice in the Early Church: A Documentary Reader* (New York University Press, 2001), edited with commentaries by Steven A. McKinion.

There is now a vast literature on the role of women in the early Church, but good recent studies include Deborah F. Sawyer, *Women and Religion in the First Christian Centuries* (Routledge, 1999), D. M. Scholer, *Women in Early Christianity* (Garland, New York, 1993) and Ben Witherington, *Women and the Genesis of Christianity* (Cambridge University Press, 1990). For Christian attitudes to homosexuality from the ancient to the late medieval worlds, John Boswell, *Christianity, Social Tolerance and Homosexuality* (University of Chicago Press, 1980) remains fundamental.

For religion in the Roman Empire, and especially relationships between traditional polytheism and Christianity, Robin Lane Fox, *Pagans and Christians* (Viking, 1986) is unsurpassed in both its learning and style. But see also Keith Hopkins, *A World Full of Gods: Pagans, Jews and Christians in the Roman Empire* (Weidenfeld and Nicolson, 1999); but beware, this is not a conventional approach to writing history, as he interjects fictional passages, some including time travellers, into the text. For more general studies of the Empire see Martin Goodman, *The Roman World 44BC–AD180* (Routledge, 1997), especially the section on 'Humans and Gods'; and Averil Cameron, *The Later Roman Empire AD284–430* (Fontana Press, 1993). For a fascinating insight into Roman views of Christianity, Robert Louis Wilkin, *The Christians as the Romans Saw Them* (Yale University Press, second edition, 2003) is a brief study of Christianity's main intellectual critics. For the Christian side of the debate, based around the writings of many early Christian Fathers, see the same author's *The Spirit of Early Christian Thought: Seeking the Face of God* (Yale University Press, 2003).

For the growth of Christianity the classic study is Adolf Harnack, *The Mission and Expansion of Christianity in the First Three Centuries* (Williams and Norgate, two volumes, 1908). However, the modern work to read is undoubtedly *The Rise of Christianity* (Princeton University Press, 1996) by Rodney Stark. Challenging and original in approach, it must, however, be read with caution and a critical eye. There are a number of articles relating to this book in the *Journal of Early Christian Studies* (Johns Hopkins University Press) Number 6, 2, 1998, that are well worth reading.

On the subject of martyrdom, W. H. C. Frend, *Martyrdom and Persecution in the Early Church: A Study of a Conflict from the Maccabees to Donatus* (Basil Blackwell, Oxford, 1965) has long established itself as the classic text. But again it has become somewhat dated with the passage of time, not least from the fact that it is clearly written from a very sympathetic Christian perspective. It should now be supplemented by newer works, especially Daniel Boyarin, *Dying for God: Martyrdom and the Making of Christianity and Judaism* (Stanford University Press, Stanford, 1999) who has a very different view of the Jewish context to Frend's, and G. W. Bowerstock, *Martyrdom and Rome* (Cambridge University Press, 1995) which explores the specifically Roman background.

A book which covers the miracles and missions aspect is Ramsay MacMullen, *Christianizing the Roman Empire (AD100–400)* (Yale University Press, 1984) although some readers might find the style a little informal for so academic a work.

On the concept of orthodoxy a good modern study is the collection of essays edited by Rowan Williams, *The Making of Orthodoxy: Essays in Honour of Henry Chadwick* (Cambridge University Press, 1989). Another excellent study, based heavily on the original sources, is Jaroslav Pelikan, *The Christian Tradition: A History of the Development of Doctrine, Volume I: The Emergence of the Catholic Tradition (100–600)* (University of Chicago Press, 1971).

The literature on the New Testament, and especially the emergence of the canon, is extensive. A good starting point for the study of the New Testament in general as well as the canon in particular is Arthur G. Patzia, *The Making of the New Testament: Origin, Collection, Text and Canon* (Inter-Varsity Press, 1995) which covers both practical and theoretical aspects. More specifically on the canon itself, Harry Y. Gamble, *The New Testament Canon: Its Making and Meaning* (Fortress Press, Philadelphia, 1985) is both succinct and lucid. Hans von Campenhausen, *The Formation of the Christian Bible* (Adam and Charles Black, 1972) is magesterial, covers the Old as well as the New Testament, but is now a little dated. Bruce M. Metzger, *The Canon of the New Testament: Its Origin, Development and Significance* (Clarendon Press, Oxford, 1987) is hugely scholarly and detailed, and should only be approached after reading the books by Patzia and Gamble. For the views of a distinguished ancient historian, who is also an atheist, Robin Lane Fox, *The Unauthorized Version: Truth and Fiction in the Bible* (Viking, 1991) is well worth reading. Covering the whole history of the Bible he sometimes comes to conclusions that many modern biblical scholars and theologians would now find uncomfortably conservative, but which can be surprisingly refreshing.

For commentary on the New Testament books themselves, the literature is not only vast, and the text of the New Testament has probably the longest and most extensive critical bibliography of any literary work, certainly in the Western world. The first commentaries appeared as early as the mid-second century and have continued down to the present day. It is thus difficult to know where to begin, but perhaps Raymond E. Brown, *An Introduction to the New Testament* (Doubleday, 1997) would be a good starting point, although this is still a substantial volume. Specifically for the letters of St Paul there is also a seemingly endless stream of commentaries. However, a good, and this time short, starting point would be E. P. Sanders, *Paul: A Very Short Introduction* (Oxford University Press, 1991). Both of these contain good bibliographies for those who wish to pursue their reading further. For a somewhat different approach the short introductions to each book of the New Testament by Tom Wright are written from a firmly Christian perspective and are as much spiritual reflections as they are commentaries. They are in a series called *For Everyone*.

For Christian writings not in the New Testament, the standard work is now J. K. Elliott, *The Apocryphal New Testament: A Collection of Apocryphal Christian Literature in English Translation* (Clarendon Press, Oxford, 1993) which replaces the volume by M. R. James first edited in the 1920s. For a shorter collection of texts mentioned in this introduction, such as the First Letter of Clement, the Letters of Ignatius, and the *Didache*, see *Early Christian Writings: The Apostolic Fathers* (Penguin, second edition, 1987) edited by Maxwell Staniforth and Andrew Louth. *Against the Heresies* by Irenaeus can be found in an excellent modern English translation in Robert M. Grant, *Irenaeus of Lyons* (Routledge, 1997). There is an equally excellent modern English translation of *Eusebius: The History of the Church from Christ to Constantine* (Penguin, second edition, 1989) by G. A. Williamson and Andrew Louth. This is perhaps the single most important primary source for the first three centuries of Christianity, mainly because about one-fifth of the book consists of earlier texts collected by Eusebius in the fourth century.

PART ONE

Christ and Caesar: Christianity *c.* 300–*c.* 500

1

Imperial Christianity

For he must reign until he has put all his enemies under his feet. (1 Cor. 15:25)

To mark the conclusion of the great Council of bishops and their representatives who had gathered from all over the Christian world in the city of Nicaea on the Asiatic side of the Bosphorus in 325, and also to celebrate the twentieth anniversary of his accession, the Emperor Constantine held a lavish banquet to entertain and honour the bishops. This was an 'event beyond all description. Guards and soldiers ringed the entrance to the palace, guarding it with drawn swords, and between these the men of God passed fearlessly, and entered the innermost royal courts.'

What had happened to transform Christian leaders from being despised, persecuted and at the margins of Roman society into the honoured representatives of a faith worthy to receive such lavish imperial favour?[1]

New Empire, New Faith

The idea that the Empire itself could be transformed into an instrument fit for divine purpose was one with a long Christian pedigree. Justin Martyr in the mid-second century had argued that Christians were far from being politically seditious, actually praying for the Emperor and his Empire. Bishop Melito of Sardis (died *c.* 190) had perhaps been the first Christian writer to point to a chronological convergence between the Empire and Christianity, both emerging in the same generation. And in the following century Origen looked to a time when all humanity would recognize the truth of the gospel, within a Christianized Empire able to defeat its enemies by the power of prayer and divine intervention. This line of argument was to culminate with

Eusebius in the early fourth century who saw the Empire as part of the workings of divine providence, and having a common destiny with Christianity itself in bringing humanity to unity and concord.[2]

The political instability which had plagued the Empire in the middle decades of the third century began to ease in 284 when the army in the eastern provinces proclaimed their general, Diocletian, as Emperor, and within a year he had won control of the west as well. Diocletian was aware that at the heart of imperial instability lay the interlinked problems of space and time; the vast geographical extent of the Empire's territories, and the comparative lack of any sense of continuity in their rule. By 293 he had devised a complex plan to attempt to alleviate these by creating a multiple system of overlapping rule through a tetrarchy. The Empire was divided into eastern and western halves with an Augustus as supreme ruler in each; since 286 he had been the senior Augustus in the east, with Maximian as his junior Augustus in the west. Now below each Augustus he further subdivided each half of the Empire by creating a Caesar as a deputy and unofficial heir for each Augustus, Galerius in the east and Constantius in the west. In theory an order of succession of four Emperors had been created, dynastically linked through a series of marriage alliances; Constantius, for instance, had put aside his first wife, Helena, and had married Theodora, a daughter of Maximian. Furthermore, to cement the unity of Empire and tetrarchy, these four figures had been invested with a sacred character, Diocletian and Galerius taking Jupiter as their protector, and Maximian and Constantius the heroic offspring and instrument of his divine will, Hercules, thus endowing the tetrarchy with an imperial theology.

At the same time, Diocletian also initiated a wholesale reconstruction of the Roman world at its military, economic and social levels. The army was gradually increased in size to perhaps half a million men, a huge and now permanent demographic burden on the Empire requiring conscription and heavy taxation to maintain. Problems of inflation were tackled through the minting of new gold, silver and bronze coins, and by a brief but unsuccessful attempt at imperial control over the prices of a range of key goods. Administration was streamlined, but at the same time expanded, by doubling the number of provinces to about 100, to make each one smaller, but then grouping these provinces into twelve dioceses, with each Emperor directly administering three. Roman law, the Latin language and the worship of the traditional deities were now all utilized to achieve the desired goal of cultural unity across society.

Where did Christianity fit into this new imperial scheme? By the end of the third century, with its rapidly growing numbers and emerging sense of its own organizational identity, this was one minority no Emperor could afford to ignore. For most Christians, however, improving political, economic and social stability were as welcome as they were to the 'pagan' population at large. This term, derived from *pagani* meaning rustics or country dwellers, was the unflattering shorthand that Christians used to denote that bewildering array of religious groups and philosophical schools that had developed over the centuries around the Mediterranean. This is a word I have deliberately avoided using until now as it has obviously acquired negative and inaccurate overtones with the passage of time, was not a word the 'pagans' themselves used, and implied a unity of belief and practice at variance with reality. However, it was in the attempt to revive traditional paganism in its religious sense that the gravest problems for Christianity were to arise in this new and more autocratic Empire. Ultimately Christianity could not be accommodated within this vital aspect of the imperial scheme of reconstruction.

This started to become clear as early as 297 when formal pagan sacrifices were ordered to be performed throughout the army, which presented Christian soldiers with a stark choice of disobedience to either Emperor or faith. This dilemma came to a head two years later when an animal sacrifice failed to provide clear signs for the priests to interpret on the entrails, and this disaster was blamed on Christian soldiers standing nearby who had made the sign of the cross on their foreheads as a protection against this demonic rite. A purging of Christians in the army and at the imperial court followed. Then, in February 303, having consulted the oracle of Apollo at Didyma, which warned him that the Christians were (perhaps somewhat conveniently for the oracle) preventing the god from speaking the truth, Diocletian issued an imperial edict ordering the destruction of Christian buildings, books and liturgical vessels throughout the Empire. Over the following few years a further series of edicts intensified the persecution which was to last intermittently for a decade. After two generations of relatively peaceful coexistence this renewal of persecution is now seen more as an aberration than an inevitability, and more the result of political machinations than religious hostility, with Galerius as its main instigator, using it as a device to enhance his status within the tetrarchy.[3] But whatever its motivation, despite the deaths of thousands of Christians, and the apostasy of an even greater number, the attempt to force them into religious and cultural conformity ultimately failed. For one thing, it now seems clear that most pagans did not share the fanatical hatred of those around Galerius, and many examples of Christians being hidden by sympathetic pagan friends and neighbours point to a lack of popular support for the policy.[4]

In any case there were marked differences between the east and the west in the severity with which persecution was implemented. In Britain, Gaul and Spain the Caesar, Constantius, was much more in tune with this popular sentiment, and, apart from some token gestures, little seems to have been done to disturb the life of Christians under his rule. This has led to some modern speculation that his relative tolerance was derived from much deeper, if secret, sympathies for the faith, and to the possibility that he and his family were actually to some degree members of the Christian community.[5] Whatever the truth of this, it is certain that his son, Constantine, was acutely aware of the contrast between his father's policy and that of Galerius which he had personally witnessed in the east during its initial unfolding.

The abdications of Diocletian and Maximian in May 305, however, set in motion a train of events that was to transform the fortunes and status of Christianity within the Empire. Galerius and Constantius were now elevated to Augusti in east and west respectively. But the promotion of Maximin in the east and Severus in the west as the new Caesars produced dynastic instability in the reconstructed tetrarchy, as the claims of the sons of both Constantius and Maximian had been overlooked. Within a year, however, Maxentius, the son of Maximian, had replaced Severus, and reappointed his father as Augustus after the death of Constantius. Then, following a failed attempt to invade Italy in his capacity as senior Augustus in 307, Galerius lost the capacity to impose his will on the western provinces, while Constantine, proclaimed Emperor by his legions at York after his father's death in 306, bided his time, and continued his father's policy of comparative religious toleration.

By 311 Maximian was dead and Galerius dying. Virtually on his deathbed the latter had issued an edict formally ending persecution, although the eastern Caesar, Maximin, was to continue with it for a while longer in the provinces under his control. In the west this growing instability was to be ended by a final military conflict between Maxentius and Constantine. In 312 Constantine led his army, by all accounts much smaller in number than his opponent's, into northern Italy, and in a brilliant campaign of battles and sieges defeated much of Maxentius's superior forces and arrived within striking distance of the virtually impregnable walls of Rome. Instead of waiting prudently behind these defences, Maxentius took the fatal decision to come out and meet Constantine in pitched battle. At the Milvian bridge he was defeated and drowned in the Tiber, allowing Constantine to enter Rome in triumph.

But the Constantine who now marched into the imperial city was, in one vital respect, a changed man from the one who had entered Italy a few months before. At some unknown point before the climatic battle he had had an encounter with divinity, an epiphany that was to permanently affect both his personal destiny and that of the Roman world. Two years earlier there had been stories of a vision that Constantine was supposed to have had of the god Apollo.[6] But now, as he awaited Maxentius outside Rome, he began to muse on the role of the divine in political and military affairs, and to argue with himself that those who appealed to many gods had foundered, while his own father, who recognized a single god, had been more fortunate. Now he began to pray to this one god to reveal himself and help Constantine in the coming battle, all concepts familiar to anyone in the ancient pagan world.

And so, out of a clear blue sky, Constantine had his new vision, followed by a confirmatory dream. But the god who had now revealed himself to Constantine was none other than the God of the Christians, and by his sign of the cross Constantine was promised his victory. Like Paul on the road to Damascus, Constantine had been singled out by God and endowed with unchallengeable charismatic authority to lead the Roman world to Christ (Document 5).

What are we to make of this imperial epiphany? First of all, we should not confuse a modern reaction with an ancient one; a vision or dream of a god was neither particularly novel nor disturbing in the ancient world. Great rulers especially were almost expected to experience such things, as the account of Constantine's encounter with Apollo in 310 makes clear. The first tetrarchy had also associated itself closely with pagan divinities, and looked to them for help and protection. But clearly, what seemed ordinary and natural to the ancient world may appear far less so to a modern audience. Consequently much time and ink have been expended in the attempt to explain, or explain away, this event that Eusebius and ancient Christians accepted as miraculous. One problem with the account given by Eusebius that has been noted is the obvious difference between it and the earlier one by the prominent Christian convert, Lactantius, probably written in 314–15, much nearer to the events than Eusebius writing in the 330s. Lactantius briefly recorded a dream only, not a preceding vision, in which Constantine was advised to mark his soldier's shields with a 'heavenly sign . . . a slanted letter X with the top of its head bent round'.[7] This has led some to the conclusion that Eusebius's much more extensive and elaborate account must be an invention either in whole or in part.[8]

Not surprisingly it has thus also led to much modern speculation that what Constantine might have seen could be explained in scientific rather than miraculous terms. Could the sign against the sun be accounted for by the rare, but scientifically demonstrated, effect of sunlight on ice crystals? Was his dream the product of the extreme levels of tension and stress naturally experienced before a decisive battle?[9] What we can say, however, is that Constantine's behaviour after his vision, dream and victory were very different from his behaviour before them. Upon entry into Rome, Constantine refused to offer the usual sacrifice to Jupiter; the language used by the panegyrist to celebrate his victory, and the wording on his eventual triumphal arch, were both strangely ambiguous when discussing the precise divinity which had given him success; and Christian bishops rapidly joined the imperial court in some numbers.[10] In the years which followed, Constantine also shifted from his pre-312 policy of relative toleration to one of outright support for Christianity, showering the Church with huge gifts and deliberately elevating the status of the clergy. And the Christian talisman that he had ordered to be made, the Labarum, continued to be carried with his armies during subsequent campaigns. Clearly Constantine believed, and acted as if he believed, that something had happened to him in the period immediately before the battle at the Milvian bridge. And in his account of the 330s, Eusebius stresses both that he received his information personally and directly from the Emperor, and that the events were witnessed by more people than just Constantine.[11]

Whatever view is taken, it is the consequences that flowed from Constantine's experience that are of real historical significance. And in order to understand them we must first of all appreciate the context in which Christianity now moved from the periphery to centre stage in the life of the Empire, in the sense of the symbiotic relationship between the state and religion universally accepted in the ancient world. It was virtually impossible for people in that world to conceive of a significant religious institution separate from the state. Christianity had, of necessity, grown and developed independently from the Empire, and so long as that Empire worshipped false gods, Christians would be obliged to keep their distance. But at the same time many Christian thinkers, as we have seen, naturally looked forward to a time when their faith and the Empire could join forces for a common purpose. But that could only be on Christianity's terms. With the unexpected and quite unpredictable miracle of Constantine's conversion, the first and crucial of those terms had been met. This helps to explain the apparently remarkable lack of hesitation on the part of Christians, from their leaders downwards, in accepting the new role and status conferred on their faith by an Empire that had only recently been bent on forcing their compliance with its pagan culture. Now Christians saw an opportunity to reverse this, and transform the Empire itself into their ally; a two-way process in which the Empire was made fit for divine purpose and at the same time the Church would ensure the Empire's peace, prosperity and victory over its enemies through its prayers and intercessions with the true God. Constantine shared with his polytheistic predecessors this conception of the success of the Empire stemming from its correct worship of divinity. For him, the confirmation that he had chosen the true divinity was his own continuing success, from the Milvian bridge to his final triumph over the eastern Augustus, Licinius, in 324, to bring the whole Roman world once more under a single ruler.[12]

The process of Christianizing this Roman world, however, required far more than just the conversion of a particular Emperor. In any case, in 312 a Christian Emperor ruled only the western half of the Empire; in the east, where most Christians lived, the Augustus remained a pagan. So the gifts of money or land that Constantine lavished on the Church, or the exemptions from taxation or expensive public service which he granted to the clergy, only affected a minority of Christians before 324. Nor did his own conversion trigger a wave of mass conversions among his pagan subjects; even by the time of his death in 337 it is probable that Christians still remained a minority, if by then a considerable one, within the Empire as a whole. A century after his death, pagans themselves still existed in significant numbers, and in the early 390s remained strong enough to launch a military rebellion against the Christian Emperor, Theodosius, only quashed at the battle of the river Frigidus in 394. So the degree to which Constantine could Christianize his Empire remained relatively limited. Indeed, a distinction must be made between the Empire at the state and government level, and the Empire at the demographic and cultural levels. We can, perhaps, speak of a Christian government under Constantine, but not yet of a Christian empire in the fullest sense of that term.

So Constantine had to advance slowly and carefully in a number of stages in his Christianizing programme. Until his final victory in 324 this was largely limited at the official level to the terms of the so-called Edict of Milan issued jointly by Licinius and himself in 313. This document effectively ended persecution throughout the Empire, restored confiscated property to the Church, and allowed it to hold common property under Roman law; in addition, while it granted freedom of worship to all faiths, it specifically singled out Christianity as a religion particularly favoured by the state. This was a compromise designed to establish the joint rule of the two Augusti on as broad a religious base as possible. But after 324 Constantine was able to 'openly and actively propagate Christianity while he barely and reluctantly tolerated paganism'.[13] Christians were increasingly favoured for government posts, officials were dissuaded from offering pagan sacrifices, temples were looted for their treasures, and bishops gained extensive legal powers as judges in a range of cases.

Nowhere was this strategy of Christianization more literally visible than in the vast building programme initiated by Constantine. Indeed, he may well have been the greatest of the Roman imperial builders, a distinction rather obscured by the passage of time as so many of his projects have either been destroyed or rebuilt over the centuries. But as we saw in the Introduction, it was the lack of grand, purpose-built structures for worship in comparison to the extensive temple complexes which allowed many polytheists to dismiss Christianity as a serious religion; it just did not look the part. The first generations of Christians themselves further emphasized this distinction. It was the people in the assembly who were holy, not the buildings they worshipped in; divinity resided inside the individual and was not to be sought at a geographical location (Acts 17:24; 2 Cor. 6:16). Constantine's building programme began to modify and reassess this viewpoint.

At one level, then, new church buildings could be seen as a form of propaganda for his new faith, changing the urban landscape of the Empire as profoundly as the first Augustus had done three centuries earlier. But there were also deeper layers of meaning expressed by these visible signs of Christian advance. Roman cities had always had a sacred geography of temple, forum, circus, palace or theatre proclaiming the links between public and religious life. Truly to take possession of the Empire, Christians would now have to do the same; speak the same language as the pagans, as it were, and annex urban geography for their faith. This process began soon after Constantine's capture of Rome itself. Here, he and his architects effectively created the pattern for church building that has predominated throughout subsequent Christian history. They deliberately avoided the form of the pagan temple but instead used as their model the building type known as the basilica, a long central hall with colonnades, side aisles, and apsidal end, that across the Empire was the city assembly room, court house and audience hall in one structure. This they now transformed into a new type of sacred space. Avoiding the pagan centre of Rome, Constantine effectively ringed the city with eight massive Christian basilicas, including St Peter's, St John Lateran, and St Paul's Outside the Walls. His Christian mother, Helena, during her famous pilgrimage to the Holy land in 326–7 similarly initiated construction of more basilicas, including the Holy Sepulchre over the recovered tomb of Christ to celebrate the resurrection, and the Church of the Nativity in Bethlehem around the cave in which Jesus was supposed to have been born. In addition, great imperial cities such as Trier, Nicomedia and Antioch all received new Christian basilicas. And all of this building work culminated and climaxed in a new imperial city. On the European shore of the Bosphorus, on a magnificent site, in 324 Constantine began the reconstruction of the old Greek city of Byzantium, and, like Alexander the Great and Julius Caesar before him, renamed his city after himself: Constantinople. Here a new palace, forum, hippodrome and churches were laid out along wide avenues, secured on three sides by the sea, and on the landward side by a new defensive wall, and, like the original Rome, divided into fourteen districts.

But over time, it was the dedications given to these new church buildings, and what Christians placed inside them, that did as much as anything to transform their meaning. As well as creating a new sacred geography, these buildings were also concerned to preserve and celebrate sacred time; to memorialize for ever the history of their own community and faith, and to replicate the history of human salvation. These were ambitions that stemmed from the very nature of a religion of incarnation. God had entered time and space himself and made them potentially holy. This pattern of salvation was now to be laid out on the ground in order to tell the greatest of all stories. This began with the naming or dedication of churches, at first by recounting events in the biblical narrative as with Helena in the Holy Land; but as the fourth century progressed this moved on to the commemoration of the age of the martyrs. Salvation history itself now included the great heroes of the faith. Most dramatically of all, the physical remains of martyrs were now moved, or 'translated', from their place of original burial and brought inside these new churches, and laid to rest beneath the altars on which the Eucharist was celebrated, linking the crucifixion of Jesus to the sacrifice of those who had died for their faith in him, and transforming remains into sacred relics. The church building now became a meeting place of the living with the dead, the point at which heaven and earth met, a visible symbol of an ongoing tradition.

In the changed historical circumstances of the fourth century, Christianity could proclaim its message in ways thought impossible and inappropriate in the first. Without losing that sense of distinction between the holiness of the people rather than the buildings, these new structures could be seen as shifting the meaning of Christian buildings into a language more familiar to the worshippers in pagan temples, in a way analogous to the earlier shift associated with the acceptance and use of Greek philosophy to help explain Christian mysteries. This was a new language expressed now in stone. In its turn, these developments encouraged a new form of sacred travel: the pilgrimage. Again, this was a concept not unfamiliar in the pagan world. As we have already seen, countless numbers of pagans had made a similar journey to their own sacred sites for centuries. Helena was not alone in the fourth century in wishing to experience with a physical immediacy the sites of the great events of her faith. From this developed pilgrimages to the tombs of the new heroes, the martyrs, in the hope of transforming the inner spiritual life of individuals as they symbolically travelled along the pilgrimage of life to its ultimate destination arrived at so violently by the martyrs. And these new martyr shrines captured for ever the faith of those who had remained steadfast even unto death in an age of considerably diminished perils. Thus in so many new ways the Christian movement not only continued to develop itself but also in the process continued reinterpreting and making new so much in the life of the ancient world.[14]

Diversity and Division

The Christianity that Constantine encountered after his conversion in 312, and more especially after his conquest of the east in 324, was far from a uniform and homogeneous faith. As we have already seen in the Introduction, diversity was very much a hallmark of early Christianity. Under the stress of persecution, diversity had sometimes been so stretched that a number of open divisions had torn apart the fabric of the Christian body in many regions. The most significant of these in the west, and the one which Constantine would have to struggle with first, had occurred in north Africa. Here the church in the great city of Carthage, the second largest in the west, and in its hinterland, especially the province of Numidia, was divided and in a state of open schism. This had first erupted in 307 when a new Bishop of Carthage, Caecilian, had been elected and then consecrated by African, but crucially not Numidian, bishops. Now power politics, personality clashes and social and regional jealousies came to the surface. All of these in their turn had been exacerbated by the persecution and its aftermath. How should apostates be treated, and especially those who had handed over the sacred scriptures for burning? Numidians took a much harsher and rigorist line, calling for the re-baptism of these *traditores*, reviving the still-unresolved dispute between Cyprian of Carthage and Stephen of Rome in the previous century. When one of the bishops who had consecrated Caecilian was claimed to be a *traditor*, the Numidians declared his election and consecration invalid, and chose their own candidate as Bishop of Carthage, Majorinus. Now altar was raised against altar as rival clergies claimed the same jurisdictions, and parallel bishops began to emerge in city after city, as Numidians cast doubt over the validity and efficacy of sacraments performed by previously apostate clergy. When Majorinus was succeeded by the determined and charismatic Donatus, a local dispute blossomed into a full-blown schism that was eventually to take his name: Donatism.

Constantine was obliged to become involved in this bitter and escalating dispute when the Donatists appealed to him for judgement in his capacity as their new Christian Emperor. His own conversion was recent, and his knowledge of Christianity still largely unformed; but he was now plunged into the complex world of ecclesiastical politics and was obliged to take actions and make decisions far earlier in his career as both Emperor and Christian than was desirable.[15] He was thus influenced by bishops nearer to him, such as Ossius of Cordoba or Miltiades of Rome; and in addition the Donatists appeared to be the heirs of Tertullian and his vision of a defensive Church based on purity and rigour. Constantine would naturally have favoured the more open and outward-looking model as the one best attuned to the project of Christianizing his Empire.

However, he agreed to a formal judgement as the Donatists requested, but to be held in Rome under the supervision of its bishop. Donatus and Caecilian each brought ten episcopal supporters, three more bishops came from neutral Gaul, and fifteen more were selected from Italy by the Roman bishop. When this Council, perhaps not surprisingly given its weighting, found against Donatus, he appealed again to Constantine, who then convened a yet larger gathering at Arles in 314. Some 33 bishops and many other clergy met and upheld the judgement of the Roman Council. When the document purporting to demonstrate that one of the consecrators of Caecilian was a *traditor* was demonstrated to be a forgery, Constantine finally lost patience with the Donatists. Starting with an order to confiscate their property in 316, imperial persecution was once more unleashed, but now for the first time in support of one group of Christians against another. But like all previous attempts to obtain conformity by coercion, this one too proved a failure in the face of the grim intransigence of the Donatists, who positively rejoiced that martyrdom had now returned to prove and test the purity of their faith. They fed and grew fat on the poison meant to kill them. By 321 Constantine was obliged to call off this renewed persecution, and Donatism continued to flourish as an alternative Christian organization in Africa for many generations.

Among the more numerous Christians of the east, however, Constantine was to encounter divisions that surpassed Donatism in both their extent and significance, and challenged Christians to locate and identify with greater precision what should be universally believed and practised within an ideally undivided organization. Ignatius of Antioch back in the first decade of the second century had first employed the term 'catholic', derived from the Greek adjective *katholikos* meaning universal. Again, like the word pagan, I have consciously avoided using this term as it has also acquired deeply controversial status, especially since the sixteenth century. But Christians had employed the word since the time of Ignatius to mean those beliefs and practices employed by a single body that were meant for universal application by all Christians. But the very diversity of early Christianity, and the lack of any mechanism by which both orthodoxy and its related concept of catholicity could be defined, yet alone imposed, left the term as much as an ideal as orthodoxy itself.

With the arrival of an almost unbroken succession of Christian Emperors, however, the fourth and fifth centuries were to witness intense struggles to turn idealism into reality, and at last to locate with precision the organization which taught, in the words of Bishop Cyril of Jerusalem (*c.* 315–87) 'universally and without omission all the doctrines which ought to come to human knowledge', the body which God himself willed and ordained 'should exist throughout the whole world', as Augustine (354–430) was later to express it.[16] In other words, to set limits on the degree of legitimate diversity and so distinguish between the true body teaching the true faith, as opposed to sectarian distortions.

If Carthage and North Africa presented Constantine with serious problems of ecclesiastical division, those which had spread from Alexandria and Egypt to much of the eastern Empire before his conquest of 324 were of a different order of magnitude, involving not only schism but also a profound doctrinal divergence between competing claims of orthodoxy and catholicity. Problems had first arisen in Egypt in 306 during a lull in the persecution. The Bishop of Alexandria, Peter, drew up a list of canons or rules for the treatment of those who had apostasized in various ways. In all cases, after appropriate penance, both clergy and laity were readmitted to the fold. This relative leniency, perhaps not surprisingly, did not satisfy some of those who had remained steadfast, and their champion emerged in the person of Bishop Melitius of Lycopolis, who began to ordain clergy untainted with apostasy, but, crucially, without the authority of his nominal superior, Bishop Peter. As with the rigorous Donatists to the west this quickly resulted in a schism, and by the time Constantine gained political control of the east in 324, two parallel and overlapping church organizations existed across much of Egypt, with those dissenting from the authority of Peter's successors eventually called Melitians.[17]

This organizationally divided Church had, however, further fragmented with the emergence of a profound doctrinal dispute, itself originating from one of the greatest theological questions that early Christianity had to grapple with: the problem of reconciling monotheism inherited from Judaism with an acknowledgement of the divine status of Jesus and the Holy Spirit. This incipient Trinitarianism in its turn involved a sophisticated examination of the person and nature of Jesus of Nazareth; what precisely was his relationship to God, and in turn to the rest of humanity? This still ongoing debate is known as christology, and will be examined in more detail in Chapter 3. However, in about 318 a cleric of the Egyptian church called Arius (d. 336) was unwise enough to put his views into circulation in a popular poem called 'Thalia' in order to bring them to a wider and predominantly non-clerical audience. This quickly came to the attention of Alexander, Peter's successor as Bishop of Alexandria. He detected more than a whiff of heresy in this work, for it appeared that Arius had asserted that while God the Father was eternal, the Son was not, in that he was a creature of the Father's making, and thus inferior to God in character, essence or substance. A Council of Egyptian bishops was convened by Alexander, which affirmed that the Son was co-eternal with, and equal to, the Father. Arius, however, refused to retract and appealed first to the intellectual pedigree of his ideas. Indeed, as modern scholars have argued, the theses of Arius can all be found in the impeccable Christian writings of the previous century, above all those of Origen.[18] Second, Arius appealed to Christians beyond Egypt, and two further Councils of bishops, one in Bithynia in Asia Minor and another in Palestine, had by 321 affirmed the orthodoxy of Arius's statements in the sense that they fell within the then-permitted spectrum of legitimate diversity. Thus, by the time that Constantine conquered the east in 324, what he inherited was a dispute that had spread beyond Egypt and was now profoundly dividing Christians across the whole of the eastern Empire. What was he to do?

It has often been argued that one of the attractions of Christianity to Constantine was that it had the potential to be one among several other instruments of unification within his sprawling and possibly unmanageable Empire. Although modern scholars have injected a note of caution in seeing this as a motivation as early as 312, at the same time it was clearly an idea that grew in his mind over time. Church and Emperor both sought unity for their respective organizations as a desirable goal, if for somewhat different reasons.[19] But a Church fragmenting into rival theological groups, all claiming to be orthodox and catholic, was equally clearly a threat to the integrity of both institutions as they grew further together. However, the methodology for achieving Christian unity was in some vital respects different and more subtle than that for achieving imperial unity. In the political realm Constantine deliberately sought inclusive and ambiguous language in his edicts and other pronouncements. Here imprecision was a virtue. But, as he was to discover, it could become a vice when dealing with the complex subtleties of theological language. Lack of precision invited diverging interpretations, with potentially disastrous consequences for Church unity. This was not a point entirely grasped either by Constantine or his immediate successors; for them the seemingly obscure doctrinal issues involved in the christological debate were essentially trivial and insignificant. Here were two different perceptions. For Emperors, wholeness derived from the political search for compromise and consensus; for churchmen, it could mean rather a concept of purity and precision of definition.[20]

However, Constantine shared with them the belief that the essential instrument for maximizing Church unity and minimizing dissent was the Church Council. Originating in the apostolic councils of the first generation of Christians (Acts 15), and continued by periodic gatherings of their episcopal successors, local and regional Councils had become established mechanisms for resolving disputes and asserting authority, as Constantine had already discovered with the Donatist controversy. He now sought to elevate this concept onto an entirely new level. Before the arrival of a Christian Emperor neither the means nor the necessity of expanding this conciliar model had been available or desirable. Now they were. For the first time the whole world, the *Oikoumene*, could be gathered in one place through its episcopal representatives. Constantine thus presented the Church with the dizzying vision of the Christian *Oikoumene*, of all the local churches, from across the Empire and beyond its frontiers, summoned to join together for the first time in their history to settle their disputes in a way that would present them with a definitive and unchallengeable authority. At a stroke the age-old dilemma of defining and asserting orthodoxy and catholicity might at last be solved.

At the time, however, it is doubtful if more than a minority of bishops shared quite such an elevated vision. When this first Ecumenical Council (from *Oikoumene*) eventually gathered at Nicaea in 325, therefore, they were probably fewer than 300 in number, the west sending only a handful of representatives, as the theories of Arius had as yet barely penetrated their half of the Empire. But crucially it could be argued that every constituent part of the Church Catholic was in some way represented at this episcopal assembly, although partly because of its novelty the universal status of its authority would still take time to be widely accepted.

After a formal imperial opening ceremony, the ensuing debates were chaired by Bishop Ossius, with Constantine occasionally asserting his charismatic authority to control the proceedings and steer them towards a constructive conclusion. The bishops eventually decided to issue a statement of faith along with twenty canons to regularize ecclesiastical practice. This statement of faith was itself based on already existing baptismal declarations, but with some modifications, crucially the inclusion of the word *homoousios*, meaning of one, or the same, substance or essence to describe the relationship of the Son to the Father. This was a problematic term as it had no biblical precedent and had actually been condemned by an earlier, if local, Council in 268. However, almost all the bishops at Nicaea believed that it was the best way to confound the propositions found in *Thalia*, while leaving room to interpret the statement from a variety of perspectives. Eventually all but two of the bishops signed this statement of faith, or Creed as it has come to be known from the opening of the Latin version, *Credo*. Those readers familiar with the modern vernacular translations of this so-called Nicene Creed found in contemporary liturgies may be puzzled at the obvious differences between these later versions and the original. The reason for this is that this original version was to undergo a further revision at the later Council of Constantinople in 381 (Document 6).

Constantine now believed that the hoped-for unity had been achieved. But subsequent events were to prove this to be premature. If anything, the attempt to define faith more precisely led on the contrary to an intensification of divisions. Some bishops did not accept interpretations placed on the Nicene formula by other bishops. Personal and inter-city rivalries became mixed up with the theological disagreements. And the result was that for decades the eastern provinces of the Empire especially remained in a state of shifting fragmentation. The conventional division between pro-Nicene and Arian parties, however, would now be seen by scholars as too simplistic and failing to do justice to a much more complex patchwork quilt of doctrinal and geographical variations, and implying a sense of unity which was largely untrue for either side. Once again, a better model than competing parties would be a spectrum representing a much more diversified and graduated series of interpretations. It was to take several generations, a series of further Councils, and the emergence of a number of theological schools of thought before the areas of that spectrum deemed to be orthodox and catholic could be distinguished, at least by the vast majority of Christians, from those that were not.

And at the centre of these disputes during the reign of Constantine and his immediate successors was a figure who will reappear on a number of occasions in subsequent chapters: Athanasius, Bishop of Alexandria from 328 until his death in 373. He was a controversial figure in his own lifetime and has remained so for most of the subsequent centuries. For some, like John Henry Newman in his *Arians of the Fourth Century* of 1834, a hero, for others, such as Eduard Schwartz at the beginning of the twentieth century, a villain; a defender of a precious but precarious orthodoxy against heretical Emperors and bishops, or an intransigent and power-hungry obstacle to unity. The present generation of historians now portrays him as a very human character, brilliant but fallible. Indeed, it might be argued that here was a classic example of that phenomenon described so graphically by Paul, a heavenly treasure entrusted to an earthen vessel.

Five times he was to be exiled as a result of imperial displeasure, either externally from his native Egypt, or in hiding within it. Stubborn in defence of the Nicene formula against any attempt which, in his view, sought to distort or minimize its meaning, the battles that he fought represent at their most extreme, perhaps, those differences in perception that could separate church-men from Emperors in their common search for unity: the contrast between precision and compromise.

But in his writings Athanasius is now seen by many historians as very much lacking in that quality of scholarly precision himself. He systematically distorted and misrepresented both the arguments and characters of his opponents, selected his evidence in a totally one-sided way, could be evasive and incomplete in his descriptions of events, suppressed vital pieces of evidence inconvenient to his position, painted himself as unjustly persecuted, and portrayed attacks on himself as attacks on the whole Catholic Church. Unrelenting in his defence of what he conceived to be Christian orthodoxy, he was frequently lacking in many of the virtues extolled by his faith such as humility or patience. In his own city of Alexandria he was also quite prepared to employ intimidation and physical violence, unleashing organized gangs of thugs onto his local opponents. Athanasius was never one to turn the other cheek.

Compared by some modern historians to twentieth-century gangsters, and certainly behaving in some ways like the popular concept of a Mafia boss, Athanasius has yet to a large degree been vindicated with the passage of time. His manipulation of events, arguments and personalities had both 'a far nobler motivation, and far more enduring success' than that of any leader of a modern criminal conspiracy.[21] He must also be seen in the context of an age where his opponents were equally prepared to use the same techniques and methods as Athanasius. He was often just rather more effective in their employment. And clearly it is his view of what constituted orthodoxy that has been the far more enduring and widely accepted concept than any of those of his opponents. The history of Christianity might well have taken a very different course had it not been for Athanasius. Some modern scholars, indeed, have pointed to the potentially individualistic nature of Arianism both theologically and politically, highlighting that self-choice that was at the heart of heresy, and that the Nicene formula by contrast 'provided theological support for an autocratic political order' as well as a firmer base for Christian unity. If individualistic Arianism had prevailed it would have presented 'dangers for the church of today, as it did for Christians of the fourth century' and might have resulted in a quite different 'Christian world-view concerning the relation of the individual to authority both secular and divine'. Thus the opponents of Athanasius, albeit often unwittingly, presented a serious threat to the authority and organizational integrity of Christianity as well as to theological orthodoxy. If they had prevailed, Christianity might have fractured permanently along a series of fault-lines that would have left the faith in a hopelessly divided and consequently severely weakened condition. However questionable the methods employed to achieve it, this was what Athanasius and his supporters helped to avert.[22]

A Mixed Legacy

So what, then, were the most significant longer-term consequences of Constantine's conversion? For one thing it marked a further stage in the expansion of episcopal authority. Constantine was not only converted to a faith but also through that became a member of an organization. Although not baptized until a few days before his death, in itself not unusual in the fourth century, and in his particular case possibly delayed as a consequence of some of the actions he had had to take such as the murders of his son Crispus and second wife Fausta, Constantine was certainly accepted as a member of the Church in his lifetime. Although by the early fourth century that Church was, by later standards, still frail and vulnerable in some aspects of its structure, at the time it was probably the best organized institution in the Empire. As we have seen, necessity had obliged it to find ways to hold its disparate local manifestations together. It had developed techniques to withstand state persecution, it was the fastest-growing religious body in the Empire, and had at least begun the process of potentially acquiring the mechanisms to define orthodoxy and propagate it. And perhaps above all, in its episcopate it had developed a unique form of lifelong leadership, with its authority independent of political, economic or social status. It was thus natural for Constantine to turn to the bishops as the executors of his Christianizing policies. He gave them wealth to dispense as charity, extensive legal privileges, and vast new buildings in which they now began to adapt imperial court ceremonial in more elaborate liturgies.

As the fourth century progressed, so bishops exercised more and more authority not only within the Church itself but also in secular terms within their own cities and regions. Athanasius required a firm power-base within Alexandria and Egypt in order to operate effectively on a wider stage, just as in turn he needed a clear sense of orthodoxy beyond Egypt in order to have an ideological focus around which his local church could be mobilized. It was very much a two-way process. And by the late fourth century the bishops 'acted as effectively as they did because they found roles into which they could step with confidence', roles and ground already prepared for them by the traditional élites with whom they now shared a common cultural background.[23] Thus many modern historians have come to stress that the Christianizing of the Roman world in the fourth century was also itself a two-way process; Christians were as much influenced by the world of the educated Roman élite as that world was affected by Christianity, 'a dynamic process in which both sides' were changed.[24] Even to speak of two 'sides', Christian and pagan, is now itself being questioned by scholars. The idea that the fourth century witnessed a dramatic struggle between two competing cultures in which finally the Christian triumphed, is now widely interpreted as a construct of fifth-century historians, but unfortunately one sometimes too readily adopted by some of their modern counterparts.[25] What all élite Romans had in common was often more crucial than what divided them, and among these was an educational background or *paideia*, giving them a shared culture of courtesy, restraint and toleration. This was essential in a world of great religious diversity.[26] Thus during the fourth century Christians developed to the point where they 'spoke and wrote the rhetoric of empire' as naturally as they professed their religious faith, another essential ingredient without which they 'would never have become a world religion'.[27]

In the church of St Pudenziana in Rome there is one of the oldest surviving Christian mosaics. It dates from the late fourth century and depicts Christ and his apostles in the same contemporary artistic fashion as an Emperor and his senate.[28] What is this image telling us? Had Constantine and his successors turned the Church into little more than a department of state? Certainly, for many nineteenth-century historians such as the Swiss Jacob Burckhardt in his book *The Age of Constantine the Great* of 1853, this was essentially the case. In Burckhardt's view Constantine cynically used the Church for his own political ambitions and in reality cared nothing for religion. Later nineteenth-century German historians extended this concept and compared the Church of the fourth century to their own day, seeing it as very much at the mercy of Emperors, a concept that came to be called 'Caesaropapism'.[29] Then in a short but seminal lecture in 1929, Norman Baynes reasserted Constantine's religious motivations, a position now broadly accepted by most scholars who emphasize instead the inseparability of the spheres of religion and politics in the ancient world. A truer contemporary understanding of the mosaic is provided by Eusebius, who saw the Christian ruler and his Empire as a *mimesis*, a copy, mirror or imitation of God's rule in the heavens.[30] Constantine himself emphasized this connection between the earthly and heavenly when he prepared for his own entombment in the new Church of the Apostles in Constantinople. Alongside the twelve symbolic tombs of the apostles he placed his own, eventually acquiring the title *Isapostolos*, the equal of the apostles in his eastern territories. Such concepts of Christian monarchy and empire were to have a profound effect on the later Byzantine period of the eastern Empire, and, to a lesser extent, on the Latin west of the Middle Ages.

But even before the fourth century came to its close, some Christians were expressing doubts about the wisdom of such a close identification of Church and Empire. There were dangers as well as opportunities in such a relationship. Those churchmen retrospectively seen as the champions of orthodoxy had had to oppose Emperors as well as heretics in their battles for the purity of the faith. Then for twenty terrible months between 361 and 363 the Emperor Julian, known as the Apostate, had announced his abandonment of Christianity and re-embracing of paganism. He unleashed a programme which aimed to reverse all the Christianizing polices of the previous half-century. These conflicts between Christian and imperial authorities came to a head in the late fourth-century clash between the impeccably orthodox Emperor, Theodosius, and the Bishop of Milan, Ambrose (*c.* 339–97). In 390 imperial troops massacred about 5,000 citizens in the city of Thessalonica in reprisal for having their general lynched by a local mob after he had imprisoned a charioteer who had insulted him. Ambrose, by then Bishop of the city that had effectively become the western capital, demanded that Theodosius do penance for this massacre, and actually confronted him personally in the basilica during the Eucharist and forbade him from receiving Communion until a satisfactory penance had been performed. This event has been seen by one modern authority as 'a pivotal moment in the history of church and state in the west'.[31] No senator, however prominent, had ever dared to rebuke an Emperor as this bishop now did, and these events were to be a harbinger of later medieval clashes between Emperors, kings and their bishops.

For a bishop was ultimately possessed of a different kind of power from that of senators, generals or even Emperors themselves. The authority of a bishop was sacramental, conferred upon him for life by the Church as the ultimate wielder of divine authority. The power of a bishop was quite beyond the reach or competence of any secular individual or body to grant or remove. And this demonstrated that in some respects and in certain instances Church and Empire could be potentially rival powers in their demands for the loyalty of their subjects. Inclusion within the Empire did not necessarily always mean identification with it. The shift from the enthusiasm of Eusebius to the caution of Ambrose with regard to an imperial Christianity stands like a pair of contrasting bookends at the two chronological extremes of the fourth century. By its final years some Christians had already come to argue that 'the new imperial Christianity was largely a symptom of misplaced opportunism'.[32]

Suggested Further Reading

In addition to the general books on the history of the early Church included in the Suggested Further Reading section at the end of the Introduction, there are a number of texts which cover the later period more specifically. A good starting point might be Peter Brown, *The World of Late Antiquity AD150–750* (Thames and Hudson, 1971) which obviously covers a rather longer time-span, but is useful in putting the fourth and fifth centuries into a broader context; it is also lavishly illustrated. *The End of Ancient Christianity* (Cambridge University Press, 1990) by R. A. Markus is an excellent and sophisticated study of much that we will be covering in Part One. It is a work based on extensive scholarship but divided into manageable sections, and all held together by consistent themes of change, seeing how late antiquity led into the beginnings of the Middle Ages. Equally sophisticated and learned is Averil Cameron's *Christianity and the Rhetoric of Empire: The Development of Christian Discourse* (University of California Press, Berkeley, 1991). Like Markus's book, this one is also concerned with change, more specifically how Christians became the natural inheritors of the Roman Empire, and how the processes involved helped to transform both. Two further, and shorter studies by Peter Brown also examine this process: *Power and Persuasion in Late Antiquity: Towards a Christian Empire* (University of Wisconsin Press, 1992) and *Authority and the Sacred: Aspects of the Christianisation of the Roman World* (Cambridge University Press, 1995).

Among modern biographical studies of Constantine, the recent one by Charles Matson Odahl stands out. *Constantine and the Christian Empire* (Routledge, 2004) is based on a lifetime of scholarship and is greatly enhanced by almost 100 illustrations, many being photographs taken by the author himself. It makes a strong case for the sincerity of Constantine's Christianity and championing of his faith. A number of other recent studies of various aspects of the relationship between Emperors and Christianity should also be mentioned. H. A. Drake, *Constantine and the Bishops: The Politics of Intolerance* (Johns Hopkins University Press, 2000) is a long, perhaps too long, and certainly repetitive reassessment of Constantine's reign which argues that it should be seen more from a political than a theological perspective. It utilizes a host of modern political concepts and terms ('message' and 'spin' among others) and can sometimes fall into the same trap which he himself criticizes previous studies for, namely interpreting the past through present eyes. Timothy D. Barnes in his *Athanasius and Constantius: Theology and Politics in the Constantinian Empire* (Harvard University Press, 1993) is an intense and closely argued interpretation of the writings of Athanasius and others, and is an excellent example of modern historical documentary techniques in action, showing how we can no longer take the great Bishop at his word. His earlier work, *Constantine and Eusebius* (Harvard University Press, 1981) is partly an exercise in the establishment of context by looking at the whole career and all the surviving works of Eusebius, but is also at the same time excellent on Constantine. T. G. Elliott in *The Christianity of Constantine the Great* (University of Scranton Press, 1996) presents a controversial reinterpretation based on a closely argued reappraisal of the sources, which is notable for dating the origins of Constantine's Christianity well before his 312 conversion, which Elliott believes is a complex piece of fiction devised by Eusebius; few scholars have been convinced, however. Still worth reading is the seminal essay by Norman H. Baynes, *Constantine the Great and the Christian Church: The Raleigh Lecture on History 1929*; this was reprinted by Oxford University Press in 1972, with a new Preface by Henry Chadwick. This was the lecture in which Baynes reasserted the primacy of religion as a motivation for Constantine's actions in opposition to the nineteenth-century rationalists. Samuel N. C. Lieu and Dominic Montserrat have edited a collection of essays on the legacy of Constantine with the title *Constantine: History, Historiography and Legend* (Routledge, 1998). As with many such collections, some essays are more relevant than others to the issues covered in this book.

Among the primary sources available in translation, two stand out. *Eusebius: Life of Constantine* (Clarendon Press, Oxford, 1999) is an excellent modern translation with an introduction and extensive explanatory footnotes, by Averil Cameron and Stuart G. Hall. It is something of a model for how this type of source should be presented to a modern readership. Lactantius' *De Mortibus Persecutorum* (Clarendon Press, Oxford, 1984) is edited and translated by J. L. Creed in parallel Latin and English texts, with another fine Introduction.

2

City and Desert

But he would withdraw to deserted places and pray. (Luke 5:16)

In the modern Western world many people assume that aspiration to such things as the ownership of a large house, the purchase of fashionable clothes, the eating of sophisticated food, the earning or winning of as much money as possible, and the unrestricted expression of sexual desire, are all normal manifestations of individual freedom and choice. Some even go so far as to assert that whatever laws or conventions constrain them in the pursuit of their desires or ambitions are to be repealed or avoided as obstacles to the right of the physical cultivation of the self. Movie stars, rock singers, prominent sportspeople or large lottery winners who have achieved these material goals in the most spectacular or ostentatious ways are often heroes to millions who both envy and seek to emulate them in their success. The suggestion, therefore, that true human freedom and fulfilment are to be found, by contrast, in the control and disciplining of mental and physical gratification, sometimes to the point of outright renunciation, is thus both bewildering and not a little distasteful to many modern Western people.

Yet significant numbers of ancient Christians deliberately abandoned conventional family life, sought poverty, fasted, renounced all forms of sexual practice, and believed that in so doing they had discovered a path to a higher freedom that would lead them to the ultimate fulfilment of human destiny. What led them to this conclusion, and what were the consequences for both Christianity and the Roman Empire?

A Desert of the Heart

Until fairly recently, the origins of what eventually became Christian monasticism were usually presented as relatively straightforward and clear-cut. This was seen as a phenomenon that began in the deserts of Egypt, possibly in the mid-third century during the Decian persecution with the flight of harried Christians, was given further impetus during those mid-third-century decades of supposed crisis with some Christians, for instance, escaping the burdens of excessive taxation, and then attained its definitive forms under Antony (*c.* 251–356) and Pachomius (*c.* 290–346), the respective originators of the concepts of the hermit and the monastic community. Sometimes mention was made of inspiration either from earlier Jewish practice or from the example of more contemporary philosophical schools such as Stoicism, and all rounded off by suitable quotations from the New Testament such as the ones describing Jesus's 40 days retreat into the wilderness after his baptism by John the Baptist (Matt. 4:1–11; Mark 1:12–13; Luke 4:1–13).[1]

The present generation of scholars, however, has become extremely sceptical about these, and other, relatively simple cause-and-effect explanations. They question, for instance, whether the beginnings of monasticism were either uniquely Egyptian or located exclusively in deserts. Syria clearly had its own, quite independent monastic history, and just as ancient as that of Egypt. Even in that latter country there is now abundant evidence of a long tradition of Christian asceticism to be found within, or on the fringes of, cities, towns and villages. Neither Antony nor Pachomius were originators or inventors of particular types of monasticism; at best they introduced innovations into already existing traditions. The links between martyrdom and monasticism previously stressed by many authorities are also now seen as much more complex, the latter not developing out of the former as had been claimed in the past, nor as its substitute in the more settled conditions of the fourth century. Rather, both derived from a common set of motivations, parallel and complementary rather than sequential. Indeed, the very notion of searching for the 'origins' of Christian monasticism has itself been challenged as a misconception derived from uncritical reading of ancient literary sources such as Athanasius's *Life of Antony*, which in reality were composed more for polemical than historical purposes.[2]

Early New Testament evidence such as 1 Corinthians 7 or Acts 4:32 demonstrates that in the first generation of Christians there were already those who believed that their new faith was leading them to adopt alternative ways of living and practising, even at the cost of breaking up conventional households. For some, the demands of living out their new creation led to the practice of virginity, among them Paul himself.[3] In other words, for some

Christians the imperative to live and practise their faith at a deeper level and in more radical ways had always existed. In that sense, asceticism and monasticism did not have identifiable origins in later time or space, but were rather co-terminus with the arrival of Christianity itself, and in their turn shared an identity with martyrdom in having the same motivation of giving up earthly life as a sacrifice to obtain an eternal one. Particular historical circumstances or contexts moulded and directed such motivations into particular concrete forms. In addition it has also been argued more recently that the relatively settled conditions experienced by Christianity in the fourth century led to a great consolidation and stability across a range of Christian charisms, including both the episcopate as we saw in the previous chapter, and the developing institutionalization of the ascetic practices that became monasticism.[4]

The elements that were eventually to cohere as monasticism were thus integral parts of the very dynamic of Christian history itself, evolving and developing alongside a range of other Christian manifestations. Reading the pages of Eusebius's *History of the Church* illuminates some of these points. He does not link the flight to the desert during persecution with Christian asceticism; indeed, he sees martyrdom as quite independent of asceticism, the latter emanating in his view far more from the solitude required in the search for the Christian life of philosophical enlightenment, the kind of life that might be perfected in a final call to martyrdom, but very much preceding it.[5] On the other hand, the rapid expansion of Christianity during the third and fourth centuries would in itself have resulted in a similar growth in the numbers pursuing an ascetic life. And there is some evidence to suggest that as by the middle decades of the fourth century conversion had become for some more a matter of conformity to the prevailing direction of imperial preferences than motivated by deeply held convictions, and thus for many Christians life was often indistinguishable from the conventional norms of family life in the Empire, some would have sought an escape from these through the adoption of more enthusiastic and demanding forms of Christian living.[6]

So in order to understand how and why Egyptian monasticism evolved in the third and fourth centuries we must first explore briefly the historical context within which this happened. This was certainly one of social and economic upheaval and disruption, caused as much by the policies of Diocletian as by any supposed mid-third-century crisis. His reforms led both to a greater integration of the local Egyptian society and economy within the larger Empire in everything from taxation and trade to a growing urbanization and the subsequent creation of new and powerful local élites in a world of unsettling social mobility. Some responded to these disturbing times with flight, either from taxes or into bands of outlaws. Others moved into the expanding towns of the Nile valley at the expense of the villages. More positively, these towns themselves showed evidence of a vibrant cultural and intellectual life, with flourishing education, at least for the growing numbers who could afford it, leading to a basic understanding of the Greek language and philosophical ideas among a perhaps surprising number of the population. Hellenism was certainly not the sole preserve of the great city of Alexandria, and we must not imagine an absolute divide between a sophisticated Greek-speaking élite in that great port and a primitive, Coptic-speaking and largely illiterate rural hinterland. Ideas flowed as freely as trade up and down the length of the Nile.

Not surprisingly, novel religious ideas were among those seeping into this world. Alongside the surviving practices dating from the time of the Pharaohs were other more recent arrivals, among them Christianity. But again, at a time when the distinction between orthodoxy and heresy was at best blurred and indistinct, Egyptian Christianity covered a very wide spectrum, including Gnostic ideas, and, from about 270, those of the religious teacher, Mani (*c.* 216–76). He was a Persian whose teachings derived from an amalgam of Jewish, Christian, Gnostic and other faiths. Mani's teachings were, like those of the Gnostics, dualistic, and based on the concept of a fundamental conflict between light and darkness. The main objective of his religion was to release the particles of light stolen by Satan and imprisoned in human minds and certain matter such as vegetables like cucumbers. A series of teachers including Buddha, the Jewish prophets, Jesus and finally Mani himself had been sent to effect this release. And one of the necessary preconditions for this was strict asceticism, including vegetarianism. It also presupposed a distinction between an enlightened Elect who practised a more advanced austerity, and the main body of Hearers.

However strange and irrational many of these ideas now seem, at the time they attracted the sympathies of many intelligent and well-educated inhabitants of the late Empire. Perhaps stranger still, Mani's followers saw themselves as very much a part of the mainstream of Christianity, just as much as those who interpreted it in a more Gnostic way. Between all of those who called themselves Christians was the common ground of belief in individual salvation, the practice of asceticism to some degree, the stress on a heavenly as opposed to purely earthly citizenship, a common use of Greek philosophical ideas, especially those derived from Plato, and traditions coming out of the Jewish scriptures.[7]

It was from this complex, not to say potentially chaotic, maelstrom of social and intellectual ferment that Egyptian monasticism emerged. In its towns and villages more and more individuals were practising *anachoresis* or withdrawal, not only from such burdens as excessive taxation, but also from the demands of conventional family life, and so beginning to shift the meaning of the term from its secular origins to a more spiritual one. These people were living alone, and thus initiating another change in language, with the emergence of the word *monachos*, 'one who is alone', as a technical term for a spiritual as well as geographical state, its earliest known use in this sense found in a papyrus dated from 324, and the origin of our word 'monasticism'. Yet we must be careful not to associate it at this stage with all the later accretions that have come to typify the word 'monk'. These village ascetics sought spiritual enlightenment, but followed no rule, obeyed no superiors, had little or no concept of orthodoxy or heresy, and did not live in defined communities. Rather they continued to live in, or on the fringes of, towns and villages and maintained a range of social and economic contacts with their inhabitants. However, the monastic literature of later generations effectively 'airbrushed' them out of the historical record, as they did not fit the model of 'proper' monks living in organized communities under rules and clerical superiors. Their importance for the early history of monasticism, therefore, has only recently been recovered by the work of scholars discovering and interpreting sources beyond the standard literary ones.[8]

How, then, did the asceticism practised by these early Christians differ from that of the classical philosophical schools such as Stoicism? The word 'ascetic' derives from the Greek *askesis*, denoting the training or practice that an athlete would undergo to discipline his body in preparation for competitive games. Paul had seen a connection between this and the Christian life: 'Athletes exercise self-control in all things; they do it to receive a perishable garland, but we an imperishable one' (1 Cor. 9:25). Philosophers had also seen the similarities with their training of the intellect. However, it was Christianity that applied the concept in new and specifically religious ways that themselves originated in Christian views of the relationship between the body and the soul. For most Hellenists the body was perceived as in many ways an impediment to the soul, some going so far as to compare the body to a prison or tomb from which the soul would only be released finally at the moment of death. Through the practice of moderation or self-control, however, the worst excesses of physical distraction could be minimized and the body become a more fitting vehicle for the soul.[9]

The Christian doctrines of incarnation and resurrection represented a fundamental challenge to these views. God had become a human being, with a human body as well as a soul, and through the actions of this body, principally suffering death by crucifixion, had achieved a profound spiritual transformation in which the body participated as well as all the other parts of the human entity, as evidenced by the resurrection appearances recorded in the Gospels. From now onwards both body and soul were inextricably linked in the Christian view of the process of salvation. As Clement of Alexandria had written, the human person 'attains its destined end through the body, the soul's consort and ally'.[10] And as the modern historian, Peter Brown, has remarked of this new Christian attitude: 'Seldom had the body been seen as more deeply implicated in the transformation of the soul.'[11] Thus Christian *askesis* did not spring from a negative view of the body as an irrelevance to be discarded, but rather from a positive one in which it had become the temple of the Holy Spirit. In addition, Athanasius argued that the *Logos*, the Word, had dwelt in a human body and thus demonstrated that all human bodies were now capable of spiritual and moral reformation, a recovery of control over the passions, even to the point where fear of death itself was removed. The victory of Jesus in the crucifixion and his resulting physical transfiguration in resurrection, was now possible for all Christians by the power of their spiritual recreation, and demonstrated equally through the self-control of the ascetics as it was in the suffering and death of the martyrs.[12] Christian asceticism was thus not based on hatred or loathing of the body but rather in the effort to lovingly begin the refashioning of it into the form of its supreme model, the risen and triumphant Christ.[13]

Just as the goals of philosophical and Christian asceticism were radically different, so too the methods, although sharing certain superficial similarities, were also clearly distinguishable in their intention and purpose. The fasting, vigils, silences, poverty, manual labour and chastity practised by Christian ascetics were undertaken to gradually but ineluctably bring the self face to face with its own disordered will, twisted out of focus, as it were, by the fall of Adam. Once the desires of the body had been brought under control then the ascetic would begin to reach the core of his inner being, his heart, the seat of his deepest self, and here the realignment of his own will with the loving will of God could begin. Here he would lose one self and find another, his true reordered self, his Christ-like being, his ultimate destiny. Having ruthlessly cleansed his disordered will just as the wind and sand scoured nature to produce a sterile desert, so the Christian ascetic would journey to the desert of his own heart and in its stillness and silence would find the peace and freedom of Christ.[14]

For in Christianity was a new type of freedom different again from the philosophical freeing of the soul from the body. To be distracted by the affairs of the world was a symbol of the bondage to sin consequent upon Adam's disobedience to God and fall from his favour, recoverable only through the power of Christ, the second Adam. Just as the physical desert was feared by all, pagans and Christians alike, as the natural abode of demons who could lure the unwary ascetic with enticing visions, so the world was also regarded as the scene of temptation; the only place where true freedom could be found was the ascetic's cell. Here in poverty, fasting and solitude he would discover the paradoxical truth that was first taught by Jesus, that true freedom was only to be found when the cares and pleasures of the world were abandoned and replaced by total dependence on God (Matt. 6:25–34). As one modern commentator has written: 'The concrete act of physical privation was a means of fulfilling the true meaning of asceticism: to be free from care.'[15] Here the innocence of paradise could be rediscovered in a renewed intimacy with God. And at the same time a new compassion for fallen humanity would be kindled which itself flowed from this experience of the love of God, and resulted in an outpouring of love for his creation. Physical detachment from the world actually led to another paradox: a deeper spiritual commitment to it.

Nowhere were these paradoxical truths more starkly revealed than in the ascetic's sexual renunciation. This is perhaps the aspect of Christian monasticism that can cause most amusement, bewilderment or even loathing on the part of many in the modern Western world, and can consequently lead to some profound misunderstandings. For one thing, what was to emerge as the orthodox Christian teaching, as opposed, for instance, to the dualism of the Gnostics or Manicheaens, was the affirmation of the essential goodness of God's physical creation, and supremely of the human body. As Athanasius stressed in his fourth-century *Life of Antony*, all ascetic renunciations, whether of sex, food or wealth, were not based on a hatred of creation but in the attempt to reorientate the individual into a proper relationship between the spiritual and the physical, the soul and the body.[16] In the following century Augustine was equally at pains to stress the complementary nature of virginity and marriage, both pointing to the final unanimity of the redeemed in the heavenly Jerusalem.[17] Many other Christian writers and apologists of these centuries were also to argue that sexual renunciation was only one, and sometimes far from the most important, of a number of similar self-denials. For many fourth century ascetics it was actually abstaining from food that was seen as the more fundamental surrender of self, as it helped to reverse the first sin of Adam in eating what was forbidden to him.[18] One of the greatest Christian preachers of the early Church, John Chrysostom (*c.* 347–407), once delivered a series of sermons on the Gospel of Matthew in which almsgiving, poverty, avarice and wealth appeared far more frequently than sexual sins.[19]

Yet at the same time the virgin state summed up the true meaning of all acts of renunciation for early Christian ascetics, and 'was to complete the transformation of the heart'.[20] For Gregory of Nyssa (*c.* 330–*c.* 395) the virgin body was like a mirror in which the immense purity of God could be glimpsed; and for Ambrose, Christ's sexless birth and chaste life were a bridge between the present fallen state of humanity and its potential for resurrected transformation, a token of human nature as it should be.[21] Ambrose also emphasized the further paradox of the intact virgin womb barring entry to all who would violate its purity, and the consequent openness of the mind and heart of the virgin to Christ, the scriptures and the poor.[22] He then went on to apply this paradox to the whole Church, an equally pure and intact body yet endowed with the capacity for growth and nurture through which the lost solidarity of humanity would be regained.[23] Above all for Ambrose it was the virgin womb of Mary the mother of Jesus through which God himself had entered the world, made possible by her act of total obedience to the mysterious will of God, which symbolized the human will and the body being brought into complete harmony. Not surprisingly, many Christian ascetics of the fourth and fifth centuries thus looked upon the conquest of sexual temptation as a kind of measure, or, as Peter Brown has expressed it, a barium-trace, through which they could probe the deepest and most private recesses of the will. And here we must remember that our post-Freudian concept of sexuality as the primary instinctual drive was not shared by early Christians; for them it was more a secondary reaction to a whole range of passions and desires. So for John Cassian (*c.* 360–430), a Western monastic writer, sexual temptation was the measure by which he eliminated the extent of the remaining spiritual dis-orientation within the will of a monk.[24]

Virginity, then, encapsulated the Christian virtues of faith, hope and love, a sign that, unlike the great cities of the Empire, the Church did not have to rely on sexual procreation for its continuity; it proclaimed, rather, its faith and hope in a promise of divine love that would carry it into a glorious future.[25]

Cities Old and New

Famously, in chapter 14 of his *Life of Antony*, Athanasius described how 'the desert was made a city by monks' during the early decades of the fourth century.[26] This simple but audacious claim quickly entered into Christian mythology, and the physical wasteland of the desert became one of the abiding symbols of monasticism, the alternative city of true Christian living. As late as 1966 it provided the inspiration for the title of Derwas Chitty's classic study of early Christian monasticism, *The Desert a City*. The present generation of scholars, however, has challenged this assumption, and does not now see the endless swirling sands of the desert as the unique location of what was to become Christian monasticism.

Just as the earlier heavy reliance by scholars on a limited number of literary sources such as *Lives* of early monks, for instance, usually composed after their subject's death, has now been augmented by more recent discoveries of a much wider range of sources in reinterpreting some aspects of the theology of monasticism, so too the practice of monasticism is now seen in a somewhat different light. Much of the literary evidence was not only composed much later than the events or personalities depicted in it, and thus often reflects a more mature and developed concept of monasticism which was then 'read back' into the earlier, formative, period, but it was also often designed for rhetorical or polemical purposes. Modern scholars have attempted to get back 'behind' these sometimes distorting literary images and have in consequence recovered a different and often contrasting picture of early monastic practices. Like the modern interpretation of the first generation of Christians, what has been uncovered in the world of the early monks is a much more diverse set of practices than was previously thought to exist.

This is nowhere more so than in the case of their geographical location. The *Life of Antony* established the ideal of the hermit living a solitary existence in the deep desert as the prototype of Christian monasticism. We now know that this was far from the case. Historically the practices to emerge as monasticism not only significantly pre-dated Antony, but also owed far more to urban settings than they did to the desert. From the widows and virgins supported by urban churches in the earliest days of Christianity, through the village ascetics, to the first fixed communities along the fertile zone of the Nile, out to the remotest hermit in a desert cave, the practices of early monasticism, like the beliefs of early Christians, covered a very wide spectrum. Even when desert monasticism did begin to grow in the fourth century, it must be understood that there was also a similar and parallel growth of pre-existing urban monasticism as well. By going into the deep desert, Antony was not inventing anything. He took a set of ideas and practices that had already established a recognizable tradition and, in conformity with that Christian concept of tradition, by moving them into a new physical location, helped them to further evolve. In any case, we must also be careful with the use of the word 'desert' itself. This could just as well mean a small, inhospitable space like a rock outcrop within the fertile zone of the Nile valley, or an area just beyond that fertile zone, as it could the deep desert itself.[27] Thus, in the telling words of Peter Brown, the desert to which Antony withdrew 'created the asceticism of the fourth-century monks as little as the inhospitable woods of the New World created the Puritanism of the Pilgrim Fathers'.[28]

If we compare passages from the *Life of Antony*, perhaps the most famous literary source for an understanding of early monasticism, with the seven letters which he himself wrote, we can begin to see how this new interpretation of monastic beginnings has evolved in recent years. The Athanasian authorship of the *Life* has itself recently been challenged, but most authorities would accept that Athanasius was the author, but that the version we now possess was perhaps one later amended by the author himself. However, it will come as no surprise, in the light of what was said about Athanasius in the previous chapter, that his portrait of Antony is now universally distrusted by scholars as an accurate historical account. The Antony that speaks to us in the *Life* is very much one moulded, one might almost say manipulated, by Athanasius into his view of the ideal monk, simple and guileless, relatively uneducated, but firmly orthodox (in Athanasius's view of that concept), and hence staunchly anti-Arian, but touchingly obedient to his clerical superiors. In presenting Antony in these terms, Athanasius had clear theological and political motives; for one thing, he effectively sought to recruit the dead hermit, and through him wider Egyptian monasticism, as allies in his campaigns against clerical and imperial opponents. A passage at the opening of the *Life* illustrates some of these points (Document 7).

Here is an Antony whose roots in a Coptic-speaking, rural world are stressed. He is described as shunning formal education, thus emphasizing his lack of Greek in terms of both the language and philosophical concepts; rather, he is shown as both intellectually and spiritually dependent upon scripture for his knowledge. He is obedient to legitimate authority, whether parental, scriptural or in the form of his first ascetic teachers. His early need for solitude, and lack of dependence on luxuries such as food, are emphasized. He is portrayed as clearly a person specifically chosen by God for a particular purpose. But at the same time Athanasius is unable to eliminate entirely evidence for the pre-existence of ascetic practices and communities in Egypt; Antony entrusts his sister to a community of virgins, and is himself clearly dependent for his initial training on those very village ascetics discussed earlier.

How realistic is this as a portrait of Antony? It is probably an amalgam of accurate reporting, with some deliberate suppressions or reinterpretations – very much what one would have expected from Athanasius. Take, for instance, his account of Antony's education, or rather lack of it. From what we now know of the existence of schools teaching Greek language and ideas in rural Egypt in the third and fourth centuries, is it likely that a boy like Antony from a relatively prosperous background would have been allowed to miss out on such an opportunity? In a later passage of the *Life*, Antony is described as debating with Greek-speaking philosophers, if conveniently through an interpreter (chapters 72–80). Athanasius accounts for this ability by stressing Antony's natural wisdom: 'It was a marvel that although he had not learned letters, he was a shrewd and intelligent man.'[29] The implication is that Antony was inspired by a divine wisdom that was marvellous or beyond human understanding, and was acquired through the discipline of his ascetic training which gave him such an intimate and natural knowledge of God.

Yet the evidence of the seven letters reveals a very different Antony, a person well versed in the basics of philosophy, a teacher of wisdom whose knowledge is as much derived from human as it is from divine sources. Such an Antony might well have been perceived as a potential threat rather than an ally by Athanasius. The long-established catechetical schools and other study groups in Alexandria were exactly the speculative world that had fostered Arius, and were a continual thorn in the flesh of episcopal authority. A monasticized version of these groups might well have been seen by Athanasius as a further potential challenge to his sometimes precarious grip over the Egyptian church. Hence Antony had to be portrayed in the *Life* as the uneducated but obedient monk;[30] a monk who was also conveniently available not only to dispute with philosophers but also with Athanasius's theological opponents, all branded by him under the label 'Arians'. 'In things having to do with belief, he was truly wonderful and orthodox' declared Athanasius of Antony (see chapters 68–9).[31] And significantly, as his life drew to its close, it was to Athanasius that Antony bequeathed his last possessions of any significance, his sheepskin and the cloak on which he lay, making the bishop the designated keeper of these relics and, by implication, of his legacy as well.[32]

In contrast to the *Life*, which, within a couple of generations, had established the conventional view of Antony and Egyptian monasticism, both in the Greek-speaking East and through Latin translations in the West, the letters remained largely unknown, and their authenticity widely doubted. This was mainly because they presented such a different Antony from the one in the *Life*, and also the precarious nature of their transmission through a series of partial translations, not only in Coptic, Greek and Latin, but also Syriac, Georgian and Arabic. The modern Swedish scholar, Samuel Rubenson, has, however, presented a powerful case for their authenticity, recovered a working text, and produced a pioneering and revolutionary study of them. As he remarks of their significance: 'They oblige us to redraw not only the image of Antony, but also much of the established picture of early Egyptian monasticism.'[33]

Nowhere is this more startling than in the comparison between the unlettered, Coptic-speaking rustic of the *Life*, and the sophisticated writer of these letters, the latter a man of some education, well versed in Platonic philosophy, and at ease with terms such as *gnosis*, using it to help explain his understanding of the spiritual life, very much in the Alexandrian tradition of Clement and Origen. And like Origen, the Antony of the letters also presents the demons that are the manifestations of temptation as internal, psychological forces, not the externalized creatures of the *Life*, and the delight of many later generations of painters.

Since it is clear that these letters were written for the benefit of other monks, it is also obvious that at least some of these early ascetics formed part of an intellectual tradition, and thus casts further doubt over the idea that this generation of monks were all uneducated peasants. Rather, it emphasizes the point that Hellenistic culture was far from the sole preserve of sophisticated

Alexandria. As Rubenson comments about late third-century Egypt in the light of these letters: 'New religious movements such as monasticism were not the product of people on the margin of society, but of intellectuals dissatisfied with what tradition had to offer.'[34] Although that tradition was that of the old pagan gods, such people clearly presented the representatives of any fragile replacement organization, such as the episcopate, with potentially dangerous alternative sources of charismatic authority. No wonder that Athanasius wished to see such groups removed from the vicinity of Alexandria to the comparatively remote safety of the desert.

Pachomius, that other great founding icon of Egyptian monasticism, has, like Antony, also undergone something of an interpretative transformation in recent years. Previous views of Pachomius were similarly largely informed by a study of literary works whose origins were located well after his death, including those by the Western writers Palladius (*c.* 364–420/30) and Jerome (*c.* 345–420).[35] The picture that emerged from such sources was of a Pachomius who was famous as the founder of coenobitic monasticism, that is of monks formally organized in specific communities under common rules and in precise geographical locations. We now realize that this was as much a distortion of his role as earlier concepts ascribed to Antony. Pachomius did not invent coenobitic monasticism; he inherited it. And his *Rule* was largely a construct by later generations. As one scholar, James E. Goehring, has commented:

> The image of Antony and Pachomius as respectively the fathers of anchoritic and coenobitic monasticism is a fiction that grows out of and beyond the depiction of these two figures in the literary sources. While both were influential, their insights were at best innovations and not creations.[36]

In the case of Pachomius the main innovation was the grouping of a number of monastic communities into a kind of federation, a *koinonia* of ascetics. At his death in 346 he had nine such communities, perhaps numbering as many as 3,000 monks within his *koinonia*, but of those, some three had not been founded by him but had voluntarily joined, thus demonstrating the pre-existent nature of this form of monasticism.[37] At the same time other coenobitic communities continued to flourish outside the Pachomian *koinonia*, for instance at the White Mountain, which, under its leader, Shenoute, developed into the chief monastic site of Upper Egypt.[38]

In other ways, too, Pachomian monasticism stands in contrast to the mythical desert isolation. Indeed, it has been argued that one of his other innovations was to leave the desert entirely in favour of the fertile Nile valley.

On top of that, his occupation of 'deserted' villages has also been reassessed. In reality his monks probably occupied only parts of villages that had been depopulated, while most of the remaining village continued to be inhabited; indeed, the very presence of a Pachomian monastery may well have attracted people back into these small urban sites. One of the reasons for this was that in reality these monasteries were hives of economic activity, encouraging agricultural life beyond their enclosing walls, and also themselves being centres for the manufacture of mats, baskets, ropes and sandals. Boats regularly traded their goods along the Nile as far north as the city of Alexandria itself, and from there all across the eastern Mediterranean. All of these activities were under the control of stewards who met in the mother house at Pbow for an annual financial reckoning. Thus Pachomian monasticism, far from being just another example of the pervasive influence of the desert, was in actual fact derived from, and a development of, that earlier village monasticism.[39]

This powerful monastic *koinonia* was also not under the formal or direct authority of the bishops of Alexandria, themselves raised to the status of Patriarchs along with the bishops of Rome and Jerusalem by the Council of Nicaea. The dangers, as well as the advantages, of siting monastic communities at a distance from that city, no matter how grand the new honorific title of its bishop might now be, were evidenced by the rather less than precise nature of the monks' theological pursuits. Pachomius himself was not concerned with the niceties of what did or did not constitute orthodoxy. He was far more concerned with the charismatic diversity that made up a successful community. And the willingness of these communities to utilize a similar diversity of religious texts is demonstrated by the Gnostic finds at Nag Hammadi, physically located within the orbit of a Pachomian house, and, in the view of some modern scholars, probably part of the reading material available to the monks. Rival charismatic authority here combined dangerously with heretical reading in a way that would have alarmed a bishop like Athanasius. Only with the eventual arrival of Theodore as successor to Pachomius, a man from a wealthy urban background, could Athanasius at last exert his influence on these monks.[40]

Charism and Hierarchy

Standing on top of a 60-foot column, with his arms outstretched in prayer to his crucified Lord, his emaciated and broken body attracting vast crowds, both Christian and pagan, calling for his intercession on their behalf, the figure of Simeon, the great Syrian ascetic of the fifth century, symbolized in its most dramatic form what the episcopate feared from this expanding monasticism: a rival charismatic authority.[41] It was this charismatic power that attracted crowds even to see the most remote of hermits. Such was the case of John of Lycopolis, the most famous hermit of the Thebaid in southern Egypt; he was not only besieged by crowds of supplicants, but was also said to have given advice to imperial generals and to have predicted the deaths of Emperors.[42] Many ascetics were also credited with having performed exorcisms in which their power over the infecting demons had been demonstrated and the truth of Christianity proclaimed. Some, especially in Syria, had come to be seen as the natural protectors of local communities.[43] In all of this there were clear links and similarities with the martyrs and confessors, extending further to the similarly lowly and relatively insignificant social origins of some of the early ascetics, who were virtually all lay people, and thus potentially as threatening to the social hierarchy as they were to the clerical.[44]

Even Antony in his letters is revealed as a charismatic teacher of spiritual *gnosis*, with an authority almost comparable to that other great early Christian writer of letters, Paul himself. And if monasticism was a movement tinged with incipient Gnostic heresy, other deviant individuals and groups, such as Marcion, Tatian and their followers, had in their turn advocated sexual renunciation like the ascetics. There are even instances where widows supported by the Church had taken on the role of prophetesses, and in a few extreme cases going so far as to perform baptisms and celebrate Eucharists, actions deeply unlawful in the eyes of the male hierarchy.[45] And some early monastic communities in Egypt showed a toleration of schismatics that was anathema to the bishops of Alexandria; we now know of at least one monastery, at Labla in Upper Egypt, where Melitians were accepted members of a supposedly orthodox community. Indeed, the Melitians not only had a parallel episcopate of their own, but also monastic communities.[46] So revered a founder of communities as Pachomius was himself summoned before a Council towards the end of his life to answer charges that he was a dangerous visionary.[47]

The threat to ecclesiastical unity and episcopal leadership inherent in monasticism was thus as clear as it had been in the case of martyrdom. As one modern historian has summed it up, in the case of Pachomius what was primary to him 'was his understanding of the charismatic authority inherent in the monastic enterprise and the distinction of this authority from that of the Church'.[48] What was true of Pachomius was also surely true of many other monastic pioneers. Just as the episcopate, threatened by the rival attractions of the confessors and martyrs, had found ways to bring their enthusiasm within the control of the hierarchical Church, so now too it sought both to assert its authority over, and at the same time harness the undoubted power of, the monastic movement. Clearly one way was to physically remove monks to isolated communities away from the main urban centres and seats of episcopal authority, and hence the official approval of the mythology of the desert. But as we have seen, that carried with it the danger that isolation could lead to subversion. One way around this problem was by ordaining some prominent monks so as to place them and their communities under clear episcopal authority. One of the most amusing incidents in early monastic history is that of Pachomius hiding in the reeds along the banks of the Nile, secretly watching Athanasius as he sailed south, partly in search of the elusive Pachomius and with the intention of ordaining the famous monk. Pachomius successfully evaded the descent of the patriarchal hands and preserved his spiritual independence.[49]

But perhaps best of all was the burgeoning monastic literature. And here again there were comparisons with the oral transmission of the faith by the earliest Christians and the necessity of preserving and fixing the teachings of the apostles in writing. While they too lived, the great monastic founders were themselves like the apostles before them, sources of authoritative teaching. But after their deaths their ideas and commands had to be transmitted eventually in written form. Here was the opportunity for clerical authority to mould that literature in the direction it wished it to go: hence Athanasius's *Life of Antony* which quickly established the model for subsequent monastic Lives. Orthodoxy, and conformity to episcopal authority, became defining elements of authentic monasticism. Earlier diversity of both belief and practice were effectively silenced.[50] This literary impulse was to lead to the composition of Rules under which monastic communities were to live, in the West eventually producing the most influential of these, the Rule of St Benedict in the 540s. But as one modern historian has noted: 'Once that teaching was written, the reins of tight control slipped from the fingers of the masters themselves.'[51] And long before Benedict came to compose his Rule, the episcopate itself had assimilated some of the ascetic charisma by increasingly adopting elements of the radical lifestyle of the monks themselves, often in the form of the growing impulse towards clerical celibacy. Just as the relics and with them the charisma of the martyrs were now being brought physically within the jurisdiction of basilicas and their bishops, so too monk-bishops were now appropriating that of the ascetics.

But monasticism also posed another threat, this time not only to the orthodoxy but also to the catholicity of the early Church. Martyrdom had led to schisms such as that of the Donatists and Melitians, groups with a strong tendency to see the martyrs as forming an élite of Christian purity not to be sullied by the muddy waters of re-admitted apostates. Gnostics and Manichaeans also divided their adherents into groups of ordinary and élite followers. There was thus the potential for monasticism to similarly see itself as an élite form of Christianity, with the inherent danger of separation from the mainstream of the Church. At its most extreme there were those who proposed that only the celibate could be saved. It has also been argued by modern writers that the emergence of a hierarchical concept in early Christianity encouraged a view in which virginity could be seen as the highest and purest state of Christian virtue.[52]

Again the clerical leadership sought to promote the egalitarianism and integrated nature of the Church to combat this by utilizing monasticism as an ally in the concept of hierarchical service. This was true, for instance, of the work of Basil, the fourth-century Bishop of Caesarea in Asia Minor, and himself a significant figure in the history of early monasticism. But Basil's asceticism always had a social and primarily urban dimension. Following a famine in his province of Cappadocia in 369 he began to transform Caesarea into a 'new city' that would break down social distinctions and care for the poor, sick and destitute. He constructed a new hospital and other buildings, and set an example of service by personally dressing the wounds of the sick. Basil's concept of the Church was that of an extended family with all its members, clergy, laity or ascetics, employed in a joint venture. For as Basil argued in his *Homilies*: 'Humans are political beings, used to living together. In their common experience of public life and in their dealings with one another, they have to show a generosity directed towards improving the lot of those in need', and he affirmed that 'all are related, all are brothers, all are the offspring of a single father'. Basil used the example of the martyrs not simply to encourage individual ascetic efforts, but rather as a rallying point for the whole Christian community. As he preached: 'The city of the martyrs is the city of God.'[53]

In his more specifically ascetic writings Basil further stressed that there were not different types of people in the Church but rather Christians at different stages of development. Any ascetic withdrawal had to be interior and not geographical; these enthusiasts should remain open and ready to serve the wider community. He was not so much interested in the establishment of separate institutions and never employed the word 'monk', maintaining instead a vision of a socially integrated Church and city.[54] As a modern biographer has written of Basil: 'He functioned as a member of an élite; but it was an élite that he constantly strove to inspire with his own ideals, so that they became co-workers in a Christian enterprise.'[55]

A generation earlier, in the city of Alexandria, Athanasius had also sought to promote the integration of asceticism within the larger purposes of the Church. He had a similar concept to Basil of the diversity of gifts within the Christian community, and often quoted the parable of the sower (Matt. 13:1–8) and Paul's concept of being all things to all men to illustrate this (1 Cor. 9:22). Whatever ecclesial or political motives Athanasius may have had for wishing to integrate and control monasticism within his Alexandrian church, it is clear that he also held a very high and developed theological concept of asceticism and was a genuine admirer and promoter of that life. For him, ascetics were a sign of the truth of the Gospel message; ascetic transformation of some Christians demonstrated the extent of moral perfection made possible through the power of Christ for all Christians.[56] Essentially he pointed to the practice of virginity as a demonstration of the power of the incarnate Word; the chaste body of Jesus was both a model to imitate and, at the same time, a vehicle to be accessed as a source of spiritual strength to achieve virginity.[57]

Indeed, Athanasius stressed that the union of the virgin bride to her bridegroom, Christ, paralleled the archetypal union of Word with flesh in Christ, a point central to his incarnational theology and disputes with Arius. For Athanasius, the Word had effectively 'divinized' human flesh, thus enabling all humans to freely and permanently control their passions, among them the sexual drive. And here he entered into dispute with another ascetic pioneer, Hieracas, who taught that after the incarnation marriage itself was no longer possible, relegating sexually active Christians to an inferior grouping within the Church. For Athanasius, this implied that some Christians had a nature that led to celibacy while others did not. He totally rejected this. Virginity was a matter of free will, of choice enabled by the grace of Christ, not a different nature. Virginity was thus just another, if transcendent, form of marriage within the diversity of the Christian community. The incarnation had potentially freed humanity from slavery to the commands of a fallen and corrupted nature. Thus marriage between men and women was not different in kind, but only in degree, to the spiritual union with Christ consummated in virginity.[58]

But, not surprisingly, Athanasius was also clear that the burgeoning groups of female virgins in Alexandria should be firmly under episcopal control. In the fourth century there was as yet no uniform system or pattern for such communities. Some continued to live with their parents, some independently, others under the control of a male ascetic. This latter form has been called 'spiritual marriage' by modern scholars and was the one least approved of by Athanasius. Apart from the obvious dangers of sexual temptation, there was also again the potential for forming groups or schools of deviant theology. Thus he worked to bring all communities of virgins directly under episcopal control, and to regularize and unify their practices such as prayer, fasting, the singing of psalms, and the times at which they could be seen in public, the latter normally in Church during the liturgy, and then discreetly veiled.[59]

But while he strove to integrate asceticism into the wider life of the Church, he also encouraged movement in the opposite direction, to extend ascetic practices, in however limited a way, to Christians at large. This was perhaps best illustrated by Lent. Fasting, vigils and other ascetic practices such as sexual renunciation were at least temporarily extended to all Christians, reaching an intensity during Holy Week leading up to Easter Sunday.[60] This was also one of the motivations behind his ordination of selected monks, even to the point of creating the first Egyptian monk-bishops.[61] By the late fourth century this concept of the monk-bishop had spread to the West with the work of Martin, elected Bishop of Tours in 371. In the early decades of the fifth century this process was to be greatly extended when monks from the community on the island of Lérins near Cannes started to become bishops of some of the prominent cities of southern Gaul.[62]

For by this point monasticism had become an accepted and permanent feature of Christianity in both the East and the West. There was now a growing number of ascetic communities living under a Rule and a superior, points of intensity that radiated the light of Christian living to the wider Church. They were microcosms of what the Gospel promise made possible for the whole of humanity, living proofs of the truth and power of the incarnation and resurrection, and demonstrated that the imperial Church 'was not a counter-cultural sect, eager to keep its members pure and perfect amid a godless society, but rather a culture-creating institution, eager to embrace even the imperfect'.[63] It was, perhaps, after all not so much a matter of the desert being turned into a city, as monasticism being part of that Christian transformation of the cultural life of imperial cities themselves.

Suggested Further Reading

A good modern general introduction to the history of early monasticism is the one by Marilyn Dunn, *The Emergence of Monasticism: From the Desert Fathers to the Early Middle Ages* (Blackwell, Oxford, 2000). Manageable in terms of length, this is achieved by being almost note-like in places; however, it is an authoritative and readable starting point.

There are a number of modern studies that have fundamentally reoriented our understanding of the origins and early development of Christian monasticism. Among the most significant of these are: *The Body and Society: Men, Women and Sexual Renunciation in Early Christianity* (Columbia University Press, New York, 1988) by Peter Brown. This is brilliantly evocative with a wonderful use of metaphor, massively scholarly, and taking the reader into a world different not only from our own but also that of the medieval monastic experience as well. It is an indispensable work, if long and often complex. David Brakke's *Athanasius and the Politics of Asceticism* (Clarendon Press, Oxford, 1995) is a revised version of a Yale doctoral thesis and, while it cannot entirely hide these origins, is an important reinterpretation of Athanasius, Antony and early monastic life. James E. Goehring, *Ascetics, Society and the Desert: Studies in Early Egyptian Monasticism* (Trinity Press International, Harrisburg, 1999) is a series of reprints of articles by the author first published in journals mostly in the 1990s. However, they do not make for a dry and obscure academic read. On the contrary, they represent one of the most significant and radical reinterpretations of early Egyptian monasticism, and more than fully justify their republication in book form in order to reach a wider audience. In *The Letters of St Antony: Monasticism and the Making of a Saint* (Fortress Press, Minneapolis, 1995) Samuel Rubenson has produced a similarly radical reinterpretation of Antony himself, challenging the idea that he was an unlettered peasant, as first presented to the world by Athanasius, and demonstrating how he, and, by implication, other early monks were actually cultured and well read. It is closely argued and not always an easy read, however. Finally Vincent L. Wimbush and Richard Valantasis have edited a collection of essays simply entitled *Asceticism* (Oxford University Press, 1995); based on the contributions to an international conference held at Union Theological Seminary, New York, in April 1993, this covers a very wide thematic spectrum, including some entries on non-Christian examples of asceticism. Like many such collections it should be read selectively. However, all previous studies of early monasticism should now be reviewed carefully in the light of these modern ground-breaking works.

Among these is perhaps the classic twentieth-century account by Derwas J. Chitty, *The Desert a City: An Introduction to the Study of Egyptian and Palestinian Monasticism in the Christian Empire*, first published in 1966, and subsequently in a 1977 edition by Mowbray. Written in what already by the 1960s was a somewhat old-fashioned style, very anecdotal, but still full of the knowledge that came from extensive familiarity with the sources and the geography, it is still capable of giving an excellent flavour of the lost world it describes. In similar vein, the two sets of translations, *The Sayings of the Desert Fathers* by Benedicta Ward (Mowbray, Oxford, 1975) and *The Lives of the Desert Fathers* by Norman Russell (Mowbray, 1980) must now be studied very carefully as many scholars now argue that the texts that have survived are often the product of later observers 'reading back' their own ideas or times onto the earlier period, or the re-working of later editors, and so may not be an accurate reflection of the thoughts of the first monks. This is also a criticism that has been made of Douglas Burton-Christie's *The Word in the Desert: Scripture and the Quest for Holiness in Early Christian Monasticism* (Oxford University Press, 1993), a too uncritical acceptance of the sources at face value.

Three studies by Philip Rousseau are also well worth reading. *Ascetics, Authority and the Church: In the Age of Jerome and Cassian* (Oxford University Press, 1978) is based on his Oxford doctoral thesis, and traces how the developments that began in Egypt culminated in the West with John Cassian, and how the latter's writings represented a point of departure for the future. *Pachomius: The Making of a Community in Fourth-Century Egypt* (University of California Press, Berkeley, 1985) is particularly good on the spiritual and practical life of Pachomian monks. *Basil of Caesarea* (University of California Press, Berkeley, 1994) deals mainly with the Bishop as a thinker, and is thus rather a sophisticated book, but it clearly unites his theology with his more practical actions.

Among primary sources in translation, Athanasius' *The Life of Antony* is crucial. There is a good modern translation with an introduction by Robert C. Gregg, published by SPCK in 1980.

3

The Great Debate

When the Spirit of truth comes, he will guide you into all the truth.
(John 16:13)

The Synoptic Gospels record Jesus asking his apostles a fundamental question: who do you think I am? (Matt. 16:13–20; Mark 8:27–30; Luke 9:18–20). This question of Jesus's identity was to absorb some of the greatest minds of the early Church, and in the fourth and fifth centuries stimulated one of the most profound debates in Christian history. It was to become the central issue at all four of the Ecumenical Councils of the period, Nicaea in 325, Constantinople in 381, Ephesus in 431, and Chalcedon in 451, and to result in the promulgation of two of the Church's essential statements of belief, the Nicene Creed and the Chalcedonian Definition. At the same time this debate intensified and focused in sometimes dramatic ways a number of the characteristics of early Christianity that we have already encountered, from its diversity and search for orthodoxy, to its assimilation of Hellenistic learning and Roman imperialism. It has also left a number of legacies that still affect Christianity to this day. For one thing, the search continues to find possible answers to the question Jesus first put to his apostles on the way to Caesarea Philippi, and has blossomed into the branch of theology known as christology. More negatively, the origins of the most lasting divisions within Christianity can be traced directly to this debate. So, then, why did early Christians consider this question to be so vital that they spent so much of their time and energy in the attempt to find an answer to it?

Questions and Problems

In the long search to suggest answers to this basic question of Jesus's identity, it can sometimes appear that the difficulties raised and the attempted solutions offered take on the mind-numbing complexity of three-dimensional chess. Yet this was no game. At stake behind the seemingly endless subtleties in the arguments and counter-arguments that flew back and forth across the Mediterranean world was the very nature of Christianity itself. For instance, all Christians accepted certain basic principles as taught by their faith. One of these was that Jesus had come to save humanity from the consequences of the Fall and sin, and to restore people to a right relationship with God. Yet clearly only God can save; no human being, however spiritual or enlightened, can do that. Thus Jesus had to be, in a real sense, divine; in the words of the New Testament, the Son of God. As Paul wrote of Jesus: 'For in him the whole fullness of deity dwells bodily' (Col. 2:9). And in a famous series of letters written by the cultured pagan, Pliny the Younger, to the Emperor Trajan around the year 112, we have one of the earliest non-Christian sources of evidence of this basic belief of the new sect in the divinity of its founder.[1] Thus any christological formula that compromised the full divinity of Jesus was in danger of calling into question that very salvation of humanity that was at the core of the faith.

On the other hand, however, was the equally important assertion that Jesus was like us, fully human; not only was he the Son of God, he was the Son of Man as well, in the words of the letter to the Hebrews: 'For we do not have a high priest who is unable to sympathize with our weaknesses, but we have one who in every respect has been tested [or tempted] as we are, yet without sin' (Heb. 4:15). This was a basic principle accepted by all Christians. As Origen had argued, only a whole man could redeem other whole men, a fundamental belief that was to find its brief but classic formulation in the fourth century by Gregory of Nazianzus (330–90), from the province of Cappadocia in central Asia Minor: 'the unassumed is the unhealed'.[2] God's salvation had to extend to human need in its fullness and wholeness, body, mind and soul; if Jesus was only partly human then that again called into question the extent of human salvation. Whatever we are that makes us truly human, Jesus had to share, and share fully.

Beyond that, a further series of questions and problems flowed from this fundamental principle that Jesus had to be both truly divine and fully human. Who were Christians praying to? Prayer to a solely human Jesus would surely be both blasphemous and ineffective. But at the same time, in the Eucharist Christians believed that in a real sense they were eating and drinking the body and blood of their Lord. In order to be able to do this, however, Jesus would equally have had to have had a human body made of real flesh and blood. Further, in their baptism as well as their acts of penance, Christians made certain assumptions about Jesus and his relationship both to God and to themselves. Thus who Jesus was, the nature of his relationship to God and to humanity, went to the very heart of Christian belief and practice. A saviour disengaged either from his divinity or from the process of history was no true saviour at all.

Answers to these questions were to prove neither easy to attain nor simple in their formulation. At the outset it might appear to be rather like a problem of how to get two different pints of liquid into a single one-pint vessel. How can a single individual contain within himself both the fullness of divinity and the wholeness of humanity? Any attempted answer, for instance, however intellectually subtle in its formulation, that started from the assumption that God had, as it were, 'taken over' a human body would not suffice. This would imply that Jesus had been little more than an automaton manipulated by divinity; at its most extreme this had led to Docetism, a belief in a Jesus who only *seemed* to be human but in reality was not. In a less extreme form it could also imply that Jesus was little more than divinized flesh, without a human soul or free will. This was the charge to be brought against another influential fourth-century Christian thinker, Apollinarius (*c.* 310–*c.* 390); in the intensity of his desire to defend the divinity of his Lord he had effectively discarded Christ's human soul and so left him a less than whole man.

At the other end of the spectrum was a theology that started with the assertion of the full humanity of Jesus. But this too could lead thinkers, however subtle their arguments, into the opposite trap. Paul of Samosata, for example, who had become Bishop of Antioch in about 260, was an early exponent of this approach. His insistence, absolutely correct in itself, that Jesus must have experienced the whole range of human emotions, temptations and sufferings, led him to imply, at least in the eyes of his opponents, that Jesus was little more than a man with a uniquely divine inspiration; that God dwelt in him as a quality but not as a person. In other words, it seemed that Paul of Samosata was arguing that Jesus was like the Old Testament prophets in being divinely inspired, even if in his case that inspiration was continuous rather than fleeting and momentary. But Jesus was clearly different not just in *degree* but also in *kind* from the Jewish prophets. How could the bishop of Antioch's Jesus be a divine saviour? He was certainly a Jesus who could be understood and appreciated in a world in which pagan gods were assumed to speak through human oracles, but this was not the Jesus worshipped by Christians. This line of reasoning was to find, perhaps, its most developed exponent in Theodore of Mopsuestia (*c.* 350–428). Theodore's great achievement was to stress the psychological temptations and sufferings of Jesus, not just his physical ones;

that salvation had to reach to the fullest extent of human need. But in so doing he was in danger of seeing the incarnation in moral rather than material terms, leaving divinity a somewhat secondary role.

Thus there was to be no single thinker who alone solved these problems; no one had a 'Eureka moment' in which all the pieces of this complex jigsaw suddenly snapped into place. Each one, even those subsequently regarded as heretical (and in some cases this was not until long after their deaths) had some crucial insights that slowly, piece by piece, added to the overall emerging picture. Rather like the modern struggle to overcome disease, where no over-arching cure has been found, the disease slowly retreating before a long series of small advances and breakthroughs, interspersed with false trails and setbacks, early christology advanced and retreated and advanced again across the Christian world. How could divinity live with humanity in the same individual without one impairing, or at its worst, effectively obliterating the other?

Part of the problem faced by Christian thinkers in these centuries was one of language. How could they find the words and phrases to compose formulas that would do justice to both the divinity and the humanity of Jesus, and at the same time explain the union of these two elements? The apostle Paul himself had hinted at the problem of using human language to convey divine truth (1 Cor. 4:20; 2 Cor. 3:3) and had sometimes reverted to metaphor to express his meaning (Eph. 5:30–2). Without initiating a lengthy discussion on the subject of the philosophy of language, clearly there is a distinction between God on the one hand, infinite and eternal, and human language on the other which is finite and particular. How can the latter adequately communicate meaning about the former?

Yet from Paul himself onwards Christians have expended countless words in the effort to explain their faith. Without anticipating a point we shall have to return to later, however limited they may be, words remain one of the chief means of communication that we possess. They can never, of course, tie God down, as it were. He will always remain beyond our limited powers of understanding and communication. But at the same time they are essential in the effort to convey meaning. As we have seen, christological writing still continues today, but along lines often determined by the great debates of the fourth and fifth centuries. Why? Perhaps it is because language can have a negative quality. Words act like signposts: they are just as essential in stopping the traveller from taking the wrong route as they are for pointing in the right direction. They can never take you to the end of the journey, but they can help in preventing you from taking a wrong turning or entering a dead end. It is no accident that much of the language used in the Chalcedonian Definition is itself negative. The right words can help in keeping Christians on the right track in their exploration of the faith.[3]

One way to attempt to get around the dilemma faced when trying to express the infinite through the finite was for early Christian thinkers to follow the example of the New Testament and employ the language of imagery, metaphor and analogy. Justin Martyr employed such techniques in his *Dialogue with Trypho*, a Jew. To help explain the generation of the Son from the Father, Justin used the analogies of the sun sending out its rays, or a fire kindling other fires.[4] This approach was taken up by authors in subsequent generations. In his *On First Principles* Origen famously introduced the metaphor of the iron in the fire. Here he compared the iron to the soul of Christ immersed in the fire of God; just as heat removes cold so Christ was thus incapable of sin.[5] The problem with such language, however, was that it did not describe a stable relationship. When the iron is removed from the fire it will inevitably cool. So was Origen describing a permanent and substantial union between God and Jesus, or only a moral one? Yet, as Gregory of Nazianzus was to remark later, the distinctive message of Christianity could sometimes better be served by evocative images than logical systems.[6]

However useful or not the language of image and metaphor might have been, by the fourth century Christian thinkers had two fundamental literary sources which they could exploit in their quest for christological understanding. One of these was obviously the canon of the New Testament. As we have seen, by the fourth century this consisted of a universally accepted core of texts that made up the bulk of an agreed canon. Thus any christological statements or formulas had to be in accord with the meaning of the New Testament, or at the very least not in contradiction to it. But here arose another potential problem, that of interpretation. Docetics, for instance, could use the biblical language of 'appearance' (Titus 2:11; 3:4) to justify their view of an insubstantial human Jesus. Later, Arians could also quote the New Testament in support of their christology (e.g. Heb. 1:4, 3:1; Acts 2:36; 1 Cor. 15:24–8; Col. 1:15). There could even appear to be contradictory statements within a single book of the New Testament: 'The Father and I are one' seemed to be contradicted by the statement 'the Father is greater than I', both sayings of Jesus recorded in John's Gospel (John 10:30, 14:28). On top of that the New Testament writers could make assertions without offering explanations for them. Jesus is called the Son of God, but exactly *how* he is this is never explained.[7]

Hence the early Christians turned to a second source of writings to aid them in this problem of interpretation: the literature of Hellenism. From the time of Justin Martyr, Clement of Alexandria and Origen, Greek philosophy had been seen as a legitimate storehouse to be plundered in defence of Christian teaching. Nowhere is this more notable than in the christological debate, which demonstrated the degree to which the classical inheritance had become assimilated into Christian dialogue. Indeed, the very intensity of this debate in the fourth and fifth centuries was only possible once both the canon and Hellenism had been so thoroughly absorbed into Christianity. In any case, if Christian thinkers were to appeal to their pagan counterparts, it had to be in a language that the latter would understand. However, it must always be remembered that Greek thought was only an interpretative tool; the primary authority remained biblical. But at the same time this was the best vehicle available at that time for offering such a tool to Christian thinkers.

Yet it is also at this point of contact that some of the most complex problems in christology arose. This was not only a pre-Freudian world, it was also a pre-scientific one as well in our modern sense of that term. In borrowing a series of words, mainly from the various branches of Platonism, we should not assume that ancient Christians thought in quite the same precise and narrow way that we tend to when it comes to technical terms. Words were aids to thought, not exact mathematical equations. This was then further confused as some terms could become virtually synonymous with each other, could shift their meaning over time, or be used by different Christian writers to mean somewhat different things. However, this was the terminology available, and as such it has entered into the accepted vocabulary of christology.

One of these key words is actually very familiar, if only in translation: *Logos*. At the opening of the Prologue to his Gospel, John writes: 'In the beginning was the Word, and the Word was with God, and the Word was God' (John 1:1). In each case the original Greek *Logos* has been translated as 'Word'. He has taken over a concept long familiar to Hellenistic thinkers and applied it to Christianity. *Logos* could just as plausibly be translated as 'Reason'. As early as *c.* 500 BC the Greek philosopher Heraclitus saw the *Logos* as the universal reason governing and permeating the world, a concept later adopted by the Stoics. The Old Testament writers had not dissimilar ideas, and the Greek *Logos* was effectively paralleled by their figure of Wisdom. The Hellenized Jew, Philo (*c.* 20 BC–*c.* AD 50) saw the *Logos* as the divine pattern from which the material world is copied, the divine agent in the process of creation and effectively an intermediary between God and humanity. Thus in associating the *Logos* with the divine, John was doing nothing extraordinary. However, a little further in his Prologue he makes an assertion that would have been quite unimaginable to the Greek mind: 'And the Word [*Logos*] became flesh and lived among us' (John 1:14). This *Logos*, transcendent and fundamentally outside the material creation, has now been brought into it, and not in any theoretical way but in a very concrete individual, Jesus of Nazareth, the Son of God himself. How was this possible? Whatever the answer to that question, all christology starts from this incarnation of the *Logos*, of the transcendent becoming immanent. But what John does not go on to explain is the precise mechanism by which this has come about.

A little earlier in time than John, Paul had offered his own description of this process, itself possibly based on an even earlier Christian hymn, and viewed it, perhaps, rather more from the human perspective, when he wrote of Jesus:

> though he was in the form of God, [he] did not regard equality with God as something to be exploited, but emptied himself, taking the form of a slave, being born in human likeness. And being found in human form, he humbled himself and became obedient to the point of death – even death on a cross. Therefore God also highly exalted him and gave him the name that is above every name, so that at the name of Jesus every knee should bend, in heaven and on earth and under the earth, and every tongue should confess that Jesus Christ is Lord, to the glory of God the Father. (Phil. 2:6–11)

For John the already exalted *Logos* has taken flesh (*sarx*); for Paul the exaltation is the result of the self-emptying (*kenosis*) of divinity in becoming human (*anthropos*). Thus already in the biblical descriptions we have the origins of two, hopefully complementary, ways of looking at the incarnation: a *Logos-sarx* (Word-flesh) and a *Logos-anthropos* (Word-humankind) Christology. To rather over-simplify, the former begins with the exalted, transcendent being who has been with God in eternity coming down to take a human form; the latter sees a lowly man exalted because of the self-emptying of God into his person, rising to divine glory.

Beyond these words the Greeks also had a series of terms which reflected their view of the different levels or states of being within things. Early Christian thinkers applied them to Jesus, his divinity and humanity and the means by which they were united in one individual. Here, there are problems that can lead to some confusion as there is often no exact or precise English equivalent, and to some extent modern people no longer think easily in such categories. However, we have already encountered one of these terms when considering the statement of faith issued by the Council of Nicaea in 325: *ousia*. This is often translated as 'substance' or 'essence', and means that which stands underneath something and gives it reality. In the Nicene Creed it appears as *homoousios*, 'of the same substance' when speaking of the relationship of the Father to the Son. As we noted, a major hesitation in using this word existed because it was not biblical in origin, and further suspect as it had been used by Paul of Samosata and thus condemned by an earlier, if local, Council. And another problem raised by *ousia* was whether its use was in a generic or particular sense. If the former, it tended to obliterate the individuality of the Father and Son, and hence other terms for other levels of being would have to be used to help identify them in a more particular sense.

One of these was *hypostasis*. Confusingly, this could either be taken to mean something not dissimilar to *ousia* itself, or it could mean something more like the individuating principle.[8] This ambiguity could lead it to be associated with other terms, often with *prosopon*. This word originally meant 'countenance' or 'face', the means by which something appears, or its distinctive characteristics. In some usages it could mean the masks worn by actors in the ancient theatre, and was normally rendered into the Latin *persona*, and hence into the English word 'person'.[9] However, we should be careful not to ascribe to *prosopon* the full psychological meaning that we now normally attach to 'person', at least not until its use more in this sense by the Chalcedonian Definition. And further associated with *hypostasis* and *prosopon* was the term *physis* (or *phusis*), normally translated as 'nature', which can be used in a static sense, but in christology came to be more dynamic, meaning a way of acting, or the self-determination in a being, that which gives a thing its distinctive characteristics.

Thus given the subtlety of meanings often contained in a single word, it is perhaps not surprising that Christian writers did not always use them as precise technical terms, but more as aids to thinking. But this in itself held the danger that different authors could mean either the same thing but use different words for it, or use the same word but mean different things by it. This was essentially the problem in the extended and increasingly acrimonious exchanges in the late 420s and early 430s between Cyril, Patriarch of Alexandria (d. 444), and Nestorius, Patriarch of Constantinople (d. after 451). It took the authority of the Ecumenical Council of Chalcedon in 451 to clarify what by then was in danger of becoming a hopeless tangle of variant words and meanings. Earlier, in the 360s, Athanasius himself had already warned against not fighting 'about words to no useful purpose, nor to go on contending with such phrases, but to agree in the mind of piety'.[10] However, these words were the best tools that early Christians had at their disposal, and, rightly used, could be hugely beneficial in the task of interpretation.

But there was also the further danger that the philosophical terms could take over, as it were, from the biblical or theological understanding they were attempting to elucidate. For instance, the Cappadocian writers of the fourth century, Gregory of Nazianzus, Basil of Caesarea and Gregory of Nyssa (c. 330–c. 395) used Stoic theories about the mixing of two natural things which permeate each other, but without either one losing its own nature, and applied them to the divine/human 'mixing' in Jesus. While on one level insightful, on another it could be viewed as too materialistic a concept, and did not give a clear enough distinction between the substance and its concrete manifestation as *prosopon*.[11] In addition, the too rigid adoption of Platonist concepts of divinity, especially the idea that God is immutable or unchangeable, could also present problems for Christian writers. If the Platonist concepts are assumed, how do you then explain the *Logos* entering a changing world, especially in uniting himself to a particular human being who experiences birth, suffering and death?

This could lead to apparently quite contradictory solutions to christological problems, but in reality stemming from the same common philosophical root. Arius, for instance, in conforming with Platonism, argued that God is incapable of change or suffering. But in Christ the *Logos* became incarnate in a man capable of change and suffering, so that the *Logos* could be said to suffer too; but the corollary of this is that the *Logos* could not thus be truly described as divine, and so in what sense is Jesus the Son of God? This leads to the conclusion that Jesus is not the *natural* Son of God, but only a Son by adoption.

Then later in the fourth century Apollinarius was to challenge this, but from the same Platonist conceptions. Jesus must be truly God, he argued, but if God cannot change or suffer, then Jesus cannot really have suffered, at least in that part of himself which experiences spiritual and psychological as opposed to merely physical suffering, namely the soul. Therefore Jesus cannot have had a human soul, which correspondingly calls into question the fullness or wholeness of his humanity. Either way, divinity is disengaged from history, and salvation itself is clearly called into question, as only God can save, but that salvation itself must reach to the fullest extent of human need.

So, the adaptation of Greek philosophical concepts and language to the interpretation of the Christian message found in the New Testament canon was a two-edged sword. Used in the wrong ways, even with the best of intentions, it could confuse and mislead, at worst arriving at those dead-ends in the journey of Christian exploration that have come to be called heresies. So how, then, could this language be used as signposting on the route to orthodoxy?

Proposals and Limitations

It has become customary to organize contrasting christological methodologies in the fourth and fifth centuries into two groupings: those who followed a *Logos-sarx* approach and those who adopted a *Logos-anthropos* model. It has also become customary to assign the former to an Alexandrian school of christology, and the latter to an Antiochene one. However, many modern scholars have argued that such a bold, black and white division is more misleading than illuminating. For one thing, it is quite incorrect to impose so precise a geographical identification; and for another it is an oversimplification to refer to them as 'schools'. These were far from being organized groups of theologians in imitation of the Greek philosophical schools. Most Christian thinkers worked and wrote as individuals, sometimes acknowledging influences from other individuals, but in no sense should the term 'school' be applied to such loose associations, with its implication of a systematic or homogeneous approach. Theologians who have been ascribed to one 'school' sometimes utilized approaches and techniques more often associated with the other 'school'. Furthermore, it is now seen as problematic to speak even in the loosest sense of Antiochene christology much before 400, and to see the two contrasting approaches in any sort of open conflict or competition before the exchanges between Cyril and Nestorius. That there were different method-ologies in the examination of the question of Jesus's identity is not in doubt; but to limit them to only two contrasting 'schools' is patently incorrect. In some ways this is just as misleading as describing all the opponents of Athana-sius as 'Arians'; he may have wished to group them together under such a tainted label for his own polemical purposes, but it made no more sense than referring to his supporters as 'Athanasians'.

In his detailed analysis of christology in the early Church, Aloys Grillmeier has re-labelled the contrasting approaches as 'frameworks' based around the *Logos-sarx* and *Logos-anthropos* methodologies. Perhaps even this credits them with a sense of common purpose that they did not in reality possess, and that a better word might be 'tendencies'. Whatever one's preferences in labels, however, it does remain broadly the case that the biblical titles 'Son of God' and 'Son of Man' for Jesus did lead to a tendency for particular individuals to start from, or emphasize, one or the other, even if their intention was to show that neither should be seen as the predominant characteristic of Jesus. Gerald O'Collins has described the *Logos-sarx* tendency as highlighting the Johanine theme of 'the Word becoming flesh', and the *Logos-anthropos* as 'the eternal Word assuming the man Jesus'. Distilling this down still further, perhaps it would be useful to speak of a God-man and a Man-assumed as the two contrasting approaches.[12]

Both approaches or tendencies, however, carried within themselves both the potential for extraordinary insights, and the danger of exaggeration or elimination of one or more vital elements. If we examine the christology of Athanasius, for instance, we shall find both these positives and negatives present. Athanasius is clearly an 'Alexandrian' in that his emphasis is on the God-man, divinity entering human history by the means of human flesh. His insight is clear: only if the divine enters our world of time and space can we truly be saved. As he wrote in his early treatise *On the Incarnation*:

He has been manifested in a human body for this reason only, out of the love and goodness of his Father, for the salvation of us men. We will begin, then, with the creation of the world and with God its Maker, for the first fact that you must grasp is this: *the renewal of creation has been wrought by the self-same Word who made it in the beginning*. There is thus no inconsistency between creation and salvation; for the One Father has employed the same Agent for both works, effecting the salvation of the world through the same Word who made it at the first.[13]

Here, Athanasius has taken up the biblical Pauline theme of recreation and linked it to the original creative act of the *Logos*. This will eventually lead him to a declaration of another of the great, insightful themes of many early christological writers, that the destined culmination of humanity's salvation by recreation is to be with God in a peculiarly intimate way by experiencing *theosis*, deification: that 'God assumed humanity that we might become God'. While Jesus is the *natural* Son of God, it is we who become his children by adoption (Document 8).

However, the language that Athanasius uses to describe the God-man leaves an impression that this 'divinization' had already taken place at the incarnation, that in a sense the *Logos* 'took over' or merely 'inhabited' a convenient body: 'Existing in a human body, to which He Himself gives life . . . His body was for Him not a limitation, but an instrument . . .'[14] Was Jesus no more than instrumental flesh, *sarx*? If so, what of his human soul through which he experienced more than the physical pain of a material body alone, but also the mental and spiritual anguish of the garden of Gethsemane and the sense of abandonment on the cross? If, as Athanasius implies, it is the *Logos* which animates the flesh, then, in effect, the *Logos* has taken the place of the human soul in Jesus. Influenced as he seems to have been by Stoic views of the *Logos* and the soul, Athanasius, at least in the view of one modern authority, assumed that the human, rational soul is the most perfect copy of the *Logos* within the earthly, corporeal creation. It fulfils towards the body the function which the *Logos* has in the cosmos. It is a *Logos* in microcosm, and therefore also a way to him and to the Father. Athanasius's view might be put in these words: where the original itself appears with all its power, the copy, with its secondary and derived power, must at the least surrender its function, even if it does not give place altogether.[15] Athanasius himself is perhaps rather more ambiguous than this, but his failure to discuss a role in salvation for the human soul of Jesus did leave the way open for Apollinarius to be far more explicit: 'The human race is not saved by the assumption of a mind and a whole man, but by the taking of flesh . . . An immutable Mind was needed which would not fail through weakness of understanding.'[16]

Was humanity indeed so weak that it could not be trusted in its wholeness to assist in the process of its own salvation? Was it only the passive instrument of the active agency of the *Logos*? Are we only saved by a divinity who in the ultimate resort is external to us; or, rather, by a God who so loves, understands and values us that he truly enters inside our very being? While Athanasius,

Apollinarius and others who represented the God-man approach would not have agreed that their understanding of salvation was from the outside only, their language too often implied this. What was needed was a balance to this tendency, and this was provided by theologians using Man-assumed language.

Gregory of Nazianzus also used the terminology of divinization, but in his work there is a subtle shift in that the *theosis* of humanity is an idea 'for which the divinization of Christ's human nature is to supply the theological foundation'.[17] In other words, there is here a realization that human nature is not just the passive recipient of the *Logos*, but is itself raised to stand alongside divinity in the process of salvation. Between the divine and the human there is a 'mixing' or 'conjunction'. In some way the two have come together. But was it possible to find a language or terminology that would do justice to this unity while at the same time preserving the distinction of the two entities, but without going so far as to imply that they were divided?

One linguistic method that had been employed from an early date in the christological debate to emphasize the unity of human and divine in Christ was the so-called 'exchange of predicates' (*communicatio idiomatum* in Latin) or the interchange of properties. What this meant was that there were certain things that could be asserted of Jesus as a man, just as there were others which could be claimed for him as God. But if he was both human *and* divine, then what was true of one was equally true of the other, or as Origen had expressed it: 'the divine nature is spoken of in human terms, and at the same time the human nature is accorded the distinctive epithets proper to the divine'.[18] Thus one could legitimately say that Jesus as Son of Man died on a cross, and just as legitimately that as Son of God he was also crucified. Yet the problem with this kind of language is that while death clearly marks the termination of earthly existence for human beings, God must be eternal, with no beginning and certainly no termination.

That raised the further question of the sense in which one could speak of God experiencing all the things that humans do from birth, through growth, to the point of death. Yet the New Testament was clear that Jesus had encountered the full range of human experience including temptation (Heb. 4:15) and growth in wisdom (Luke 2:52) as well as birth and death. And as we have seen, it was one of the central insights of the Man-assumed tendency to emphasize the absolute necessity of a fully human Jesus able to experience all that other humans do. Could the terminology of Hellenism be of any help in trying to explain how Jesus can both be truly human and divine, and how these two states could co-exist in one individual in perfect harmony?

It was during the first half of the fifth century that this question of the manner of the human/divine union reached a climax. One crucial argument centred on the birth of Jesus, and especially concentrated on the person of his mother, Mary, and her precise role in that event. Diodore, Bishop of Tarsus (d. *c.* 390) had written of Jesus as Son of God by nature and Son of Man by grace, but by this effectively implying that there were somehow two Sons, divided not united. Mary was thus not the mother of a divine individual but a human one in some way joined to divinity. The problem was that for generations at both the intellectual and popular levels Mary had been accorded the title *Theotokos*, the 'God-bearer'. In what sense, then, could it be asserted that God had been born, since clearly his eternal status meant that he had no beginning?

This was one of the crucial points at issue between Cyril and Nestorius. The Patriarch of Constantinople was a determined opponent of what he considered to be heresy, especially of the type emanating from the rival Patriachate of Alexandria in the form of Arianism and Apollinarianism. His position has been neatly summarized by Frances Young: 'To attribute birth and suffering and death to the Logos is to fall into pagan thinking and follow the heresies of Apollinarius and Arius.'[19] Nestorius by contrast was at pains to uphold the full humanity of Jesus; that at the incarnation God saves humankind through a particular human being, so that divinity must take a humanity that is congruous with all human beings. Thus, Nestorius argued, God became incarnate by the means of his *prosopon* making a human *prosopon* his own in a great act of condescension.

Nestorius criticized Cyril for appearing again to leave out the human soul of Christ and to see him more in terms of universal humanity than a concrete individual. On the other hand, Cyril considered that Nestorius had not accounted sufficiently for the unity of divinity and humanity in Jesus and thus ascribed to him two *prosopa*. For his part, Nestorius saw in the term *theotokos* the danger of Apollinarianism and preferred the word *christotakos*, the 'Christ-bearer'. The issue was debated at the Ecumenical Council of Ephesus in 431 and *theotokos* upheld as a legitimate and orthodox title for Mary.

For Cyril had seen that there was a way around the problem of speaking about God being born, and that the terminology of Hellenism could elucidate it. It depended on what one meant by saying that God had been born. Here there had to be a clear distinction between God as Holy Trinity who had clearly not entered the virgin's womb. But the divine *Logos* was a different matter. Here Cyril made an original and imaginative philosophical leap. Just as John in his Gospel had seen that the *Logos* had become flesh in defiance of traditional Greek thinking about divinity, so now Cyril saw that in *kenosis*, self-emptying, God had willingly passed outside the limits of his own nature as that was conceived by the philosophers. He had literally poured himself out into his own creation, the supreme act of *agape*, self-giving love, something so tremendous that it stretched human understanding and imagination almost to breaking point in the attempt to contemplate its enormity. Thus, argued Cyrial, it was possible to speak of a double generation of the *Logos*, once begotten of the Father in eternity, and then born of a virgin in time and space. And so Mary had indeed become the mother of the person of the *Logos*, where divinity and humanity met. Here Cyril seemed to be taking up the challenge implied in the words of the Western writer, Tertullian, two centuries earlier: 'the Son of God died; it is by all means to be believed, because it is absurd. And he was buried, and rose again; the fact is certain, because it is impossible.'[20] What seemed to be an absurd and impossible paradox to the conventional Greek mind, God had been able to achieve, and by approaching it in an unconventional way Cyril had been able to offer an explanation.

But, perhaps not surprisingly, the arguments of the early fifth century produced as much confusion as they did clarity. Cyril's great concern was to preserve the unity of the human and divine in Jesus (1 Cor. 8:6); the basis of that union was the 'person' of the divine *Logos*, in which Christ is not plural but singular, one out of both *prosopa*, one single mode of existence. The danger here was in a potential failure to preserve the distinction between the human and the divine. If the union was at the prosopic or hypostatic level, did it also mean a union at the other levels of *physis* or *ousia*? Where Nestorius could be accused of ambiguity in seeming to imply two 'persons' in Christ, did Cyril fall into the opposite trap of so emphasizing the unity that the two 'natures', human and divine, also became one? This was effectively what a monk from Constantinople, Eutyches (*c.* 378–454) was accused of teaching in the 440s – that after the incarnation the divine *physis* merged with the human *physis*, and thus Jesus effectively had only one, divine 'nature'. Clearly this so-called Monophysite position implied that Jesus was not fully and truly human.

Finally, in 451 at the fourth Ecumenical Council of Chalcedon, the attending bishops issued a defining statement which sought to clarify what had become potentially tangled language and terminology. They were helped in this by the arrival in the east of a lengthy letter from Leo I, Bishop and Patriarch of Rome, addressed to the Patriarch Flavian of Constantinople, and popularly known as the Tome of Leo, the most significant Western contribution to the debate. The resulting Chalcedonian Definition appears to be relatively straightforward in its language; but that is a deceptive simplicity. Once one is aware of the generations of theological debate that lie behind it, the momentous nature of its sonorous phrases takes a whole new dimension of meaning. The tortuous lineage of each of its statements, both the positives and the negatives, leap into focus, and the greatest insights of Alexandria and Antioch meet in harmony (Document 9).[21]

Broader Contexts

There is always a temptation to see great intellectual questions such as those involved in the christological debate being carried on, as it were, in a hermetically sealed thought-bubble quite isolated from what was happening outside in the rest of Church and the world. But this was far from the case. Both secular and ecclesiastical politics intervened at a number of points and levels during the progress of the debate. Obviously, since the conversion of Constantine in 312 there had been a constant imperial dimension to the search for orthodoxy. This was nowhere more clearly manifested than in the manoeuvrings that led up to the summoning of the Council of Chalcedon.

In 448 a local Synod in Constantinople had declared firmly against the Monophysite position of the monk, Eutyches. But he had friends at court, and the Emperor Theodosius II was persuaded to assemble what he hoped would be recognized as a new Ecumenical Council at Ephesus in 449, mainly with the object of rehabilitating Eutyches. About 140 bishops attended, but the proceedings were dominated by the presence of intimidating numbers of monks gathered for the purpose by Eutyches and his allies. Not surprisingly, the proceedings were effectively hijacked by them, and the Roman envoys, for instance, prevented from reading or presenting the Tome of Leo. Some 113 bishops duly declared Eutyches perfectly orthodox.

His victory seemed complete. And with his triumph that of Monophysitism in the east also now seemed assured. But the Emperor's sister, Pulcheria, was a bitter opponent of the monk, and upon the sudden death of her brother in July 450, assumed the imperial title herself. The new Empress promptly began a purge of pro-Eutycheans at court, received Leo's Tome with great reverence, and quickly married another opponent of the Monophysite position, the general Marcian. The imperial couple then moved to undo the damage done by the 'robber' Council of Ephesus, and summoned the bishops to meet once again, this time at Chalcedon. Here the reluctance of those episcopal delegates to draw up another declaration of faith that might appear to go beyond those of Nicaea and Constantinople was overcome under further imperial pressure. Thus it was that the accidents of imperial death and succession amid court intrigues helped materially in producing one of the most fundamental doctrinal formulas of Christian history.

Imperial intrigue was not the only type of political activity at work that helped to mould the course of the debate. The Church was equally as capable of producing rivalry, faction and underhand plotting on its own account. This formed the rather unsavoury background to the conflict between Nestorius and Cyril. Neither seem to have been particularly attractive characters. Stubborn, convinced of the rightness of their own positions, and totally unwilling to listen to criticism, these personal characteristics proved fatal when added to the long-standing rivalry between their two bishoprics. At the Council of Constantinople in 381 the 'new' Rome had been added to the old one along with Jerusalem, Alexandria and Antioch as a fifth Patriarchate. Not only was this seen as a potential threat by Alexandria which had previously had sheer size on its side, but it also appeared to be an ecclesiastical affront too, as, unlike the other four, the new Patriarch of Constantinople could not claim an apostolic foundation.

In 403–4 Theophilus of Alexandria had achieved a great victory for his Patriarchate when he secured the deposition of John Chrysostom as Patriarch of Constantinople. Cyril was Theophilus' nephew, and in his disputes with Nestorius of Constantinople in 429–31, hoped to land a further body-blow on the upstart see. Nestorius for his part was just as eager to obtain revenge for his own city. This intense rivalry was also to reappear again in the years leading up to Chalcedon when Diosculus of Alexandria again helped to engineer the deposition of another Patriarch of Constantinople, Flavian, in 449. And in 431 Cyril had been materially aided in his victory by intrigues that bore fruit when the Patriach John of Antioch abandoned Nestorius to his fate. Both sides had used equally questionable methods, reminiscent of those employed by Athanasius and his opponents in the previous century. As Frances Young has commented: 'Cyril poses the age-old problem: how can a man apparently be both saint and sinner – or in his case perhaps we should say, great theologian and moral blackguard'.[22] Both Athanasius and Cyril are canonized saints celebrated with feast days in the Church's calendar. Once again, frail and fallible human beings, even in their weaknesses, can be seen as divine instruments by the Christian community.

Something similar could also be said for the words and philosophies that they employed. As we saw earlier, language has its own limitations when used as a vehicle for expressing truths about God. Christian thinkers had turned quite naturally in the early centuries of their faith to the philosophical schools of Hellenism to aid them in their interpretation of the Christian revelation recorded in the New Testament. But however useful they were, at certain points 'Christian problems burst the bounds of any one system'.[23] It was only by making imaginative leaps that often challenged some of the basic presuppositions of Greek thinking that theologians such as Cyril could make significant breakthroughs. It was sometimes necessary to be prepared to think 'outside the box' as we moderns would put it in order for christology to move forward. For what was clear was 'the inadequacy of all attempts to approach the divine majesty' and that 'God infinitely surpasses our human categories'.[24] The workings of God remain mysterious, not totally unknown or unknowable, and revealed, Christians believe, at their most profound in the person of

Jesus; but there is a point beyond which even the most agile of human minds cannot go in understanding and communicating that understanding. Here we 'see in a mirror, dimly' and it will only be when we pass beyond the gates of death that we 'will see face to face' and know the mysteries of God as profoundly as he knows us (1 Cor. 13:12). And Christianity is not only about thinking but also about worshipping and praying: *Lex orandi lex credendi* ('the law of prayer is the law of belief'). 'The personal union of divinity and humanity entailed by the incarnation exceeds our conceptuality, and cannot be clarified in plain descriptive language in such a way as to be positively intelligible.'[25]

Early Christian thinkers were themselves acutely aware of this. Basil of Caesarea told the faithful of his city that: 'One has to observe, therefore, how far the word falls short of the truth', but at the same time acknowledged to a correspondent that: 'words are the images of the soul'.[26] As Philip Rousseau has commented on Basil's view: 'language provided a reliable if transient, map of reality . . . To speak accurately, therefore, was to know profoundly'.[27] Words were thus signposts on the journey of faith. But they were not the only ones. As Frances Young has paraphrased the writings of the theologian Theodoret (*c.* 393–*c.* 460): 'I cry out with wonder at the Christian mystery, that our faith is beyond mental grasp, beyond words, beyond understanding. The only suitable response in the end is praise.'[28] Even the Chalcedonian Definition itself with all its careful and precise use of words can in the end only point towards the mystery; it cannot explain it. This was a mystery equally experienced by the Christian ascetic in his life of dedication and prayer, going out within himself on the vast ocean of divine silence to search for the God made man. It was also to be found in the liturgical life of the Church, in its art and architecture and ritual:

> For Christian language, like Christian art, was trying to express mysteries that were essentially inexpressible except through symbol . . . For if the goal of the human spirit was to be defined as a process of divination achievable only in contemplative union with God, if the human and divine worlds display the harmony of God through an all-embracing system of signs, the ultimate reality necessarily lay beyond words.[29]

Words could point towards God, but his reality was daily being experienced by Christians in their baptism and participation in the liturgy where Christ dwelt under the eucharistic signs of bread and wine.

The christological debate is also significant for the light it sheds on other aspects of Christian history, most notably the understanding of tradition and orthodoxy. If tradition in the Christian understanding of the word is not the defence of a static view of faith, but rather a living thing that looks as much to the future as to the past, then the arguments, tensions and resolutions inherent in the christological debate should shed further light on this concept. The use of the term *homoousios* in the Nicene statement of faith, or Cyril's leap beyond the confines of his inherited intellectual horizons, were necessary in order that christology could move forward. In the words of Rowan Williams: 'continuity was something that had to be re-imagined and recreated at each point of crisis'.[30] What sometimes appeared to be innovation was in reality renovation. The explanation of tradition could mean a re-formulation in unfamiliar language, as in the case of Cyril to 'recycle the traditional inheritance' in order to respond to the dynamic progress of the evolving controversy.[31] For Gregory of Nazianzus this demanded a radical break with his own deeply Platonic education and culture. The good and the perfect in Plato's vision was timeless, static and transcendent; for Gregory perfection came to be seen rather in constant progress. 'This notion of perpetual progress is grounded in Gregory's most fundamental theological perceptions: man's mutability, making possible constant change and progress, and God's incomprehensibility, ensuring that never can he be wholly grasped; true knowledge of God is the seeing which consists in not seeing.'[32] It was sometimes the very attempt to hold fast to tradition in the static sense that could lead thinkers into error; such, it could be argued, was the case with Arius, Theodore of Mopsuestia, and Nestorius.[33]

Language and terminology had to change to reflect and speak to changing times. But the problem was to find the innovation that both responded to present demands, but at the same time remained faithful to, and helped to clarify, the truth inherited from the past. Innovation and change in themselves could not be rejected, but, to return to the musical metaphor used in the Introduction, new variations had to remain consistent with the original theme. The formulas of the Chalcedonian Definition may seem a long way from the language of the New Testament, yet, as Grillmeier has remarked: 'The dogma of Chalcedon is ancient tradition in a formula corresponding to the needs of the hour', and a concept like *hypostasis* 'is determined precisely by the way it is used in Hebrews 1:13'.[34] This leads him to the conclusion that all the technical terms and complex formulas 'are intended to preserve the Christ of the gospels and the apostolic age for the faith of posterity'.[35] Or as the twentieth-century Catholic theologian Karl Rahner argued, Chalcedon was not so much an end as a beginning.[36] Perhaps, though, it was both; a consummation of all the long arguments that had gone before it, and a preparation for those that were to continue into the future.

For orthodoxy is itself a dynamic concept in Christianity. It will always be a 'work in progress' rather than a completion. The latter will only come with the *parousia*. That Spirit of truth that John wrote of in his Gospel will, so

Christians believe, continue to guide them into all truth until the end of time itself. And it will do it through fallible human beings and the diversity of words and works they create. That very diversity that we have noted as one of the hallmarks of early Christianity was clearly in evidence once again during the christological debate of the fourth and fifth centuries. It could be one of the greatest strengths of Christianity. As Peter Brown has noted: 'The early Church was so creative largely because its most vocal members so frequently disagreed with each other.'[37] Tensions could be fruitful; but they could also be destructive. Diversity could equally lead to division. For Christian history there is also a darker legacy to the Chalcedonian Definition. Not all Christians found it possible to accept it in the generations which followed, and those who became labelled as 'Nestorians' or 'Monophysites' gradually separated from other Christians who appropriated to themselves exclusive claims of orthodoxy and catholicity. Yet the tragedy was that in the mid-fifth century people like Cyril and Nestorius were actually far nearer to each other doctrinally than sometimes even they, and certainly later generations, imagined. Indeed, much of the research undertaken during the twentieth century on the christological disputes of the fourth and fifth centuries was done so with the ecumenical intention of rehabilitating and explaining with unbiased eyes many of those figures from the past subsequently labelled as heretics. However, the fact remains that from Armenia in the north to Ethiopia in the south there are still many millions of Christians in a variety of 'Non-Chalcedonian' churches still awaiting the means of reconciliation between themselves and their Orthodox, Catholic and Protestant brethren.

Suggested Further Reading

This is obviously a subject of enormous complexity in which too often, perhaps, the devil does lie in the detail. There is really no way to simplify the issues and their subtleties. However, among general modern treatments of christology two good starting points would be Gerald O'Collins, *Christology: A Biblical, Historical and Systematic Study of Jesus* (Oxford University Press, 1995) and Hans Schwarz, *Christology* (William B. Eerdman, 1998), Catholic and Protestant writers respectively, both of whose books contain sections on the controversies in early Church set within broader treatments. Also, many of the general works on the early Christian history mentioned in the Suggested Further Reading section at the end of the Introduction contain accounts of varying levels of detail; the most thorough is probably in the relevant chapters of Henry Chadwick, *The Church in Ancient Society: From Galilee to Gregory the Great* (Oxford University Press, 2001); but be warned; like much else in that book some readers will find it heavy going.

The most detailed account of early christology is to be found in Aloys Grillmeier, *Christ in Christian Tradition. Volume One: From the Apostolic Age to Chalcedon (451)* (Mowbray, revised edition, 1975). A monumental work of scholarship, making few concessions to readers (it assumes an understanding of Greek and Latin) and excellently translated from the German by John Bowden, at some points it does, however, betray the deeply Catholic faith of its Jesuit author, and has not been above criticism for still retaining too sharp a distinction between Alexandrian and Antiochene christologies. And even in its nearly 600 pages of text it cannot hope to cover all the complexities of the subject, as the author himself acknowledges.

Frances Young, *From Nicaea to Chalcedon: A Guide to the Literature and its Background* (SCM Press, 1983) is about more than just the christological debate, but is excellent in expanding the reader's understanding and appreciation of many early Christian authors. But, like Grillmeier, she does not always make life easy for readers unfamiliar with the classical languages. Rowan Williams, *Arius: Heresy and Tradition* (Darton, Longman and Todd, 1987) obviously focuses on Arius, but has much to say of significance that goes far beyond that one individual or his times. Closely argued, deeply philosophical and theological in content, it is an outstandingly insightful study that rewards careful and patient reading.

4

The African Pilgrim

We speak God's wisdom, secret and hidden, which God decreed before the ages for our glory. (1 Cor. 2:7)

One summer's evening in the year 386 a man sat in a garden in Milan. From Eden to Gethsemane, gardens had been the settings for some of the greatest of spiritual dramas. Now once again the scene was set for the climax and resolution of another, but this time intensely personal, conflict. Having asked his friends to leave him in solitude, this man, in his early thirties, his body wracked with emotions and tears pouring from his eyes, seemed to be on the verge of what we would now call a nervous breakdown. What had brought him to this place in such a condition? And why was this small personal drama to be of such significance not only for early Christianity but also for the future history of the Latin West?

The Restless Heart

Thagaste was a small provincial town in Roman north Africa, now called Souk Ahras and in modern Algeria. About 200 miles from the Mediterranean, it was on the southern fringes of the fertile belt whose produce helped to feed the great city of Rome. Here in the mid-fourth century a minor pagan landowner, Patricius, married a Christian wife, Monica, and subsequently produced three children, two boys and a girl. One of these sons, Aurelius Augustinus, born in 354, was clearly a boy of some intellectual promise. Educated in Thagaste itself, and subsequently in the somewhat more prominent nearby town of Madauros, at the age of fifteen this academic progress was temporarily halted for about a year while his father sought for the funds to continue it in the far more prestigious, but expensive, Carthage. During these months of relative idleness the boy had his first serious encounter with a garden. As part of a gang of youths he stole pears from the orchard of one of his father's neighbours. This adolescent exploit was later to cause the mature man much spiritual questioning; he saw it as a parable of original sin, his theft of the inedible pears a minor repetition of the stolen fruit of paradise. But eventually the greatest landowner in Thagaste, Romanianus, supplemented his father's meagre means, and in 370 at the age of sixteen he at last set out for Carthage, the great port and regional capital of north Africa, the only city in the West that could even begin to rival the magnificence of Rome or Alexandria.

Here over the next few years he was to make his first lifelong friendships, engage in his first sexual exploits culminating in the taking of a concubine and the birth of a son, Adeodatus, to discover Cicero, and lose one religious faith and find another. Technically a catechumen, he had almost been baptized when his life seemed to be in danger from a childhood disease, and he had continued to attend the first part of the Christian Eucharist. His reading of Cicero's *Hortensius*, however, both turned his mind to a more serious pursuit of philosophy and reawakened his religious instincts. But, as he returned to reading the Christian scriptures, his profound disappointment with their poor style in comparison to the great classical authors, especially in the abysmal Latin translations then available to him, led to disillusionment with the faith of his mother. In 373 at the age of nineteen he experienced his first religious conversion: to Manichaeism. He was to remain a Hearer for nine years. The claims of the Manichees that their beliefs were founded on reason, their repudiation of the Jewish scriptures, and their dualistic explanation of the problem of evil, seemed to present better answers than Christianity to many of his pressing problems.

By 376 he had completed his formal education and was now himself a teacher in Carthage. His continuing religious questionings, however, were leading to his first doubts about Manichaeism and its ability to answer not only his questions but also those of his closest friends Alypius and Nebridius. This fresh disillusionment was compounded when the famous Manichaean Bishop, Faustus, visited the city and was quite unable to satisfy these young intellectuals when confronted by their probing examination. Carthage in any case was proving to be too restricted a stage for the fulfilment of their ambitions, and so in 382 they set sail for Rome and wider horizons. Here in Italy he would find the patrons he needed among the wealthiest aristocrats of the Empire. One of these, the prominent pagan senator, Symmachus, arranged for him to be appointed as professor of rhetoric in the city of Milan, now effectively the main centre of government in the western half of the Empire. He moved there in the autumn of 384, eventually to be joined by Alypius, Nebridius, his concubine and son, and his mother, Monica.

Milan was not only the residence of the Emperor, however; it was also the episcopal city of Ambrose. Never before had the African encountered a Christian like him. From a wealthy aristocratic family, he had been elected Bishop against his wishes in 373 while still an unbaptized provincial governor. Our young African went to the basilica to hear him preach, initially more out of secular interest, to experience a master of oratory, rather than for the religious content of the sermons. But what he heard had a profound effect on him. Here was a man of lofty social status, with an intellect and education to match his own, who for the first time presented to him a spiritual interpretation of the Jewish scriptures which not only satisfied him on an intellectual level but also offered an effective refutation of their dismissal by the Manichaeans. Ambrose was also a thinker and orator who began to show him how the philosophy of the Platonists could be used in defence of his mother's faith. Under Ambrose's influence he returned again to a study of the great followers of Plato, men like Plotinus and Porphyry. In comparison to their sophisticated religious thought the Manichaeans again appeared crude and inferior; God and evil began to seem far more sophisticated concepts than he had previously conceived. Once again he felt his imagination swept up into something far greater, just as he had done all those years before when he had first read Cicero's *Hortensius*.

Now, at the beginning of 386, he was on the one hand withdrawing more and more into himself in an intense and emotional course of study; on the other hand the world and ambition were calling. He put aside his lover of sixteen years and became formally engaged to a girl of only twelve. Respectable marriage was essential if he was to find promotion in imperial service. However, sexual renunciation was not yet for him, and he quickly took another, if temporary, partner.

But this absorption in philosophy was not his only intellectual pursuit. A prominent Christian priest, Simplicianus, eventually to succeed Ambrose as Bishop of Milan, introduced him afresh to the Christian scriptures, which he now read in the light of Platonist philosophy; and indeed in the person of Jesus the *Logos* made man, the ultimate goal and fulfilment of philosophy. Just like Justin Martyr more than two centuries earlier, he was now being led ineluctably towards an acknowledgement of Christ as the final end in which Hellenistic as well as Jewish thought ultimately culminated. Simplicianus also told him of others who had taken this route before him, especially the great intellectual Marius Victorinus, the translator of Plotinus and the leading light of the Platonism of his day. In old age he too had read the scriptures and had become convinced of the truth of Christianity, had humbly gone through the preparation of a catechumen and had been baptized.

His friend, Alypius, was also coming to a similar conclusion, if by a somewhat different route. One day a fellow African had introduced him to

Athanasius's *Life of Antony*, and told him that such a monastic community actually existed just outside Milan, and further reported to him that others who had abandoned the prospect of bright worldly careers had joined another community in Trier. The friends were shaken by the concept of these men, learned and unlettered alike, taking heaven by storm. His intellect now convinced, still our African resisted. By the summer of 386 the two parts of him, his intellect and his will, were at war with each other. Like rising waters slowly building behind a great dam, everything told him that a final abandonment of his will to Christ was the only answer. That dam must break, but still it held, though under intense and increasing pressure. The psychological strain of this inner conflict led to even his physical health deteriorating, and he began to experience repeated difficulty with his breathing. Would he ever find release from this growing torment?

And so we come to the garden in Milan. Here, sitting under a fig tree that again echoed not only the distant tree of Eden, but also the pear orchard of his youth as well, he sat in an agony of mind and body, nearing the point of complete breakdown, and seriously contemplating suicide as the only possible release. And then, suddenly, as if floating on the air itself, he heard a voice singing, the sweet, innocent voice of a child, associated by everyone in the ancient world with the pronouncements of oracles. He heard this angelic voice gently chanting: 'Pick up and read, pick up and read.' The random opening of a book, perhaps Virgil for a Latin pagan, the Bible for a Christian, and reading the first sentence that the eye fell on was a common practice in antiquity for finding miraculous words that would answer or resolve a problem. Perhaps this was what he was now meant to do. He recalled how Antony himself had resolved upon the ascetic life after hearing the words of Christ in the Gospel, seemingly addressed precisely to himself.

Quickly he rose, brushed away his tears, and walked over to where Alypius was sitting. Here he had left a copy of the letters of Paul. He opened the book, and looked. Immediately his eye fell on two verses from the letter to the Romans: 'let us live honourably as in the day, not in revelling and drunkenness, not in debauchery and licentiousness, not in quarrelling and jealousy. Instead, put on the Lord Jesus Christ, and make no provision for the flesh, to gratify its desires' (Rom. 13:13–14).

At the reading of those words the dam finally burst and the waters flowed into his soul and all doubts were washed away, and he had his first glimpse of the great truth of the Christian God, that our hearts are restless till they rest in him. Then Alypius followed his example and he too picked up the book and read the next verse: 'Welcome those who are weak in faith' (Rom. 14:1) and saw these words as directed to himself. In those few minutes their world had changed for ever. Alypius and the man we know as St Augustine had completed the first stage of their Christian pilgrimage. Now they could turn to the next.

That began with baptism. In the dark early hours of Easter Sunday, 387, the two friends and Adeodatus removed their clothes and walked down into the baptismal pool attached to the great basilica in Milan to hear Ambrose invoke the Holy Trinity over them. As they moved from death with Christ into his new life, they were anointed with oil and clothed in the symbolic purity of white garments. Then they were led with the other newly baptized Christians into the basilica itself to experience the eucharistic feast for the first time. Augustine would never forget the experience of being greeted by a shimmering sea of lighted candles held in the hands of the assembled faithful, as he too moved from darkness to light, nor the inexpressible beauty of the chanted hymns, a musical practice copied from the Greek East and introduced to Milan by Ambrose himself. By now all thoughts of respectable marriage or brilliant public career had been abandoned, and by September, 388, Augustine and his circle of friends were back in Africa, initially settling in Thagaste to begin the first experiment in monastic living on African soil.

His mother had already died before he had left Italy. By 391 his son, Adeodatus, had followed her, as had his friend, Nebridius. Emotional bonds tying him to his past were snapping, which made the new ascetic life of his little community all the more appealing. But by now the site of this experiment had shifted to the port of Hippo Regius. Here a preliminary foray to discuss the possibility of founding a community there took a surprising turn when the assembly at the Sunday Eucharist pushed Augustine forward and demanded his immediate ordination. Like Ambrose and others before him, the Christians of Hippo knew a prestigious catch when they saw one! This was now the price he had to pay for a small house and another garden in which to re-found his community. By 395 he had been elected the unwilling assistant to the elderly bishop, and within a year had succeeded him upon the latter's death. Here Augustine was to remain as Bishop of Hippo for the rest of his life.

We know so much about his life because he now composed what was to become his most read work, the *Confessions*. This told the story of his early life culminating in his conversion to Christianity. At the heart of this book was the idea that his own experiences were a paradigm of what was possible for the whole human race (*Confessions* II, iii, 5), and that people find God only by truly finding themselves first. Or as Augustine was to express it in one of his sermons: 'Our whole business in this life is to heal the heart's eye by which God is seen' (Document 10).[1]

Yet the *Confessions* is not a straightforward autobiography. It is unique in the literature of antiquity, both as a masterpiece of artistry and style that helped confound any lingering pagan doubts about the ability of Christianity to nurture great literature, and at the same time as a totally new and original conception. It was in part a description of that renewal and reformation in the new creation of Christ which Paul had first introduced and which Augustine encapsulated vividly in one of his letters: 'Our Maker is our Re-maker'.[2] But the *Confessions* also had some classical influences as well, most notably in the philosophical soliloquies such as that of the Emperor Marcus Aurelius, or in the epic poem the *Aeneiad* of Virgil telling the story of the journey of Aeneas from the ruins of Troy to the foundation of Rome. Augustine's journey, however, was a spiritual one, and his agonizing over his separation from God was at a great emotional distance from philosophers who thought that reason alone could bring them near to the divine.[3] Augustine was rather the prodigal son returning to a loving father, and his book owed as much to the *Lives* of the Christian ascetics as it did to pagan authors for its literary precedents. It is also a vast, extended prayer in which the reader, as it were, overhears a Christian soul in dialogue with his maker. In that sense it is more a work of theology than autobiography. Indeed, it can be read on so many levels that these multiple readings can give it a very modern feel. Its themes of memory, redeemed human nature and the grace of God working on individuals have found echoes in a wide variety of later works, from spiritual autobiographies like those of Teresa of Avila in the sixteenth century or John Henry Newman in the nineteenth, to novels such as that by Marcel Proust or *Brideshead Revisited* by Evelyn Waugh. Not surprisingly it has recently been described as 'one of the most influential books of western European culture'.[4]

Controversies

In his own time, however, Augustine's reputation was largely built on his lengthy career as an apologist for orthodox and catholic Christianity, forged in a series of disputes with opponents both outside and within the Christian fold. One of the first of these was the contest with the proponents of the faith of his first conversion, the Manichees. It was their explanation for the existence of evil, their claims to be a religion of reason, and their rejection of the Jewish scriptures which had initially attracted Augustine. What he gradually came to see was that their analysis not only of divinity but also of humanity was defective: far too simplistic and unable to offer explanations for the complexities and conflicts he felt within himself. 'The Manichees had avoided the tensions of growth on all levels . . . With all their talk of "setting free", the Manichees had no room, in their religious language, for the more subtle processes of growth – for "healing", for "renewal".'[5] It was a static faith in stark contrast to the potential dynamism of Christianity, one that left Augustine feeling trapped: 'I had already lost hope of being able to advance higher in that false doctrine' he wrote later of the Manichees in the *Confessions*, his own potential for spiritual progress thwarted (*Confessions* V, x, 18). As he was to discover, their boast of reason dissolved into a series of complex myths, and their criticisms of the Jewish scriptures were easily answered by Ambrose with the help of Platonism and the application of typology.

At the heart of the problem, however, lay their account of creation and their explanation for evil. Their dualism, the idea that created matter was inherently evil because the product of darkness, effectively absolved the God of goodness and light of responsibility. But, as Augustine discovered, this did not really accord with reality as he had found it; creation contained much within it which was manifestly good. Again it was the Platonists who began to lead Augustine towards a solution. For them, evil was effectively non-being. From this he went on to argue that Christianity's analysis was easily superior to the Manichaean one. In its origin all creation was good because made by the one supreme God of goodness. Evil had arisen not as a force in its own right, but as a corruption of what was originally good, and the ultimate cause of evil was sin, and the responsibility for sin rested with human beings, not with God. Evil thus had no existence of its own; it is literally nothing.

Yet of their own free will human beings have chosen this path of corruption, and the only way back is to recognize that we are utterly dependent on the grace of God, even for that primary initiative of believing in him at all. Here Paul took over from the Platonists. What the grace of Christ offered Augustine was precisely that growth, that dynamic re-creation of his nature that he found so frustratingly lacking in the Manichees. And in a series of public disputations and in his many writings, Augustine presented them with a stream of counter arguments based on a much more sophisticated analysis of both God and humanity.[6]

A far more potent foe within his north African church was represented by the Donatists, however. By Augustine's day they had become entrenched, and in some areas were probably in a majority. One of the reasons for his election as priest and then Bishop of Hippo was that the non-Donatist assembly in the city felt intimidated by a dominant Donatist presence, and they looked to Augustine to use his intellectual skills to combat this. Both churches laid claim to the title 'catholic', and so the debates in which Augustine was to be heavily engaged have become fundamental for the history of the struggle to achieve the defining characteristics of that concept.

The Donatists presented one potential model of catholicity. In this they claimed to be the legitimate heirs of Tertullian and Cyprian, and thus appeared to have the advantage of appealing to local traditions and feelings. Their notion of catholicity was defined in terms of purity and exclusivity. They made no distinction between the present, historical Church, and the future eschatological one that would follow the *parousia*. Among other things, this view depended crucially on how certain passages of the New Testament were to be interpreted. 'His winnowing-fork is in his hand, and he will clear his threshing-floor and will gather his wheat into the granary; but the chaff he will burn with unquenchable fire' John the Baptist was reported as foretelling of the Messiah (Matt. 3:12). The problem was to decide when this 'gathering' was to happen. For the Donatists it was a present reality; they had already been formed into a 'gathered' Church. This idea originated in their rejection of those bishops and other clergy who had compromised with the imperial authorities during the Diocletian persecution, and was extended to those 'contaminated' by succeeding them or collaborating with them, including those outside Africa. Thus their concept of catholicity extended to the sacraments celebrated by these two groups; sacraments too had to be 'pure' and uncontaminated by the sin of apostasy. A fullness of purity in clergy, people and sacraments was thus the defining mark of catholicity for the Donatists.

Augustine saw in such arguments that same essential flaw that he had previously isolated in the Manichaeans. Donatism also left no room for growth, either individually or collectively. Its ideas led once again to a static view of the faith, deriving from its essentially defensive posture. Donatism 'was immobilized by anxiety to preserve its identity'.[7] What was the Church? Was it a refuge, an alternative to the larger and impure society around it, or a vital part of that society seeking to transform and redeem it from the inside? Augustine took the latter view, and saw the Church as the vehicle through which humanity could strive to recover its lost sense of unity consequent upon the Fall. As such, the Church was inevitably going to be a mixture of saints and sinners; the wheat and the chaff had yet to be separated. In any case, as Augustine was frequently to observe, not all Donatists were that holy or morally pure anyway.

The Church on earth was never going to be a monolithic structure, but was rather in constant dynamic tension with itself and the world. For Augustine the imperative of catholicity that flowed from this was growth and expansion, both within the individual and in the wider community. People strove for moral purity aided by the grace of Christ, and the Church ever sought new members for itself. The Donatist church was locked into the past and the present; Augustine's Church was one forever looking to the future. The logic of the Donatist argument was that catholicity would also be limited in space as well as time, confined to its African homeland. Augustine argued that that confounded the very command of Jesus to his followers to 'make disciples of all nations' (Matt. 28:19); catholicity by its very nature was universal in the sense of being international and not the unique preserve of one people or region of the world. In his own words: 'The untroubled globe of the world judges those men not to be good, who separate themselves from the whole world, in a particular part of the world.'[8]

And thus it also followed that if the Church was morally mixed, the validity and efficacy of its sacraments could not rest on the subjective purity of those administering them. Sacraments depended not upon the holiness of human beings, but upon that of their originator, Jesus himself, the only person without sin, who sanctifies the sacraments through his ministers. Thus the validity of the sacraments of baptism and Eucharist, and the ordination of those celebrating them, rested instead upon the objective holiness of Christ. Once given, they could never be removed; baptism or ordination remained valid whatever the precise 'purity' of the priest or bishop administering them.

It was one thing, however, to challenge the Donatists on the intellectual level, quite another to combat them on the ground. By the late fourth century they had long been a powerful and established alternative to the official, imperially approved Church in north Africa. Augustine preached sermons against them not only in Hippo but also in Carthage and other cities, he issued a stream of writings, and engaged in public debate with their bishops, culminating in a great conference held in Carthage in 411, attended by 284 Donatist bishops and 286 of their opponents. The problem, however, was not so much winning arguments as inducing Donatists to return to the fold. As they were technically schismatics it was impossible to apply the imperial laws against heresy to them until an Edict of 405 equated schism with heresy. The crucial questions, however, were how far the imperial authorities should become involved in any process of persuasion or coercion, and what form or degree of coercion should be adopted. For many years Augustine was deeply reluctant to use even the mildest of physical force against the Donatists. However, in the years after 405 he became convinced that mild coercion was not only morally permissible, but also appeared to work empirically in the sense of persuading Donatists to abandon their church for his. Theologically he justified this on the grounds that humanity's fallen state required restraint, and that biblical passages such as the one about compelling people to come in also seemed to condone some level of physical inducement such as fines or other economic sanctions (Luke 14:23). What he would never agree to, however, was the use of either torture or capital punishment. But his attitude, however mild in the context of his age, has not endeared him to later generations, and he has sometimes been seen as the 'father' of the medieval Inquisition, and selective quotations from his works were used as a justification for the torture and execution of religious opponents during the Reformation. What is now clear is that such accusations, or out-of-context employment of his ideas, are clearly anachronistic, and would undoubtedly have horrified him.[9]

His combat with the Donatists secured Augustine's reputation as a theologian and controversialist within north Africa; what was to expand that into international recognition was the controversy that was to occupy much of the last years of his life, that with the Pelagians. But here his legacy is even more mixed than that resulting from the Donatist conflict. The issues at stake again raised fundamental questions about orthodoxy and catholicity, but this time centred on the moral condition of humanity, the degree to which our wills have been affected by original sin, and the consequent need for divine grace. Any reading of the *Confessions* makes it clear that Augustine viewed grace as the essential element in the healing process needed to begin to restore humanity to a right relationship with God. What did Augustine mean by this grace? As he conceived it, grace was 'a supernatural aid personally granted to the Christian through the essential and exclusive mediation of Christ'.[10] This was a totally free and unmerited gift; as Augustine himself wrote: 'The grace of God would in no way be grace if it were not in every way purely a gift.'[11]

The British theologian, Pelagius, had severe doubts about this line of argument. For him, human nature was nowhere near so corrupted and unable to fend for itself as he assumed Augustine to be implying. Genesis had described a human nature originally good in its essence; but clearly humanity's moral imperfections and failures could not be denied. Pelagius effectively argued that each human being was born into the same primal innocence as Adam, but that over time each individual was constricted by the weight of past habits and the corruption of society. Baptism restored the freedom of moral action and removed the necessity to follow the example of Adam. Thus grace was a useful *aid* in an individual's moral progress, not the essential originator of it and accompaniment to it.[12] Augustine on the other hand argued that Adam's sin was far more fundamental for the human condition. Where Pelagius saw Adam as providing his descendants with a bad example to follow, Augustine conceived of original sin as an inherited disease passed down the generations; in the graphic words of John Henry Newman in the nineteenth century, 'the human race is implicated in some terrible aboriginal calamity' from which no human beings can free themselves.[13] For Augustine, the implication of the Pelagian argument was that we can attain moral perfection largely through our own efforts: 'If God has made you man, and if you make yourself righteous, you are doing better than God has done!' retorted Augustine in one of his sermons.[14]

In Augustine's view, the initiative always lay with God, a God who 'makes us righteous not through our own righteousness, but through his, so that our true righteousness is that which comes to us from him'.[15] True freedom was not the state taken for granted so lightly by Pelagius, but only the final end of a long process; baptism put you on the road to convalescence, it did not cure you. 'Men choose because they love; but Augustine had been certain for some twenty years, that they could not, of themselves, choose to love. The vital capacity to unite feeling and knowledge comes from an area outside man's powers of self-determination.' Or in Augustine's own words: 'From a depth that we do not see, comes everything that you can see.'[16] This thing that we cannot see, but can experience, is grace which can 'lift our being up to the Being of God, because it can lift our love'.[17]

So far, so good. But further problems arise when considering Augustine's doctrine of grace. To what extent is humanity free to resist the gracious initiatives of God? If individuals are not able to choose to reject God's advances, then what is left of human free will? To this Augustine then posed a counter question: what is free will for? Is the possession of free will the same as being free? By choosing evil, humanity has effectively rejected God's gift of free will and it can itself only be recovered through the gracious action of God, for 'if the Son makes you free, you will be free indeed' (John 8:36). For Augustine, the ultimate liberty of the saints is to lose the freedom to sin. But in so arguing he remained clear that grace did not override human free will; humanity remained free to accept or refuse God's grace, but ultimately cannot defeat God's ends by so choosing.[18]

This leads on to the further question: what are God's ends? What is the purpose and ultimate end of creation, above all of the creation of humanity? What does God will for humanity? Here we reach one of the most fiercely contested of Augustine's ideas, that of predestination. Briefly, this asserts that God has selected, or elected, only certain individuals for ultimate salvation, endowing them with the gift of saving grace. As Peter Brown has commented, this was a concept well suited to its time and place. Its emergence could clearly be interpreted in the light of the exclusive nature of north African Christianity going back at least to Tertullian, and ironically seemed to echo the basic impulse of the Donatists in this respect. And it also clearly spoke to the context of the early fifth century, a time of barbarian invasion and imperial disintegration in the West, where people would look for a sense of refuge, security and survival in a rapidly changing world. In this interpretation Brown presents perhaps one of the most favourable modern treatments of the origins of Augustine's concept of this doctrine.[19]

Other commentators are much more critical. Serge Lancel, for instance, sees the doctrine emerging as an extreme reaction on the part of Augustine to the ideas of the prominent Pelagian, Julian of Eclanum. And with it, he argues, Augustine placed himself 'on the frontiers of heresy'.[20] Gerald Bonner sees a paradox between Augustine's concepts of divine love and divine predestination, one that he frankly admits he is unable to reconcile. As he remarks, few modern theologians would maintain Augustine's concept of predestination in its full rigour.[21] Bonner and John Burnaby are also in agreement in arguing that Augustine was too much influenced by another historical context, that of ancient notions of justice, punishment and retribution as practised by the secular legal authorities.[22] And several commentators have noted that there remained a fundamental scriptural stumbling-block to Augustine's concept of predestination.

In the first letter to Timothy, God is described as a saviour 'who desires everyone to be saved and to come to the knowledge of the truth' (1 Tim. 2:4). This idea of a divine desire for *universal* salvation seemed to contradict Augustine's more pessimistic view of an elect only receiving the gift of saving grace, and even in his own day he was heavily criticized in these terms by John Cassian and other monastic writers from Gaul. Some modern authorities remain as convinced as Cassian that Augustine never succeeded in defending his views adequately in the light of this biblical passage.[23] But at the same time Gerald Bonner makes it clear that there is a distinction between this Augustinian doctrine and that of the Church; predestination, as understood by Augustine, never became the official teaching of the Latin Church of his day, nor of the Middle Ages, but remained no more than the opinion of a distinguished theologian.[24]

A further distinction has to be drawn, however, between Augustine's concept of predestination and that of the sixteenth-century Protestant theologian, John Calvin. Technically, Calvin is supralapsarian in asserting that God's decree of election, and by implication damnation, was made *before* Adam's fall, while Augustine is infralapsarian, in that the decree is a *consequence* of the Fall which God foresaw but did not compel. In addition, Calvin was to stress the total and complete corruption of human nature as a result of the Fall, while Augustine had defended the more limited extent of the disaster, humanity in his view retaining something of the divine likeness in which it had originally been created. For Calvin, goodness had died in humanity with Adam; for Augustine, it was wounded but capable of convalescence.[25] Although at first sight these distinctions may appear somewhat trivial, the significance and implications are in fact far reaching and clearly set a gulf between the two theologians.

Two Loves

For centuries, educated Romans had quoted the famous lines from Virgil's epic poem the *Aeneid* reflecting the belief in the eternal destiny of their great city and Empire:

> To them no bounds of empire I assign,
> Nor term of years to their immortal line.[26]

As we have already seen, in 248 the Empire had celebrated the millennium of Rome's foundation, again seeming to reinforce this everlasting destiny. Even when, in the fourth century, that Empire had shifted its religious allegiance to Christianity, Eusebius had, in a sense, done no more than reinterpret the old idea. He saw that destiny itself now subsumed into the larger picture of an earthly Empire reflecting the eternal kingdom of God himself. Perhaps the high-watermark of this concept of the eternal Christian Empire came in the reign of Theodosius I from 379 to 395. During these years paganism was finally and definitively outlawed, temples were destroyed or secularized into cultural monuments, the pagan revolt in reaction to these measures quashed, and orthodox Christianity proclaimed as the only official religion of the Empire. To many, even to Augustine himself, it seemed that the future of their Christian world looked bright.

But Theodosius had come to power in the wake of a disaster, the humiliating defeat of a great Roman army at Adrianople, not at the hands of the military forces of another great Empire, but by the barbarian Goths. Their subsequent pacification by Theodosius seemed to have reversed this catastrophe. But barbarian pressure on the Empire's frontiers had been building for generations, and Adrianople can now be seen rather as the harbinger of further disasters to come. More and more barbarian groups were being settled inside the Empire, partly to offer protection to them from other barbarian peoples pressing them from the east, and partly to supplement a declining population in the Empire itself and so provide the legions with desperately needed troops. As the ethnic composition of the imperial army gradually shifted in favour of the barbarians, so more of their leaders attained high rank in that army. By the early fifth century the writing was on the wall for those with eyes to read it. Many of the western provinces of the Empire were now effectively at the mercy of barbarian tribes whether external or internal, and the situation was rapidly deteriorating from year to year.

Then, finally, the unthinkable happened. In 410 the barbarian king, Alaric, at the head of a coalition of tribes supposedly in the service of the Empire, besieged and then broke into the eternal city of Rome itself, sacking and ravaging it and its inhabitants. Following that, his army moved south down the Italian peninsula driving further floods of refugees before it. The first ones to cross the sea and arrive in the relative safety of north Africa brought news that could scarcely be comprehended. It is almost impossible for us now to appreciate fully the sense of psychological trauma induced by these events. There is nothing in our more recent historical experience comparable to it; the fall of Singapore to the Japanese in 1942 undoubtedly damaged the presumption of British invincibility in the Far East, and the collapse of the Berlin Wall in 1989 heralded the end of Soviet domination in Eastern Europe. But these events are but pale and distant echoes of the catastrophe of 410. Rome was the symbolic heart of an Empire and culture that had lasted not for decades or generations but which had endured for a millennium. The fact that it was no longer the political capital of the Empire was not the issue; it was the living, vital heart of a whole world that, until 410, had seemed eternal and inviolable. Something sacred to all Romans, pagan or Christian, had now been violated, and that by those very barbarians who Rome had successfully kept at bay for centuries.

Why had this happened? For many of the remaining pagans, the answer seemed clear. So long as the gods of Rome had protected their city, she had been secure. Their abandonment in favour of the alien religion of Christianity had directly led to this, the greatest of all disasters imaginable. Only with a return to the worship of the gods could it be repaired.

Augustine shared with his fellow Romans that initial sense of shock when the news first reached him in Hippo. That other great Christian intellectual, Jerome (*c.* 345–420), had written of his own reaction: 'If Rome can perish, what can be safe?'[27] A few weeks after the sack, Augustine told his shaken congregation: 'The world is dying, the world is growing old, the world is overcome with weakness, it has the gasping breath of old age'.[28] But his analysis of the reasons for this calamity differed from the pagan one, and he believed there was an answer to Jerome's question. Rome's sack was a punishment for the sins of humanity; and in another sermon preached in its wake he compared humans to olives pressed to make oil, but with the spirit of humanity now turned to pure oil in this pressing. Even in the midst of disaster, he found reason for hope. 'Do not lose heart brethren, there will be an end to every earthly kingdom.'[29]

In these revolutionary words lay the kernel of a great idea that had been brewing inside him for some years. The sack of Rome merely confirmed that growing disillusionment he had been increasingly feeling for the Theodosian concept of Christian Empire. In 412 he sat down to write what was to grow over the following fourteen years into 22 books that we collectively know as *The City of God.* Here Augustine not only answered the pagan critics of Christianity, but more significantly also presented a vast panorama, a vision of an alternative to the Eusebian concept of the relationship of the heavenly and earthly realms. For the Christian, argued Augustine, ultimate citizenship did not reside in any earthly state, even Rome itself; the destiny of humanity lay far beyond this, in the truly eternal citizenship of the kingdom of heaven. Our lives on earth are but a temporary existence in which we are never really at home, but aliens passing through, pilgrims in a foreign land. The only eternal city is the city of God himself.

On one level there is, however, little that seems particularly original in

Augustine's thesis. The very title *The City of God* was itself taken from a theme that appears in a number of the Psalms (Ps. 46, 48 and 87), and is repeated again in the New Testament, especially in the book of Revelation (e.g. Rev. 3:12, 21:2, 21:10), and at a number of other points (e.g. Heb. 12:22; Gal. 4:24–6; Phil. 3:20). This concept of Christians as aliens with respect to earthly states was one also found in a number of early Christian writers; Tertullian, for instance, describing a Christian as 'an alien in this world and a citizen of the city on high – Jerusalem', a concept also repeated by Origen, Clement of Alexandria, Hilary of Poitiers (*c.* 315–68), Jerome and Ambrose.[30] In addition, while we have seen that there was a Christian tradition of interpreting the Empire in a positive light even before the conversion of Constantine, always alongside that was also a continuing counter tradition of seeing it in a very different light. This began again in Revelation with the presumed identification of a persecuting Rome with the beast of chapter 13, or the harlot of chapter 17. This view also had its later proponents, such as Hippolytus, who interpreted the Empire as a satanic imitation of the universal and eternal kingdom of Christ.[31] Indeed, Augustine's very use of the terminology of the two cities probably came from a renegade Donatist, Tyconius, a strange individual who broke with his former Donatist allies but never joined their opponents.[32]

However, *The City of God* is far more than just a re-presentation of old ideas. Its breadth, detail and sense of vision, all informed by the urgent necessity of responding to the events of 410 and the escalating collapse of an entire world, lift *The City of God* onto an altogether more elevated plane. Never before had a Christian writer scrutinized the historical records of both Judaism and Rome in such critical detail, and used them to construct and justify a vast thematic interpretation of the human spiritual and moral condition. *The City of God* goes beyond any supposed philosophies of history or politics to explore the fundamental human conditions upon which such philosophies themselves ultimately founder in their failure to recognize humanity's ultimate destiny. For at the heart of his concept, and lying behind the terminology of the two cities itself, Augustine identified two contrasting dispositions in humanity, which he characterized as two loves; 'self-love reaching the point of contempt of God . . . the love of God carried as far as contempt of self' (*The City of God*, XIV, 28). For him, the whole of history, sacred or secular, and the construction of all political systems, took their starting points from, and were the ineluctable developments of, these two primary loves (Document 11).

Augustine identifies the origins of this fractured humanity as commencing at the very inception of both Jewish and Roman history. For him, it is no accident that both begin with acts of fratricide. In chapter 4 of Genesis, Cain is described as murdering his brother, Abel, and then, significantly for Augustine, as founding the first earthly city (*The City of God*, XV, 1). Later, he sees this initial crime reflected in the murder of Remus by Romulus, and the subsequent foundation of the city of Rome by the latter (*The City of God*, XV, 5). For him this new city of Rome was but a further manifestation of the great city of Babylon and the Empire of Assyria (*The City of God*, XVI, 17; XVIII, 22). Thus at a stroke Augustine challenges the widely held beliefs in the eternal and unique destiny of Rome and its Empire. History is dynamic and God is its author. Rome, like all other empires or states, has had its failures, military defeats and catastrophes; the sack of 410 was thus placed within a broader historical context, and Christians clearly absolved from the blame for its misfortunes.[33]

Augustine's answer to Jerome's question about where safety and peace are to be found was simple. Anyone looking for these in the ever-changing and impermanent fortunes of earthly states he calls a fool, for:

> such is the instability of human affairs that no people has ever been allowed such a degree of tranquillity as to remove all dread of hostile attacks on their life in this world. That place, then, which is promised as a dwelling of such peace and security is eternal, and reserved for eternal beings, in 'the mother, the Jerusalem which is free' (Gal. 4:26) . . . It is in the longing for this reward that we must lead devout lives, guided by faith, during this troublesome pilgrimage. (*The City of God*, XVII, 13)

And here Augustine enfolds one of the central themes of the *Confessions*, the idea that the human heart will be for ever restless in this life on earth, into that of the *The City of God*, where the only rest is conceived as eternal, in the true city of God, the heavenly Jerusalem. On earth those true lovers of this eternal destiny will remain as aliens and pilgrims in a foreign land.

From his protracted conflict with the Donatists emerged other ideas that are also further developed in the *The City of God*. One of those was that the citizens of the earthly and heavenly cities are not clearly differentiated until the end of time and the final judgement. Augustine never identified the heavenly city with any earthly institution, not even the Church. 'In this situation, many reprobates are mingled in the Church with the good, and both sorts are collected as it were in the dragnet of the gospel; and in this world, as in a sea, both kinds swim without separation, enclosed in nets until the shore is reached' (*The City of God*, XVIII, 49). It is in this inevitable mixing that Augustine sees the origins of states and empires, in their reversal of the heavenly principles of love, unity and mutual tolerance: 'hence human society is generally divided against itself, and one part of it oppresses another, when it finds itself the stronger . . . The result has been . . . that some nations have been entrusted with empire, while others have been subdued to alien domination' (*The City of God*, XVIII, 2). The one exception to this pattern of mixture, domination and subjection was the monastic life, where individuals could choose freely to associate with one another in a new type of community which sought to reverse these, and establish a rule based on love. But Augustine was also clear that while monastic communities might to some degree prefigure the heavenly city more than any other human institutions, they certainly did not constitute a viable model to be imitated, but rather their very existence discomforted conventional society by presenting a fundamental challenge to it.[34]

But this did not mean that the citizens of the heavenly Jerusalem should stand aloof from the affairs of this world. However, it was equally clear that Augustine conceived the role of the secular state in much more limited terms than was usual in ancient society. Basically he saw the role of the state as one of minimizing social disorder through its laws and their agencies. Yet these in their turn had to be just, for if justice is removed from the state 'what are kingdoms but gangs of criminals on a large scale?' (*The City of God*, IV, 4). The Christianity that Augustine envisaged was a fundamentally questioning, not to say revolutionary, force in that it rejected all forms of utopia based upon worldly hopes, and was quite clear that 'the quest for perfection and happiness through politics is doomed'.[35]

In this latter point *The City of God* represented a fundamental and final abandonment of a concept that went back at least to the writings of Plato, that the *polis*, the earthly city, was the place where humanity would find its happiness and fulfilment, an idea that had expanded from encompassing a single city to the whole Roman world. The concept of the Empire as a divinely instituted and blessed institution, whether by pagan divinities or the Christian God through his imperial vice-regent on earth, the Emperor, was replaced by the more limited and modern-sounding concept of states as purely human institutions which were, in religious terms, neutral. To the question of whether or not the Empire could be re-formed into the image of God and heaven on earth, Augustine's answer was clear; that reformation happened in the human heart, where the only true recreation into the image of God could happen.

This disengagement of the secular state from divinity in any form was to be one of Augustine's greatest legacies for the future of the West. It gave Latin Christianity an essential counterweight to the Eusebian conception of the divinely ordained Empire. However close the Latin Church came to identifying itself with the barbarian or feudal kingdoms that eventually succeeded the Roman Empire in the West, there always remained the warnings implicit in *The City of God*. In the 1140s, for instance, one Otto of Freising took up many of Augustine's themes and even entitled his universal history *The Two Cities*.[36]

As Augustine lay dying in 430, however, it seemed that his life's work was now going up in flames. Two years earlier a vast army of barbarian Vandals had crossed the straits of Gibraltar from Spain and entered north Africa. For so long secure from these hordes, now these last provinces too began to succumb to the ravages that had afflicted so much of the West for so many decades. Encountering little resistance as they marched and plundered their way east-wards, by 430 the city of Hippo itself was now besieged, and Augustine was to die literally with the barbarians at the gates. Yet his work was to survive. The great bulk of his writings were preserved from destruction as the Empire in the West disintegrated, culminating with the formal abdication of the last Emperor in 476. He was to emerge as not only one of the most revered thinkers in medieval Christendom, but was also to become one of the great inspirations of the Reformation through his influence on Martin Luther. Even today his voice remains strong; Pope Benedict XVI has acknowledged Augustine as his greatest teacher. In a real sense our world too changed with Augustine's in that garden in Milan.

Indeed, if we review the history of the last century with all the political, economic and social 'isms' that so attracted so many people, whether, at their most extreme, the lure of the promise of a thousand-year Reich, or the inevitability of the dictatorship of the proletariat, and then see the scale of the consequent misery, destruction and death that followed in their wake, can we say that Augustine does not have a message for our times across the sixteen centuries that separate him from us? His analysis of the restless human heart and the divided self, reflected in a divided humanity that flows from it, and his consequent assertion that our ultimate hope can never be fulfilled in this world, least of all by political ideologies and the states they create, remains a timeless one.

Suggested Further Reading

Augustine was one of the most prolific writers of the early Church, and a vast amount of that writing has survived into modern times, including dozens of substantial treatises, commentaries and other major works, along with hundreds of sermons and letters, some of which are themselves the length of minor works. Consequently we have only been able to concentrate on two of those major works, albeit probably the most widely read and influential, in this chapter.

An excellent introduction to both the life and thought of Augustine is provided by Henry Chadwick's *Augustine: A Very Short Introduction* (Oxford University Press, 2001). Originally published in the Oxford 'Past Masters' series, it has now been reprinted under this new title with an updated bibliography and the addition of some illustrations. It is written with great clarity and a simplicity that somewhat belies the massive learning behind it.

Also recently reissued is what has for many years been regarded as the standard biographical study of Augustine in English. Peter Brown's *Augustine of Hippo: A Biography* was first published in 1967; the revised edition of 2000 published by Faber and

Faber wisely leaves the original text unamended, but adds an extensive epilogue which takes account of more recent specialist scholarship, and especially the discoveries in 1975 and 1990 respectively of previously unknown letters and sermons by Augustine. This is an elegantly written and scholarly life of Augustine, which deals both with his interior intellectual and spiritual development, and attempts to place them within the broader historical context of his times. Although not a study of his theology as such, it does make quite a few assumptions about the reader's prior theological knowledge.

More recently the French scholar Serge Lancel has produced an even more detailed study. First published in France in 1999, and subsequently in an English translation by Antonia Nevill for SCM Press in 2002 that is not only very clear but also at times quite lyrical, Lancel's *Augustine* does incorporate the newly discovered letters and sermons as well as the most up-to-date research in the main text. It complements rather than replaces Peter Brown's biography, however, partly by presenting a Gallic rather than Anglo-Saxon interpretation. It too deals with both Augustine's life and ideas in a broadly chronological order; the drawback with this is that because so many of Augustine's ideas overlap from work to work, it can lead to some repetition.

Among those studies dealing more specifically with Augustine's theology, the one by Gerald Bonner, *St Augustine of Hippo: Life and Controversies* (Canterbury Press, third edition, 2002) has become something of a standard starting place since its first publication in 1963. It has stood the test of time well. Insightful and written with clarity when dealing with highly complex and sophisticated issues, it is largely constructed around extensive quotations from, and references to, the writings of Augustine himself. For those who have already familiarized themselves with the basic outline of Augustine's life from other sources, the initial biographical chapters could be safely skipped.

Perhaps the 'classic' English study of Augustine's thought, however, is by John Burnaby, *Amor Dei: A Study of the Religion of St Augustine* (Hodder and Stoughton, 1938). For obvious reasons somewhat dated in style, and written at a time when its author could assume a more extensive knowledge of Latin than now prevails, it is not only extraordinarily perceptive but also a surprisingly easy read. In the view of Henry Chadwick it remains the greatest intellectual biography of Augustine, but is not so overwhelmed by the eminence of its subject as to avoid criticism or disagreement where that is deemed appropriate by the author.

Of the two works by Augustine himself introduced in this chapter, there is an excellent modern translation of the *Confessions* published by the Oxford University Press in its 'World's Classics' series in 1991, beautifully accomplished by Henry Chadwick with an introduction and wealth of useful footnotes. There is also a good, short, modern commentary by Gillian Clark, *Augustine: The Confessions* (Bristol Phoenix Press, 2005). This contains a very useful up-to-date bibliography that goes beyond this one work in its scope. For *The City of God* there are two very good modern translations. The one by Henry Bettenson, originally published by Penguin in 1972, was reissued in 2003; and Cambridge University Press published an alternative by R. W. Dyson in 1999. There is also a commentary by Gerard O'Daly, *Augustine's City of God: A Reader's Guide* (Oxford University Press, 1999) which contains a detailed book-by-book analysis with surrounding chapters of discussion. While excellent, it can prove a little dry to read, given its approach and level of detail.

Finally, R. A. Markus, *Saeculum: History and Society in the Theology of St Augustine*, first published by Cambridge University Press in 1970 and reissued in 1988, is a brilliant study of Augustine's evolving views on the Roman Empire and the general relationship between the secular and the sacred. Heavily based on *The City of God*, there is again some almost inevitable repetition of ideas, and sometimes it does not translate Latin words and phrases; however, it traces the growth of Augustine's thoughts in this area quite thoroughly, and also argues for their continuing relevance.

PART TWO

Expansion and Order: Latin Christendom c. 1050–c. 1250

5

Roads to Canossa

See, I am sending you out like sheep into the midst of wolves; so be wise as serpents and innocent as doves. (Matt. 10:16)

The winter of 1076–7 was particularly severe, and in many parts of Europe snow, ice and frost made travel hazardous. Despite this there were, however, two particular groups for whom journeys that winter were imperative. One had set out from the city of Rome and had headed north intending to cross the Alps by way of the Brenner Pass and so into Germany in order to be present at a great Church Council. For this party was headed by none other than Pope Gregory VII, Bishop of Rome. But he was to be frustrated in his efforts and forced to take shelter in the ancestral castle of Countess Matilda of Tuscany situated at Canossa in the foothills of the Apennines. The other, much smaller group, consisted of a few horsemen who had succeeded where the papal party had failed; they had come south from Germany itself in great haste, as desperate to find the Pope as he was to avoid them. They were led by the 26-year-old Henry IV, King of Germany, Italy and Burgundy. He needed the Pope not only to perform his imperial coronation and place upon his head the crown of the Holy Roman Empire, but also more urgently to lift from him the sentence of excommunication which that same Pope had pronounced in the February of 1076.

Gregory VII's declaration that Henry was barred from the sacraments of the Church and that his feudal vassals were released from their oaths of fealty to him, was unprecedented. Never before had a Pope excommunicated and effectively dethroned an Emperor-elect. The news of the promulgation of the sentence had sent shock waves across Latin Christendom. But as a result many of the princes of Germany, both lay and episcopal, had deserted Henry, and told him that he had to persuade the Pope to absolve him within a year of the sentence, or face deposition. By the opening of the new year of 1077 he knew he had but weeks to save his throne and dynasty.

At last, on 25 January, he caught up with the Pope at Canossa. Here, fasting, bare-headed and unshod, dressed in the garb of a penitent, the most powerful secular ruler in the West came for three consecutive days to stand in the bitter cold before the gatehouse of the castle. Inside, Gregory VII, armed only with a great religious idea, finally relented, and at the end of the third day formally re-admitted Henry to the communion of the Church.

This meeting at Canossa in the winter of 1077 was one of the most dramatic set-pieces of medieval history, and its significance has been debated endlessly by historians. How had the Bishop who claimed direct spiritual succession from the apostle Peter, and the foremost secular ruler of Latin Christendom, been brought to this fateful confrontation? Did it represent a victory for the papacy, or did subsequent events reveal that Gregory VII had foolishly overreached himself to the detriment of his office? And where did the events at Canossa fit in the broader sweep of the history of Christendom? For the two winter journeys of Pope and Emperor-elect were, in a sense, small parts of the much longer journeys that had been taken by the Church and the various secular successors of the Roman Empire after its demise in the West at the close of the fifth century. In order to understand how and why these two men were brought to Canossa we must thus stand back from the events of 1077 and survey briefly the longer roads that had led from the final days of imperial Rome to what is called the Middle Ages.

The Petrine Office

When discussing some of the issues central to the concerns of Christians in the early centuries of their faith in the previous chapters, the bishops of Rome made little more than fleeting appearances. This was partly deliberate; but at the same time it did reflect the fact that they were rarely more than peripheral to much of the historical development of early Christianity. Yet at the same time Rome and its bishops were always the unseen presence off-stage from the main dramas. They might be active participants in great events on rare occasions only, but in terms of honour and prestige their passive role was widely acknowledged.

This consciousness of the special status of the Petrine office was first enunciated in the New Testament documents. In all the lists of apostles recorded in the Synoptic Gospels Peter was always placed first, an ordering that was far from accidental, but rather deliberate and hierarchical. Peter was always shown to be present also among the 'inner core' of apostles at many of the most significant events in the life of Jesus, such as his transfiguration (Matt.

17:1–8) or the agony in the garden of Gethsemane (Matt. 26:37). And at the crucial moment on the road to Caesarea Philippi when Jesus asked his apostles who they thought he was, it was Peter who made the breakthrough with his declaration that Jesus was the Messiah and the Son of the living God, which elicited from Jesus the announcement that Peter was the rock on which the Church was to be built (Matt. 16:13–20). In John's Gospel, in the post-resurrection accounts, it was Peter who was again singled out for a special role when Jesus asked him three times for a declaration of his love, and followed each with the command to feed his sheep and a prediction of his martyrdom (John 21:15–19). In the first half of the Acts of the Apostles it was Peter again who was shown exercising decisive leadership on a number of occasions, such as speaking to the crowds to explain the meaning of the strange events that they had just witnessed on the day of Pentecost (Acts 2:14–42),or when brought before the Jewish Sanhedrin with John (Acts 4:1–22). Peter was also the first apostle to perform a miracle in the name of the risen Jesus, whose very shadow could heal the sick (Acts 3:1–10, 5:15). Yet Peter was also a figure of contradiction. His three-fold declaration of love for Jesus was but a reversal of his three-fold denial of him in the hours leading up to the crucifixion (Matt. 26:31–35, 69–75). Peter was, perhaps, the supreme New Testament example of the flawed human material that Jesus chose to work with and through.

It was, however, the intimate association of Peter, along with Paul, with the city of Rome that was crucial in the history of early Christianity. Yet historically neither of them were the founders of the Church in Rome, and neither exercised any episcopal function in the city. Indeed, the Christian community in Rome was already one of the largest in the Mediterranean world before they arrived, and any concept of a monarchical episcopate there had to wait until both apostles were long dead. However, it would clearly not be beyond the realm of probability that they exercised some form of leadership in the Roman community; they were, after all, the only apostles ever to travel to the West. And it was their martyrdom in the city, probably under Nero in 64, and the continuing presence of their relics in the city that were of the greatest significance for later generations of Christians. By the time of Irenaeus, writing in the 180s, the claim would be made that the current bishop of Rome was the twelfth in succession to Peter (a conveniently apostolic number) with the sixth successor appropriately called Sixtus. While such a list is clearly 'suspiciously tidy' it does reflect the continuing and unchallenged tradition of the unique Petrine office exercised by the leadership of the Roman Church.[1] By 258, just a few years after the massive celebrations for the supposed millennium of Rome's pagan founders, Romulus and Remus, the Church there had instituted a feast on 29 June for Peter and Paul, the alternative and rival founders of Christian Rome. Shrines over their graves had existed since 165, the centenary of their martyrdom, and this had attracted a growing stream of pilgrims to visit these unique relics.

This primacy in terms of prestige and honour was reflected in other lists, namely those of the Patriarchates, drawn up by the Ecumenical Councils of the fourth and fifth centuries. Eventually five cities emerged as the supreme examples of Christian leadership, but in each Council the list was always headed by Rome, the only church with a double apostolic foundation. And when at Constantinople in 381, and again at Chalcedon in 451, the Church of Constantinople was included in the list as the 'new' Rome, the older city protested that the criteria for inclusion had never been political but always religious, namely biblical and apostolic. Indeed, at Chalcedon, when Leo's Tome was read to the assembled bishops, they had been recorded as crying out that Peter himself had now spoken through Leo his successor as leader of the Roman Church.

However, this acclamation for Leo was personal rather than institutional. The Roman Church and its bishop were accorded a primacy of honour and prestige within a collective episcopate, not a primacy of authority which set either him or his Church in a position superior to other bishops or churches in any doctrinal or jurisdictional sense. And yet history was to be kind to Rome. It was, first of all, the only apostolic foundation among the churches of the West, and thus the only Patriarchate in the West. The other four were in the Greek-speaking East, which inhibited any one from emerging as supreme. Then the destruction of Jerusalem by the Romans in 70 and again in 135 helped to downgrade what in the first generations had been the natural and obvious 'mother Church' of Christianity. Persian, and then Arab invasions in the seventh century took both Antioch and Alexandria out of the Christian Empire and left their churches somewhat beleagured outposts in an alien world. That left only Constantinople as a serious rival for the leadership of the Christian world, but a rival handicapped by the lack of an apostolic connection. Even Carthage, the second city of the West, eventually fell to the Arabs, and with that its Christian significance rapidly declined. Even the disappearance of the Roman Empire in the West as a living reality at the end of the fifth century favoured the Roman Church and its bishop; as the generations passed it was increasingly seen as the only surviving link in the West back to the Christian Empire, and so catholic Christians would naturally look to it for security in a hostile world of heretical barbarians.

For despite its prestige, the Roman Church in the generations after the fall of the Empire in the West was in a far from secure position. For one thing, most of the barbarian tribes which now occupied the territories of the old Roman Empire were Arians or pagans. Their conversion to catholic Christianity was a painfully slow process. One of the earliest of the pagan leaders to convert was Clovis, the leader of the Franks who had overrun much of Gaul; he accepted baptism as a catholic Christian in about 500. But the Visigothic kings in Spain did not abandon their Arianism until the late sixth century, and the Lombards, who had conquered much of northern Italy, took another century to be converted from Arianism. It was thus not until about 700 that all the former provinces of the Western Empire were firmly committed to the same form of Christianity as the bishop of Rome.

Partly because of this, the political orientation of the Roman Church and its bishop was Eastwards. They shared with their fellow catholics a loyalty to the surviving Christian Empire and its ruler in Constantinople. Indeed, for long many in the West hoped for the reconstruction of that Empire, and in the mid-sixth century their dreams seemed to be nearing fulfilment when the Eastern Emperor Justinian launched an attempted military re-conquest of the West, regaining territory in Italy, north Africa and Spain. But the imperial presence in Italy could present its own problems. For one thing, the long and bitter campaign had resulted in a further deterioration of urban life. It has been estimated that by about 500 the city of Rome, once the greatest in the Mediterranean world with perhaps nearly a million inhabitants at its height, was already reduced to about 100,000. The conquests of Justinian may have caused it to decline further to as few as 30,000, although there is evidence of recovery by the end of the century.[2] On top of that the spiritual independence and doctrinal integrity of the Roman Church could be compromised by the imperial presence in Italy. As late as the 650s one Bishop of Rome, Martin I, was arrested, put on trial in Constantinople, and subsequently died in exile in the distant Crimea when he refused to accept the heretical teachings then dominant in the imperial court.

Steadfast doctrinal integrity was, indeed, one of the proudest claims of the Roman Church. While the great churches of the East in Alexandria, Antioch or Constantinople had at times willingly lapsed into heresy, Rome and its bishops had not, apart from rare occasions when imperial physical coercion had been applied as in the cases of Bishops Liberias in the fourth and Vigilius in the sixth centuries. The one problem case was that of Honorius I in the early seventh century who, writing in a formal letter to the Patriarch of Constantinople, had unwisely used the expression 'one will' in Christ; this seemed to contradict the two natures christology of Chalcedon, and to support the Monothelite (one will) party currently engaged in fierce theological dispute with the subsequently orthodox 'two wills' party in that city. At the second Ecumenical Council of Constantinople in 681 the 'two wills' formula was accepted as orthodox belief and anathemas pronounced against Honorius. If not totally impeccable in its doctrinal orthodoxy, then, the Roman Church had at least a far less compromised record than any of the other Patriarchates, if for no other reason than that it was far less theologically sophisticated or imaginative.[3]

The dangers inherent in an unreflective policy of loyalty to the Eastern Empire, combined with the untapped potential for Christian expansion in the West, slowly turned the face of the Roman Church towards the setting sun. The first key figure in this lengthy process of reorientation was Gregory I the Great, Bishop of Rome from 590 to 604. One of the crucial initiatives that Gregory took was to despatch a party of about 40 monks under Augustine who landed in England in 597 and began the conversion of the Anglo-Saxons to the Roman version of Christianity. Although Gregory certainly had no master plan for the long-term reorientation of the Roman Church westwards, this papal mission proved to be the first of many which led progressively to the conversion of Germans, Danes, Norwegians, Czechs, Magyars and Poles to catholic Christianity. By about 1000 not only were the former provinces of the Roman Empire once more firmly within the communion of the Latin Church, but vast new territories beyond the old imperial frontiers were now either converted or in the process of conversion.

But not only was Latin Christendom expanding geographically; at its heart the claims of the Roman Church and its bishop were also developing, shifting from just a primacy of prestige and honour to one of spiritual and jurisdictional authority. While the bishops of Rome had always asserted their apostolic succession directly from Peter, a position in itself largely unchallenged in the first centuries of Christianity, its significance and meaning could become matters for controversy. For instance, during the clash between Stephen of Rome and Cyprian of Carthage in the 250s, Stephen became the first Roman bishop to unambiguously use the passage in Matthew chapter 16 to claim superior authority over other bishops.[4] The question centred on whether Jesus's gift of the keys, the power of binding and loosing, had been given only personally and specifically to Peter, or whether, as his heirs and successors, the subsequent bishops of Rome had inherited those spiritual and jurisdictional powers from him. What is certain is that from a remarkably early date the claims for a centralization of powers on Rome were 'clear and unrelenting'.[5] Over time these claims became more specifically articulated. Innocent I, Bishop of Rome 402–17, argued that whenever a major decision was to be taken in any province of the Church, however geographically remote, before coming to a final conclusion it should be referred to Rome 'so that every decision may be affirmed by our authority'. His successor, Zosimus, claimed: 'Such then being our authority, that no one can revise our sentence'. The Roman Church, then, already saw itself, as it were, as the final court of appeal for Christendom.[6]

Leo I carried on these claims during his reign from 440 to 461, arguing, for instance, that while each bishop ruled those entrusted to him specifically,

'Peter especially rules all whom Christ also ruled originally'. Leo was also the first to claim for the Roman bishops *plenitudo potestatis*, the fullness of power; while all bishops receive apostolic powers, only the bishop of Rome has a universal leadership role, partly derived from Jesus's promise to Peter that his faith would never fail and that he was to strengthen his brethren (Luke 22:32). Two things, however, are noteworthy in Leo's arguments. First of all, his insistence that in claiming sweeping powers for himself as Roman bishop and successor of Peter, he was no innovator. As he himself wrote in one of his letters, he was not seeking to 'start something new, but to renew the old', harkening back not only to the New Testament record itself, but also the writings of others contemporary with it, such as the letter of Clement from Rome to the Corinthians, and subsequent writings in which the role of the Roman Church and its bishop had been elaborated. Thus Leo saw the evolving position of Rome as a matter of tradition, in the sense of the musical metaphor of original theme and progressive variations.

Second, Leo stressed that this guiding and ruling Petrine office was not one of domination but of service, and thus a divine gift to the universal Church: 'Thus in Peter the courage of all is fortified and the aid of divine grace is so arranged that the strength which comes to Peter through Christ, through Peter is transmitted to the apostles.' In this, Leo was utilizing a concept found in Roman law, that the person who inherits steps straight into the shoes of the person from whom the inheritance derives. Thus Leo was not the successor of Sixtus III (432–40) but the *direct* successor of Peter, inheriting the totality of the apostle's powers.[7] The bishop of Rome stood at the apex of the Christian hierarchy, but it was truly a hierarchy of service. This was a concept to be encapsulated succinctly by Gregory I when he became the first Bishop of Rome to ascribe to his office the expression *Servus servorum dei*, the servant of the servants of God, in future generations to become an official title of his successors. The exaltation of the office of Roman bishop depended entirely, then, on the paradox that he was the lowest of the low.[8]

However, it was the reign of Gelasius I (492–6) that represented perhaps 'the high point of papal claims in Antiquity'.[9] He was the first Roman bishop to use the expression 'vicar of Christ' for the Petrine office, although this was not a term that was to enter regular use until the twelfth century, and he further repeated the claim that the successor of Peter 'has the right of judging the whole world'.[10] It was in his famous letter to the Emperor Anastasius in Constantinople, however, that he most clearly summarized Roman views of the relationship between spiritual and secular power. This concept was to be of immense importance for the future of the West, and eventually came to be known as the theory of the two swords, representing spiritual and temporal power respectively, and derived from Luke 22:38 (Document 12).

Papacy and Empire

Despite its claims to universal spiritual authority the Roman Church remained physically vulnerable and potentially at the mercy of whichever political power predominated in Italy. The Eastern Emperors, for instance, were not only seen as increasingly unreliable as spiritual guardians, they were also weakening in terms of military power. The advance of the Arabs in the seventh and eighth centuries had wrenched many provinces from the Empire, and twice, in 674–8 and 717–18, they had besieged Constantinople itself. Not only that, but also in the 720s the Emperor Leo III had launched an imperial campaign to stamp out the veneration of icons. This move was condemned by Rome in 731 and, in retaliation, the Empire confiscated lands owned by the Roman Church in its territories in Italy and the Balkans.

In the following year of 732, however, the Franks defeated another Arab army that had invaded their territory from Spain at the battle of Poitiers. They were led to victory not by a Frankish king, but rather by the mayor of his palace and effectively his leading minister, Charles Martel. By this point the weak and ineffectual royal house of the Franks, the Merovingians, had relinquished power to their hereditary palace mayors. So when in 739 the Lombards sacked Rome and the imperial forces failed to protect the city, the writing was on the wall; effective protection of the Roman Church could no longer be looked for from Constantinople, but possibly lay nearer at hand with the Franks.

The turning point came in 751 when, with the explicit authority of Rome, Charles Martel's heir, Pepin, had the Merovingian dynasty overthrown and himself crowned as king of the Franks. By 754 the Lombard advance in northern and central Italy had overwhelmed the last imperial enclaves of territory there governed from the city of Ravenna. The Empire wanted its Italian lands back and expected its loyal bishop in Rome to help. The latter, however, travelled to France to meet Pepin and came to a historic agreement under which the Franks would re-conquer the imperial territories in Italy from the Lombards, but instead of restoring them to Constantinople, would hand them over to the Roman Church. Pepin publicly showed his reverence for the bishop of Rome by performing the *stratoris officium*, leading the bishop's horse by the bridle in the lowly office of a groom. In return he was anointed in an act of spiritual confirmation of his newly acquired royal status, along with other key members of his family, thus establishing his line as the legitimate Frankish sovereigns. By 756 Pepin had defeated the Lombards and duly handed the former imperial territories to the Roman Church to form what was to become the Papal States. Thus the bishop of Rome, now unique in the West in using the title 'pope', had at a stroke acquired not only a small but significant territorial state of his own, but also the prospect of a realistic protector in the shape of the new Frankish dynasty.

In 773 this role was put to the test when the Lombards once again besieged Rome. True to their word the Franks, under Pepin's son Charles, entered Italy, defeated the Lombards and absorbed their territories into the Frankish kingdom. Following further conquests over barbarian tribes in the east, on Christmas Day 800 the pope placed a new crown on the head of Charles in St Peter's basilica in Rome, uttering the fateful but in the West long redundant word *imperator*, 'Emperor'. But what was Charles the Great, or Charlemagne, Emperor of? Was it a revived Roman Empire? Was he to be the new Constantine? The ambiguity of the title and its relationship to the papacy were to remain a problem for the West for centuries. After Charlemagne's death in 814 popes continued to anoint and crown his successors until the early tenth century. But the death of this powerful Emperor left his descendants fighting over the territorial spoils, and thus within half a century of his death the new imperial protection of Rome was little more than a pious fiction. Deprived of external protectors, the papacy fell victim to internal power-politics and between 872 and 1012 about one-third of popes died in suspicious circumstances, the victims of feuds between Roman aristocratic families trying to outmanoeuvre one another in the effort to secure the papal prize.[11] Not surprisingly the result of this urban in-fighting was a papacy 'at one of the lowest ebbs in its history'.[12] Even the revival of the Empire with the coronation of the German King Otto I as Emperor in 962 did little more than make the papacy a further battleground in European power struggles. Of the 25 popes in the century 955 to 1057 some thirteen were the appointees of local aristocrats, and the other dozen the candidates of these new Holy Roman Emperors in Germany. As Eamon Duffy has rightly observed: 'At the opening of the eleventh century the papacy was a contradictory mixture of exalted theory and squalid reality.'[13]

Reform

As the political shape of Europe shifted under the Carolingians and then the Ottonians, so too did its social construction, with the emergence of what we have come to call feudalism. This is a notoriously contentious historical subject as its origins are far from clear, it had many local variations, and generally tended to change its nature over time. However, at its heart was land, the ownership of which for most of recorded history until modern industrialization had been the main source of wealth, conferer of social status, and determinant of political power. What helped to make the feudal system of land ownership distinctive was its military aspect. It was, in part, a system designed

to raise armies. This was based on the feudum or fief, a grant of land in return
for military service. Under this arrangement a lord granted land to a vassal
who in turn swore an oath of fealty to his lord, paid homage to him, and
agreed to render not only military service but also to attend his court to offer
advice and receive justice. So alongside land went a deeply personal relationship between individuals. Its most basic unit was known as a manor, a village
or group of villages with sufficient fields to produce enough agricultural
wealth to support a mounted fighting man and all his necessary equipment.
These villages were populated with many families who were tied to the land
through the system of serfdom. While not technically slaves, they were often
in reality little more than one degree removed from slavery, obliged to render
a certain number of days of manual labour to their lord and unable to leave
their village without his permission.

As feudalism spread across Europe, perhaps not surprisingly the Church
became enmeshed into its system. Many bishops and monasteries were themselves great landowners, and in return for these lands granted to them by great
secular lords, effectively became their vassals; in the reign of the Emperor Otto
II many German archbishops and bishops were responsible for raising
anything from 40 to 100 armed men each, and some even personally led their
forces into battle.[14] But the connection between the Church and the Empire
went beyond this basic military obligation. Bishops and abbots were also
obliged to attend the royal court to render advice; in effect, as churchmen
tended to have if not a monopoly of education then the next best thing to it,
many of them took on an overtly political role and became royal servants and
the chief administrators of whole kingdoms. At lower levels too many abbeys
or parish churches were the property of nobles, so-called proprietory
churches, and while not rendering military service to their lord, they still
contributed economically to the feudal system.

We must be careful, however, not to look upon this through the moral eyes
of later generations. The German historian, Gerd Tellenbach, in particular has
warned against the tendency to see such arrangements as corrupt in themselves. As he has pointed out, alongside any economic or military considerations, one of the main motivations for powerful laymen endowing churches
or abbeys was faith. In return for praying for the donor, his family and descendants, the abbey or priest would acquire the protection of a lord, just like any
other vassal. Indeed, it is difficult to see how, given the strength and extent
of feudalism, the Church could have avoided becoming intimately involved
in it.[15]

Yet increasingly it had its critics. By the eleventh century some influential
voices, especially originating in the monasteries, were starting to be raised
against certain aspects of the feudal links between the Church and secular

society. But again we must be careful. As Tellenbach has commented: 'In all periods of Church history there have been voices which in warning tones have depicted current times as ones of decline from original ideals.'[16] In the eleventh century, however, there was clearly a growing, if unco-ordinated, clamour for 'reform'. As we have already observed, this has tended to be a loaded word in Church history. The concepts of reform and renewal at an individual level have been built into Christianity since the time of St Paul's letters in the middle of the first century, and have helped to give the faith its sense of dynamism. But what can sometimes also happen is that reform and renewal can shift from being primarily individual to collective or institutional ideals. After all, communities and institutions are made up of individual people, and when sufficient of them feel a personal call to reformation, that can create a momentum. Bearing in mind all the necessary reservations and qualifications, this is what seems to have happened in the eleventh century. Whether or not this constituted a 'movement' for reform is largely a matter of semantics. What is clear is that some influential, and other not so influential, voices were beginning to be raised against certain aspects of the contemporary Church. And these came to rest initially on two main concerns: simony and clerical continence.

The term 'simony' was derived from the account of the sorcerer Simon Magus who tried to obtain spiritual powers from the apostles by offering them money (Acts 8:9–24). Thus simony is the buying and selling of things spiritual. As such it was frequently condemned in the early centuries of Christianity, the Council of Chalcedon in 451, for instance, outlawing the practice of exchanging money for ordination. By the time of the Middle Ages, however, it had become a very wide and imprecise term covering everything from sacraments to proprietory churches. The danger inherent in this was that simony could be claimed as 'the principal crime of whomever happened to be one's opponent'.[17] Thus by the middle of the eleventh century objections were being raised to a range of practices which had by then been current in the Church for generations. But attacks on it were symbolic of one aspect of the cry for reform, a feeling that the laity, especially its more powerful members, had far too much influence over the affairs of the Church.

Linked to that was a growing desire to assert the differences between laity and clergy. And the main focus came to rest on the sexual practices of the latter. As we have already seen, in the early Church celibacy had been elevated as an ideal, driven especially by the growth of asceticism and monasticism. However, by the eleventh century, while celibacy remained one of the characteristic features of those taking monastic vows, the 'religious', clerical marriage or openly living with women not their wives remained widespread among the parochial, or 'secular', clergy. Again the reasons for this were partly economic. Many rural clergy could not afford to pay for servants, and thus wives and children were a necessity in order that the priest's fields were farmed and his house kept in order. This led in turn to the not infrequent practice of 'hereditary churches' where a son would succeed his father as the ordained priest to continue supporting the family. And while the episcopate was mostly unmarried, many clergy attached to their cathedrals or other urban churches were far from celibate. For reformers, this not only made the clergy appear to be too much like the laity around them, but also compromised what might be termed their 'ritual purity' when celebrating the sacraments, especially the Eucharist.

Thus by the early decades of the eleventh century the first voices began to be heard calling for a radical change; not just personal renewal, but institutional refashioning as well. Among these were hermits like Peter Damian (1007–72), or mixed groups of clergy and laymen who were calling for the radical overhaul of the Church in Milan and other Italian cities; these 'rag-pickers' or Patarini were to be a feature of Italian religious and political life for several decades. Even the pious Holy Roman Emperor, Henry III, was touched by these new demands and in 1022 at a synod in Pavia helped to push through stern measures against clerical marriage and concubinage, although with little practical effect.

The fundamental turning point came, however, in 1046. By that year there were no fewer than three claimants to the papal throne as a result of the aristocratic in-fighting that plagued Rome. Henry III now came south from Germany and summoned another Synod, to Sutri just outside Rome. Here the Emperor brushed aside all other contenders and placed his own candidate firmly on the throne of St Peter, and followed him with others, all Germans. But each of them had not only their nationality in common; they were also men of a different calibre from the Italian aristocrats who had fought each other for the office over the previous century. Their very names spoke deliberately of a different, and earlier, age of the Church: Clement, Damasus, Leo and Victor, all redolent of a time of spiritual heroism and the first formulation of papal claims.

Not only that, but they now reached out across Europe to find and bring to Rome some of the leading advocates of reform. Peter Damian was plucked from his hermitage and created a cardinal; so too a monk from Lorraine was summoned to become cardinal Humbert of Silva Candida; Hildebrand, a native Roman of decidedly non-noble blood, was similarly elevated as cardinal archdeacon of the Roman Church. The arrival of these men, and others like them, many from monastic backgrounds, and all equally dedicated to the successors of Peter and the reform of the universal Church, meant that in the years after 1046 the heart of the Roman Church began to beat with a new, energetic rhythm. Regular Synods began to enact a stream of reforming decrees; between 1041 and 1122 there were to be more than 100 such Synods held in Rome. And popes became travellers again, taking their message outside the eternal city; in 1049, for instance, for the first time since 878 a reigning pope set foot once again on the soil of France.

For in Rome a number of elements had now come together. The revived papacy looked back into its own past and began once more to announce its ancient claims to spiritual authority and jurisdiction in the new conditions of the feudal age. At the same time the rejuvenated papacy became the natural ally of clerical reform; at the 1059 Synod the gift of churches from laymen was condemned. The sweeping theoretical powers of the papacy were now to be thrown behind the drive for reform. And in order to try to ensure that the papacy itself did not once again become the prisoner of aristocratic intrigue or imperial power politics, that same 1059 Synod began the process of reordering the method of papal election by giving it exclusively to the cardinal bishops.

Gregory VII

Then in 1073, and momentarily putting aside the new electoral procedure, cardinal Hildebrand was swept onto the papal throne by popular acclamation during the funeral of his predecessor, taking the name Gregory VII, a conscious act of homage to the first pope of that name.

Seldom has a more charismatic, but also controversial, individual, sat on the throne of St Peter. For above all he had an intense sense of personal identification with the apostle, combined with an ascetic temperament (he continued to wear his monastic habit throughout his pontificate), a commitment to reform and a sometimes startling indifference for the opinion of others. He could inspire both the most devoted loyalty and also the most extreme personal loathing. His motivations were deeply and intensely religious, often at his lowest moments throwing himself on the mercy of Jesus and St Peter, and with a profound veneration for the scriptures. Yet his actions could also provoke the most bitter of political disputes. In so many ways, just like Peter himself, Gregory VII was a figure of contradiction. In the words of his most recent biographer:

> The comprehensiveness of his vision marked him off from the past, while its formation upon ancient models marked him off from the future. In such terms, he was, indeed, the great innovator in the history of the papacy, who nevertheless stands alone. He was the towering fore-runner and prophet of the papal monarchy of the central Middle Ages, but not its architect or builder.[18]

So what was his vision for Christendom? Above all this was summed up in the concept of liberty: 'liberty was the birthright of the Christian religion in which Christ founded it and in which it must always be renewed'.[19] In his final encyclical letter written in exile in 1085, having been driven from Rome by his enemies and with his vision seemingly in ruins, he wrote: 'My greatest aim has been that holy church, the bride of Christ, our lady and mother, should return to her true glory and stand free, chaste, and catholic.'[20] The only lordship that Christians should be subject to was that of Christ; as he had written to the clergy and people of Chartres in 1077: 'Do not allow the yoke of iniquity, or any lordship, to be in any way imposed upon you to the destruction of your souls, knowing that, in this cause, papal authority and defence will never let you down.' The Roman Church and its bishop had regained their liberty and were now to lead all Christians into true freedom in Christ.

This would be achieved by Roman leadership of a radical programme of reform and renewal, nothing short of 'the moral rearmament of Latin Christendom'.[21] Simony should be assaulted wherever it was to be found, and chaste and pure clergy encouraged. But for Gregory himself all his hopes and fears for a free and renewed Church came to centre on what was called Lay Investiture. This was the act by which a layman handed to a cleric the symbols of his office. For a bishop or abbot these were the pastoral staff, symbolizing his role of shepherd, and the ring, the symbol of his marriage to Christ and his Church. With these the bishopric or abbey were effectively gifted from the donor to the recipient. The central problem with this was that it gave what we would now call a 'mixed message'. These were symbols of *spiritual* authority, but received from a *secular* source. Thus the impression given was that the origin of episcopal or abbatial authority was the layman, often a king, and not from the free gift of the Church.

This was further complicated by the method of selection of the candidate for office; by the eleventh century this was normally made by the same person who performed the investiture, namely the king or prince, and who had granted the *regalia* to the bishop or abbot, namely his lands and other properties, rights and duties under feudal law. Thus the free election by the Church, and the investiture of the symbols of spiritual authority became, alongside the attack on simony and promotion of clerical celibacy, central to the programme of papal reform. Perhaps as early as 1075, but certainly unambiguously by 1078, Gregory had condemned lay investiture.[22]

Yet this was still only a background noise in the growing cacophony generated by the relationship between Gregory and the young king of Germany and would-be Emperor Henry IV. The son of the pious Emperor Henry III he had succeeded to his father's German throne in 1056 at the tender age of six after the untimely death of the Emperor. As cardinal Hildebrand, Gregory had known and admired his father, and felt a personal sense of responsibility for the son. Yet, in a travelling court, surrounded by plotting dukes, counts and archbishops, the young Henry IV had developed some decidedly unpleasant character traits. He early learnt to be cunning and secretive; but then, after being proclaimed of age in 1065, he added depravity, promiscuity and cruelty to his other vices, in 1069 attempting unsuccessfully to obtain a papal divorce from his wife. Thus even before Hildebrand became pope, Henry was widely regarded as lacking in terms of character and conduct: 'By chivalric, no less than ecclesiastical, standards, he was unfitted to be king.'[23]

Ideas of clerical reform had also been making their way into Germany during the middle decades of the century, and had begun to cut across the political grain of imperial rule. Secular magnates had taken the opportunity of the comparatively feeble royal position during Henry's minority and early years of rule to strengthen their own regional power bases in what was already a highly decentralized feudal state. Not unnaturally, Henry sought to counter this by appointing loyal followers to bishoprics; but clearly the problem with this was that loyalty to the ruling house did not necessarily go with deep spirituality, and outright simony could sometimes creep into these appointments. In 1072 a meeting of lay and ecclesiastical princes had started to push the ideas of the reformers more vigorously in Germany, and clearly saw such traditional royal practices as increasingly unsatisfactory.

Gregory VII, however, was prepared to be patient and lenient with the young king. He had hopes that Henry would change his ways and follow the more spiritual course of his father. As the new pope began his reign, however, Henry faced outright rebellion from some of his princes, notably in Saxony. Thus he could not afford to add the pope to his list of enemies. Friendly letters were exchanged. Henry promised personal reformation, especially the removal from court of certain excommunicated counsellors. By 1074 two papal legates had been sent to Germany to help initiate widespread reform and reconciled the king to the Church. All seemed set fair when the king did public penance for his past misdeeds and received the blessing of the legates.

Henry and Gregory needed each other, but for very different reasons. Henry wanted a friendly papacy that would endorse his ecclesiastical appointments, and ultimately confer what only a pope could, the imperial title through coronation and anointing as Holy Roman Emperor. This would give him the prestige that would make opponents hesitate before rebelling against God's, and St Peter's, chosen vessel. Gregory on the other hand was only willing to grant the imperial title to someone spiritually and morally worthy, and who would have enough political weight to be a decisive influence in the campaign for Church reform. At the same time many senior ecclesiastics in Germany were far from committed to this reformation, and rather saw increasing papal involvement as an intrusion into their spiritual as well as temporal powers; while on the other hand some secular princes sought alliance with the papacy as a political counterweight to an ambitious monarchy.

By the beginning of 1076 Henry was militarily in a stronger position, having defeated his Saxon rebels; thus his need for papal support was consequently lessened. In January two archbishops and 24 bishops went so far as to renounce their obedience to Gregory, citing the illicit manner of his election, in effect a convenient excuse. Henry joined in the orchestrated clamour by also demanding that Gregory stand down; the pope's irritating demands for reform, personal as well as ecclesiastical, and the removal of excommunicated but essential advisers had not lessened over the intervening months.

But Henry's position was itself far from secure. Many lay magnates smouldered with resentment at his treatment of them, and some, at least, of the churchmen who had demanded papal abdication had done so under royal coercion. Thus when the royal messengers arrived in Rome in February carrying news of royal and episcopal rebellion against the papacy, they were met with uproar at the Lent Synod. On 22 February Gregory responded with one of the most extraordinary papal pronouncements of the Middle Ages. In a public letter addressed personally to St Peter, and couched in ringing tones, he excommunicated Henry IV, many of his leading bishops, and released his subjects from obedience to him (Document 13).

While technically not deposing Henry, this blast of righteous papal fury was unprecedented, and sparked a battle inside the German nobility, lay and ecclesiastical, for their loyalty to king or pope. By October Henry was effectively losing this struggle, with many leading ecclesiastics, from the archbishop of Mainz downwards, abandoning him, as much for political as for spiritual reasons, and rebellion brewing once again in Saxony. At the same time he was now presented with a chilling ultimatum: be reconciled to the pope within one year of the pronouncement of excommunication, or face potential deposition by his own German nobility. Thus 'Henry's single concern was now to become reconciled to Gregory.'[24]

Gregory was now on the road himself, making for the Brenner Pass and Germany, to take charge of a great ecclesiastical Council scheduled at Augsburg in the new year. By 28 December he had reached Florence, but a combination of appalling winter weather and the non-appearance of an official escort from the German princes obliged him to make for the ancestral seat of his great ally and friend, the Countess Matilda of Tuscany. It was there at her castle of Canossa on 25 January 1077 that Henry caught up with him.

Not only had king and pope travelled along many difficult roads that winter to this fateful confrontation; so too had what they each represented, the ecclesiastical and secular forces that had also journeyed along difficult paths since Rome had ceased to mean so much an empire and had come to embody a spiritual ideal instead.[25]

The Meaning of Canossa

What, then, was the significance of this confrontation at Canossa? Historians have debated that question at some length over many generations, but without reaching a generally accepted consensus. The question itself raises a further set of issues. Was there a clear 'victory' for one of the protagonists? A question which, in its turn, must lead to an examination of the objectives that either wished to achieve. Further, which time-frame is being considered, the immediate events and outcomes in late January 1077, or the continuation of the struggle down to the death of Gregory in 1085, or an even longer period of time? Should it be viewed in exclusively spiritual terms, or were the political ramifications the crucial issues? And what were the personal motivations involved in the events, and to what extent did they shape them?

First of all, it is probably true to say that both Henry and Gregory achieved at least some part of their goals. Henry had gained his most pressing objective: to obtain papal absolution before the deadline of February 1077 expired. Thus he avoided the immediate prospect of deposition by his own princes. He had bought some time, some room to manoeuvre and to rebuild his position in Germany. But some ambiguities remained. Was he still the undisputed king to whose loyalty all his vassals were now obliged to return? Had the pope absolved Henry the personal penitent, or Henry the king, or both? Was he brought back to the communion of the Church just as an absolved penitent, or was his political status also restored as well? Certainly not all of his vassals accepted the latter position, as political and military resistance to him continued inside Germany, with an alternative royal candidate, Rudolf of Swabia, receiving much of their support. Gregory's position was one of neutrality between the two contenders; for him the size of either's political following or extent of military success were not the crucial factors, but rather their spiritual suitability for so exalted an office. The fact that he eventually rejected Henry in favour of his opponent would tend to demonstrate that Gregory himself did not interpret the matter as settled at Canossa.

From Gregory's perspective the events at Canossa also contained clear elements of achievement. In the view of the modern historian I. S. Robinson, one of these was 'the public acceptance of the unprecedented claims which Gregory VII had made for the papal office'.[26] This, in his view, was the price that Henry IV had paid for his tactical success at avoiding the danger of deposition, a consequence of his own overestimation of his imperial authority and political weight. This view clearly implies that Henry had most at stake, and thus to lose, at Canossa. At the same time Gregory, in the opinion of H. E. J. Cowdrey, had made a first clear move in the direction of bringing Henry to a 'right mind' in both spiritual and political terms, a fact publicly demonstrated by the king's penitential austerities. Cowdrey is at pains to stress that the events at Canossa must be viewed through medieval eyes; how people at the time saw it rather than how later generations, with different conceptions, interpreted it. In that light we must avoid seeing Henry's penitential actions in the modern sense of personal humiliation or degradation. In the Middle Ages true penitence was seen as ennobling and exalting the individual, a positive spiritual experience that all present would have understood and responded to in that way. At the same time there was also a political element. There was a well-understood convention, almost a formal ritual, known as *deditio*, the surrender or capitulation of a person or town to superior strength, an action performed with a sense of chivalric honour by both parties. The surrender was accompanied by the equally well-understood corollary of mercy and justice being done by the victor to the vanquished. This also normally followed the equally formal pleading by others on behalf of the party offering surrender. We know that inside the castle at Canossa, as well as the pope, there were other powerful individuals present including not only the Countess Matilda of Tuscany, but also, among others, Abbot Hugh of Cluny, another ally of Gregory and perhaps the most prominent monastic churchmen of his day. As Gregory himself wrote of what occurred, in absolving Henry and restoring him to communion, he was responding to two interlinked actions: 'Overcome at last by the earnestness of his penitence and by the prayers of all who were present.'[27] Thus it seems reasonable to surmise that certain key individuals interceded for the king during those three crucial days, and became a chorus of actors in what was, to some extent, almost a piece of ritualized theatre, with lines and actions already rehearsed and their meaning well understood.[28]

But that then raises further questions. For one, did Gregory have any realistic alternative but to absolve the penitent king? Given that, to some extent, the events were stage-managed and the script well known by all the participants, he surely had little choice. In any case, from both the spiritual and political perspectives, any other outcome would have been almost unthinkable in the Middle Ages. Gregory would have needed clear and unquestionable evidence of Henry's insincerity to refuse absolution; in that sense he was in the same position as any priest faced with an individual who had successfully performed all the necessary demands of penitence. To have refused absolution would have deeply shocked contemporary religious sensibilities and potentially damaged the spiritual claims of the papacy as the keeper of the keys given to St Peter by Christ himself, with powers both of binding and loosing. Having bound him as an excommunicant in 1076, Gregory could hardly have withheld forgiveness to someone who had sincerely performed the accepted acts of penance.

But that raises the question of Henry's sincerity. This neither Gregory nor anyone else was able to judge *at the time*. The king's subsequent actions, however, made it clear to Gregory, at least, that there were severe questions over Henry's sincerity, and the extent to which he was, in reality, merely play-acting at Canossa. By 1080 Henry's actions had obliged Gregory to excommunicate him again, which in its turn led to a series of imperial sieges of Rome and Gregory's eventual flight into exile in 1084. To adapt terms more familiar from christology, Henry wore a mask of penitence, but how much did this conceal or reveal about his real substantial penitential orientation?

And then there were the political considerations. By performing an act of *deditio* Henry would have gained sympathetic understanding from many nobles, lay and ecclesiastical, in Germany. The evidence would suggest that at the beginning of 1077 there were many of them who had yet to decide irrevocably between king or pope. If Gregory had refused absolution this might well have polarized opinion in Germany to an alarming extent, rather than bringing together two still persuadable groups to unite behind a king who had received papal approbation as a reformed sinner. It was certainly not in papal interests, politically or spiritually, to ferment a bloody civil war in Germany.

Thus it is easy to understand why different historians have come to different conclusions about Canossa. For Eamon Duffy it was 'an astonishing victory for the papacy, with the most powerful monarch in Christendom suppliant at its gate, and the political unity and stability of Germany in the pope's hands'.[29] But this was a victory which 'rapidly turned to ashes'. By remaining in a state of ambiguity over which royal contender to acknowledge, Gregory's actions could be seen as betrayal by both sides. Indeed, the strength of the enthusiasm for Gregory in Germany, or rather the lack of it, was perhaps already strongly hinted at when the escort to lead him over the Brenner Pass failed to materialize in the weeks before Canossa. This was no formality. In the conditions of incipient civil war, with all parties armed and on a nervous guard in Germany, a full military escort was a necessity before Gregory could attempt so hazardous a journey. The total absence of one speaks volumes. The pope was a useful and desirable ally so long as he kept his distance. The last thing the vast majority of the princes wanted was a pope on their soil meddling directly in their affairs, spiritual or temporal. The princes looked for papal validation of their actions, not arbitration between them.

But then looking forward still further, beyond the limits of the immediate protagonists, Duffy sees Gregory as, if not the victor, then at least the crucial architect of subsequent papal policies: 'If he was defeated in the short term, the spirit of papal reform owed everything to him, for after him the papacy never receded from its claims to freedom from secular and political control in spiritual matters.'[30] Other historians, however, are not quite so sure that the issues are as clear-cut as this. I. S. Robinson sees the longer-term consequences of what became known as the Investiture Contest between papacy and Empire that dragged on for several decades after Gregory's death, as disastrous: 'The truth of the matter was that the papal party had sacrificed the unity of the Church to its own narrow factional interests.'[31] F. Donald Logan is in substantial agreement with this verdict: 'The pontificate of Gregory VII was a failure, perhaps even a monumental failure. He disturbed the forward progress of reform by picking unnecessary fights with secular rulers.'[32]

Perhaps what remains at issue is as much a matter of semantics as of history. What is meant by victory or defeat, success or failure? What constitutes Christian unity or division? Were the interests of the papacy identical with, or distinct from, those of the wider Church? Did Gregory pick fights with secular rulers in an aggressively proactive way, or, in the circumstances of the time, and with the particular personalities involved, were they unavoidable? What is, perhaps, capable of being asserted without contention is that Gregory VII was a monumental figure who, for good or ill, decisively affected the fortunes of the Church and society in his, and later times to such an extent that the period from the mid-eleventh century onwards for a number of generations to come bears his name: the Gregorian papacy. It is to the fortunes of that papacy in that subsequent period that we must now turn.

Suggested Further Reading

An excellent starting point among general surveys of medieval religious history is Bernard Hamilton's book *Religion in the Medieval West* (Edward Arnold, second edition, 2003). This makes few assumptions about a reader's prior knowledge, and is written in a clear and approachable style with a talent for explaining complex issues in simple terms. The book that has established itself as something of a 'classic' is *Western Society and the Church in the Middle Ages* by R. W. Southern, first published by Penguin in 1970. It is beautifully written by a great medieval scholar, if now somewhat dated. Among more modern introductions is Joseph H. Lynch, *The Medieval Church: A Brief History* (Longman, 1992). It is very concise, sometimes reading like a series of summaries and a bit clipped in style, but nevertheless a good modern starting point. John F. Thomson, *The Western Church in the Middle Ages* (Arnold, 1998) is a clear, straightforward study, which again neatly summarizes complex topics, but like most textbooks of this kind is probably too ambitious in trying to cover so much ground both chronologically and thematically in such a concise format. One relatively short general introduction that I believe achieves a good balance between narrative and themes, and with excellent summaries of the most significant areas, is *A History of the*

Church in the Middle Ages (Routledge, 2002) by F. Donald Logan. It also contains excellent, up-to-date bibliographies at the end of chapters.

Somewhat more substantial, and concentrating specifically on the period from 900 to 1125, is Gerd Tellenbach, *The Church in Western Europe from the Tenth to the Early Twelfth Century* (Cambridge University Press, 1993). This is the final result of decades of research and thinking, written by a scholar in his eighties. He emphasizes the continuities as well as the changes in the period, and relies heavily on a wealth of German scholarship generally unavailable to many other historians. First published in Germany in 1988, it is well translated by Timothy Reuter.

Among the lengthier treatments of the period from 1050 to 1250, that by Colin Morris stands out. *The Papal Monarchy: The Western Church from 1050 to 1250* (Clarendon Press, 1989) has established itself as perhaps the most authoritative general study of the Church in the central Middle Ages. Alongside this book should also be mentioned one by Malcolm Barber, *The Two Cities: Medieval Europe 1050–1320* (Routledge, 1992). This is an excellent and detailed general history which puts Christianity into a broader context; it contains substantial passages on the Church, which in itself indicates just how important an institution it was in the Middle Ages.

Among books specifically on the history of the papacy, an excellent introduction is provided by Eamon Duffy, *Saints and Sinners: A History of the Popes* (Yale University Press, revised edition, 2001). Elegant and crisp in style, it is written for a wide audience, has some brilliant summaries and often cuts through the complexities to reveal the heart of important issues. It also contains a detailed bibliography. For an equally excellent summary of the papacy in the early centuries of Christianity, Robert B. Eno, *The Rise of the Papacy* (Michael Glazier, 1990) is a clear synthesis of scholarship at the close of the twentieth century.

For Pope Gregory VII, one work now towers above all others. H. E. J. Cowdrey, *Pope Gregory VII 1073–1085* (Clarendon Press, 1998) is a truly majestic work of over 700 pages. It is one of those rare books that is a privilege to read; the result of a lifetime of scholarship, it rehabilitates Gregory as a pope primarily motivated by his spiritual and moral precepts rather than as a manipulator of medieval politics. At the same time it draws the reader into the whole world of the eleventh century in a quite absorbing way.

6

Keepers of the Keys

Jesus said to him, 'Feed my sheep'. (John 21:17)

The history of the Gregorian, or Reform, papacy of the central Middle Ages raises a whole series of questions and issues that were crucial both at the time and also of significance for later generations. These centre on two characteristics of the medieval papacy: it was both a centre of unity helping to hold Latin Christendom together; and at the same time a sign of contradiction, a force rivalling other centres of unity in the West and so potentially causing both spiritual and political instability. At the same time, its claims to universal authority in terms both doctrinal and jurisdictional, were undoubtedly a key element in the growing rift between the Latin West and the Greek East. We have already seen how the christological debate of the fourth and fifth centuries led to the first substantial division between Christians. These medieval centuries were to witness a second great schism between the churches linked to Rome and Constantinople respectively. And they were to look forward to the third great divide, that within Latin Christendom itself in the sixteenth century, when the issue of the papacy was again to arise as a major cause of controversy; for some a divine gift of unity for Christians, for others a curse that had led to the deformation of the original message.

And in that lies the key to these characteristics. Did the Gregorian papacy launch itself on a career of unwonted innovations that took the Church as well as itself away from the gospel; or was the gospel itself the inspiration for the direction taken by Rome? Did the medieval popes betray the command of their Lord to feed his sheep; or were they the guardians of a faith that cannot fail and is there to strengthen all Christians (John 21:15–19; Luke 22:32)? Was this the Peter who denied Jesus three times before the crucifixion, or the faithful apostle and leader of his flock who faced martyrdom rather than deny his Lord again?

It is not the function of history as an academic discipline to offer definitive answers to such questions; they are beyond its purpose, scope or capacity. What it can do, however, is contribute to an informed debate by showing how, why and when these issues arose, and what people at the time thought about them. Clearly, in these medieval centuries the old concerns about tradition and authority resurfaced, if in different historical circumstances. An exploration of them will help to put the larger theological and ecumenical questions within their historical context.

Papal Government

Whatever else can be said about papal government in the central Middle Ages, one thing is above dispute: it expanded enormously in size. At the same time, that expansion was accompanied by, and partly the consequence of, another characteristic of the medieval papacy, and that was the attempt to impose a Roman conception of order on the Western Church. However, this expansion and ordering must be rooted firmly within its historical context. First of all it was not the product of any later conception of the personal attribute of infallibility ascribed to popes. The Roman Church as an institution was generally recognized as the model of orthodoxy and focus of catholicity, and her bishops were honoured as the successors of Peter in the role of leadership of that Church. Indeed, for most of these centuries, the term 'vicar of St Peter' was more usually ascribed to them than the more expansive 'vicar of Christ' which only acquired common currency during the course of the thirteenth century. The first pope to use the latter expression in the sense of a formal title implying certain attributes different from the former was Innocent III (1198–1216); but merely the employment of a title does not in itself signify universal assent to all its implications at that time.[1]

On top of that, many modern historians also use the expression 'papal monarchy' when discussing the Gregorian popes. This can be equally misleading if used uncritically. It must be born in mind that the Middle Ages had a particular concept of monarchy, namely a feudal one, and that the later ideas of an absolute or constitutional monarchy were then quite unknown. Thus, while the relationship between the papacy and various kings and princes of Christendom was fundamentally spiritual, this was often expressed in feudal language in the surviving sources.[2] And one of the features of feudalism was a contractual relationship between lord and vassal, in which there were clear limitations to the lord's authority, expressed in legal terms, and a relationship between them based on mutual obligations and rights. These were the terms in which people thought and wrote at the time.

However, the fact of the expansion of papal government in the central

Middle Ages is undisputed, and there are a number of ways in which this can be demonstrated and, to some degree, quantified. One of these is through the growth and ordering of the Church's law: Canon law. Before the emergence of the Gregorian papacy the power of the Church was severely weakened by the absence of any common or unified codification of its laws; there was no universally accepted standard to which to refer, each province having its own collection of Canon law, with often substantial variations between them.[3]

The Roman Church had early begun evolving its own system of Canon law, probably from the late fourth century, based on concepts taken from the Roman imperial legal system, and the content derived from decretals, or papal letters, normally written in response to a particular question of legal dispute. By about 500, these were being collected and systematized, but at that stage purely for local use within the dioceses subject directly to the bishop of Rome. Thus, rather like English common law, papal Canon law was case law built upon precedent. As such it was dynamic and capable of being shaped to fit changing conditions.[4]

Yet at its heart remained the assumptions and methodologies of classic Roman law. This had received its final and most authoritative statement in the four books of the Emperor Justinian's *Corpus Iuris Civilis, the Body of Civil Law,* produced in sixth-century Constantinople. Of these four books the most important for Western Canon law was the first, the *Digest,* the private law of the Roman jurists. About 1070 a copy of the *Digest* was rediscovered in the West and, combined with the new techniques of the dialectical method pioneered by Peter Abelard (1079–1142) in such works as his *Sic et Non* ('Yes and No'), this led to the first great collection of Canon law in the West by Master Gratian of Bologna in about 1140, in a work known as the *Decretum.* This sought to reconcile legal differences through the dialectical method of argumentation. Although the *Decretum* was an entirely private, academic exercise in no way authorized by the papacy, it steadily began to influence Canon law across Latin Christendom, and led to further developments. For instance, in 1190 Bernard of Pavia produced his *Compilatio Prima,* the first attempt to assemble the legal material by subject, including ordination, marriage and matters affecting the clergy only.

By now one of the main sources for these ever-expanding compilations was papal decretals, and thus the Canon law of Latin Christendom was increasingly becoming papal law. However, the first 'official' compilation, made with the papal stamp of approval, was the *Compilatio Tertia* of 1210, by Peter Beneventanus Collivaccinus. This process finally culminated with the *Libra Extra* by Raymond of Pennaforte in 1234, specifically commissioned by Pope Gregory IX (1227–41) which, with periodic revisions, was to remain the main source of Roman Canon law until the early twentieth century.[5]

Thus during the central Middle Ages the papacy became the source and interpreter of the law of the Church. As such it had helped to bring order out of chaos and in the process turned Canon law into a science and a recognized academic discipline, centred on the great university in Bologna. Many areas of human thought and activity were brought within its domain, from the liturgy and the sacraments, to the administration of Christian marriage, and the distinguishing marks of orthodoxy and heresy. In the words of the distinguished papal historian, Walter Ullmann, it represented 'the legalization of the faith'.[6] Or to quote a contemporary, John of Salisbury (*c.* 1115–80): 'the whole function of the law is religious and holy'.[7]

Rome, however, was not only the great centre of legal theory, it was also increasingly the final court of appeal as well. As Roman Canon law became effectively the law of the Western Church, so more and more litigants began to flock to Rome to have their cases judged by the highest court in Christendom. Thus one of the major functions of the medieval papacy became that of a universal law court. Decade by decade the volume of legal business brought to Rome either to be heard and judged personally by the pope, or, as time passed more likely by the ever-expanding army of judges employed by the papacy, could, on occasion, virtually bring the whole system of papal government to a grinding standstill. James of Vitry, the Bishop of Acre in the Holy Land, noted in a letter of 1216 that at the papal court: 'People were so intensely occupied with temporal and worldly affairs, with kings and kingdoms, with lawsuits and quarrels, that it seemed hardly permissible to talk, even only a little, about spiritual matters.'[8]

This was the price that had to be paid for what Pope Innocent IV (1243–54), himself an outstanding Canon lawyer, saw as the function of the law, the right ordering of society on earth as a reflection of the divine law of God.[9] And it was also a measure of 'the extraordinary success of the papacy in establishing its claims to a universal jurisdiction' of the Church.[10] Theory had now been put into practice on a scale that no one before the Gregorian papacy would have thought possible. Thus, just as Christianity had earlier assimilated and so helped to preserve much ancient Greek thought, so now the medieval papacy did the same for another great legacy of the ancient world, Roman law, and in so doing became a powerful instrument not only for the ordering of the Church and its faith, but also a force for the ordering of civil society and the expansion of the intellectual and cultural worlds as well.

Beyond the exclusively legal there were also other ways in which the role of the papacy in the central Middle Ages could be seen to be expanding. One of these was the increasing influence that it exercised over the monastic world. The next chapter will deal in more detail with medieval ascetic life, but for the moment it will be sufficient to make the point by noting, for instance, the vast increase in the number of religious houses that placed themselves under the protection of St Peter, in effect under the guardianship of the Roman Church. The monastic world was at the heart of the movement for reform in the Church, part of whose programme was to secure its liberty from what was seen as lay interference; in the case of abbeys from the control of their founding noble or royal families, or from bishops less committed to a deepened spirituality than the monks. One way to achieve this freedom was to petition Rome to have St Peter named as official protector; if granted, a letter would be issued from the papacy to the abbey in question, framed in terms similar to this one sent by Gregory VII in 1081: 'Therefore we command by apostolic authority that no one shall presume henceforward to trouble the aforesaid place, fortified by apostolic defence, but that it shall remain in peace and free from any disturbance under the protection of St Peter, to whose jurisdiction it belongs.'[11]

During the course of the eleventh century some 270 religious houses of all types received such papal letters of protection. But during the following century there was a staggering acceleration to something in the order of 2,000 grants of papal protection. As I. S. Robinson has commented, these statistics demonstrated two things: first a growing confidence on the part of religious communities and their founders in the power of St Peter and his vicar to protect them in a realistic and meaningful way; this was no mere formality. Second, that this confidence in the protection of the papacy in its turn contributed to the expansion of papal authority in Western Christendom, partly through demonstrating that this willingness to accept the jurisdiction of Rome was, in itself, a model of the obedience which the whole Church, at least in theory, owed to the successors of St Peter.[12]

Indeed, it was perhaps not surprising, given the common commitment to reform, that the papacy and monasticism were so intimately linked in this period, with no fewer than eleven out of the nineteen popes in the century and a quarter from 1073 to 1198 being former members of religious orders. On top of that, numerous cardinals also originated from the same source. Of the 66 cardinals created by Pope Paschal II (1099–1118) about a third were former monks; one abbey alone, the Cistercian monastery of Clairvaux, produced eight cardinals during the course of the twelfth century, one of whom became pope as Eugenius III (1145–53).[13]

Yet another way in which the Gregorian papacy extended its influence over the Western Church was through the summoning of Synods and Councils. We have already seen how regular Synods in Rome were used by the papacy as instruments of reform in the eleventh century, starting at Sutri in 1046. But this concept could be extended beyond Rome itself as popes travelled further afield to hold such gatherings. Urban II (1088–99), for instance, a former protégé and supporter of Gregory VII, summoned eleven Synods during his reign, only three of which were held in Rome. This peripatetic papacy helped extend its influence by bringing unprecedented numbers of bishops and other senior ecclesiastics into personal contact with the pope, and at the same time transformed these gatherings into instruments for publicizing the reform programme.[14]

But perhaps above all it was the revival by the papacy of the holding of Ecumenical Councils that most dramatically illustrated its enhanced prestige and authority. Not since the fourth Council of Constantinople in 869–70 had Rome recognized any Council as having ecumenical or universal status. However, in a period of less than a century the popes were not only to summon four such Councils, but they were to be the first held in the West. Indeed, the papacy breached a further convention of the ancient Ecumenical Councils. All previous such Councils had been summoned by Roman Emperors from Constantine at Nicaea in 325 onwards. The Gregorian papacy now assumed the authority previously recognized as a uniquely imperial privilege and summoned four Councils to meet in its Lateran palace in Rome in 1123, 1139, 1179 and 1215. Not surprisingly, the surviving Roman, or by this point what has come to be called the Byzantine Emperor in Constantinople, did not accept this, as he saw it, papal usurpation of his authority. Thus no Greek bishops attended these Councils and the Orthodox Churches of the East do not recognize their ecumenical status to this day.

Be that as it may, by the time of the fourth Lateran Council in 1215 over 400 Western bishops, along with hundreds of other churchmen, did attend, to make it the greatest gathering of its kind since the fall of the Roman Empire in the West. Nothing could speak more eloquently of the virtually unchallenged supremacy of the papacy within Latin Christendom by the early thirteenth century.

It was not only popes themselves, however, who travelled across Europe and summoned Councils. This increasingly became the function of the papacy's main representatives to the local churches, the legates. Again, bare statistics begin to point to the increasing importance of this instrument of papal authority. During the 150 years from 900 to 1050 we only know of about 50 papal legations. However, in one later 30-year period alone, from 1130 to 1159, no fewer than 109 legations left Rome for various parts of Western Christendom.[15] At the same time these travelling legations were also supplemented by permanent legates, normally senior archbishops, such as Gebhard of Constance, the permanent legate in Germany from 1089 to 1110, or Bernard of Toledo, permanent legate to the Spanish kingdoms from 1096.

These legates, of whichever kind, had a variety of functions. One of the most important of these was again the promotion of reform. They could summon local Councils to pass reforming decrees, depose bishops opposed to the reform agenda, or promote those who accepted it. At the same time they could straddle the religious and the political worlds; for instance no fewer than nine legates were employed by the papacy at various points in the negotiations surrounding the dispute between King Henry II of England and his Archbishop of Canterbury, Thomas Becket, leading up to the latter's martyrdom in 1170. Or they could perform purely political functions, such as fostering alliances with sovereigns, or others like the Lombard League of Italian cities in the mid-twelfth century, a grouping favourable to the papal cause; or they could be employed countering alliances less well disposed to the successors of St Peter. They could organize holy wars, such as those against the Muslim princes in Spain, or accompany Crusades, as Adhemar, Bishop of Le Puy, did for the First Crusade in the 1090s. Not surprisingly, therefore, legates became in the twelfth century 'the foremost executors of papal policy'. Even the level of resistance they sometimes encountered from local prelates indignant at this intrusion into their own spheres of activity, and the denunciations of them for avarice when they successfully collected taxes due to the papacy, but often years in arrears, demonstrated their very effectiveness. If they had been ineffective servants of St Peter, there would have been nothing to complain about.[16]

All of these spheres of increasing papal activity and influence in the Church themselves would have been impossible, however, without a correspondingly significant expansion of the machinery of government in Rome itself. Just as all medieval monarchs ruled and governed through a *Curia Regis*, or Royal Court, so too the papacy based its government of the Church on the papal court, its own curia. And at the heart of this were the enhanced roles adopted by the cardinals from the mid-eleventh century.

The word 'cardinal' was derived from the Latin *cardo*, meaning a hinge on a door. Divided into three orders of cardinal bishops, priests and deacons, the first of these probably dating back to the seventh century, their initial functions were liturgical, assisting with the services in the Lateran basilica. By the central Middle Ages there were seven cardinal bishops from the dioceses around Rome, 28 cardinal priests who presided over titular churches within Rome, and eighteen cardinal deacons. From the mid-eleventh century, however, their functions steadily shifted from liturgical to administrative, and by about 1100 they effectively formed the government of the Church alongside the pope himself; by that time they had also evolved from being primarily Romans into an international body. Peter Damian in about 1065 was probably the first person to make the comparison between the cardinals and the ancient Roman senate, calling the cardinal bishops 'the spiritual senators of the universal Church', arguing that just as the ancient senate used all its skill and energy to subject the peoples of the Empire to its rule, so now the new senate should 'subject the human race to the laws of the true Emperor, Christ'.[17]

In order to achieve that, the cardinals took on ever-expanding roles inside the Roman Church. One of the first key dates in this process was 1059 when the cardinal bishops were given the theoretical monopoly of papal elections. Gradually the cardinal priests and deacons were also admitted to this electoral college, and at the third Lateran Council in 1179 it was first decreed that a candidate for the papal office required a two-thirds majority in order to achieve election. By employing a relatively large international body of electors it was hoped that undue influence in the election process by either the Roman aristocracy or a foreign power could be, if not eradicated entirely, then at least effectively neutralized. The further refinement of the two-thirds majority was to guard against the possibility of a papal schism in the case of an evenly divided electoral college.

In addition to their voting duties the cardinals also effectively ran the most important departments of the papal government. This included the crucial institution of the Consistory. This was created partly to take over the legal functions of the Synods as Rome increasingly became the legal centre of Christendom; it was the Consistory that was to try some of the most spectacu-lar cases of the Middle Ages, such as its condemnation of the teachings of Peter Abelard in 1141, and the case against the christology of Peter Lombard in 1179. The Consistory also became the body which advised the pope on a range of political matters, from the making of treaties to the deposition of kings.

Cardinals also staffed other departments such as the *Camera*, founded by Urban II following the example of the system of financial regulation instituted by the great abbey of Cluny; for any institution as substantial as the papacy the effective collection and distribution of revenues was to be of supreme impor-tance. Also the *Cancellaria* or Chancery, the secretariat in charge of the written documents issued by the curia, and the Registers which preserved an authen-tic copy of them. As such, the Chancery emerged as a powerful organ of papal propaganda, combining functions that we would now call public relations and press office along with its more formal role of issuing documents; during the reign of Innocent III, for instance, we know that it issued at least 6,000 letters. And in addition to staffing all of these departments, the cardinals also took on other occasional roles, most notably as papal legates.[19]

It is no wonder that the modern historian Bernard Hamilton has estimated that the curia grew ten-fold in size in the three centuries after 1050, as the sheer volume of business executed by the papal government expanded at a similar rate.[20] At the same time it has long been recognized that not only was there a quantitative expansion of the curia in the central Middle Ages, but also in terms of quality it remained unrivalled. Walter Ullmann claimed that the papal curia 'was infinitely better organized and had more ramifications than its royal counterparts'.[21] Its Registers and other archival material gave its access to what might be termed the longest and most substantial 'collective memory' in Christendom, a huge and sometimes vital resource in disputes with kings or local churches. Staffed by some of the best educated minds of their day, with levels of efficiency that most royal governments could only dream of, the papal curia was a potent weapon in the process of putting the theories of universal papal jurisdiction and authority into practice, and allowed the papacy and its territorial states to 'punch above their weight' in the Europe of the time.

Thus, as Eamon Duffy has noted: 'By the end of the twelfth century, the finger of the papacy lay on every living pulse in the Church.'[22] A whole range of matters which in 1000 had been the concern of local churches exclusively had by 1200 been centralized in a vastly expanded papal government in Rome. These included such things as the process of canonization; in 1000 the making of saints had been local, informal and usually involved an element of acclamation by the laity. By 1200 it was a formal legal process involving regulations for the collection and evaluation of the evidence of witnesses, and reserved exclusively to the papal government in Rome. The same was true of the process of determining the validity of relics; this was again an exclusively papal function by 1200.[23] Thus across a vast and expanding range of human activities, from high politics and international relations to the minutiae of who could marry whom, Rome was no longer a distant theory but rather a living reality for the people of Latin Christendom.

Papal Weaknesses

Without wishing to diminish the extraordinary growth and achievements of medieval papal government, at the same time those must be balanced against the equally powerful limitations inherent in it. Rome could not always get its own way, and sometimes that was for reasons entirely beyond its control.

Among these were the facts of geography. Rome might have been more and more at the centre of Latin Christendom in a spiritual or administrative sense, but it certainly was not in terms of time and space. Rome was situated on the southern fringes of Christendom and this presented a number of problems. By modern standards travel was slow and laborious in the Middle Ages; but the only means of communication, whether orally or in written form, was dependent on the speed of the fastest horse. With Rome days, if not weeks away in terms of the time it would take for messages or instructions to travel from even the nearer parts of Christendom, this could cause problems, especially if political events moved faster than Rome could react to them.

The danger for the papacy was always one of losing the initiative in often complex negotiations with or between secular rulers. Rome could be left ill-informed and its legates forced to take decisions on the spot not always subsequently approved of by the papacy. This was a problem which always beset Gregory VII in his relations with Henry IV and Germany. As H. E. J. Cowdrey has commented, Gregory often showed a 'lack of comprehension of the political and ecclesiastical realities of the German kingdom'; he was heavily dependent upon what others told him, and the accuracy and impartiality of their information.[24] Even by the thirteenth century and the much more developed system of government available by then, a pope like Innocent III could still lose control over the actions of his legates in Germany, as happened in 1200 when, without obtaining prior papal approval, they established a tribunal of princes to decide between rival claimants to the imperial throne, thus giving to mere princes the authority which Innocent believed was the sole prerogative of the pope.[25] During the Fourth Crusade of 1203–4 the breakdown of communication and control which Innocent had hoped to exercise over the expedition led to one of the most catastrophic events of medieval history; indeed, keeping Crusades on what the papacy saw as their correct course was to prove a perennial problem for it.

These problems were, in their turn, compounded by the extraordinary amount of time medieval popes were absent from Rome, whether for reasons of war and politics or papal schisms. It has been calculated that in the century from 1099 to 1198 popes were absent from Rome for more than half the time, and from 1198 to 1304 were away for two-thirds of the time. Governing a church while in exile or on the hoof clearly had its problems.[26]

Part of the reason for these protracted papal absences from Rome lay in the periodic failure of the cardinals to elect a pope acceptable to enough of them. In the century and a quarter from 1073 to 1198 there were no fewer than three papal schisms, the first initiated by the dispute between Gregory VII and Henry IV. Following the latter's second excommunication in 1080, he retaliated by promoting an anti-pope, 'Clement III' who, with a number of short-lived successors, was to perpetuate a divided papacy until 1121. Then in 1130 a disputed election led to another eight-year papal schism, and a further eighteen years of division followed the disputed election of 1159. This was the reason that the Third Lateran Council introduced the two-thirds majority system for papal elections in 1179, to try to ensure sufficiently overwhelming support for a single candidate. It certainly had the desired effect in the central Middle Ages with undisputed elections until 1378, when the system again broke down.

A divided curia could also produce governmental paralysis in other ways. One of these occurred in 1193 when the college of cardinals split over how to deal with the thorny problem of King Richard I of England, the Lionheart, then a captive of Henry VI of Germany and held to ransom. Richard was returning from the Third Crusade when he had accidentally fallen into the hands of his enemies. As a Crusader he was technically under the protection of the papacy and thus in normal circumstances could have expected the pope to issue threats of spiritual sanctions against his captors. However, a strong party of cardinals resisted that, as they were politically more in sympathy with the German sovereign, and other groups of less committed cardinals feared throwing the German Emperor into a deeper alliance with Richard's other enemy, Philip II of France, and so reducing papal influence in both kingdoms.[27]

In their role as legates the cardinals could also sometimes be as much of a hindrance as a help in advancing papal government. We have seen already how legates could make themselves, and through them the papacy, deeply unpopular when they attempted to collect papal revenues in arrears. But perhaps more fundamentally there were occasions when legates clashed openly with senior ecclesiastics in territories they had been sent to. One of the most protracted of these occurred during the pontificate of Gregory VII. Archbishop Manasses of Rheims caused almost endless problems for the pope and his legates, especially over issues of keeping ecclesiastical appointments vacant so that the archbishop could collect the revenues which reverted to him in periods of vacancy, or of uncanonical or simoniacal appointments. Finally the papal legate, Hugh of Die, excommunicated the truculent archbishop. Even after travelling to Rome to be personally reconciled by Gregory, Manasses continued as a thorn in the side of the legates by deliberately trying to evade them and deal directly with Rome.[28]

The fundamental reason why bishops like Manasses caused so many problems was that they bitterly resented what they saw as unauthorized interference in their spheres of activity. Before the middle of the eleventh century the papacy was viewed as an institution worthy of the greatest reverence, with sweeping claims, but incapable of exercising them in a realistic way. Indeed, the exercise of a more centralized form of Church government was generally seen both as unnecessary and certainly undesirable. Bishops and abbots were part of the political élite, often directly related to the nobility, and in a few cases to royal houses themselves. Most shared the common assumptions of that élite, namely that the local and the noble were the best people to understand and govern the affairs of their churches. Secular princes were, in any case, more immediate powers than distant Rome. And when that remote city began to seek a more practical role in governing the universal Church, some bishops saw that as the exercise of sweeping claims that were themselves novel, unprecedented or even sacrilegious. The freedom and liberty of the papacy that was claimed by the reformers seemed, in the way it was sometimes exercised, more like tyranny to others. The attitude of many bishops in the years before the papal reform movement began was well illustrated by a bishop of Constance who, in 1033, publicly burnt a papal bull that had arrived in his diocese.[29] Thus some historians such as Walter Ullmann have seen episcopal opposition to the full deployment of the principles of papal government as more fundamental an obstacle than either royal or imperial displeasure.[30]

But it was also clear that however real the disquiet caused in the ranks of the episcopate by a revived and renewed papacy, one of the fundamental weaknesses of that papacy was political. To have withdrawn from any political involvement was not an option, however, for the Gregorian papacy; to be engaged with the medieval world meant having a political role in it, and any attempt to remain above the political sway would have made no sense whatsoever to that medieval world. The idea that the papacy's spiritual prestige would have been tarnished by the employment of temporal means to achieve its religious ends is a very modern notion, and one that, again, would have been meaningless at the time.[31] For good or ill the papacy had to pursue as much a political as spiritual agenda. It was an impossibility for the popes to have existed solely as religious leaders even in their immediate territorial sphere.[32] Indeed, the very existence of a spiritual role within Latin Christendom was, it could be argued, itself dependent on political and military means. Given the condition of the feudal world in which it found itself, the forging of things like a territorial state of its own, and alliances with powerful protectors, were actually essential means of ensuring its spiritual independence.

The problem was that both of those goals, however desirable, were notoriously difficult to achieve. For one thing the Papal States, which had existed as a territorial entity since the donation of Pepin in the eighth century, were extremely unstable. Even in theory they were never substantial enough to be counted as more than a small- to medium-sized state, certainly not by themselves generating the financial or military strength needed to protect the papacy unaided from potential enemies like the Holy Roman Emperor. On top of that, they were periodically subjected to invasion by more substantial military forces both to the north and south of them, and thus subsequently condemned to fluctuating frontiers. The long papal absences from Rome led to the further deterioration of the pope's control over his own feudal vassals within the States, and to a virtual collapse of his capacity at times to even gather taxes due to him from his own territories. It was not until Innocent III instituted a wholesale reconstruction of the administrative and financial bases on which they were theoretically built that they could really be seen as a useful tool of papal policy.

The very fragility of the papacy as a territorial and political ruler had led it to seek the aid of more powerful external kingdoms from the time of the fall of the Western Roman Empire onwards. Initially, as we have seen, the bishops of Rome naturally turned eastwards to the surviving Emperor in Constantinople. But, as the papacy was to discover throughout its medieval history, a presumed protector could become either an actual oppressor or an extremely weak defender. The Byzantine Emperors fluctuated between both. In the eighth century this had led to the alliance with the Franks. But after the death of Charlemagne in 814 his empire rapidly disintegrated and the popes became puppets in the game of Roman aristocratic power-politics. The resurrection of the empire and the coronation of a German Emperor in 962 again proved to be a double-edged sword. However, perhaps ironically, it took decisive imperial action at the Synod of Sutri in 1046 to kick-start the papacy on the road to reform and freedom. Yet that very policy brought Gregory VII and Henry IV into open conflict. This left the papacy with one remaining external protector it could turn to: the Normans.

The Normans were descended from Viking raiders ('Northmen') who had been granted substantial lands on the north coast of France in the tenth century: the Duchy of Normandy. It was famously a later Duke, William, who sailed from his Duchy to conquer the entire kingdom of England in 1066. But other Norman raiders had also sailed south into the Mediterranean and set about conquering other possessions from the Arabs and Byzantines in Sicily and southern Italy. By 1059 they were well enough established for the papacy to enter into an alliance with them by which the papacy gave them a semblance of legitimacy for their conquests in return for a promise to protect the pope from his local opponents in central Italy. It was, indeed, the Normans who intervened to rescue Gregory VII from the Germans in 1084, and took him south with them to die as an exile in Salerno the following year.

Yet the Normans were to prove as equally unreliable as any of the papacy's other allies. Part of the reason for this lay in the very nature of their agreement. From the perspective of the papacy the south, the *Regno*, was part of the Patrimony of St Peter, and thus each Norman prince only held his lands and titles at the grace of the pope; these were definitely not hereditary rulers, but individuals who could only remain so long as they demonstrated their 'suitability', *idoneitas*, in the eyes of the pope, a combination of moral worth and political effectiveness.

But the perspective of the Norman princes was totally at variance with this. Like Duke William in England, they saw themselves as hereditary rulers of the *Regno* by right of conquest, something merely confirmed and blessed by the papacy in a way similar to the papal blessing given to William in 1066, conveyed by the papal gift of a banner of St Peter to his expedition.

This mutual misunderstanding of each other's preconceptions always brought an element of instability into the relationship. Yet so long as they had a common enemy, whether the Byzantines to the east always looking to recover their former Italian lands, or the German Emperor to the north who saw all of Italy as his natural territory, the alliance held. Indeed, from 1080 to 1127 relations between them remained generally harmonious, with Urban II spending almost one-third of his pontificate in Norman territory, and several Church Councils also being convened under their protection. A number of Norman princes were also noted for their pious furtherance of reform within their territories. Yet these periods of harmony were sometimes interrupted by violent clashes. On three occasions papal armies had been defeated by the Normans and the reigning pope subsequently held captive by them, in 1053, 1139 and 1156. The ambitions of Roger II, the Norman King of Sicily, to bring all the lands in the south under his rule, resulted in his excommunication in 1127. Then in 1189 the last Norman King, William II, died childless and his throne passed at least in theory to his heir, his aunt Constance, a daughter of Roger II. Unfortunately for the papacy she was already married to the German Emperor, Henry VI, and the prospect of a German–Sicilian union threw the papacy into a state of terror, with the nightmare scenario of potential political and military threats from north and south simultaneously. After papal attempts to promote an alternative king of Sicily failed, and the birth of an heir, Frederick, to Henry and Constance in 1197, the nightmare seemed to be materializing as a waking reality.[33]

The political problems of the papacy, however, were not just confined to the unsuitability of its allies. Even at the most exalted, theoretical level, the papacy was not alone in claiming a divine commission. German Emperors could employ their own propagandists to counter the unique and universal claims of the papacy during the Investiture Contest. One, Benzo, Bishop of Alba, in arguments reminiscent of Eusebius, saw the Roman Empire, not the Roman Church, as the ultimate expression of universalism, and thus the revived Emperors in the West were the images of God and the true regulators of ecclesiastical life. Such claims had already, of course, come under the critical scrutiny of St Augustine. However, another writer, known as the Anonymous of York, devised a more original challenge based on an alternative interpretation of such Gospel passages as Matthew chapter 16. Here, the phrase describing Peter as the rock on which the Church was to be founded, was seen as applying to all the apostles and not just Peter; and in any case, argued the Anonymous, the only true head of the Church was Christ himself. At the same time Christ was also the true king and model of kingship, and thus earthly kings were the true vicars of Christ. Ingenious as such theories were, however, ultimately they did not establish themselves in the consciousness of Christendom as firmly or widely as the papal interpretation of the text.[34]

Far more potent, however, than any theoretical challenge to papal primacy was the much more practical problem of unco-operative kings who could do much to block the reform agenda of the papacy. With some sovereigns, the papacy had to be pragmatic and settle for what it could realistically achieve. William I of England was a case in point. Here was a king sympathetic to the reform of the clergy, but who insisted on keeping a tight rein over all aspects of his kingdom, including his bishops. So William insisted on reading papal letters to them first, would not allow the Church to initiate legal proceedings against one of his barons without royal consent, and saw no need for visitations by papal legates. Yet his relations with the papacy remained cordial as Rome accepted him as the *de facto* ruler of the English church so long as he continued to favour clerical reform.[35] Strong kings like William I were always a greater problem than relatively weaker ones like the Capetian dynasty in France; with a less developed system of central government papal legates normally had an easier time in France calling Councils to promote reform.

In Germany the effectiveness of the papacy depended upon the fluctuating fortunes of its kings. As an elected rather than hereditary monarchy, the German sovereigns could periodically face challenges from rival claimants, in an ironically similar way to the papacy itself. So long as German kings faced realistic rivals to their throne they needed the papacy as an ally and were thus more amenable to its demands. But usually no sooner had they achieved unchallenged authority than they became much more difficult to deal with so far as the papacy was concerned. This was not only the case with Henry IV and Gregory VII, but also later with Otto IV and Innocent III. Powerful German kings like Frederick I Barbarossa (Red Beard) who reigned from 1152 to 1190, could often defy Rome for years; only his military defeat at the hands of the Lombard League of Italian cities in 1176 forced him to be more amenable. Indeed, for a decade alliance with the League was the cornerstone of papal diplomacy and its key to political survival.[36]

At an even more basic level as well kings could prove to be deeply entrenched in their control of their churches. In the Spanish kingdom of Leon, for instance, something like one-third of the bishops were normally former royal servants. So long as they were pious and open to the ideas of reform this was no major obstacle; but if their royal loyalties came into conflict with their papal ones, then that could spell trouble.[37] And so far as the Scandinavian kingdoms were concerned, geographical remoteness from Rome meant that effectively even a pope like Gregory VII could be no more than reactive in his relations with them.[38]

However much the political fortunes of the medieval papacy fluctuated between frustration and success, there was one constant weakness that remained to inhibit the papacy no matter who sat on the throne of St Peter, and that was financial. In theory papal revenues were extensive. They consisted of taxes from the Papal States; special taxes such as Peter's Pence, consisting of one penny every year for every house of a freeman in England, a system subsequently extended to Poland and Scandinavia; fees for the vast volume of legal work carried out in Rome; the offerings of pilgrims at the great basilicas in Rome; and a series of special gifts or donations from abbeys, cathedrals or kings. However, in practice such revenues were extremely uncertain and irregular. The problem with taxation was collection. In an age long before a modern revenue system, all governments were dependent on local agents who collected taxes on their behalf, taking a commission from the proceeds. For centuries such tax-collectors had been understandably unpopular, like St Matthew who collected taxes for the Roman occupiers of Palestine (Matt. 10:3). However, most kings were able at the least to threaten and punish their own dishonest tax-collectors. Not so the papacy. Geographical distance or the lack of the means of effective coercion meant that it was always at the mercy of its own agents, or indeed of greedy kings and nobles. Thus normally only a fraction of the taxes due to it ever reached the eternal city. The same was largely true also for the legal expenses paid by litigants in Rome. Much stuck to the fingers of officials before it ever reached the papal treasury.

The medieval papacy was thus almost always short of money. The stream of satires criticizing the avariciousness of the papacy that continued over the generations was paradoxically symptomatic of a poor rather than a wealthy institution, taking desperate measures to extract what was owed to it. Papal legates were thus not only the butt of vicious jokes for attempting to claw back local taxes sometimes years in arrears, but also because the sometimes considerable expenses of their missions had to be found by the local churches as well. All this made for a papacy with nothing remotely comparable to a king like Frederick Barbarossa in terms of material resources, and which had led some historians to argue that the greatest long-term weakness of the medieval papacy was financial.[39]

The Crusades

Nowhere were both the achievements and the limitations of the Gregorian papacy more vividly exposed than in the phenomenon we know as the Crusades. The origins of them were long in duration and diverse in nature, and their subsequent course protracted and tortuous. Obviously the long-term trigger that eventually set them into motion was the military conquest of the Arabs who carried with them their new religion of Islam, taking Jerusalem from the Byzantines in 638. By the middle of the eighth century a vast swathe of Islamic conquests stretched from Iran in the east to Spain in the west. In the centuries that followed, the religious and cultural unity of this Empire was accompanied by political fracture, and by the eleventh century the Islamic world presented a kaleidoscope of often rival states.

Into this complex picture erupted the Seljuk Turks, themselves newly converted to Islam, capturing large parts of the Middle East and threatening the eastern borders of the Byzantine Empire in its provinces in Anatolia, roughly equivalent to modern Turkey. Stung by a series of raids into its richest and most populous provinces, the Byzantines resolved to crush the Seljuks once and for all. To that end they assembled a great army which captured the fortress of Manzikert near Lake Van on the eastern extremities of Anatolia. Subsequently surrounded by a vast horde of Seljuks, the Byzantines now saw an opportunity to deal them a mortal blow. But instead of the defeat of the Seljuks, what followed was perhaps the single most disastrous day in Byzantine military history. The day of 26 August 1071 witnessed not only a catastrophic defeat for the Byzantine army but also the capture of its Emperor on the battlefield along with the slaughter of most of his finest troops as the Imperial Guard fought to defend him. This left the eastern provinces wide open, and in the following years the triumphant Seljuks raided virtually at will across Anatolia, subduing it to their political as well as military control.

What could the Byzantines now do? Defeated in the east by the Seljuks and in the west by the Normans, the shrunken Empire was incapable of launching a counter-offensive exclusively from its own depleted resources. Thus in 1074 letters arrived in Rome from the Emperor in Constantinople asking for the aid of the Pope, Gregory VII, in persuading Western kings or their soldiers to travel east to aid the wounded Christian empire. Nothing spoke so starkly of the reversal in fortunes between these two institutions as this request. And in it Gregory immediately perceived an opportunity to use this as a lever to assert once and for all the jurisdictional supremacy of the papacy over Eastern as well as Western Christendom. He wrote to Henry IV proposing that the pope himself would lead a military expedition to the east while the German king would be left as guardian of the Church in the West during his absence. The events that blossomed into the Investiture Contest overtook Gregory, however, and nothing came of the scheme. The letters went into the archives and the long memory of the curia.

Behind Gregory's thinking lay the still unresolved dispute that had arisen twenty years earlier between Rome and Constantinople. Without rehearsing the long and complex events that marked the history of the relationship between these two Patriarchates, they ultimately came to revolve in essence around two issues: one was the legitimate extent of papal authority, and the other the West's addition to the Nicene Creed. This was the phrase *et filioque*, 'and the Son', after the declaration that the Holy Spirit proceeded from the Father in the original wording, thus making a double procession of the Spirit

from the Father and the Son. These additional words had been for generations, and remain today, a bone of contention between the two churches.

But more immediately in the early 1050s the Latin use of unleavened bread
in the Eucharist had been the cause of the closure of their churches in Constantinople. In 1054 Cardinal Humbert had headed a legantine mission to
negotiate terms for their reopening. The diplomacy quickly became engulfed
in Byzantine politics and an ongoing struggle between the Emperor and his
Patriarch, and ended with Humbert and the Patriarch hurling mutual excommunications at each other. The full extent and meaning of these actions has
long been debated by historians and theologians. Were the excommunications
exclusively personal to the two individuals and their immediate entourages; or
were these anathemas directed to the two churches as institutions, thus constituting a schism? This date of 1054 is frequently cited as the precise moment in
which generations of argument, hostility and mutual incomprehension finally
resulted in an irrevocable division unhealed to this day, and as such constitutes
one of the more negative outcomes of the revived papacy.

On closer inspection, perhaps not surprisingly, it is really not quite so clear-
cut. Half a century ago Sir Steven Runciman challenged this notion, and
interpreted the events of 1054 as exclusively personal to the participants, and
argued that subsequently there was a healing process which meant that shortly
after Urban II ascended the papal throne in 1088 in practice the schism of
1054 was over.[40] The scholar who has re-trodden the ground most recently
is Henry Chadwick, and he has come to conclusions not dissimilar to
Runciman's, seeing the excommunications of 1054 as personal not institutional, and pointing out that at the time other Eastern churchmen did not
interpret it as an institutional schism either. In any case the excommunications
were technically invalid because delivered after the death of the pope, with
whom Humbert's legantine authority had also deceased.[41]

Be that as it may, there remained a long legacy of distrust between the two
churches. With the humiliating military defeat of the Byzantines at Manzikert,
and their appeal to the West, Gregory saw his moment. While he was frustrated in his efforts to exploit this, later popes retained the submission of the
Greek East to papal claims of supremacy as one of the goals of the Gregorian
reform. But another twenty years were to pass before Urban II saw an opportunity to bring this about.

The Crusades, however, had as many, if not more, Western origins as they
did Eastern. The virtually endemic warfare between lords at almost all levels of
the feudal system, for instance, produced some original ideas for its contain-
ment and diversion in the eleventh century. Two of these were the Peace of
God and the Truce of God movements. The first originated in Aquitaine and
Burgundy about 1000 as a response to private aristocratic warfare. Bishops

would establish peace councils with the authority to excommunicate any warriors who attacked churches, robbed the clergy, or molested the poor or pilgrims. The Truce of God followed later and was more far-reaching; this involved agreements to suspend fighting on certain days or for specific periods, and were again normally negotiated by bishops. By the early decades of the reform papacy these ideas were spreading across Europe.[42]

In addition, if young noble hot-heads wished to fight, then there was one sphere where this would not only be legitimate, but also desirable. In the eighth century the Arabs had conquered almost all of the Iberian peninsula, and had established a number of Islamic states there. By the eleventh century, however, the small Christian kingdoms in the north had begun a re-conquest, a long process only completed with the capture of Grenada in 1492. But in the eleventh and twelfth centuries none of these kingdoms was strong enough to attempt this alone. They not only needed to co-operate and co-ordinate military operations with each other , but they also needed outside help. Aristocratic warriors from France, or other Christian states, perhaps landless younger sons, could find ready employment and perhaps new fiefs carved from captured Arab lands in the service of the Spanish kings. The reform papacy of the mid-eleventh century became enthusiastic in its support of these holy wars to recover former Christian territories, and encouraged foreign knights to participate in them.

For the papacy, and eventually its Canon lawyers, were evolving a theory of a just war: the conditions or circumstances which would justify a Christian using organized violence, if necessary involving killing. The Christian history of such a concept goes back to St Augustine, who himself melded ancient philosophical speculations with Christian morality. Although far from being worked out in detail by the eleventh century, certain broad outlines were emerging. For a war to be just it had to have a just cause, usually a response of self-defence to an act of aggression. It must also be undertaken by a legitimate authority such as a king. And it must have a right intention, usually meaning that war was the only means for obtaining a just peace. As the Spanish re-conquest seemed to fulfil these demands, from at least the 1060s the papacy gave it its blessing. But the just-war theory opened up one other intriguing prospect for the papacy; what if the legitimate authority summoning a host to war were not royal but papal?

The papacy obviously had in its arsenal a whole battery of other spiritual inducements and rewards. One of these was the vow. Familiar for centuries in the contexts of monasticism and marriage, a vow was a promise before God and the Church to fulfil a specific action. By attaching a vow to a military expedition it could be converted into a holy war. If, in addition, an indulgence was added, remission for the penalties of sins after confession and the

performance of a penance, the spiritual nature of holy warfare would be reinforced. Pope Alexander II had granted such an indulgence to the warriors
fighting in Spain in 1063. At the same time the families and property of
departing soldiers could be placed under the protection of the Church, with
an array of spiritual sanctions available to enforce this. Finally, if the thread of a
pilgrimage could be woven into this spiritual tapestry, a Christian practice
honoured for centuries, then it would make a very impressive picture. Perhaps
fortunately the Seljuk advance in the Middle East had reached the Holy Land
by the 1090s, and their presence there was now contested by the Fatimid
rulers of Egypt, making unarmed Christian pilgrimages dangerous.

At the same time purely secular motivations also helped to lure warriors
into the service of the Church. The Spanish re-conquest had demonstrated
the possibility of booty and even lands. The Normans had gone further and
created whole new principalities and kingdoms in the *Regno*, with the retrospective blessing of the papacy. An expedition to the Holy Land thus opened
almost limitless possibilities both for the pious and the unscrupulous to attain
glory both in this world and the next.

All that was now required was a propitious moment in which all these
elements could synthesize into a great undertaking, and, crucially, one
launched at the behest and under the guidance of the papacy. This began to
approach in 1092 with the death of Malik-Shah, the Seljuk Sultan, and the
consequent internal disintegration of Turkish unity. The Fatimids of Egypt
took the opportunity to invade Palestine in 1094. And so with the Turks
weakened and distracted, the papacy once again on good terms with him, and
the Normans quiet, the Eastern Emperor, Alexius, wrote once more to Rome
asking the pope to encourage Western soldiers to come to the aid of their
fellow Christians. The letters caught up with Urban II in 1095 as he was
holding a reforming Council at Piacenza in northern Italy.

This pope had also been having his own political successes. In 1093 he had
helped to induce Henry IV's son Conrad to rebel against his father and had
thus been able to re-enter Rome the following year, a decade after his mentor,
Gregory VII, had fled the city with the Normans. From March to November
he had been planning his next reforming Council to be held at Clermont in
France. During these months a creative fusion of ideas came together in the
pope's imagination. At the Council, King Philip I of France had his excommunication for adultery confirmed, thus removing him along with Henry IV
from any practical possibility of the leadership of a Christian expedition. The
Truce of God was approved and declared effective across Latin Christendom
for three years, thus adding a further encouragement to soldiers to go abroad
to fight. Finally, on 27 November, at a concluding open-air session of the
Council, Urban announced the papal plan for a great military expedition to

the East At the conclusion of his speech many began to cut up cloth into the shape of crosses and pin it to their clothing. Thus what we call the Crusades had begun (Document 14).

Modern historians are agreed that not only in summoning this expedition but also in the sheer scale of the response, the calling of what became the First Crusade was a triumph for the Gregorian papacy. The greatest rulers of Christendom had been pushed aside as Urban II exerted the moral leadership of his office in the most spectacular of ways. No one knows exactly how many heeded his summons, but in the weeks and months which followed Clermont, as papal legates carried the message across Europe, a series of huge armies began to gather into what became the greatest military force of the Middle Ages. When they finally converged on Constantinople in the spring of 1097 an army of at least tens of thousands, perhaps even greater, had assembled. 'No secular ruler could have done as much' and as such it was 'a demonstration of the centrality of the reformed papacy in the religious imagination of medieval Europe.' Eamon Duffy further claims that it was 'the most striking proof of the transformation of the papacy into the greatest spiritual power in Christendom'.[43] For Jonathan Riley-Smith: 'The crusades were papal instruments, the most spectacular expression of the Papal Monarchy, the armies of the Christian Republic marching in response to calls from the men who on earth represented its monarch.'[44] The significance of the Crusading movement as a measure of the strength of the medieval papacy can hardly be underestimated.

But nor too can the subsequent course of the Crusades be ignored as a measure of the limitations of the Gregorian papacy. One of the problems, as we have already seen, was maintaining papal control over distant expeditions. During the First Crusade the death of the papal legate at the siege of Antioch allowed the centrifugal forces of princely jealousy and ambition to surface. During the Second Crusade of 1147 the presence of no fewer than five legates probably contributed to its confused objectives and ignominious end. The Third Crusade of 1189–92 was effectively under the control of the three greatest sovereigns of the time of England, France and Germany. The Fourth Crusade of 1202–4 was diverted from attacking the Holy Land to besieging and sacking Constantinople, an act of sacrilegious vandalism which probably did more than any other single event of the period to intensify the rift with the Greek Orthodox East. And during the course of the thirteenth century the crusading concept was used against heretics, most spectacularly against the Albigensians of southern France, as the means to convert the pagans of the Baltic region of northern Europe, and as unambiguously political weapons against Christian opponents of the papacy such as the Emperor Frederick II. Too often the papacy lost control of the very weapon it had forged, or allowed it to be diverted into some morally dubious directions. Nothing spoke more eloquently of both the power and the impotence of the medieval papacy than the Crusades.

Inspiration or Innovation?

The Crusades were but one of the novel creations of the medieval papacy, in which long-dormant theory was now consistently put into practice. And this brings us to one of the most controversial issues in Christian history: was the expansion of papal activity across Latin Christendom a legitimate development of the Petrine office, or was it a deviation from, and distortion of, the biblical and later texts? For some modern historians the contemporary arguments about the reform agenda of the papacy was *the* great debate of the Middle Ages: 'Not since late antiquity, more than 700 years earlier, had so many Christians debated publicly about such significant religious issues. The lively debates of the reform period unleashed ideas that influenced religious life for centuries.'[45] And in essence it raised once again the old controversy about what was tradition and what custom. The distinction between the two had been raised as early as 256 by a Council in north Africa (see above, p. 29). Interestingly it was Gregory VII who revived the terminology in the eleventh century. In a letter of his, but not without its authorship open to some scholarly dispute, Gregory quoted Cyprian of Carthage as the originator of this distinction, again using the words of Jesus claiming that he was not 'custom' but 'truth' (John 14:6). Thus, argued Gregory, 'a usage which is contrary to truth must be done away with'. Obviously that opened the way for the reform programme to replace customs which had developed relatively recently with what were seen as the true originals. However, as H. E. J. Cowdrey has again insisted, Gregory's words must be interpreted within their medieval context of 'the openness of custom to revision when it became necessary to establish custom upon a firm basis of law'.[46] Thus, as I. S. Robinson has observed: 'It was to uproot pernicious customs which threatened the purity of the Church that the pope exercised his right to make laws. According to Gregory VII, therefore, papal legislation had the strictly limited purpose of restoring the primitive purity and freedom of the Church.'[47] Or as a later pope, Innocent II (1130–43) was to write in 1139, taking up the theme of John 21:16–17 where Jesus commanded Peter to feed his sheep: 'The holy Roman Church, who . . . judges not only earthly but also heavenly things, is accustomed, like an affectionate mother, to fill her sons with the food of divine law and adorn them with various prerogatives.'[48]

Perhaps the most controversial document to originate from the period of the Gregorian papacy was the so-called *Dictatus Papae*, the Dictations of the Popes, compiled by Gregory VII and inserted into his official Register between documents dated 3 and 5 March 1075 (Document 15). These 27 short theses have been viewed in a variety of ways by modern historians. Some have seen them as a set of proposed chapter headings for a Canonical collection; others as a programmatic declaration encapsulating the essence of Gregorianism and as such an epoch-making expression of the concept of universal papal authority.[49] Others again have argued that while they represented nothing but wishful thinking in Gregory's day, by 1200 they had become reality.[50]

Gregory's most recent biographer H. E. J. Cowdrey is, however, rather more circumspect. He points out that the *Dictatus Papae* was an entirely private document, never in any sense published, subsequently unnoticed and unused even by Gregory himself, and only rarely cited in future Canon law collections. At best the document represented only an interim stage in the evolution of Gregory's thought and not his final position, which was better represented by the letters of the final years of his pontificate. Above all, the *Dictatus Papae* were backward-looking, 'Gregory's own attempt to sketch out headings under which ancient material might be sought, assessed, and arranged.' As such it was also exploratory and experimental; as Cowdrey points out, several of the theses, especially numbers two, eleven and twelve, would have been very hard to demonstrate from Canonical tradition. He also rejects most of the conventional explanations of the circumstances of its composition, and argues that it 'remains an enigma'.[51]

The *Dictatus Papae* does offer one vital clue, however, to the sources of inspiration for the claims of papal reformers: they came from a particular interpretation of Christian tradition. Gregory and others had a vision of the continuity of tradition from scripture, through those early Christian apologists and theologians we call the Fathers, and onwards through the first Councils down to his own day. Thus he had a purpose, 'upholding the law as it had come down to him from an immemorial past as a timeless whole, but which had sometimes been obscured or overlaid by neglect or error'.[52] There was thus an element of rediscovery involved in the process.

But at the same time there was equally a sense of that in its turn inspiring innovation: 'he also claimed authority to devise new means of implementing what old law sought to achieve'.[53] So one of the great models from the past that the medieval reformers often pointed to was the description of the first years of the Church in Jerusalem at the time of the apostles and recorded in Acts. Thus a passage such as Acts 4:32 describing the ownership of property in common could be interpreted by the reformers as the ideal for contemporary clergy, whether religious or secular. As Peter Damian wrote to Pope Gregory VI (1045–6): 'Let the golden age of the apostles be renewed and, under your presidency, let the Church's discipline blossom anew.'[54]

1. Cistercian Abbey (Fountains)

2. Folio from St John's Gospel, facsimile of Codex Sinaiticus, fourth century AD

Published by the Clarendon Press, Oxford, vol. 1 by Bible Society, London

The Bridgeman Art Library

3. View of the Roman Forum by Adeele, Jodocus Sebasiaen (1797–1855)
Private Collection/© Gavin Graham Gallery, London/The Bridgeman Art Library

4. Christ Enthroned surrounded by the Apostles and Saints Pudentiana and
Praxedis, in the Apse (mosaic) (b/w photo) by Paleo-Christian (fourth century)
Santa Pudenziana, Rome, Italy

Alinari/The Bridgeman Art Library

5. The Dream of Innocent III, 1297–99 (fresco) by Giotto di Bondone
(c.1266–1337) San Francesco, Upper Church, Assisi, Italy

Giraudon/The Bridgeman Art Library

6. Ecstasy of StTheresa (marble) by Bernini, Giovanni Lorenzo (1598–1680)
Santa Maria della Vittoria, Rome, Italy

7. Aerial view of the Greek-cross basilica, Piazza San Pietro and the surrounding Vatican City (photo)

St Peter's, Vatican, Rome, Italy/Alinari/The Bridgeman Art Library

8. Interior view of the church (photo) by Arnolfo di Cambio (c.1245–1310)
Santa Croce, Florence, Italy

The Bridgeman Art Library

9. John Wyclif (c.1330–84) (engraving) by English School (nineteenth century)
Private Collection/Ken Welsh/The Bridgeman Art Library

10. Portrait of John Calvin (1509–64) (oil on canvas) by Titian (Tiziano Vecellio)
(c.1488–1576)
The Reformed Church of France, Paris, France/Lauros /Giraudon/The Bridgeman Art Library

11. Organ panel depicting The Sitting of the Council of Trent in Trent Cathedral on 3 and 4 December 1565, 1703 (oil on panel) by Dorigati, Niccolo (1662–1750)

Museo Diocesano Tridentino, Trent, Italy/The Bridgeman Art Library

The Stake, plate 13 from 'The Miseries and Misfortunes of War', engraved by Israel Henriet (c.1590–1661) 1633 (engraving)

(b/w by Callot, Jacques (1592–1635) (after)

Thus on one level the reformers were deeply conservative, going back to search the scriptures, the Fathers and the Councils for contemporary authority. So, for instance, Canon 22 of the Fourth Council of Constantinople in 869–70 was quoted by Gregory VII for its prohibition of lay involvement in the election or promotion of a bishop and thus in defence of his policy of forbidding lay investiture.[55] But, as Brian Tierney has pointed out: 'It is no very uncommon paradox in western history that the literal application by would-be reformers of half-understood old texts from a different historical epoch can have revolutionary implications for their own times.' From secular history he cites the example of English Parliamentarians in the seventeenth century quoting medieval precedents in their controversies with the Stuart kings. From this he concludes: 'However conservative the eleventh-century reformers intended to be, the inevitable result of their activities was not to re-establish an old order of things but to bring a new order into existence.' This was true from Canon law to the Crusades.[56]

For the popes themselves, the bedrock of their authority to do so rested upon their personal identification with St Peter himself, of whom each pope in his turn was the direct successor. Each new pope began his reign with a profession of faith to the great apostle, thus establishing this intimate link. In that, the often quoted personal identification of a pope like Gregory VII with Peter is unusual only in the intensity and not the fact of this intimate relationship.[57] Guardians of the earthly relics of Peter and Paul, the integrity of the faith of the apostles passed to each new pope, an integrity of faith itself guaranteed by Roman fidelity to the teachings of the scriptures, the Ecumenical Councils, and to the continuous stream of pronouncements of past popes. Only through this particular apostolic succession of faith did the contemporary Roman Church gain direct access to the promises and gifts bestowed upon it by Christ himself, and thus through that particular church to all the churches of Christendom in communion with Rome.

Yet the Petrine office was seen by many popes more as a gift to the Church than as a means to dominate it. Jesus had commanded Peter not only to strengthen his brethren but also to feed them, as Innocent II stressed in his letter quoted above. Pope Innocent III took up this theme in a sermon, possibly delivered at his installation as pope in 1198, on the words of Jesus as recorded in Matthew 24:45: 'Who then is the faithful and wise slave, whom his master has put in charge of his household, to give the other slaves their allowance of food at the proper time?' Innocent was clear that he was that faithful slave or servant, again echoing the Christian concept of the hierarchy of service and the words of Gregory I in calling himself the servant of the servants of God. In Innocent's own words: 'Now you see what kind of servant he is who commands the household, truly the vicar of Jesus Christ, the successor of Peter, Anointed of the Lord, God of the Pharaohs, who is the mediator between God and man, placed below God but above men, who is less than God, but greater than man.' Innocent's modern biographer, Helene Tillman, has pointed out that unless seen in their right context this sentence, especially its second half, could easily be misunderstood. The very authority and exaltation of the Petrine office depended, argued Innocent, on the simultaneous abasement of its holder as a servant or slave of his master, Jesus Christ.[58]

It was on this basis as the loving servant who feeds his Lord's household, as the pastor whose faith cannot fail, and the rock upon which the Church itself is built, all derived from the words of Jesus himself in the Gospels, that the Gregorian papacy saw itself as the natural leader of biblically inspired reform. In other words, what appeared to be innovations in the expansion of papal government in the central Middle Ages were in fact nothing more than Christian traditions rightly understood and put into practice after long ages of neglect. Papal monarchy and ecclesiastical renewal were thus the two sides of the same coin.

Yet, as we have seen, there were those both at the time and subsequently who disagreed with this justification for the expansion of papal power. From the time of Gregory VII himself some objected that he was preaching novelties unprecedented in Christian history: 'It was unprecedented for a pope to use the power of binding and loosing to depose a king and absolve his vassals from their fealty to him.'[59] Gregory retorted that there was a precedent, the papal sanction for the removal of the last Merovingian king of France and his replacement by Pepin in 751. At the same time Gregory also argued that kings must in addition be judged by their usefulness and suitability on moral as well as political grounds.[60] Was this, then, a legitimate reinterpretation of the powers of binding and loosing entrusted to Peter by Jesus in Matthew chapter 16, the exploitation of ancient ideas in new ways because of the changing demands of different times?

The same could be said of the papal alliance with the monasteries. The Council of Chalcedon in 451 had made monks subject to episcopal oversight, part of that clear campaign in the early Church to assimilate the enthusiasm of the ascetics into the hierarchical institution. So was the placing of so many religious houses under the protection of St Peter, effectively the papacy, an act of disloyalty to one of those very Ecumenical Councils the papacy claimed to champion? As I. S. Robinson has commented:

> The role of the religious in the service of the papacy, their special relationship with St Peter, was completely at odds with the norms of ancient Canon law, as expressed in the Council of Chalcedon. There could be no more striking demonstration of the pope's powers 'to make new laws'

– to adapt existing institutions to the changing needs of the Church – than the papal alliance with the religious orders.[61]

Here was the essence of the issue. To what extent was it legitimate for the papacy to adapt ancient ideas or practices to the needs of the contemporary Church? And at what point did inspired adaptation become outright, and unauthorized, innovation? Their defence of their adoption of papal protection, argued the monks of the great abbey of Cluny in Burgundy, was that they were not contravening the Canons of Chalcedon as they had put themselves under the authority of a bishop, and that the greatest one possible. Popes like Gregory VII also argued that papal protection was essential to defend reformed monasteries from the malice or incompetence of unsympathetic diocesan bishops. In whatever way it was to be judged, however, direct papal protection of literally thousands of religious houses did undermine local episcopal authority.[62]

While the Gregorian papacy had largely won most of the arguments by about 1250, critics had not been entirely silenced. Once the papacy as an institution weakened again in the fourteenth century, those criticisms came back to the surface, and questioned whether or not 'the Christian Church took a disastrous turn when it permitted one of its ministers to elevate himself to the position of an emperor'.[63] Such questions, and many others like them, were to be asked again in the sixteenth century when reform was to be once more a vital issue for Christians. Modern historians, however, must remain silent in the face of such issues. It is not their function to offer answers to such speculative questions, but only to inform the debate. But what history can say, in the words of one of its modern practitioners, is that: 'Few people in European history have had as much impact on their world with as few material resources, as have able popes.'[64]

Suggested Further Reading

In addition to the general works mentioned in the previous chapter, among the more specialist works on the papacy of the central Middle Ages the one by I. S. Robinson stands out. Focusing on the papacy as an institution and its emergence as a powerful political force, *The Papacy 1073–1198:Continuity and Innovation* (Cambridge University Press, 1990) may be very detailed and scholarly, but it is also highly readable. Logically arranged into sections, it is easy to follow its train of thought. It is based on a vast number of original sources as well as the works of other modern historians, and offers some new and refreshing interpretations.

Rather older, written in a lofty style, and massively scholarly, *The Growth of Papal Government in the Middle Ages: A Study in the Ideological Relation of Clerical to Lay Power* by Walter Ullmann was first published by Methuen in 1955, with a final revised third edition in 1970. As the title implies, it deals with the evolution of ideas, and can appear rather detached from concrete events. Some of the arguments now seem both rather dated and quite sweeping in their scope, but in its day it was a pioneering work. Unfortunately it was also written in an age when an author like Ullmann could assume a working knowledge of Latin on the part of his readers; don't expect him to make life easy by translating.

Also by I. S. Robinson is *Authority and Resistance in the Investiture Contest: The Polemical Literature of the Late Eleventh Century* (Manchester University Press, 1978). It is a detailed investigation of the propaganda of the period in which it is possible to see through a window into the thought-world of the protagonists, one so different from our own. Massively scholarly, but a surprisingly easy read. Also on this subject is Brian Tierney, *The Crisis of Church and State 1050–1300* (Prentice-Hall Inc., 1964). Essentially a collection of documents preceded by a series of short introductory commentaries. Some of the interpretations are now rather dated.

Pope Innocent III has received attention from a number of biographers. Unfortunately there is not one as magisterial as that of Gregory VII by H. E. J. Cowdrey. However, a good introduction to this other towering figure of the medieval papacy is by Jane Sayers, *Innocent III: Leader of Europe 1198–1216* (Longman, 1994). Well packaged into manageable chunks and an easy read, it can sometimes lack depth and detail, but that is to be expected given its relatively short length. More substantial and very up-to-date is John C. Moore, *Pope Innocent III (1160/61–1216): To Root Up and to Plant* (Brill, 2003). Despite its somewhat curious title it is a very scholarly book, based on Innocent's own Registers, and with lots of substantial quotations. It is written in an attractive and lively style, and chronological rather than thematic in arrangement. This can lead to some repetition, and the dictates of chronology can overwhelm the analysis. However, the final chapter of evaluation is thoughtful and provocative.

The book that is still regarded as the most authoritative interpretation of Innocent III is the one by Helene Tillmann, *Pope Innocent III*. Originally published in German in 1954, it has been translated into English and published by the North-Holland Publishing Company in 1980. It is rather dated in style, and frankly hampered by an awful translation by Walter Sax, veering between tenses within a single paragraph and with some very inelegant expressions. We are in urgent need of a new standard Life of this great pope.

James M. Powell has edited a collection of essays on Innocent III, *Innocent III: Vicar of Christ or Lord of the World?* (The Catholic University of America Press, expanded edition, 1994). Dating from the 1850s to the 1980s in origin, some of these essays are more useful than others, as is to be expected in such an undertaking. But they do give a flavour of non-English scholarship, and the editor's introductory essay is excellent, well worth reading just for itself. J. C. Moore has also edited another, more modern collection, covering a wide variety of aspects of Innocent III, some rather esoteric in nature, and entitled *Innocent III and his World* (Ashgate, 1999).

For the Crusades there is an excellent short introduction by a leading scholar in the field, Jonathan Riley-Smith, *What Were the Crusades?* (Palgrave, second edition, 1992). For a more substantial (500 pages) single volume the French historian Jean Richard, *The Crusades c. 1071–c. 1291* (Cambridge University Press, 1999) would be a scholarly but approachable work, well translated by Jean Birrell. The modern classic remains the three-volume set by Steven Runciman, *A History of the Crusades*, first published by Cambridge University Press in the 1950s but frequently reissued since then. Although now somewhat dated in certain aspects, it remains a magnificent read.

7

The Enthusiasts

All of them were filled with the Holy Spirit. (Acts 2:4)

For many centuries the port of Dover has been one of the main entry points into England and, as such, it has frequently witnessed the arrival of some strange, exotic or suspicious-looking travellers. One such group stepped off a boat from France on 10 September 1224. This party consisted of nine men, dressed only in patched, frayed and threadbare tunics held together with cords around their waists, and all of them barefoot and penniless. They would undoubtedly have attracted attention, and quite possibly some hostility. Who were they?

They did not look like respectable monks in flowing habits, riding on horses and paying good money for their food and lodging. These men walked on bare feet and did what no monk would consider it seemly to do: they begged for their bread and a roof over their heads. In that fashion they made their way across Kent to their first destination, the great cathedral city of Canterbury. And as they proceeded they occasionally halted in market squares to preach the gospel of Christ to all who would listen. Itinerant and unauthorized preaching, combined with begging, aroused deep fears of the wandering heretics who had afflicted Latin Christendom for decades. Passing through London, where they deposited some of their number, the remaining ones continued their journey until they reached their final destination, the nascent university town of Oxford.

For this small, eccentric group of men were the first lappings of a great tide that had been spreading out from central Italy for several years and had now at last reached the shores of distant England. They were, in fact, the first Franciscans to set foot on its soil; hundreds more were to follow in the coming decades. Their journey from Dover to Oxford both heralded and symbolized a number of transformations that had affected both Church and society in the previous generations.

Starting about 1000 the West had begun its slow, painful recovery from the multiple shocks of the fall of Rome and the barbarian invasions. As the last of those destructive marauders, the Vikings, began to settle as neighbours rather than plunderers and to accept the faith of their former victims, Europe began to recover economically, socially and demographically from the long series of disruptions that had begun in the fifth century. The population began to grow again, new villages were planted in the countryside, towns and cities expanded even faster, and with them trade and commerce began to revive and flourish once again. Gold and silver coins once more appeared and wealth began to multiply.

By 1200 the West was experiencing a prosperity unknown for centuries. The new urban merchants, bankers and manufacturers could afford to educate their sons in the classical heritage of Greece and Rome. And with this new mobility, geographical and social, this rising wealth and expanding education, both feudalism and the Church that in part reflected it, were increasingly questioned and challenged. In 1176 a group of northern Italian cities, the members of the Lombard League, had defeated the Emperor Frederick Barbarossa in battle. But it was not only feudal armies that were crumbling before this new urban reality; so too were many of the old religious assumptions. The stable world of royal court and monastic cloister were both under siege. Across Europe in the course of the twelfth century small but intense movements of enthusiastic religious protest led by the urban laity were presenting both Church and state with escalating problems.

Should they be combated or contained, or should their message of dynamic enthusiasm be embraced? The Church of the central Middle Ages in the end adopted a mixture of both methods, with Inquisition and Crusade brought to bear upon them on one side, while on the other, popes led by the example of Innocent III began the process of reconciliation and assimilation that was to culminate with the new Orders of Mendicant, or begging, friars led by the Franciscans and the Dominicans. Here was a new type of asceticism tuned to the needs and demands of a sophisticated and literate laity, urban and educated, questioning and open to new ideas. Radical poverty, impassioned preaching, and finally the conquest of the new learning itself in the first universities made the friars the perfect instruments in the reconciliation of a new world with an old faith.

But at some moments, and in a few places, it had been touch-and-go whether or not orthodox Christianity in its Latin version would survive the onslaught. In the end, though, the Church and its new friars were able to capture and then inject this lay spirituality into the bloodstream of Western Christianity, renewing and rejuvenating it and avoiding the prospect of wholesale division.

The New Monasticism

The early Church had successfully tamed the ascetic enthusiasms of some of its members, institutionalizing them into the system of monasticism, firmly under the supervision of the episcopate. It had been one of the greatest examples of the process of integrating the charismatic inspiration of individuals and minorities within an enfolding hierarchic organization in a mutually fruitful way. In the five centuries following the fall of Rome in the West it was the *scriptoria*, the writing rooms, of these monasteries where the painstaking task of copying helped to preserve so much, if far from all, of the heritage of the classical past. At the same time, slowly but surely, it was the Rule of St Benedict, first composed in Italy in the 540s, that became the crucial document governing the lives of virtually all the monks in the West. About the length of an MA dissertation, it was to become 'one of the central statements of Christian living', an attempt to set out in an ordered and codified form the main tenets of the gospel (Document 16).[1]

It was Charlemagne and his successors in the ninth century, for instance, with the help of the abbot Benedict of Aniane (*c.* 750–821) who began the process of standardizing monastic life within their realms around this sixth century Rule. By about 1000 they had been so successful that virtually all monks in the West, with the addition of local customs, followed the life prescribed in the Rule of St Benedict. Yet to use words like 'Benedictine', let alone 'Benedictine Order', would be quite anachronistic. Benedict himself had absolutely no vision of those later concepts and his Rule was designed for a single, self-governing community. And that was how most monks lived for most of those centuries.

But during the course of those same centuries Europe also became more and more organized on a feudal basis, and monasticism adapted to this new social and political order. It was not only at the most visible level of the ownership of vast tracts of land worked by dependent serfs and owing the feudal duties of vassals to lords that abbeys resembled the secular world. In deeper and more hidden ways they assumed much of the ethos of the world around them.

The monastic vows, for example, especially obedience to the elected abbot and stability within one community for life, were seen in feudal terms, like the vows of a vassal to his lord.[2] Indeed, the medieval world viewed stability and obedience as positive social values in themselves, reflecting a largely stable, relatively static society free from unnecessary innovations in which such values could be passed on timelessly from one generation to another.[3] The very architecture of the great abbeys reflected the eternal and the timeless.[4] At the same time the vow of poverty was not then understood in the predominantly economic sense familiar to the modern world. In the Middle Ages it meant primarily a sense of powerlessness, and so too was capable of a feudal interpretation in the sense of one individual dependent upon another in a hierarchically ordered society, whether of vassal to lord or monk to abbot.[5] Even the spiritual life of monks was to some extent a reflection of secular society. They were seen as the spiritual warriors of Christendom, defending its borders and those of its constituent kingdoms as really as any mounted soldier with lance and shield.[6] At a more personal level, monastic communities prayed for the souls of their founders and benefactors, and their families and descendants yet unborn, not only for success in this life but also for salvation in the next.[7]

Monasticism was thus an essential part of the medieval world-view, an élite of spiritual soldiers at the apex of the Christian hierarchy, just as the kings and their nobles were in the secular sphere. They were the two sides of the same feudal coin. And as such it was not surprising that so many of the secular nobility also staffed the cloisters of the great abbeys as they did the corridors of royal palaces. The Rule of St Benedict assumed the presence of young boys in a monastic community and, before the twelfth century, it was a common practice for royal and noble houses to offer at least one of their sons to an abbey as a child oblate, entering the cloister between the ages of five and seven. One modern study has estimated the size of the French nobility at 3 per cent to 4 per cent of the total population; assuming that about 1 per cent of that total population lived in monastic communities, that would mean that one quarter to one-third of all French nobles lived under monastic vows.[8] Even if this is something of an exaggeration, it does demonstrate the clear linkages between feudal society and its nobility and monasticism.

Readjusting those links as society itself changed was to be a slow and sometimes painful process. Christianity had already successfully managed the transformation from being an alien culture to the official religion of the Roman Empire. It had then survived the fall of that Empire in the West and accomplished another transformation into the spiritual conscience of the feudal world. In that capacity it had striven to tame the wilder excesses of a warrior élite, not least in diverting some of their destructive energies into more constructive channels such as the Peace and Truce of God movements, and into the ritualized spiritual warfare of the monks. As such, medieval monasticism was, in the words of one modern historian, 'a system designed to make an autocratic government function righteously'.[9]

Now Christianity and more especially its ascetic component would have to manage a further transformation as society began to shift from a predominantly rural and feudal world into one where the values of the expanding urban centres would have to be accommodated. Monasticism would have to become as appropriate and meaningful to the new conditions as it had been to the old. As Lester K. Little has observed, a map of western Europe in 1000 would have emphasized monasteries rather than towns as centres of power, jurisdiction, communication and culture; but by the thirteenth century those centres had shifted to urban areas.[10]

One of the earliest and most significant signs of change came in 909 when Duke Willian of Aquitaine founded a new abbey at Cluny in Burgundy. In itself the fact of a great prince establishing a monastic community was certainly nothing out of the ordinary. What was novel, however, was that he effectively renounced the usual feudal rights over the house, allowing the monks a genuinely free choice in electing their abbots, free control of their lands and properties, and, most significantly of all, vesting the protection of the abbey in Saints Peter and Paul through their successor on earth, the pope. Under a series of outstanding abbots Cluny was to flourish during the tenth and eleventh centuries, and to become the centre of a network of communities across western Europe that was inspired by its early attempts at restoring Benedictine life as that had been understood by Benedict of Aniane. Further, a series of papal privileges encouraged this distinctive Cluniac form of monasticism; in 931 the pope allowed a relaxation of the vow of stability enabling other monks to leave their communities and join Cluny in search of a stricter observance, and in 1024 another privilege effectively removed Cluniac houses from local episcopal oversight, placing them under the sole supervision of the abbot of Cluny. Not surprisingly, Cluniacs became the natural allies of the Gregorian papacy in its drive to purify the clergy and free the Church from what it saw as the unwarranted interference of powerful lay nobles. Indeed, in 1088 a former prior of Cluny became pope as Urban II.

Cluny not only grew in the strength of its association with the papacy, but in many other ways as well. One was in the physical size of its buildings. Over time, three churches were built for the monks at Cluny, each one larger and more magnificent than the one it replaced, culminating in 1130 when Pope Innocent II consecrated the third church, then the largest in Latin Christendom, vaster even than St Peter's in Rome itself, and designed to serve a community of 300 monks. By that point hundreds of abbeys and priories had affiliated themselves to Cluny in some way, either by placing themselves under the direct control of the abbot of Cluny, or by copying its customs and practices while retaining their own independence. Great abbeys like Gorze near Metz, first founded in the eighth century, but then restored from 933 following the Cluniac pattern, went on to found or influence another 160 houses across Lorraine, north-west Germany and the Low Countries. The abbey of Hirsau in Swabia adopted Cluniac observances in 1079, and was at the centre of its own 'family' of 60 reformed houses. However, all of these relationships varied too much, from total control from Cluny through a series of much looser associations, for it to be described yet as an Order.

The other great expansion associated with Cluny was liturgical. The Rule of St Benedict envisaged the monastic day as one punctuated by regular communal prayer, which was to become the eight monastic offices of varying lengths and probably accounting for about one-quarter of a monk's time, the other hours being taken up by manual labour, study, meals and a variety of other administrative tasks. However, during the early Middle Ages liturgy steadily became more important and took up increasing amounts of time. The noble families who founded abbeys expected the monks to chant extra psalms especially for their spiritual benefit. And while Benedict had originally envisaged a community largely consisting of laymen, the proportion of ordained priest-monks in communities steadily grew, necessitating more chapels and altars for them to be able to say Mass, as the Eucharist was now more normally called.[11]

While Cluny was clearly 'reforming' in some aspects of its life, it certainly was not so when it came to liturgy. One of the hallmarks of Cluniac monasticism became lengthy and elaborate liturgies which, especially on feast days, could effectively take up a whole day apart from sleeping and eating. On such days a Cluniac monk could easily spend eight hours in the choir chanting and praying. Yet this itself satisfied one of the basic precepts of tenth- and eleventh-century Latin Christendom; that the world was a sinful place, and that monks formed a spiritual élite which performed an essential service in unending prayer for fallen humanity. Thus, in a sense, the more monks there were praying for longer amounts of time, the better it was for the world. However, one of the obvious casualties of this almost obsessive drive for liturgical prayer was that other ingredient of monastic life as originally conceived by Benedict: manual labour. Eventually Cluniac monks effectively abandoned that aspect of the ascetic life.[12]

Not surprisingly, as the eleventh century drew on, there was a reaction against what some began to see as the distortions introduced by Cluniacs and others into the ascetic life. The first stirrings of this were seen in a growing attraction for the life of the hermit. Modern scholars have interpreted this in a variety of ways. Brenda Bolton, for instance, sees it as a sign of dissatisfaction with the ways in which traditional monasticism had become ossified, concerned more with the form than the spirit of ascetic life, and an example of a new type of private, individual spirituality in contrast to the unrelenting communal chanting of Cluny.[13] Lester K. Little agrees that it was indeed in part a reaction against existing monastic forms, but adds another element: a rejection of, and flight from, the new urban world, back to the idealized desert of the early Egyptian hermits.[14] Whatever the motivations, the eleventh century is notable for the numbers of both individual hermits and communities, most notably in Italy at places such as Camaldoli, Fonte Avellana or

Vallombrosa, and then later in France with individuals such as Robert of Arbrissel (*c.* 1055–1117) who founded the great abbey of Fontevrault, or Stephen of Muret (*c.* 1052–1124) who founded the community of Grandmont.[15]

However, the movement that perhaps best exemplified, encapsulated and synthesized the reaction against Cluny, the flight to the desert, and the reformers' search for inspiration from apostolic times and the Rule, was the new monasticism that was to come from Cîteaux. From its original Latin name of *Cistercium* was derived what we call the Cistercians, the first distinctive type of monasticism that can be identified unequivocally as an Order. Its degree of centralized organization and uniformity of practice across Latin Christendom made it, in these terms, the monastic counterpart of the Gregorian papacy.

The traditional date for the foundation of the Cistercians was 1098 when a group of about twenty monks under the leadership of Robert migrated from the abbey of Moslesme to a site at Cîteaux given to them by the Viscount of Beaune. Here they initially built some wooden huts and began, like many such groups in these decades, an experiment in ascetic living, in their case to see if it was possible to observe the Rule of St Benedict with greater fidelity to its original intentions. However, we must be careful not to impose another modern concept onto them of the literal observance of a set of rules and regulations; the early Cistercians were a group of enthusiasts seeking the essence or spirit of the Rule in a way different from Cluny. Not so much a rejection of contemporary monasticism but rather a search for the basic core values of it to be found in the one great source, the Rule of St Benedict, it was but part of that broader search involving a return to the sources of the faith whether biblical, apostolic or conciliar.[16] They were searching for purity, integrity and simplicity, not an exact apeing of the written text.[17]

So what was so special about this particular experiment at Cîteaux? It revolved around the quality of monastic living and the environment in which it was conducted. First of all the Cistercians believed that such a commitment should come from the free choice of an adult. Thus they refused to accept any boy oblates, and introduced a novitiate of one year and fixed a minimum age of entry to this novitiate; in 1134 it was fifteen years, and by 1157 it had been extended further to eighteen years. Second, the Cistercians became the first monastic group to recognize and respond to the new tide of spiritual enthusiasm that was sweeping through not only the nobility but also the agrarian peasantry, as witnessed by the extraordinary level of popular response to the calling of the First Crusade in 1095.

Traditionally abbeys had always accepted the older man who had experienced a religious calling later in life, called a *conversus*. He had always been seen as a full member of the community, and even ordination and promotion had been open to him. By about 1120, however, the Cistercians were starting to alter the status of these *conversi* as they widened their recruiting net. These new Cistercian *conversi*, or lay brothers, were generally illiterate, the sons of farmers or agricultural labourers, who would never become monks in the fully developed sense of that word; they did not sing the office, they lived in separate dormitories, would never be ordained or achieve promotion, and performed a range of menial tasks. Eventually they came to occupy the western part of the cloister, and their sleeping and eating quarters were usually behind it.[18] But they were, for all that, numerous and indispensable in Cistercian abbeys. At the time of the death of abbot Aelred of Rievaulx in Yorkshire in 1167, for example, it was estimated that the full, or choir, monks totalled 140, and the *conversi* some 500.[19]

The reason for their indispensability lay in the Cistercian attitude to manual labour. Older monasteries had come to see the spiritual life almost exclusively in terms of prayer and study which had, they believed, imperishable and eternal consequences, while manual labour was seen as perishable and of no spiritual consequence. Cistercians in contrast believed that the Rule taught them that physical tasks also had a spiritual dimension.[20] In a sense the Cistercians rediscovered the spiritual dignity of manual labour. Early Cistercian abbeys would not, therefore, use the labour of serfs tied to them as their feudal lords, but insisted on restoring the element of manual labour for the whole community found in the Rule, something like six hours a day in summer and two in winter. So while the choir monks worked in the fields or at other physical tasks, there would never have been enough of them with sufficient time to ensure that their ever-growing estates could be properly managed.

The need for additional labour was supplied by the *conversi* who, in their turn, participated to some extent in the spiritual life of the community. At the same time both benefited economically, the abbey from the additional free labour, the lay brothers in the guarantee of lifelong economic security.[21] The corollary of this renewed emphasis on the spiritual quality of manual labour was a corresponding reduction in the time given to, and thus the elaboration of, the liturgy. The offices became shorter and, above all, simpler and more austere.

And this simplicity and austerity was not only to be found in the daily life of the Cistercian monks but was also reflected in the new type of environment they created for its practice. A good way to envisage that is to imagine a series of concentric circles radiating outwards from the monk himself, starting with the clothing he wore. Traditionally Western monks had come to wear habits made of woollen cloth dyed black to create a sense of uniformity; hence the popular name for Benedictines is still 'black monks'. The Cistercians, on the other hand, simplified monastic dress still further by wearing a habit which had not been dyed. In this they were not innovating but rather following the practice of many of the Italian hermits. Initially this resulted in habits of many shades of colour from grey to brown, but eventually they too standardized this by selecting only the purest and whitest fleeces for the wool from which their habits would be made, in the process becoming 'white monks'. Once again the Cistercians gave this a spiritual interpretation, arguing that white was the colour associated with angels, with the transfigured Christ, with the glory of the resurrection, with purity and with innocence. Some of their critics, on the other hand, saw it rather as an example of ostentatious and self-conscious piety.[22]

Moving outwards from his clothing the next circle surrounding the Cistercian monk was an aura of silence. This was seen as an essential part of his fidelity to the Rule, keeping silent for all of the night and much of the day as well. However, communication was sometimes essential and the Cistercians adopted and expanded the sign language already in use in other monasteries. A monk of Cluny in 1068 had produced a list of almost 300 examples of monastic sign language.[23]

And then this austerity and simplicity was carried further into the next circle, that of the architecture that surrounded the Cistercian monks. Elaboration of liturgy had itself been mirrored in the complexity of Cluniac architecture, with massively detailed carvings on the capitals of their columns, in statues, and in the ornamented gold and silver candlesticks and other furnishings of their churches. Cistercian abbeys, by contrast, aimed for simplicity. Out went the fantastic carvings of beasts and other motifs: Cistercian columns had plain capitals; there were no sculptures, no bell towers, and the simplest and plainest of furnishings in their churches.

These simplified abbeys were then sited in a new way as well. Like the hermits of the previous century the twelfth-century Cistercians looked back to an idealized conception of the Egyptian ascetics of the fourth century and, like them, sought out the desert or wilderness. Yet, interestingly, just as the desert as a concept in early monasticism should not be interpreted in a literal sense, so too with the medieval Cistercians. Although never found in urban areas or directly on major routes of communication, many Cistercian abbeys were often not that far from them. The monks wished to reduce unnecessary contacts with the outside world, not eliminate them altogether. Hence they preferred previously uncultivated land, which in any case did not bring with it established feudal practices like serfdom. But the heart of the Cistercian spirituality of the wilderness was similar to that of the Egyptian desert hermits and monks; it was more interior than exterior. The Cistercian monk made his heart, his inmost being, a place of emptiness and desolation so that it could be filled by the love of God. Thus the Cistercian wilderness was more symbolic than geographical.[24]

The final circle radiating outwards from the Cistercian monk and his abbey was perhaps the most distinctive feature of this new type of monasticism, and that was the way that Cistercian houses related to each other. Twelfth-century Cistercians created the most developed and tightly-knit organization yet seen in monastic history; in effect, they created the first real Order. At the heart of this was their constitution, the so-called *Carta Caritatis* or Charter of Love, approved by Pope Calixtus II in its original form in 1119, but then modified and expanded over the coming years as growing experience dictated. This envisaged a collective or representative system of government for the Order based on a General Chapter of all Cistercian abbots meeting at Cîteaux. By the mid-twelfth century, with the spectacular growth of Cistercian abbeys, this could mean hundreds of abbots with their secretaries and servants descending on Cîteaux from across Latin Christendom. Although not an entirely new concept in itself, never before had the General Chapter been so important or developed; by 1155, for instance, it had added a further 92 statutes to the *Carta Caritatis*. Later, to avoid it becoming too unwieldy in size and to cut down on the time and expense involved in bringing abbots from distant lands, a steering group of Definitors generally proposed business which was then confirmed by a reduced General Chapter.

For the Middle Ages the Cistercian General Chapter was an extraordinary concept. It not only allowed a limited form of representative government, but also was an international gathering. Living in an age, as we do, when such things are almost daily occurrences we can easily forget how unusual they were in medieval Europe. In the twelfth century only Ecumenical Councils could rival the Cistercian General Chapter for the international character of the assembly.

The other concept that the Cistercians borrowed and expanded was the visitation. Every Cistercian abbot was responsible for the annual visitation, or inspection, of the daughter houses that had been founded from the mother house. Thus the entire spectrum of both the spiritual and material welfare of each abbey was open to annual inspection. As such, Cistercians ensured a high degree of uniformity of practice across the Order. Through the combination of General Chapter and visitation the Cistercians produced a balance between uniformity and autonomy quite distinct in its time, and subsequently much copied. Indeed, the Fourth Lateran Council of 1215 used the Cistercian practice as the model for the system that it ordered to be adopted by all monastic groupings.

So how large was this new Cistercian Order, and why did it experience such spectacular growth? It is rather easier to quantify the numbers of abbeys than it is actual monks in them. The boom period for the former was the quarter of a century from 1125 to 1151 when over 300 foundations were made. By that latter date there were already something like 500 Cistercian abbeys; and by 1250 this had risen further to about 650, 240 of which were in France and 120 in the British Isles. However, just like the monasteries of the Pachomian federation in the fourth century, not all of these were new found-ations. Of the 650 abbeys of the Cistercian Order in 1250, almost one-third had joined by incorporation rather then by direct foundation. Even so, that represented a formidable rate of growth.[25]

How many monks lived, worked and prayed in these abbeys? In order to be recognized as an abbey a monastic community had to have a minimum of twelve monks and an abbot, from the Gospel precedent of Jesus and his twelve apostles. Fewer than that and the community would only have the status of a priory under a prior, and not autonomous but still ruled from the mother house. David H. Williams has provided what is perhaps the best estimate of the total number of Cistercians. We know that some abbeys were relatively small, and a few very large with over 100 monks each. Williams has thus assumed an average of 30 monks for each of the 650 abbeys in 1250, making a total of almost 20,000 choir monks. Given that there were probably more *conversi* than choir monks in most abbeys, he has estimated another 30,000 lay brothers, to give a total of 50,000 from both types. To put those figures into some demographic perspective, the population of Europe at that time was probably less than a tenth of what it is today, which would imply a modern equivalent of over half a million Cistercians. No wonder that Williams has described these totals as 'a spiritual and an economic force to be reckoned with'.[26]

That comment goes some way towards explaining this quite spectacular growth. First of all the new Cistercian Order satisfied a new spiritual quest originating in that desire to return to the sources, to live the apostolic life, the *vita apostolica*, described in the Gospels and Acts, and then realized afresh in the deserts of ancient Egypt. The Cistercians tapped into this new enthusiasm felt across all classes from nobility to agricultural labourers, and the make-up of the Order reflected this social inclusiveness.[27] In the opinion of C. H. Lawrence, the Cistercians 'conveyed all the exhilarating sense of taking part in a great movement of reform, which was also a revival of a heroic past'.[28] Lawrence is also at pains, however, to emphasize that this could never be a literal or exact reproduction of a then already distant past, but rather had as much or more to do with contemporary desires: 'The remote past is a dark pool in which reformers see a reflection of their own image.'[29]

The most articulate advocate of this Cistercian reform was Bernard of Clairvaux (1090–1153), perhaps the most charismatic figure of his day. This aristocratic young man arrived at Cîteaux in 1113 with about 30 other men, all relatives and friends of his. It used to be thought that the arrival of Bernard and his party saved a failing experiment. However, that seems unlikely as the monks of Cîteaux were about to found their first two daughter houses before his arrival.[30] Nevertheless the charisma of Bernard was one of the most important factors in the subsequent growth of the Order. From his own abbey of Clairvaux he had founded no fewer than 68 daughter houses by the time of his death. Perhaps even more important was his work as a publicist for the new Order. In addition to his treatises, over 300 sermons and almost 500 letters of his have survived.[31] It was his tireless preaching tours that were the main instruments of his appeal. Tall and aristocratic in bearing, but emaciated from his relentless fasting, he had a commanding presence, and the potency of his words moved those who heard them and drew recruits after them. Like some latter-day Symeon on his column, Bernard seemed a living icon of the ascetic ideal of 'contemplation and action and of community life and solitude that corresponded to the religious sensibilities of his age' (Document 17).[32]

At the more mundane but no less important levels the Cistercians also caught 'the tide of demographic and economic change that was transforming Western society'.[33] Twelfth-century Cistercians lived in a world of growing populations and rapidly expanding cities, trade and wealth. Paradoxically, these men who fled to the wilderness to find solitude and silence were better placed than most to take advantage of these economic and social changes. Rising populations, especially urban ones, needed feeding. Cistercian agriculture was ideally suited to this, opening up vast tracts of previously uncultivated land, utilizing all the new technologies of deep ploughing, and organized on an almost industrial scale. Cistercians avoided the feudal manorial system and instead concentrated their farming into centres known as Granges where many of the *conversi* spent much of their time. Large abbeys could have 25 or more Granges scattered over their estates. The Yorkshire abbeys collectively had 72 Granges by 1220, and Burgundy boasted over 200 Cistercian farms and vineyards.[34]

But it was not only food that the Cistercians were producing to satisfy the growing market. At the same time they became one of the most significant suppliers of the essential raw material of what was perhaps the largest and fastest-growing industry of the day: textiles. In 1291 the three Yorkshire abbeys of Fountains, Rievaulx and Jervaulx had flocks of 18,000, 14,000 and 12,000 sheep respectively. These produced in their turn 76, 60 and 50 sacks of wool, with each sack containing 200 fleeces, mostly destined for the wool manufacturers of Flanders. The monks even exploited the sophisticated financial markets then developing and sold next year's production into a futures market.[35]

The very success of the new Cistercians, however, made for problems and invited criticisms. One measure of that success was the number of Cistercians who had achieved high office in the Church. By 1227 over 130 Cistercians had been created bishops, nineteen had been made cardinals and one had been elected Pope as Eugenius III (1145–53).[36] Indeed, as ardent allies of reform the Cistercian Order was naturally favoured by Rome and many of its monks had been employed as papal agents preaching the Crusade; Bernard himself was one of the main advocates of the Second Crusade.

But in some ways the Cistercians became the victims of their own early and spectacular success. Older abbeys would not only resent the obvious papal favouritism of the new Order, but also the Cistercian claims to be restoring and renewing the Rule of St Benedict; that tended to imply that the Cistercians alone were the true heirs and interpreters of this foundation document of Western monasticism. This came to a head in the mid-twelfth century in a notorious literary confrontation between Bernard and the abbot of Cluny, Peter the Venerable. It could certainly be argued that in rejecting child oblates or in creating their *conversi* the Cistercians were not being as true to the Rule as the older Benedictines. Undoubtedly what might be termed political rivalry and jealousy entered into such debates. We have already seen how the adoption of white habits with all the symbolism claimed for them could arouse hostility and accusations of self-righteousness; Cistercian insistence on austerity and simplicity, and their particular interpretation of the Rule, also led to charges of being latter-day Pharisees on the part of some critics in the later twelfth century.[37]

On the economic as well as the spiritual level the Cistercians were also encountering problems and criticisms. One of these arose with the incorporation of existing abbeys into their Order. Many of them would bring their feudal lands, including their serfs, with them. So what, then, of the purity of the Cistercians in standing apart from the feudal system? On some occasions living in a wilderness was itself something of a manufactured illusion as villages were forcibly removed to create the desired effect. And another measure, this time of internal tensions between the choir monks and the *conversi*, was the number of disturbances and revolts experienced by the Order. Although modern scholars do not agree on the exact numbers, it is clear that from at least the mid-twelfth century *conversi*-led outbreaks of revolt were running at anything from every one to three years.[38] Altogether the massive wealth of the Order, its compromises with the feudal economic system, its contacts with the secular world and its alliance with the papacy, all led to the gradual erosion of its original pristine principles and, over time, to it resembling more the traditional black monks than something so distinctive and new. As C. H. Lawrence has commented: 'Before the end of the thirteenth century, much that was distinctive in the Cistercian vocation had been lost'.[39]

The Cistercians, however, were only one of a number of similar movements of renewal within monasticism in the twelfth century, if the largest and most visible. Smaller, but no less distinctive, was the community that perhaps most successfully combined the ideals of the life of a hermit with cenobitic monasticism. Bruno of Cologne (*c.* 1030–1101) had for many years been the master of the cathedral school in Rheims, and in 1084 he seemed the ideal candidate to fill the vacant post of archbishop, but instead left to become a hermit with a small group of like-minded friends. Eventually settling in the foothills of the Alps near Grenoble, in 1090 Bruno was summoned to Rome to become an adviser to his former pupil, Pope Urban II. The nascent Order was probably saved from extinction by the arrival of Guigues du Pin, the Dean of Grenoble. He was elected prior in 1109, and in 1132 moved the little community still further up the slopes of the mountains to greater seclusion at La Grande Chartreuse, from which place the Order was to acquire its title of Carthusians, and in England the name of its houses, Charterhouses. Guigues du Pin was the author of its distinctive Rule derived from that of St Benedict but with additions from the customs and practices of the Cistercians and Camaldolese hermits. By the late twelfth century the life and buildings of the Carthusians had achieved their definitive forms. Each monk had a separate cell, rather than sharing a dormitory as in the classic Benedictine pattern, the cells ranged around the cloister, each with its own small garden and lavatory. However, Carthusian houses did have a church and refectory like a conventional abbey, but the latter was used only infrequently on festive occasions and most meals were normally eaten alone in the cell. Silence was even more pervasive than in a Cistercian abbey and conversation between the monks relatively infrequent. The diet was extremely austere, with no meat allowed, and only bread and water on Mondays, Wednesdays and Fridays. Generally each monk prayed, studied and worked alone in his cell in silence.

This was a life even more radically tuned to the individualistic piety of the central Middle Ages than the Cistercians, and the sense of distance between the Carthusian monks and the secular world was effected by their *conversi* who normally dealt with all the economic and administrative business of the house, leaving the choir monks to concentrate on their internal deserts of the soul. Perhaps not surprisingly, in view of the deliberate severity of the Carthusian life, foundations were much slower than with the Cistercians. By 1200 there were still only 39 houses, each with twelve monks and sixteen *conversi*, and even on the eve of the sixteenth-century Reformation the Order had only grown to 216 foundations across Latin Christendom. But at least the very isolation of the Carthusians from outside influences helped to preserve the original vision of their founders and their claim has always been that they have never needed reformation because they have never experienced deformation.[40]

The Cistercians, Carthusians and the other smaller Orders that evolved from the renewal of the monastic ideal in the eleventh and twelfth centuries, however, all had in common the traditional Western monastic practice of being sited in predominantly rural areas, which in some respects could be interpreted as a flight from rather than engagement with the new urban world. The growth of the towns and cities thus presented the medieval Church with a fresh challenge: how to bring the distinctive features of Christian asceticism into the urban setting and satisfy the growing attraction for the *vita apostolica* among their populations. The first attempt to do this was by the promotion by reformers from the Gregorian papacy downwards of the type of clergy known as regular canons.

One of the problems with the term 'canon' is that it can have a variety of meanings and so can potentially cause more confusion than clarity.[41] We have already seen that it can apply, for instance, to the New Testament. In the medieval world *canonicus* usually referred to a *clericus*, a 'cleric' or 'clerk', a literate person who was in Orders and performed liturgical services, most prominently the saying of Mass, usually in a cathedral or church staffed by several clergy who were named on its official list, the *matricula*, and collectively formed an *ordo canonicus*. As early as 816 the Council of Aachen had drawn up the *Institutio Canonicorum* under which each member of the cathedral clergy, the canons, who elected the bishop, held a proportion of the cathedral's usually extensive property called a preband, which was treated as feudal land. Just as the humbler, and poorer, rural parish clergy passed on their livings to their sons, so too did cathedral canons.[42]

In the eleventh century reformers urged these cathedral canons to adopt a Rule, *regula*, like monks, and to hold their property in common, sleep in dormitories, and eat in refectories together like monks. Thus was born the concept of regular canons, which was enthusiastically taken up by the Gregorian papacy. Many reformers believed that the New Testament, especially the Gospels and Acts, showed that the apostles had lived such a life and were therefore effectively the first monks. In his work *The Common Life of Canons*, the hermit and future cardinal, Peter Damian, argued that the common life was indeed evangelical in origin and thus obligatory for all clergy in cathedrals or collegiate churches. Such ideals of clerical living clearly fitted in with the Gregorian papacy's drive for a celibate clergy and an end to simony.[43]

Across Latin Christendom reforming bishops, or cathedral chapters on their own initiative, began to adopt this 'regular' way of living, in essentials not dissimilar to a monastic life. However, the ease with which this change was effected varied enormously, and in some instances resulted in often violent opposition. In some towns and cities, especially where there was no bishop or cathedral, benefactors would also found new houses of regular canons just as they had previously founded monasteries. During the course of the Middle Ages in England, for example, the number of houses of regular canons came to exceed those of Benedictine monks.[44] However, one of the main distinctions between the urbanized regular canons and rural monks was that while the latter had fields to tend, the urban canons did not. Thus the element of manual labour was diverted by regular canons into such things as the founding and running of hospitals, leprosaries or alms-houses and other charitable works.

Clearly the Rule of St Benedict was not suited to these new urban canons. There was a Rule, nevertheless, theoretically even more ancient than that, the so-called Rule of St Augustine, which did seem to be more appropriate. The earliest extant manuscript copy of this Rule that we now have dates from the late sixth century. The basis of it was derived from St Augustine's Letter 211 to his sister detailing his views on the essential requirements of a religious community. With some later elaboration this became the basis of the Rule finally given papal approval in 1118. However, like the Rule of St Benedict, this Rule was also capable of numerous interpretations and supported a variety of different ways of living it; just as there was no standard monk, so there was no uniform group of regular canons. While most regular, or Augustinian, canons were urban, there were some who used the Rule to adopt a much more monastic, even eremitic, life.

Prominent among these were the communities derived from the foundation of Norbert of Xanten (*c.* 1080–1134), a nobleman and courtier of the Emperor Henry V. In his early thirties he had had a profound conversion experience during a violent thunderstorm. After ordination and a number of experiments both living as a hermit and as a member of a collegiate church, he finally retreated to become a hermit in the forests of Prémontré near Laon in 1120. Within a year he had attracted 40 followers and adopted the new Rule of St Augustine with customs added from those of the Cistercians such as *conversi*, a General Chapter and a white habit. Thus were born the Premonstratensians or White Canons. By 1188 they had received papal approval to move into parochial ministry, to run hospitals and to teach in schools. By 1250 there were about 500 abbeys and priories of the White Canons across Western Europe.[45]

The regular canons thus represented the 'first direct religious confrontation' with the new urban society.[46] This engagement, however, was strictly limited. Obviously the regular canons were all ordained clerics and, while their hospitals, schools or alms-houses ministered to the laity, often with assistance from the laity, they could only have a limited appeal to, and provide a restricted outlet for, growing lay spirituality. The attraction of the *vita apostolica* was not confined to those in holy orders and, as the twelfth century progressed, the growing frustration of an increasingly sophisticated and educated urban laity began to mount. Not surprisingly, in some places and at some moments that frustration boiled over into outright protest and dissent. The traditional forms of the ascetic life, whether monasticism or the regular canons, could not satisfy or contain a new and very active interpretation of the *vita apostolica*.

If the model of the Christian life was Jesus and his apostles, then not only had they formed a community of prayer, but they had also gone out into the world to preach the good news of salvation. Were not all Christians called to this ministry, whether ordained or not? This new active lay spirituality was to represent one of the most profound challenges experienced by Latin Christendom in the central Middle Ages. The way the Church and its hierarchy responded to it would test it in ways unknown since the fall of the Roman Empire. Would it rise to the challenge?

The Challenge

The new active spirituality of the laity was itself a product of the new society being created in the central Middle Ages based on a number of expansions. The first of these was demographic. The size of the population of Europe during the medieval centuries can only be, at best, a matter of educated guesswork. But what does seem certain is that the decline in population during the late Roman Empire continued in the West after its fall, and that the nadir was reached around 700 when the total population of Europe may have shrunk to as little as 27 million. Thereafter there was a slow and fitful recovery to about 42 million by about 1000. However, in the generations after that the rate of increase probably doubled and by 1300 Europe may have contained as many as 73 million people.[47]

Within that overall increase what was perhaps of most significance was the much faster pace of urban growth. In the tenth and eleventh centuries European cities were but shadows of their ancient predecessors, Rome itself probably having only about 20,000 to 30,000 permanent residents. By the thirteenth century, however, there was a handful of cities starting to approach 100,000 in size, notably places like Florence, Venice or Milan, with quite a number of others in the 10,000 to 50,000 bracket. Above all, two regions in Europe stood out in terms of urbanization, namely Italy north of Rome, and Flanders from the modern French–Belgian frontier northwards to the Belgian–Dutch border area. The expansion of both was based on growing textile manufacturing and trade, and following on from them a similar growth in banking, shipping and other related industries. Although the proportion of Europeans, even in northern Italy or Flanders, that was urbanized was very small by modern standards, the economies of these towns and cities had a disproportionate and growing influence on the other, more rural sections of the population. We have seen an example of this already with the Cistercians, cultivating previously waste land to grow more crops, or breeding flocks of sheep to feed the textile industry with its essential raw material.

No part of Europe remained untouched by this commercial revolution, whether on land or sea. Venetian, Genoese and Pisan merchant fleets came to dominate the trade of the eastern Mediterranean. After the Crusaders captured the Holy land, Italian merchants established trading posts in ports like Acre or Tyre and gained access to the luxury goods of the Middle East and Asia, everything from silks to spices, and exchanged the woollen cloth, ores or refined metals of Europe for them. They were to be followed in the western Mediterranean a little later by cities like Barcelona or Marseilles. Altogether by the thirteenth century the economy of Europe was booming, and its inhabitants, at least those who could afford to, were achieving a standard of living not seen for nearly a millennium.

This new market economy based on trade, manufacturing and banking in its turn created a new dynamic and mobile society; and both of them combined to present Christianity with a series of challenges. The new economy, for instance, was much more monetized than previously. In 1000 money, in the form of coins, was relatively rare and most coins of small denominations. Expanding trade, and in its wake banking, required more coins of higher values, increasingly minted in silver and then gold. That in its turn led to revolutionary developments in areas such as credit. And all of that presented Christianity with fundamental ethical dilemmas revolving around issues of profit, lending and borrowing. Usury had traditionally been condemned as a practice by medieval Christian thinkers based on a number of Old Testament texts such as Exodus 22:25, Leviticus 25:35–8, or Deuteronomy 23:19–20. Was there a way in which Christianity could reconcile its economic morality with that of the new urban commercial society?

That new society in itself also presented novel problems. Feudal society was based on personal ties between individuals; the new society was formed from abstract concepts such as money, wages, profit and loss. It was producing winners in the form of a prosperous bourgeoisie; but at the same time many thousands of the migrants who poured into the cities from the countryside to swell their populations lived miserable existences, poorly paid and badly fed, clothed or housed. What duties or responsibilities did the emerging commercial aristocracy have to its workers? At the same time the new economy demanded higher levels of literacy and numeracy, at least from those who controlled it. Education was flourishing in the cities, with many new schools founded to supplement the traditional cathedral ones. Thus a much more educated laity was emerging; learning was no longer the preserve of the ordained clergy. And educated people tended to ask searching or awkward questions of those clergy and their privileged status. But education in its turn raised further ethical problems. For the Church knowledge had come to be seen as a divine gift which, as such, should not be bought and sold. But as urban education became more secularized, the new masters entered the market economy and charged fees for their services. Was this morally justifiable?

This mobile, thrusting urban society remained, however, a deeply Christian one. Merchants, manufacturers and bankers wanted answers to these moral dilemmas as urgently as clerics. As the Church floundered in its efforts to reconcile traditional morality with the new economy, one specific group who had become essential to the financial working of the system, Jewish moneylenders, were, tragically, to become early victims of this frustration. The out-flowing of popular piety which accompanied the First Crusade in 1095–6 produced some of the first instances of mob violence against urban Jewish communities. Some scholars have argued that the Jews took on the role of scapegoats for the failure of Christians to adapt successfully to the profit economy: 'The main function of the Jews in the Commercial Revolution was to bear the burden of Christian guilt for participation in activities not yet deemed morally worthy of Christians.'[48]

The new monasticism of the eleventh and twelfth centuries was in its turn at best no more than a partial answer to the problem, and that a negative one: flight from, rather than engagement with, the new society. Monastic virtues like poverty, obedience, stability or chastity, it has been argued, were not only not an answer to the new challenges of the urban world, but rather stood in stark contrast to them; the profit motive, the mobile society, the driving ambition of the commercial world were all virtues directly opposed to the monastic ones. The monastic world was rural and static; the commercial one was urban and dynamic.[49]

Perhaps not surprisingly, as the reformers and their allies in the Gregorian papacy turned their criticisms onto the unchaste and wealthy clergy, the newly educated urban laity followed suit. The twelfth century was to witness the emergence of groups of laity, their leaders often coming from the bourgeoisie, who combined a burning desire to follow an active life based on that of Jesus recorded in the Gospels and his apostles in Acts, with a dissatisfaction with the ordained clergy which could lead from protest to dissent. At its most critical it presented the Church with the most serious challenge to its authority that it had experienced for centuries.

Thus a potent mixture of motives has been ascribed to the protest movements of the twelfth century. These include religious explanations such as the shift from a passive to an active interpretation of the *vita apostolica* on the part of the urban laity; social explanations in the form of interpreting the protesters and dissidents as coming from both the most successful and the most disadvantaged groups in the new economy; the role of the Gregorian papacy in raising expectations of clerical renewal it ultimately failed to satisfy; its early alliance with and encouragement of such popular movements as the Pataria of Milan and other cities; a conservative reaction on the part of some of the laity to the expanding role of the Church in their lives as a result of the Gregorian papacy; the stirring of popular enthusiasm by the Crusades; the charismatic nature of some of the leaders of the protest movements; rivalries and jealousies between particular cities; and the failure of the Church to instruct either its clergy or laity properly in the faith. Thus a heady cocktail of explanations has been advanced for this explosion of protest movements. Whatever the precise mixture, one thing was clear: there was a geographical linkage between the more urbanized and industrialized regions of Europe on the one hand, with the greatest concentration of protesters and dissidents on the other.[50]

So far I have deliberately avoided the term 'heresy' when discussing the protest movements of the central Middle Ages. Although the Church was to accuse them of this and ascribe the term to them, there is clearly a vast gulf between the highly sophisticated, intellectual heresies of classical antiquity and these relatively simple movements of popular piety. However well educated their leaders might have been by contemporary standards, they bear no comparison with an Arius or Apollinarius, a Nestorius or Eutyches in terms of scholarly learning. For the most part the twelfth-century movements presented little or no direct doctrinal challenge to the institutional Church; their challenge was overwhelmingly moral and pastoral.

These points are exemplified in the life of Peter Waldes and the movement he founded which took his name: the Waldensians. Significantly, he was a wealthy cloth merchant from the city of Lyons, one of the largest and most important urban centres in southern France, a river port and major communications hub between France and northern Italy. In the late twelfth century it was an expanding city of 10,000 to 15,000 people, its wealth and demographic growth witnessed by the building of a new gothic cathedral. It was here that one day in the mid-1170s Waldes heard a jongleur or wandering player recount the popular story of St Alexis, a wealthy ancient Roman who had abandoned his family and fortune to become a beggar for the sake of Christ. So moved was Waldes that he too resolved to take the same course. In some respects he can thus be compared to the hermits of the previous century; but in other crucial ways he also represented a break with that past. For one thing he was a layman with no prospect of ordination; he was no scholar like Peter Damian. For another, he intended to live by begging which was viewed as totally unbecoming for a religious, whether monk or regular canon. Further, it was also clear that he also intended to begin a career of itinerant preaching, the special preserve of the clergy. But he was also no rebel. What he did represent, however, was 'an individualistic lay solution to a crisis of conscience rather than that provided by the more usual and institutional way'.[51] In other words, in the 1170s the Church had as yet no means of accommodating a man like Waldes who wanted to lead his life according to the active interpretation of the *vita apostolica*. He was on his own.

Consequently he paid scribes to copy and translate the Gospels and other biblical books for him to study, along with some of the works of the Fathers. His daughters were sent, presumably with the proper endowments, to the abbey at Fontevrault (history does not record their views on that!), he began giving away his fortune to the poor and needy, and wandered the roads preaching in town squares, private houses, and occasionally even churches. His fame quickly spread and he was joined by followers who acquired the popular name of the Poor Men of Lyons. He attended the Third Lateran Council in Rome in 1179, initially receiving enthusiastic support from the pope and a grant to preach with the permission of the local clergy. In effect, however, this presented him and his followers with grave problems as few clerics would wish to have relatively uneducated laymen trespassing on their preserves. In 1181 the Cistercians in Toulouse investigated his activities and, in order to continue his mission, he was obliged to subscribe to a profession of orthodoxy. The following year he was excommunicated and forced to leave the archdiocese of Toulouse, and in 1184 he and his followers fell under the blanket papal condemnation covering several groups of supposed heretics.

Modern scholars are agreed that Waldes and his followers did not represent a theological or doctrinal assault on the institutional Church.[52] Their challenge was a pastoral one; did laymen have the authority to preach or use unofficial translations of scripture? But their hijacking of these previously exclusively clerical functions could lead them on to a more wholesale criticism of the wealth and laxity of the clergy. They represented a living criticism of those secular clergy who did not fulfil the Gregorian ideals of chastity and poverty. And from that it was but a short step to a variation of the ancient Donatist position, namely that morally unworthy clergy could not celebrate valid sacraments, and thus opened the way for laymen to celebrate Mass or hear confessions. At the same time unaided study of the scriptures could lead to fundamentalist interpretations. Yet if Waldensians did lapse into heresy they represented 'the classic example of a would-be reform movement drawn into heresy by the inadequacies of ecclesiastical authority'.[53] Some modern scholars have questioned the accuracy of the word 'heresy' itself as applied to the Waldensians and similar groups. Here was instead a collection of genuine enthusiasts basically wishing to be loyal to the Church but faced with a hierarchical institution as yet incapable of finding a mechanism to accommodate and harness that enthusiasm. The strength and appeal of groups like the Waldensians was indeed witnessed by their rapid expansion, especially into the towns and cities of northern Italy and the Rhineland. Indeed the Waldensians have survived and are today a small but the only living remnant of the dissident groups of the central Middle Ages.

The Waldensians were, however, but one of several similar lay groups originating in the later twelfth century. Among these others were the so-called *Humiliati* or Humble Ones. They had no particular founder or leader but probably appeared in the cities of Lombardy in the 1170s and quickly spread across northern Italy. Similar to the Waldensians in wishing to effect personal reformation in individual lives, they were yet distinct in giving different roles to different groups within the movement. While some remained married and very much active in the world, others adopted a celibate life, and there were even some priests among their number. Like the Waldensians they again preached without authority, but their sermons were specifically directed to the defence of orthodoxy and combating of heresy. Indeed, as Malcolm Lambert has pointed out, they were the first group to have understood the potency of combining preaching with apostolic poverty when refuting heresy. It was a combination that was to have great significance for the future. Yet again they were still one of the groups that fell foul of the condemnation of 1184.[54]

One specific group that remained unaffected by that condemnation was the first to be designed exclusively for women. Starting once again in the later twelfth century, and also in urban settings, this time in Flanders, was the movement of the Beguines. Before this time there had been little provision for the religious life among ordinary women. Some nunneries did exist, but they were massively outnumbered by houses for men, and were even more exclusively aristocratic. The Beguines of Flanders were thus the first example of a form of the religious life intended for poor women as well as the wealthy. Yet unlike conventional Orders they took no vows, kept property if they possessed it and were free to leave and marry if they so desired, and were sited in urban areas; the Beguinage in Bruges, for example, was virtually a separate village within the town containing about 300 women. Clearly the desire to follow the *vita apostolica* affected not only all classes but also both sexes as well.[55]

Of all the Christian groups that originated and flourished independently of the hierarchical institution of the Church in the central Middle Ages, the one that represented the most potent challenge to orthodoxy was Catharism. This name was not derived from that of a founder or leader but rather from the Greek *katharoi*, the pure. And that gives a hint to its origins. It is now generally accepted among modern scholars that Catharism seeped into the West from Bulgaria as a result of trading links, and was derived from a group in the

Balkans known as Bogomils from their founder, Bogomil, 'Beloved of God'. As dualists they had some features in common with the ancient Manichaeans, but it is now thought that this was accidental as there is no demonstrable succession from the classical heresy. But like the Manichees, Cathars believed that all matter was the creation of an evil god and that only the soul was good. Thus the true Christian conquered evil matter by abstinence from meat and wine, or any products of coition, remained celibate, and practised a radical personal poverty. Entry into this higher state was by a form of 'spiritual baptism' (although not involving water, as that was corrupted matter) called the *consolamentum*, the comforting or consoling, and full members of the sect who had received this rite of initiation were known as *perfecti*, the perfect. Unlike orthodox Christianity there was no real distinction between a laity and a clergy; the perfect were both, and the followers who had not yet received the *consolamentum* were more like the catechumens in the early centuries of Christianity. Very few felt able to receive the *consolamentum* until they were on their deathbeds, again rather like baptism for early Christians, or the taking of the monastic habit shortly before death in the Middle Ages to secure the benefits of a monastic burial.

Indeed, it is debatable whether or not the Cathars were Christians at all. What can be said is that they claimed to be Christians, indeed went so far as to assert that they were the only true Christians; and the Church authorities certainly treated them as having lapsed into heresy rather than being outright infidels. As such they must be placed alongside other groups who were affected by the desire for the *vita apostolica* and a return to the Christianity of the early Church. The austere life of the perfect thus obviously contrasted with that of the lax and worldly clergy and attracted many followers, the first recorded appearance of their ideas being in the Rhineland towns in the 1140s. However, once again their main strength was in the urban areas of northern Italy and especially in Languedoc in southern France. Their close association with the town of Albi has led to that most concentrated and intense group in Languedoc being known as Albigensians.

In 1165 the Cathars met the orthodox catholic clergy and nobility in debate at Lombers in Languedoc. What this conference revealed was both the incapacity of the local church to combat them, and the unwillingness of the nobility to persuade the clergy so to do; indeed, it was becoming clear that some of the minor nobility of the Languedoc openly sympathized with the Cathars. By the 1170s support for them was sweeping through the region like a forest fire carried on the winds of the mistral. Here dissent found the right social and political conditions in which to thrive. Malcolm Lambert has described in graphic detail the collapse of organized political authority in the region following the departure of Count Raymond IV of Toulouse on the

First Crusade, the impotence of his successors (all, somewhat confusingly, also called Raymond), and the resulting anarchy. Here a rising population had led to the catastrophic sub-division of inheritances among older and younger sons, leading to endemic feudal warfare between petty lords with the vestiges of political authority but lacking the backing of economic security. The Church at the parochial level had been the victim of noble plunder and its organized life consequently severely disrupted. Reform had barely touched a clergy lacking the will or resources to resist, and presided over in little more than name only by an absentee archbishop of Narbonne. The enthusiasm of the *vita apostolica* and reform were thus far better represented by the Cathars.[56]

Not surprisingly, by the last decades of the twelfth century Catharism seemed to be on the verge of replacing the Catholic Church in some areas of Languedoc as the official representative of Christianity. However, we must be careful not to overestimate its success. Although figures are difficult to quantify precisely, it would seem that in most parts of the region Cathars remained in a minority, and that their expansion beyond Languedoc was extremely limited; Gascony to the west and the Mediterranean region to the east remained largely unaffected. Even in the cities of northern Italy they were spread thinly and more like a film floating on the surface of Christian life than something profoundly colouring it. Where they presented the hierarchy with a potential doctrinal threat it was at a fairly basic, not to say crude, level; few serious intellectuals ever became Cathars.

So, as Innocent III ascended the throne of St Peter in 1198 he found a Church marked by contrasts. Monasticism had experienced a century or more of renewal, and new Orders, especially the Cistercians, had blown a rejuvenating breath through an ancient way of Christian life. Yet the vitality of the new urban world with its trade, commerce and finance was largely untouched; it had produced a new, vibrant lay spirituality that craved acceptance by the hierarchy of the Church, and looked for novel methods of expression. Yet the only response it had met had been suspicion and outright condemnation as in 1184. As a result, lay enthusiasm was largely an untapped resource for a church seemingly unable to accommodate it or to produce vehicles through which it could be directed into the mainstream of Christian life.

In their absence the laity was devising its own solutions and organizations, some more orthodox than others and, at their most extreme, in direct competition, as in the case of the Cathars. Would this seepage of enthusiasm develop into an outright haemorrhage that would leave the mainstream permanently crippled; or would the Church and its leadership be capable of demonstrating the imagination and charity needed to harness the unfamiliar to the cause of tradition?

The Response

On a wall in the upper church at Assisi the early fourteenth-century painter Giotto, perhaps with the assistance of his pupils, created a fresco that told the story of a dream. The dreamer was that same Pope Innocent III, and in his fantasy he saw the mother church of Latin Christendom, a building that in the medieval world represented the Church herself, the Lateran basilica in Rome, tottering and at the point of collapse. Suddenly, walking across the piazza towards it he saw a little beggar-man dressed in rags. To the Pope's amazement this tiny figure put his shoulder to the disintegrating building and slowly, miraculously, he began to shore it up.

In this instance artistic licence accorded with historical reality. In the drama that Giotto depicted lay more than a kernel of historical truth. The two figures, Innocent III and the little beggar-man, who was of course St Francis, were to be key players in the actions and the creation of organizations that were so vital in reversing the potential catastrophe that the dream depicted. In many ways the eighteen years of the pontificate of Innocent III (1198–1216) marked the most significant papal reign of the Middle Ages. He effectively reversed the policy of ineffective condemnation of all enthusiastic groups, welcomed into the mainstream those who could be reconciled and whose energies could be redirected, authorized the foundation of new types of the religious life to harness the spiritual energies of the laity, and initiated much more effective systems for combating those who remained obdurate in their doctrinal opposition to the Church. Altogether he launched new policies which helped to rejuvenate Western Christianity and which were then developed and expanded by his successors, so that during the first decades of the thirteenth century the 'initiative passed to the Church'.[57]

In the case of the *Humiliati* Innocent III set up a committee of investigation to consider their position. As a result of this in 1201 he effectively nullified the condemnation of 1184 and established their movement as a formal type of the religious life within the Church, divided into three Orders, the First for priests, the Second monastic, and the Third Order for the laity. The first two had a new Rule composed from elements in the Rules of St Benedict and Augustine, while the Third Order, potentially the most revolutionary of the three, established regulations for reciting offices, fasting and clothing, effectively recognizing the validity of lay spirituality alongside the more traditional kind of monastic life. As a result, all the evidence suggests that in the cloth towns of northern Italy hundreds of houses of *Humiliati* flourished during the thirteenth century.[58]

With the Waldensians Innocent III could claim no more than partial success. Part of the reason for that lay in the fragmented nature of the movement itself by the early thirteenth century. Nevertheless, in 1208 and 1212 the Pope helped to reconcile two groups of Waldensians who rejoined the mainstream of the Church; the first were named the Poor Catholics under their leader Durand de Huesca, and the second group from the Languedoc under Bernard Prim. One of the most significant aspects of this reconciliation was that for the first time papal approval was given to a type of religious life that practised mendicancy, or begging. And in bringing the *Humiliati* and some of the Waldensians back under the enfolding authority of the papacy, Innocent III 'showed that he was prepared to encounter these protest movements as no other pope had done before'.[59] He demonstrated that the hierarchical institution of the Church had the vision to succeed in redirecting the energies of charismatic and enthusiastic groups.

Some, however, remained bitterly opposed to the Catholic Church, and for them Innocent III began an experimental process to discover the best means of either reconciling them or silencing them, this time by the use of coercion. The most important of these groups were the Cathars. As the local bishops and clergy in the Languedoc had proved to be so ineffectual against the Cathars, Innocent III realized that he would have to turn to forces outside the region for help. His first importation was to come from the Cistercians, who led a preaching mission in the early years of the thirteenth century. Yet this established form of the religious life also proved to be disappointingly unsuccessful. Intellectually they could easily outshine the perfect in debate; the problem essentially lay in the traditional concept of monastic poverty. Cistercian monks might individually be weak and powerless, but collectively their Order was fabulously rich and powerful. Monks on horses with servants and ample cash could not compete with the radical poverty of the foot soldiers of the perfect. A new and different approach was required if the Cathars were to be persuaded back into the mainstream of Christianity.

While this approach was in its infancy the Pope turned to other external groups who could exert force to change the minds of the heretics. This would come from the French king and the feudal nobility of northern France, and the method to be employed would be the papal instrument of the Crusade. Innocent III initiated what were to become several waves of Crusades by the northern French against the Cathars of the Languedoc. However, this proved to be a very blunt instrument indeed. For one thing, the motives of the king and his northern nobles were, to put it charitably, mixed; many warriors were as concerned to gain new lands as to fight as champions of orthodoxy, and the kings with extending their royal authority into a region that had previously remained geographically remote and thus politically beyond their effective control. Such was the violence with which these outsiders erupted into the region that many nobles who had previously remained neutral now took the side of the Cathars, as much from a desire to defend their lands from rampaging invaders as religious conviction. If force was to effect the permanent destruction of Catharism, then it would have to be more subtle and precisely focused than these Albigensian Crusades.

The new instrument that the papacy eventually forged to achieve this was the Inquisition. The very mention of that organization to a modern audience is often enough to conjure up some incredible flights of fancy: blood-soaked torturers and burning victims presided over by half-crazed clerics have become the commonplace of popular fiction. The reality, on the other hand, was often much more mundane. Innocent III had established the principles of openness towards repentant dissenters combined with persuasive force for those who were not, and these were incorporated into what became the Inquisition by his successors. Officially inaugurated by Pope Gregory IX in 1233, the objective of the Inquisition was the salvation of souls; those who received the Cathar *consolamentum* on their deathbeds died as self-condemned heretics and thus not in a state of grace (Titus 3:10–11). What the Inquisitors sought was repentance, and what was most often imposed was thus a penance rather than a sentence which would cause the guilty, or misguided, individual to return to the communion of the Church. Only those who absolutely refused to recant were finally handed over to the secular authorities for punishment, which normally meant execution by being burnt alive.

But that was surprisingly rare. One Inquisitor, Bernard of Caux, sentenced some 207 people between 12 May and 22 July 1246, and of those 184 were ordered to wear a badge in the form of a cross, 23 were imprisoned, but not one was executed. Indeed, modern scholars have estimated that even at the height of the Inquisition's campaign against the Cathars of the Languedoc, only three people a year on average were burnt, and those were normally the most intransigent of the perfect. Far more people perished at the hands of the Albigensian Crusaders than ever suffered death as a result of the trials of the Inquisition.[60]

Those statistics, however, help to explain and to put into context the real work of the Inquisition; they do not excuse all its methods. For at its heart the Inquisition was a legal mechanism, a type of court. Its procedure started with the arrival of the Inquisitors in a particular area, and the preaching of a sermon calling for heretics to repent. A period of grace then ensued during which anyone could voluntarily confess their heresy and receive a penance to reconcile them to the Church. Witnesses who were willing to give depositions against others, accusing them of heresy, were themselves given a particularly light penance. From such depositions the Inquisitors composed lists of suspects; but in order to launch a prosecution the evidence of a minimum of two witnesses was required.

Once the period of grace was over, the Inquisition became a fully fledged court, but one with some very unusual characteristics. First of all, trials were held in secret with absolutely no members of the public in attendance. Second, the accused was never informed of the names of his or her accusers. The accused could thus not cross-examine the witnesses brought against him. The accused could, on the other hand, call his own witnesses, not to demonstrate his innocence as such, but rather to show that a person or persons bore him some mortal grudge, a not infrequent occurrence in a world with a code of honour and the concept of vendetta. But this was a hit-and-miss effort. If the accusers could be shown to bear mortal enmity against the accused, then the trial was immediately stopped. Third, if the accused was found guilty the judges then did something which never happened in a secular court: they attempted even at this stage to persuade the offender to recant. If he did so, then a penance was imposed on him, ranging from the wearing of a badge, to the performance of a lengthy pilgrimage. Only if he finally proved completely obstinate was he handed over to the secular authorities for punishment, normally death by burning. The use of torture by the Inquisition was only permitted from 1252, and then only under the strictest of limitations. It was only to be used on those suspected of having information they would not otherwise give; in other words it was not used to extract a confession from the accused. It should never be used in such a way as to draw blood, cause mutilation or result in the death of the victim.[61]

The court of the Inquisition was thus a strange mixture of leniency and cruelty, and obviously open to the possibility of terrible misuse. But was it effective? Impressive in its theoretical powers, it was hampered by one major limitation: it relied on the co-operation of the secular authorities for its effectiveness. Clearly it possessed the ability to frighten, but only if its potential victims knew that the death penalty would be imposed by the temporal powers. Also, like the other instruments employed by the papacy against the Cathars, it was staffed by clergy who came from outside the region, and so independent of any local interests, and unlike the local clergy were men of the sharpest intellect, highest morals, and most advanced education.

However, modern scholars are generally agreed that in itself the Inquisition was not responsible for the decline and final destruction of Catharism; at best it did no more than accelerate that decline.[62] With internal schisms, the growing number of suicides of perfect, and thus a diminishing clerical arm, combined with the loss of much noble support, the Cathars did as much to destroy themselves as any external force did. One Inquisitor, Ranier Sacchoni, estimated that by 1250 there were only 4,000 Cathars left in Latin Christendom, and the majority of them were to be found not in the Languedoc but in the cities of Lombardy.[63] Certainly the final large-scale burning of heretics had occurred in Languedoc in the previous year.[64] By 1300, after a century of mission, persuasion and coercion, Catharism had effectively disappeared as a threat.

The Cathars had gone the way of all the dissident or heretical groups in the central Middle Ages; their enthusiasm had either been redirected back into the mainstream of Christianity, or they had been eliminated by argument or force. In the words of Malcolm Lambert: 'The history of medieval heresy is a history of failure, for none of the movements surveyed succeeded either in imposing their views on the Western Church or in gaining toleration for their opinions and practices.'[65] And the measure of that failure is, in its turn, a measure of the Church's success. For in the end the Church had risen to the challenge presented by the new, urban lay spirituality and found answers that satisfied even many of the disillusioned and dissident. But perhaps the most significant instrument of all that the papacy was to wield in that successful campaign was the one that must be counted as the greatest legacy of Innocent III to Christianity, that totally new and potentially revolutionary answer to the spiritual longings of the urban laity, a novel type of the religious life: the friars.

The Friars

It is difficult to overestimate the impact of the friars, principally the Franciscans and Dominicans along with a number of smaller Orders, on the life of thirteenth-century Latin Christendom. From small, almost insignificant beginnings they grew into the most potent institutional response to the spiritual enthusiasm of the age. As such they were to have a crucial role in everything, from the construction of a new commercial ethic, through the staffing of the Inquisition, to the revolution in the cultural and academic life of the medieval West that came to be called Scholasticism. By 1300 few aspects of Christian life had been left untouched by them in the course of their accelerating expansion.

Francesco Bernadone was born in 1181 or 1182, the son of a successful and wealthy cloth merchant in one of the rapidly growing cities of central Italy, Assisi, and thus at the heart of the commercial and urban revolution of the central Middle Ages. For more than twenty years the young Francesco, or Francis, worked with his father in the family business. But from his mid-twenties, following a series of visions, dreams and other incidents, he progressively abandoned both the commercial world and the life of a rich young man that went with it. Perhaps above all it was his experience of hearing the Gospel during Mass on the feast of St Matthias in 1208 that was the most significant turning point.

These twelve Jesus sent out with the following instructions: 'Go nowhere among the Gentiles, and enter no town of the Samaritans, but go rather to the lost sheep of the house of Israel. As you go, proclaim the good news, "The kingdom of heaven has come near". Cure the sick, raise the dead, cleanse the lepers, cast out demons. You received without payment; give without payment. Take no gold, or silver, or copper in your belts, no bag for your journey, or two tunics, or sandals, or a staff; for labourers deserve their food.' (Matt. 10:5–10)

It was as if the words of Jesus had leapt from the page and been spoken to him personally, in a way clearly reminiscent of the similar experience of Antony of Egypt in about 270. After consulting a priest about the meaning of the passage, Francis discarded his shoes and, dressed only in a simple tunic of rough material, began his career as a wandering preacher of repentance begging or doing manual tasks to earn his food and lodging. He was soon joined by other formerly rich young men of Assisi bitten by the same enthusiastic religious bug.

What attracted them to follow Francis? For one thing he was perfectly in tune with the new spirituality of the time. He conceived his movement as one predominantly lay, drawn from and ministering to the laity of the thriving towns and cities, both the wealthy and the poor, the cloth workers as well as the manufacturers and merchants, lepers and other sick and destitute persons, the occupants of hovels as well as the finest houses. His movement was to be remarkably egalitarian for its time, with no equivalent of the *conversi* of the traditional monastic Orders. Unlike them, again, there was to be no vow of stability, no fixed house which his Little Brothers would be attached to for life, but rather a freedom to move where and when they needed. His movement would thus exemplify the active interpretation of the *vita apostolica*.

It would also be in tune with the new spirituality in emphasizing the humanity of Jesus. An examination of medieval art shows a distinct shift in the way in which Jesus was portrayed from the triumphant royal figure of earlier periods to the broken, naked and desolate Christ, his head bowed in seeming defeat, his body tortured and bleeding, of the central Middle Ages. Francis exemplified and preached this human Jesus. He once heard him speak from a crucifix in the church of San Damiano telling Francis to restore his Church (which he at first took to mean the building and only later understood that it meant rather the institution) and he is credited with the invention of the Christmas crib, the human infant Jesus in the realistic setting of the stable. On a doctrinal level this armed the Church with the perfect antidote to the Cathars whose own ideas had thrown doubt upon a real, material Jesus.

In 1209, when he had acquired the apostolic number of twelve followers, he went to Rome to seek papal approval for his movement. This was the occasion of the dream of Innocent III who agreed to Francis's request. At this stage, though, his idea of a Rule for his movement was little more than a collection of sentences taken directly from the Gospels. However, he continued to attract followers, and by 1217 his movement was large enough to take the momentous decision to extend the geographical scope of its evangelical mission from central Italy to the whole world. In the next few years waves of Franciscans began to pour out across Europe; by 1224, as we saw earlier, they had even arrived in distant England. By 1316 there were over 1,400 Franciscan houses across Latin Christendom.[66]

Why were the Franciscans so spectacularly successful in terms of their growth and influence in the thirteenth century? There is no one single answer to that question, but rather the explanation lies in a powerful combination of factors. The Franciscans are often compared to the Waldensians; their founders came from similar backgrounds, and they were both movements of itinerant, mendicant preachers. Yet the relatively greater success of the Franciscans can be explained by some small, but highly significant, differences. While both were in tune with the new active concept of the *vita apostolica* the Franciscans took this in a further, more radical direction. The early-thirteenth-century observer of Church affairs, Jacques de Vitry, called them the 'new athletes', the proponents of a new and much more intense interpretation of the ascetic life.[67] They were inspired by the heroic deeds of the early monks and hermits, but reinterpreted their lives in a way appropriate to the changed historical circumstances of the thirteenth century. In a world where mainstream Christianity was under threat from everything from Cathars to the commercial ethic of the urban world, the friars were 'a revolutionary answer to a potentially revolutionary situation'.[68] They showed that a spiritual and religious life was not the preserve of a monastic élite but available to all. The ecclesiology of the monastery fitted the static world of feudalism. The friars presented a new, dynamic force in the Church more tuned to the growth of cities and commerce, and also to the new internationalism of the secular world as to the international and centralizing thrust of the Gregorian papacy.[69] In addition, originating a generation or so later than the Waldensians, the Franciscans were the beneficiaries of the mistakes the Church hierarchy had initially made when dealing with them. The Franciscans found a more open and accepting hierarchy.

All that leads on to the point that Francis was always careful to obtain the sanction of the representatives of the institutional Church. He might have conceived his movement in terms of an exclusively lay body, but he was aware that it required clerical approval. He was fortunate in that right from the earliest days of his mission he had the sympathy and encouragement of his local bishop in Assisi. And through him he gained access to the papal curia in the form of Cardinal Ugolino, who not only agreed to act as an intermediary with Innocent III, but also became the first official 'protector' of the new Order in Rome, and eventually succeeded to the papal throne himself as Gregory IX. These friends in high places were crucial in preventing the Franciscans from going the way of the Waldensians. Francis was more than willing to take an oath of personal obedience to the Pope and to keep his nascent movement within the confines of orthodoxy and ecclesial loyalty. Thus the Franciscans combined the enthusiasm of the new lay spirituality with the hierarchical and orthodox structures of the institutional Church, and became a conduit through which the quest for personal lay sanctification could be expressed anew in traditional forms. Indeed the friars of the thirteenth century were the living personification of that dynamic concept of Christian tradition itself.

Any explanation of the success of the Franciscans would be incomplete, however, without taking into account Francis of Assisi himself, surely one of the most charismatic, attractive and radiantly holy figures in the history of Christianity. It was the depth of his personal devotion to Jesus, his absolute and radical poverty, and his total vulnerability that brought him his early following. His childlike joy in physical creation revealed in his hymn known as *The Canticle of the Sun*, where he envisages the whole of creation, beginning with 'Brother Sun', praising its creator, have endeared him to later generations from nineteenth-century Romantics to modern ecologists (both, however, guilty of misinterpreting the symbolic and essentially medieval nature of the ideas expressed in the poetry).

Nothing exemplified all of this better than the manner of his death and what happened immediately afterwards. In 1226 as his death was clearly approaching, his immediate brethren brought him first to the bishop's palace in Assisi. But, at his express command, in great pain and half-blind, he had them move him from the comforts of the episcopal residence, dressed only in sackcloth, to the first church his Order had acquired, a present from the Benedictines, the simple little church of the Portiuncula in the valley of Spoleto. Here they laid him on the beaten earth floor of the church, and sprinkled him with ashes. And there he passed his final hours in prayer, awaiting the arrival of the gentle embrace of Sister Death.

Once dead, his Order then revealed to the astonished world what had up until then remained a closely guarded secret known only to a few of his closest and most trusted brethren. Witnesses were brought to examine his dead body and were shown the strange marks visible on it, five wounds corresponding to the five wounds of Christ himself, in feet, hands and side. For in 1224, during one of his many retreats up into remote mountain districts that had become characteristic of his final years, he had had another vision. He saw a man standing above him in the form of a seraph with six wings. As he looked he became aware that, just like this visionary man, he too now had wounds on his own body. And so Francis became the first person in recorded history to bear the stigmata, the wounds of Christ. Hundreds of claims of stigmata have been made since, but Francis was the first. It seemed to confirm his holy status and above all his personal identification with the crucified Jesus so typical of the spirituality of his age. Within two years he had been formally canonized as a saint by his friend and protector, Gregory IX.

Yet Francis was far more than just a conventional plaster saint. He was very much a figure of contradiction both in his own time and for subsequent historians. How do you institutionalize the vision and mission of a Francis of Assisi in a Rule or an Order? How do you express his significance as a historical figure in literary forms? For his earliest followers, Francis was seen as a figure of significance for world history; one of his early biographers, Bonaventure, identified him with the sixth angel of the Apocalypse and his Order as initiating a new phase of Christian history. One of the problems with all the early *Lives* of Francis, however, including that of his first biographer, Thomas of Celano, is to disentangle the historical Francis from the myths and legends that grew up about him (Document 18).[70]

This still remained a problem for the first modern biographical study of Francis, by Paul Sabatier at the end of the nineteenth century, who portrayed a charismatic figure whose vision was stifled by the institutional Church. But Sabatier was only reflecting one of the central dilemmas of the thirteenth century: how far had the Order of Friars Minor and its Rule been faithful to the vision of Francis? He had wanted his followers to practise absolute poverty, owning nothing either individually or collectively. He had wanted an Order of laymen who preached repentance, and who would care little for educational attainment. Yet how practical were these ideals? How could laymen preach repentance and then be unable to offer the sacrament of confession and absolution? Over time the number of Franciscans who were ordained steadily rose. In the urban setting with educated and articulate laity how realistic was the preaching of uneducated friars? Even before his death his followers were gravitating to the new universities to gain recruits and then to teach in those same universities themselves. And devices had to be invented, in essence pious fictions, whereby Franciscan property was vested in lay trustees, culminating in the papacy itself becoming the ultimate custodian of Franciscan possessions.

Was this a betrayal of their founder, or practical common sense for the real world? Some early Franciscans, called the Spirituals, indeed saw it as betrayal and sought to preserve the authentic memory of the saint in an alternative literary tradition of *Fioretti* or Little Flowers of St Francis, that so influenced Sabatier. The majority, however, the Conventuals, were willing to accept compromises for the sake of the Order. As C. H. Lawrence has argued about Francis and his Order: 'the subsequent dilution of his ideal was not a betrayal but a necessary condition for the development of a permanent organization'.[71] Brenda Bolton has further argued that Francis should be seen as an isolated figure, the originator but not the founder of an Order. As she has commented: 'The original character and message of Francis made him extraordinarily difficult either to follow or to forget.'[72] That begins to get to the heart of the paradox of Francis of Assisi; he was impossible to ignore, but equally impossible to emulate.

But in his analysis of the ills of society and in some of the methods he advocated to remedy them he was not unique. A contemporary of his, hundreds of miles from Assisi, had some remarkably similar ideas, but also employed some equally contrasting methods through which those ideas could be effected in his contemporary society. The origins of both lay in the Church's campaign against the Cathars. In the early years of the thirteenth century Bishop Diego of Osma was travelling north from Spain when he met the Cistercian missionaries, dejected from their failure to win back the heretics. In his entourage was a canon of his cathedral who had already made an impression on the Bishop when he had sold his precious books to feed the poor during a famine. This learned and gentle canon with the deep spiritual sensitivity was called Dominic. He at once saw the problem. Unless the missionaries adopted the same apostolic lifestyle as the Cathars, they would never be able to persuade them of their errors. The problem was not so much theological exposition as pastoral example. He advised the Cistercian monks to abandon their horses, servants and money bags and become wandering mendicant preachers. He and his bishop then joined them for their rejuvenated mission.

Dominic had thus established the basic principles of what was to grow into the Order of Preachers, popularly known after him as Dominicans. They should follow the active path of the *vita apostolica*, live by begging, and become itinerant preachers with no vow of stability. But at the same time the learned Dominic, the university graduate, realized that education was the essential key to successful preaching in the contemporary world. When in 1217, the same year as the Franciscans, he also ordered the dispersal of his followers from their base in Toulouse, they scattered across Europe, but quickly settled in university towns, the first ones to go to Oxford arriving in 1221, three years before the Franciscans.

Where Francis had been charismatic, Dominic was a born organizer. He and his successors as Masters of the Dominicans created an Order with an uncanny mixture of similarities to and differences from the Franciscans. Both were mendicant friars, neither took vows of stability, and they were equally loyal to the pope and the institutional Church. Yet Dominic was intensely aware of the need for organization and system, and placed study and learning at the heart of the new Order. Preachers must know how to preach effectively, and that required knowledge and skills that could only be acquired at the new universities. Thus the early history of the Dominicans was inevitably intertwined with that of the first universities.

Alongside all the other forces of expansion and ordering that we have already seen at work during the central Middle Ages was that of the intellect. Europe was not only experiencing a commercial and urban revolution, it was also undergoing an academic one. Since the American historian, Charles Homer Haskins, first coined the expression in the 1920s, we have come to accept the concept of a Twelfth-Century Renaissance. What Haskins observed was a number of similarities between what was to happen to cultural life in the fifteenth and sixteenth centuries, the phenomenon we know simply as the Renaissance, and what had already occurred during the central Middle Ages. Both of these involved far more than just a shift in artistic tastes and styles. Underlying those were new ways of thinking, the exploration of novel concepts, which in their turn were inspired by different ways of looking at and utilizing the inheritance of classical Greece and Rome in the contemporary world. The remote past had acquired an immediate relevance for both later periods, if sometimes in subtly different ways. And for the medieval Renaissance the crucial event had been the rediscovery of some key works by the ancient Greek philosopher, Aristotle.

This had come about as a by-product of the expansion of Christendom at the expense of the Arabs in Sicily and Spain. As the Arabs had swept across what had been provinces of the Byzantine Empire in the seventh and eighth centuries, they had discovered in libraries the great works of the ancient Greeks and had translated them into Arabic and so enabled them to be disseminated throughout the Arabic-speaking world, including Sicily and Spain. The Christian re-conquest starting in the eleventh and twelfth centuries had, in its turn, rediscovered these Arabic texts which, once translated into Latin, began to find their way back into the Western intellectual bloodstream. Works of Aristotle that may have been known about but remained unread because physically lost to the West were now filtering back into Western libraries. Texts such as the *Metaphysics*, the *De Anima*, the *Physics* and others were now pored over in amazement by Christian thinkers. Along with them came commentaries by great Arab scholars like Averoes and Avicenna. Initially distrusted, and even condemned by some churchmen as pagan misrepresentations of everything from creation to the immortality of the soul, their content and methodology fed a new hunger for knowledge, and the skills to exploit it most effectively, that were simultaneously emerging in the West.

Masters at both the cathedral and city schools that were growing in number in the urban world used the newly discovered Aristotle to devise new ways of teaching that sometimes departed radically in method and purpose from the older monastic tradition. This so-called Scholasticism blossomed into a method that used the texts of authoritative documents in a critical way. Lists of seemingly contradictory passages were subjected to a dialectical or logical method of enquiry to try to reveal their underlying harmony. Thus of the traditional seven Liberal Arts of the medieval curriculum, it was grammar and logic (or dialectic) that became crucial for approaching written texts in a rational manner.[73] In the structure of language and the ideas it conveyed the Scholastics hoped to discover the structure of reality itself. Thus an early Scholastic, Anselm (*c.* 1033–1109), tried to discover a logical and coherent language which would enable him to trace the grammar of reality itself, leading to rational proofs for the existence of God and the incarnation, independent of the biblical texts.

Peter Abelard (1079–1143) took this a stage further with works such as *Sic et Non* ('Yes and No') in which he placed contradictory statements by Church Fathers in a series of 150 puzzles. Critically, he separated the authoritative statements from their appropriate biblical passages, thus opening up a method of logical questioning independent of scripture. He was followed by Peter Lombard (*c.* 1100–60) who composed a similar anthology of contradictory texts, now ordered by subject, in his work *Sentences*. Such books became the set texts of Scholasticism for generations to come, and established the principles of critical but logical analysis or questioning of language, and the complementary resolution of contradictions or difficulties by discovering the meaning of the words used by the authors. Thus it was a method that was logical or dialectical, that accepted that any text could be subjected to this questioning, and that an understanding of language was a key to finding the *veritas verum*, the inner truth. It was a methodology capable of application in a range of disciplines including philosophy, law, medicine and, above all, theology. It was a hugely optimistic undertaking which elevated the reason and rationality of the human mind to a level previously unknown in the medieval world.

It was not, however, without its critics. In appearing to separate the Christian revelation contained in scripture from human intellect, and to give an autonomous field of activity to the latter, it laid itself open to attack. Famously, as early as the mid-twelfth century, Bernard of Clairvaux launched a bitter assault on Peter Abelard, accusing him of unauthorized speculation about matters that were the unique province of faith as discovered in biblical revelation. Were faith and human reason thus inevitably opposed to one another? Was the use of pagan thinkers unacceptable in Christian theology? These were questions which the Scholastics had to resolve. Anselm had already argued that theology was a quest in which faith looked for understanding, and thus implied a thinking individual.

It was to be in the thirteenth century, and above all in the works of Thomas Aquinas (*c.* 1225–74), however, that Scholasticism was perhaps to reach its height, and in which faith and reason were reconciled, and the use of pagan thinkers justified. One of the basic assumptions of Aristotelian philosophy was that all ideas start in the senses, in the human perception of the material world, a view in sharp contrast to classic Platonism with its more abstract concept of the origin of ideas. Aquinas had used this basic Aristotelian notion that knowledge and learning are essentially empirical, and at the heart of his theological questioning was the idea that grace, the gift of God that aids humanity in its spiritual and moral journey, works through nature; that grace perfects nature. Nature, the created order, is in itself good and remains essentially so even after the Fall and the arrival of original sin. Thus the material world and the human intellect remain essentially good, if impaired. So God's grace works not to overcome the natural but to bring it to perfection in a spiritual and moral sense. And so the reason and intellect of those made in his own image can pursue truth, can discover methodologies that will help to lead towards that final truth. So it could be argued that Aquinas and the Scholastics were merely doing for their age what the earliest Christian thinkers had achieved in theirs, the reconciliation and assimilation of Hellenism into Christian thinking that began with Justin Martyr and his concept of the *logos spermatikos* (see above, p. 11). Aquinas had now found ways of doing the same with the new learning of the thirteenth century.

In this, Aquinas presented a counterweight to the Platonic assumptions of Augustine. For the first time in almost a millennium the great Christian thinker and theologian of late antiquity had met his match. The contrast between the two is neatly summarized by Steven Ozment: 'For Augustine, to speak of reason was to speak of the mind of man illuminated by the mind of God. For Aquinas, to speak of reason was to speak of the mind of man naturally exercising its own innate talents.'[74] In his vast work the *Summa Theologiae* (or *Theologica*) Aquinas was to demonstrate how far the mind of a man could actually go in the desire to answer every imaginable question about the things of God. Its relentless methodology of question and answer was the masterpiece of the early Scholastic theology (Document 19).

So what has all of this to do with the friars and the new urban environment? A clue is in the religious Order that Aquinas belonged to: he was a Dominican. For in the Order of Preachers Dominic and his successors had created an organization uniquely tuned to the realities of the social and educational worlds of the central Middle Ages, in some ways more finely tuned than even the Franciscans. In the words of Brenda Bolton, the Dominicans took over 'the pastoral charge of the new civilization'.[75]

First of all Dominic created a novel kind of organization for his friars. It is perhaps no exaggeration to describe the Order of Preachers as the only institution in the thirteenth century that modern people would recognize as broadly in conformity with our notions of democracy. At every level of its hierarchy the principles of election, representation and responsibility were built into the system. If the Cistercian concept of the General Chapter was an innovation in the twelfth century, then the Dominicans went beyond it in the thirteenth. This system began at the basic unit of the priory, where each prior was elected by the brethren in chapter. The next tier was the provincial chapter, where a provincial prior was elected at a special session made up of the heads of all the houses in the province with the addition of two further representatives elected from each priory. The provincial prior, once elected, was then responsible to his chapter, and could be suspended by it. As the Order grew in size the Dominicans introduced the Cistercian practice of delegating business to a group of four Definitors elected by the full chapter on its opening day of business.

At the apex of the system was the General Chapter, normally consisting of one Definitor elected by each provincial chapter, and presided over by the Master General of the Order, who was himself elected by an enlarged session of the General Chapter and remained responsible to it. The General Chapter in its turn ran on a three-yearly cycle; every third year it was made up of the provincial priors instead of Definitors, and any new statute to be added to the constitution of the Order had to be passed by three consecutive General Chapters.

On top of that there was also a system of visitation that also ran on a three-yearly cycle. For the first two years friars were elected each year by each province to act as provincial visitors; then in the third year visitors were elected by the General Chapter of the whole Order. Thus in the words of C. H. Lawrence: 'The constitution of the order embodied a revolution in the theory and practice of government. It gave effect to the principles of representation and responsibility to an extent then unknown in either the ecclesiastical or secular world.'[76] It was far ahead of any legislature in a feudal state, even the English parliament, in the degree and scope of its representative nature: even the city republics of northern Italy had not yet moved as far as the Dominicans in this direction by the thirteenth century. All secular states were being given a lesson in the operation of representative government by a religious Order.

The purpose of this Order was to preach, and this implied the roles of teacher and pastor in the urban context in which it grew. And so alongside its structural ordering the Dominicans also had a parallel one designed to make it in effect not only the most advanced constitutional organization in Latin Christendom but also the most effective academic one as well. This originated with Dominic's concept that 'the disinterested pursuit of truth was one of the highest forms of the Christian vocation'.[77] Indeed, the motto of the Order came to be *Veritas*, truth. While earlier monastic spirituality had for centuries effectively expressed the idea that study and learning were essential elements in spiritual as well as intellectual growth, none had yet pursued this idea so relentlessly and single-mindedly as the Dominicans; the academic life was at the core of the new Order. Once again, this system started at the basic unit of the priory, each of which was to have a classroom for the lectures and disputations at the heart of the Scholastic system. Some larger priories became *studia solemnia*, or major schools, with a staff large enough to teach all the subjects of the seven Liberal Arts. Then at the apex of the Order's academic structure were the *studia generalia*, or general schools, located inside the new universities and overlapping between the Order and the other schools of the universities.

By 1247 the Dominicans had such schools at a number of universities including Oxford, Cologne, Bologna, Montpellier as well as Paris. By the middle of the century the Order of Preachers was producing masters of international reputation, culminating in the greatest of them all, Thomas Aquinas himself. This provided a graduated and comprehensive academic education for its novices and brethren beyond anything in terms of quality then available to the secular clergy or laity. As C. H. Lawrence has observed: 'This co-ordinated academic system was an extraordinary construction without parallel in the Middle Ages.'[78] The Franciscans and the other, smaller Orders of mendicant friars were obliged to replicate it in order to try to keep on equal terms with the Dominicans.

What kind of friar was this system designed to produce? Above all, Dominic wanted a system that was flexible enough to accommodate a variety of individuals. The Order had adopted the Rule of St Augustine, but Dominic saw all such Rules as purely human creations and thus as much to be moulded around the individual friar as *vice versa*. So at any time a friar could be dispensed from some particular observance of the Rule in the interests of studying or preaching. Friars had individual cells rather than living and sleeping in monastic dormitories, in order to facilitate their study; the concept of responsibility was extended from the constitutional level to that of the individual. As the modern Dominican, Simon Tugwell, has commented on the first members of his Order: 'a holy cage might make it easier to avoid temptation, but it would not make them good Dominicans'.[79] Even the recitation of the daily office was pared down to the minimum to save precious time for study or preaching, and Dominicans were encouraged to see prayer as a constant in their lives rather than merely a periodic accompaniment to the daily routine.

Early versions of the constitution encouraged Dominican novices to be 'always reading something or thinking about something'.[80] Or as the contemporary chronicler of the Benedictine abbey of St Alban's, Matthew Paris, wrote of the early Dominicans: 'The whole earth is their cell and the ocean their cloister.'[81] By the mid-thirteenth century the Order of Preachers was growing rapidly and extending its constitutional and academic system across Latin Christendom. Always smaller in number than the Franciscans, with about 500 houses in 1300 compared to the Franciscan 1,400, they had an influence, nevertheless, that went far beyond simple numbers. But what were they designed for?[82]

'First the bow is bent in study, then the arrow is released in preaching.' This metaphor drawn from contemporary military practice by an early Dominican, High of St Cher, begins to answer that question.[83] Dominicans did not study just for its own sake; study had a purpose. And that was to produce the most highly skilled preachers, teachers or counsellors possible. Not surprisingly, this was systematized as well. The Order recognized three grades of preacher. The lowest was for the friars who had only proceeded as far as a priory school, and were permitted to preach exclusively to their brethren within the priory. The next category was preacher-in-ordinary, who had to have certain minimum qualifications, including being at least 25 years of age with at least one year's study of theology; these friars could preach within the territorial district of the priory, with the prior's permission. The highest grade was preacher-general, the title of a friar with at least three years of theological study and allowed to preach within his province, but only with the specific authority of the provincial chapter.

The Dominicans were new kinds of pastors for a new type of society, and the other mendicant friars shared their ethos. The call to repentance that they delivered was now in a much more sophisticated urban setting. Friars increased not only the quantity of sermons delivered to the laity, but now also elevated the sermon itself into a science. Scholastic techniques learned in the university classroom were now given practical application in a world used to debate and argument in its secular occupations. Thus a vast literature on the preaching of sermons poured from the pens of thirteenth-century Dominicans. The early Dominican, Humbert of Romans, produced hundreds of sermon outlines designed to be appropriate for different ranks in society, and by 1293 Guy of Evreux had produced no fewer than 74 fully composed sermons for all possible occasions. Over 200 works on the art of preaching have survived from the period between 1200 and 1500, almost all of them written by friars.

The Dominicans had also produced a whole range of new tools to aid the preacher in addition to these fully developed works. The Paris Dominicans in the 1230s used the new division of the Bible into chapters devised by Stephen Langton to produce the first Biblical Concordance. A Dominican called Stephen of Bourbon took another tool, the *exemplum* or example, such as an anecdote introduced into a sermon to make a point with wit or drama, and produced the first systematic collection of *exempla*, almost 2,900 in all, between 1250 and 1261.[84]

As Humbert of Romans had written: 'As the seed is planted in preaching, the fruit is harvested in confession.'[85] For the friars the call to repentance from the pulpit was but the first part of an indissoluble whole which led from the sermon to the act of confession followed by absolution. Here again they learnt from Scholasticism to apply Aristotelian distinctions, in this case between matter and form: 'they integrated the acts of the penitent (matter) with the absolution of the priest (form) into a single, and necessary, sacrament of penance'.[86] The Fourth Lateran Council of 1215 had already placed upon each individual Christian, whether ordained or lay, the obligation of annual confession to a priest. Yet the skills and experience of most secular clergy were not up to this task. Into this vacuum stepped the friars, no longer confined to using prepared lists of penance graduated to particular sins in a rigid and mechanistic manner which was the normal practice of the seculars, but now freed by their education to engage in debate with the individual penitent, to probe and question in a logical manner, to enter more fully into motivations and other psychological explanations for particular actions, and to fix more appropriate penance. Not surprisingly, just as manuals related to preaching had been produced by the friars in great numbers, so now too a similar stream of literature and technical aids was launched concerned with the hearing of confessions. Indeed, some modern scholars have drawn comparisons here between the renewal of the central Middle Ages and the sixteenth-century Reformation. Just as the latter was accompanied and fostered by printing, so the earlier one was too by an explosion of similar literature, if hand copied.[87]

But it was not only the written word that was shaped by the friars into new forms; their spoken words influenced the design of medieval architecture as well. The urban landscape was as affected by the friars as the moral one. To take the example of Florence, one of the largest and fastest growing cities in Europe, both Dominicans and Franciscans built fine new Gothic churches in the city. But these were churches with a difference. The Dominican church of Santa Maria Novella and the Franciscan Santa Croce were built as much for preaching as they were for the performance of the liturgy. They had wide and tall naves designed to hold large congregations who could listen with unobstructed view to the preacher in his pulpit. Here was the lecture theatre of the university turned to a new sacred purpose.

It was in cities like Florence, hundreds of them across the West, that the friars were to have a crucial impact on the new economy and society. They became the vehicles through which the academic learning of Scholasticism was disseminated to the secular world. In effect they were to become the first ethical regulators of a capitalist society, and in so doing helped to integrate the activities of the new urban world into the moral order of Christianity. They were able to borrow the arguments and techniques of Scholasticism and apply them to answer the ethical dilemmas raised by the money economy, and to set the parameters within which it could legitimately operate. Ironically, the precepts of ancient philosophy, first devised themselves in the urban settings of pagan Greek city states, were to return to order the commercial lives of the renewed urban world of the Christian Middle Ages, and as such to establish some of the basic principles on which all subsequent capitalist economies have operated.

Using Aristotle as refined by Scholasticism the friars began from the presumption that both property, including money, and its potential uses were both natural and good. They were necessary instruments in the promotion of a good life and an orderly society, as they retained the essential goodness of creation marred, but not obliterated, by the Fall. The early Middle Ages had seen both property and the state as necessary evils in a fallen world, needed to control disordered human desires. Now they became good in themselves and capable of utilization to promote human happiness. How, then, did concepts like profit, fees and money-lending fit into this new ethical system?

In fixing a just price the friars argued that the starting points were Aristotle's philosophy, where he had taught that human need combined with available supply of material and labour were determinants, and in addition Roman legal principles of a market in which all parties could bargain freely. Thus by a dialectical process certain principles such as fraud, monopoly or hoarding were deemed ethically illegitimate in determining a just price for goods or labour. This then led on to the further ethical dilemma: was it just to make a profit, to prosper merely by manipulating money rather than by actual toil? The philosophical key here was the idea of intention: what did the merchant intend by making a profit? The friars argued that a merchant laboured, with his brain if not with his hands, and that therefore his profit was a form of payment for this labour. But his intention must be ordered in the right way. The accumulation of riches in itself was not sufficient cause; the right intention would include making enough money to support himself and his family, and to be able to give some away in the form of alms to help the poor. Similarly, the Scholastically trained friars had an answer for the teacher charging a fee. They drew a distinction between knowledge on the one hand, in itself ultimately the freely given gift of God, and the labour in terms of time, skill and effort used to impart it on the other. The former remained free, but it was legitimate to charge for the latter.

A far thornier problem was the practice of money-lending, which seemed to contradict the Old Testament prohibition against usury. Here the friars applied both the idea of intention and combined that with arguments derived from the concept of natural law. Generally usury was to be avoided, but they then employed casuistry, bringing general moral principles to bear on particular concrete cases, a science learnt in the schools, to find more and more instances where the general condemnation of usury did not apply. So, they used the principle found in Roman law of separating the interest paid from the original amount of the loan. Thus the interest could be seen, for example, either as a form of penalty for holding and utilizing someone else's money, or as a legitimate payment for the time in which the lender was deprived of his money based on the difference between the financial position of the lender before and after making the loan.[88]

One of the ways in which these new ethical concepts were inculcated into the new urban environment was through the adoption by the friars of an idea first employed by the *Humiliati*: Third Orders. Gradually during the course of the thirteenth century the Franciscans and Dominicans organized their lay penitents into groups or fraternities, and these eventually became formalized as Third Orders specifically for the laity.

Thus just as the Church, and particularly the monks, had helped to forge an ethic for feudal society in which the potential brutality of that world had been tempered and regulated within boundaries, so now the Scholasticism of the friars was employed to do something similar, if more sophisticated, for the new complex urban society and economy.

By the middle decades of the thirteenth century then, the Western Christian world had changed significantly from the one that had existed two centuries previously. In many ways it had grown, demographically, territorially, financially and intellectually; it was a more complex place presenting Christians with more sophisticated challenges. Yet the central Middle Ages had seen a Church and its leaders who had risen remarkably successfully to those challenges; they had grown with the world in which they found themselves. They had discovered ways to satisfy the new, but legitimate demands of an educated and wealthy laity. Above all the friars had responded to that laity and had become their pastors and allies. Christianity had renewed itself and was enabled to speak to a new society in a language that society could understand and respond to.

Suggested Further Reading

For over twenty years *Medieval Monasticism: Forms of the Religious Life in Western Europe in the Middle Ages* (Longman, third edition, 2001) by C. H. Lawrence has been deservedly seen as the best general account. It combines a clarity of structure and style with the latest scholarly research and a judicious use of original sources. The current, third edition, will probably be the last updating, however.

Among the more specific and detailed studies, Giles Constable, *The Reformation of the Twelfth Century* (Cambridge University Press, 1996) looks at the dialogue between continuity and change within the monastic world. It is a detailed and careful analysis, which places individuals and institutions in relation to one another. Ludo J. R. Milis, *Angelic Monks and Earthly Men: Monasticism and its Meaning to Medieval Society* (The Boydell Press, 1992) is a thematic study of the millennium from 500 to 1500. It confines itself exclusively to monastic orders, no friars or regular canons, and thus perhaps not surprisingly comes to the conclusion that the impact of monasticism on society was more limited than some historians have argued. It is, perhaps, a useful antidote to some more exaggerated claims. David H. Williams, *The Cistercians in the Early Middle Ages* (Gracewing, 1998) is written by a historical geographer and contains a wealth of maps, plans, graphs and black-and-white photographs. It is an exhaustive study of nearly 500 pages on every aspect of the Cistercian world, including their buildings. The reader can be selective in the chapters chosen for study. If it has a fault, it is that it tends to be mainly descriptive rather than critical or analytical. It also has a rather misleading title as there obviously were no Cistercians in the *early* Middle Ages! But it does include a massive bibliography of both original and secondary sources. Noreen Hunt edited a collection of essays on the Cluniacs back in 1971, but it still remains worthy of consideration: *Cluniac Monasticism in the Central Middle Ages* (Macmillan, 1971).

On the *vita apostolica* and the growth of heretical movements a good short introduction is by Brenda Bolton, *The Medieval Reformation* (Edward Arnold, 1983). Insightful and concise, one of its themes is a comparison of the twelfth with the sixteenth centuries as periods of reform. However, there is really too little material on the later movement to demonstrate this in sufficient detail. Malcolm Lambert, *Medieval Heresy: Popular Movements from the Gregorian Reform to the Reformation* (Blackwell, second edition, 1992) is the standard introduction to the subject. It is a substantial work, primarily written for a university readership, and thus assumes quite a lot of background knowledge, and is written in a sophisticated style. But it is invaluable as a synthesis of modern research. It broadly accepts the religious motivation of both the heretics and their opponents; not everything can be explained, or explained away, by reference to social, economic or political forces. R. I. Moore, *The Origins of European Dissent* (University of Toronto Press, 1994) is a reprint of Basil Blackwell's 1985 second revised edition. This is somewhat more limited in scope, stopping in the late twelfth century, and does not follow the course of the Crusades against heretics, the Inquisition or the friars. This work makes an interesting contrast to the one by Lambert, as it emphasizes the social, economic and political links to heresy, and those same links with respect to the responses of the secular and spiritual authorities. It is not a book for beginners in this field. Bernard Hamilton has written an excellent short introduction to *The*

Medieval Inquisition (Edward Arnold, 1981). A work of synthesis designed for the non-specialist, it is very approachable in terms of style and length.

The best introduction to the Friars is again by C. H. Lawrence, *The Friars: The Impact of the Early Mendicant Movement on Western Society* (Longman, 1994). Based on the latest scholarship, with a detailed knowledge of the primary sources, it is well written and makes its points with clarity. Lester K. Little, *Religious Poverty and the Profit Economy in Medieval Europe* (Paul Elek, 1978) is insightful, with well constructed arguments. He shows how evolving types of the religious life reflected the changes in society, especially the growth of urban living culminating with the arrival of the friars. On the Dominicans there is a brief, extremely readable and scholarly introduction by Simon Tugwell OP, *Saint Dominic and the Order of Preachers* (Dominican Publications, 2001). This book explores the inner spiritual meaning as well as the early history of the Order. For Francis of Assisi and the Franciscans, a good starting point would be Adrian House, *Francis of Assisi* (Chatto and Windus, 2000). Attractively written and based on a number of original and secondary sources, it is designed for the general reader rather than the specialist. More detailed and based on a thematic rather than chronological structure is Michael Robson OFM Conv, *St Francis of Assisi: The Legend and the Life* (Geoffrey Chapman, 1997). Kenneth Baxter Wolf, *The Poverty of Riches: St Francis of Assisi Reconsidered* (Oxford University Press, 2003) is a very scholarly work which questions many assumptions about the meaning of the word 'poverty' as applied to Francis.

For Thomas Aquinas and Scholasticism there are two excellent modern introductions. Robert A. O'Donnell, *Hooked on Philosophy: Thomas Aquinas Made Easy* (Alba House, 1995) is the shorter of the two and does live up to the claim in the title. Brian Davies OP, *Aquinas* (Continuum, 2002) is a book about twice the length of the other, and is designed for the general reader with little background knowledge. Both contain short but up-to-date bibliographies. The volume in the Oxford Past Masters Series is now a bit dated, but more than worth reading. It is by Anthony Kenny, *Aquinas* (Oxford University Press, 1980). Brian Davies OP has also written a much more substantial account, *The Thought of Thomas Aquinas* (Clarendon Press, 1992). This is not a book for beginners.

Among collections of original sources, *The Cistercian World: Monastic Writing of the Twelfth Century* (Penguin, 1993) is translated, edited and introduced by Pauline Matarasso and provides a very informative introduction. Walter L. Wakefield and Austin P. Evans, *Heresies of the High Middle Ages: Selected Sources Translated and Annotated* (Columbia University Press, 1991) is a very scholarly modern collection. Simon Tugwell OP, *Early Dominicans: Selected Writings* (Paulist Press, 1982) is a substantial volume, including the important Treatise on the Formation of Preachers by Humbert of Romans. Unfortunately they do not make for exciting reading! They are heavily academic and scholastic in nature and can seem rather dry. There is an enormous three-volume set of writings connected to Francis of Assisi and the early history of his Order. Edited by Regis J. Armstrong OFM Cap, J. A. Wayne Hellmann OFM Conv and William J. Short OFM, *Francis of Assisi: Early Documents: Vol. I The Saint; Vol. II The Founder; Vol. III The Prophet* (New City Press, 1999). There are a number of selections from the writings of Thomas Aquinas, including *Thomas Aquinas: Selected Writings* (Penguin, 1998) edited, translated and introduced by Ralph McInerny.

PART THREE

Grace and Authority: Western Christianity *c.* 1450–*c.* 1650

8

Reformations

You have been born anew, not of perishable but of imperishable seed, through the living and enduring word of God. (1 Pet. 1:23)

The sixteenth and seventeenth centuries were to witness the third great division in the history of Christianity in a series of upheavals that have come to be known as the Reformation. This term in itself, however, raises a whole number of issues. The word is in the singular, with a capital letter, and preceded by the definite article. Each of those is problematic. Reform, as we have already seen, was hardly the unique characteristic of this one period of Christian history. In addition, the assumption behind the word is that early modern Europe witnessed only one example of reform. In reality *the* Reformation was made up of a bewildering number of variations on this single theme. There was, first of all, a Catholic as well as Protestant versions of Reformation that has conventionally been described as a Counter Reformation. That description itself raises further problems as it seems to imply in its turn that the reform or renewal within those parts of Latin Christendom that remained in communion with the pope was little more than a reaction to events that had already occurred in other parts of the Latin West that had led millions of Christians to break with Rome. Many historians would now argue that that aspect only accounts for at best a part of the phenomenon, and that in essence much in the Catholic version of reform was already under way long before Martin Luther (1483–1546) or the other Protestant reformers initiated their movements. However much the energy of Catholic reform was modified or re-directed by the advent of the later reform, Catholic Reformation was very much a distinct movement that owed little or nothing to outside forces in its early stages.

Yet even the term Protestant Reformation is misleading. No more was there a single Protestant Reformation than there has ever been one single Protestant Church. Those, mostly in northern Germany and Scandinavia, who followed the teachings of Martin Luther eventually came to form a number of churches that collectively became known as Lutheran. But in other parts of Europe alternative versions of Reformation led to the establishment of rival and competing Protestant churches. Ulrich (or Hulderich) Zwingli (1484–1531) and John Calvin (1509–64), associated with the cities of Zurich and Geneva respectively, initiated reforms in Switzerland that rapidly spread to parts of The Netherlands, France, Scotland, Poland and Hungary, as well as Germany, and have been collectively labelled Reformed, or sometimes Calvinist.

The list hardly stops there. Within the first generation following the publication of Luther's Ninety-Five Theses in 1517, the traditional starting point of the Protestant Reformation, many individuals or small groups splintered from the mainstream movement to form a series of Christian communities characterized by the rejection of specific doctrines or practices. Some pointed to the indisputable fact that the New Testament does not record one single instance of infant baptism and from that argued that to be truly faithful to the earliest Christian practice only adults should be baptised. Following this line of reasoning to its logical conclusion they had themselves re-baptized, becoming known as Anabaptists (Re-Baptizers). Others rejected concepts like the Holy Trinity as late and misleading corruptions of original Christian teaching, and eventually became known as Unitarians. Still others believed that they were directly and personally inspired by the Holy Spirit, in a way not dissimilar to the Montanists in the second century. Historians now apply to all these groups the term Radical Reformation. Interestingly, one thing they also tended to have in common with each other was a generally unconscious reversion to the model of the gathered Church we first noted with Tertullian more than thirteen centuries earlier.

Variations on the theme of reform were almost endless in early modern Europe. England is an excellent example of this. Alongside the state-sponsored version, the Anglican Church, itself quite distinct but containing within it and derived from, various continental models of reform, there were minority groups, including Catholics, who dissented from the official national Church and, over time, formed their own Dissenting or Nonconformist communities, largely excluded from the mainstream of political life until the nineteenth century. And then from England, and eventually from continental Europe as well, all of these versions were transplanted to what became the United States of America, where they were to throw off yet more variations in the fertile soil of the New World.

So why did this extraordinary phenomenon we know as the Reformation happen? Why, after so successfully containing and re-directing the energies of reformers in the central Middle Ages, did the Catholic Church fail to do the same in the sixteenth century? Was there something new or profoundly different about the later reformers? Were their beliefs and practices so incompatible with those of mainstream Latin Christianity in the sixteenth century that accommodation was impossible? If not, was there a failure on the part of the official Church to respond to legitimate challenge and questioning as it had done so well in the twelfth and thirteenth centuries, and if so, why? Was the doctrinal gulf just too wide to be bridged, or was there deep-seated intransigence on all sides? And what part did changes in the political and intellectual climates play in the unfolding events?

There are no easy or definitive answers to these questions. Modern historians are still struggling to offer answers to some of them. But in order to begin an exploration of these complex and demanding issues we must first step back to examine some aspects of the historical context in which these Reformations occurred.

Contexts

If one of the characteristics of the central Middle Ages had been the expansion of Christendom in a number of areas, then this process appeared to be reversing from the fourteenth century onwards. For one thing, the Black Death killed at least a third of the population of Europe between 1347 and 1350, and left the bubonic plague as an endemic feature of life for most Europeans until about 1700. In the overcrowded towns and cities of regions such as northern Italy, the demographic losses were even more severe, with some urban centres suffering the disappearance of over half their inhabitants. Such a demographic catastrophe was in its turn bound to affect the economic and political spheres as well. Trade and commerce contracted after more than three centuries of expansion, bringing bankruptcy and unemployment in their wake. Florence was to suffer its greatest social upheaval as a result when in 1378 its cloth workers rose in a revolt known as the Ciompi. Rural areas were also affected and revolts by peasants also became a notable feature of late medieval European history, with particularly dangerous examples in France in 1358 and England in 1381. Such uprisings were markers on the long road transforming Western Europe from a feudal to a wage-earning economy, and reflected parallel developments in the refashioning of the political structures across the Continent, moving from decentralized feudal monarchies towards something beginning to resemble more the modern centralized nation state.

If the population of Christendom was declining internally, its frontiers were no longer expanding either, and in one geographical area were actually shrinking. The Ottoman Turks began their expansion from Anatolia into the Balkans in the fourteenth century, defeating an army of Crusaders at Nicopolis in 1396, and in 1453 finally capturing Constantinople itself. After eleven centuries as the capital of the Eastern Christian Empire, the city of Constantine and the Empire he had begun to transform into a Christian entity had finally collapsed and disappeared. For generations the Ottomans were to be perceived as the greatest single threat facing Christendom; by 1526 they had smashed the kingdom of Hungary in a single battle at Mohacs, and by the 1530s were threatening the city of Vienna in the very heart of Europe. From the perspective of the papacy in the early sixteenth century, the Turks appeared a far greater menace than the German monk, Martin Luther.

And the history of that papacy itself had been one of mixed fortunes since the late thirteenth century. The emergence of factions in the college of cardinals finally resulted in 1294 in the election of an elderly hermit as Pope Celestine V. A complete novice in the complex world of ecclesiastical politics, the result was chaos and paralysis only ended after several months by an event unprecedented in papal history: the abdication of a pope. His successor, Boniface VIII, was very much in the Gregorian tradition, and his bull of 1302, *Unam Sanctam,* was one of the classic medieval statements of the theory of universal papal authority and jurisdiction. But the world was changing and Boniface was no Gregory VII or Innocent III. He underestimated and alienated many of the secular powers of his day, from the aristocratic Colonna family in Rome itself to Philip the Fair, king of France. By 1303 his struggle to prevent royal taxation of clerics in France led to his seizure and brief imprisonment at the hands of the king's agents. Broken in health, he was to die within a month of his capture.

By 1309 the papacy itself had moved to Avignon, where a new papal palace was begun in 1336. For almost 70 years, until 1377, no reigning pope was to set foot again in Rome. As we have seen, the Middle Ages had witnessed many periods of papal exile from the city of Peter, so that in itself was not an impediment to a properly functioning institution. Nevertheless, the Avignon papacy was to be the longest continuous absence from Rome in the history of the institution. Traditionally this has been interpreted as a period of substantial French influence on both the curia and the popes themselves, weakening the papacy as an international force. More recently historians have questioned these assumptions however, and to some extent rehabilitated the Avignon papacy.[1]

What cannot be questioned, nevertheless, was the consequences of the long exile once the papacy returned to Rome. Within a year the election of an Italian, Urban VI, was disputed, his sanity called into question, and the French cardinals assembled to depose him and elect an alternative. From 1378 to 1417 the papacy, and with it Latin Christendom, was to experience one of the longest, and certainly the most destructive, division to date, known as the Great Schism. The papal schism developed into a major fault-line running across Christendom, with political rivalries reflected in divided allegiances, England and France for example recognizing rival claimants to the papal throne, mirroring their own ongoing conflict in the Hundred Years War. Even the religious Orders found themselves torn in two, with different provinces recognizing different popes.

As time passed and no natural solution to the schism presented itself, one suggestion that emerged was to summon an Ecumenical Council, the only conceivable body with sufficient authority to end the dispute. This the cardinals did in 1409. Although the gathering at Pisa was boycotted by both claimants to the papal throne as illegitimate because not summoned by a pope, this Council launched a series held during the first half of the fifteenth century that often proved to be reforming. Unfortunately Pisa initially made matters worse by electing a third pope without first being able to persuade the other two to stand aside. Matters were only to be finally resolved in 1417 at the Council of Constance when Martin V was finally acknowledged as the one undisputed Pope and his rivals obliged to withdraw.

This age of Councils, however, had produced a concept known as Conciliarism. Broadly speaking this elevated the Ecumenical Council into a position superior to the pope in terms of authority. Only in 1460 was Pius II able to successfully condemn the idea and bring these periodic Councils to a halt. But the legacy of Conciliarism was a papacy deeply suspicious of, and hostile to, the idea of calling another Ecumenical Council as a means to reform the Church; as late as 1512 a king of France could use the threat of summoning a Council to depose the pope as an effective political lever in a dispute with the papacy. A few years after that Luther also called for a Council to hear and judge his complaints against Rome. This fear of Conciliarism was one of the constraints which inhibited the early sixteenth-century popes from calling such a Council, an assembly which might not be under their guidance in the scope of its deliberations. It was not to be until 1545, almost three decades after Luther's initial revolt, that such a Council was finally to be summoned by a pope to the city of Trent, and which itself was to last, with long periods of enforced inactivity, until 1564. Some modern historians have seen this protracted delay as allowing enough time to pass for the exacerbating and hardening of the divisions between the first Protestant Reformers and Rome to reach a point beyond which compromise was impossible. In the opinion of Patrick Collinson: 'it was a generation too late' to heal the wounds which had now opened within Latin Christendom.[2]

It is perhaps surprising, given the institutional problems experienced by the late medieval Church, that papal schism was the only serious consequence.

That other form of division, heresy, was, with two notable exceptions, less widespread than it had been in the central Middle Ages. The two exceptions were the Lollards, largely found in the southern half of England, and the Hussites in the Czech-speaking parts of Bohemia. What distinguishes these movements, however, from the earlier outbreaks of heresy, and to some degree points to the later manifestation of Protestantism, was that they were initiated within the setting of the university and were much more doctrinal in nature.

John Wyclif (or Wycliffe), born about 1330, was a noted philosopher at Oxford University. The movement of dissent that he initiated was novel in the Middle Ages, not only in that it had no connection to any previous heretical groups, but also, and more significantly, that it was the first to combine academic questioning with a popular following. Wyclif became deeply disillusioned both with the Scholastic theology of his day and also with the state of the Church, at least as represented by the clergy. In the final phase of his life in the years before his death in 1384 he increasingly argued for scripture as the authoritative centre of Christianity, that the claims of the papacy were unhistorical, that monasticism was irredeemably corrupt, and like the Donatists that the moral unworthiness of priests invalidated their office and sacraments. By the end of his life he had come to deny the doctrine of transubstantiation, that at the Eucharist the 'substance' of the bread and wine gives way to the body and blood of Christ, and that the bread and wine remain only in their lower 'accidents', terms the Scholastics derived from Aristotelian philosophy. And he had also come to advocate vernacular translations of the Bible for use by the laity.

His academic eminence, his friends at the royal court, and a Church riven by schism, allowed Wyclif to survive, if in his final years in exile from Oxford. By that point what many of his earlier sympathizers began to perceive as his growing extremism had earned him the official condemnation of the university, and his circle of academic and court supporters had shrunk significantly. But many of his ideas, especially about lay access to a vernacular Bible and the morality of the clergy, had seeped out from their original academic setting into the population at large, at least among those who were literate, including members of the lower clergy, craftsmen and artisans. Here, in secret underground reading circles, the Bible was studied, and preachers, clerical or lay, listened to. However, the revolt of Sir John Oldcastle in 1414, a Wyclif sympathizer, lost the movement much of its remaining élite support as it appeared to be associated with political sedition. But the Lollards, or 'mumblers', continued as a small underground movement into the early sixteenth century when they were largely absorbed or replaced by Protestantism.

Their numbers, however, must not be exaggerated. Oldcastle's revolt, for instance, probably attracted fewer than 300 supporters.[3] In the middle decades of the fifteenth century Lollard numbers declined still further, and only staged a moderate recovery in the decades before the Reformation. In the Diocese of Lincoln in the decade 1511–21 the Church courts dealt with about 300 cases of suspected Lollardy. To put those numbers in perspective, that was an average of 30 cases a year spread geographically over the eight counties that made up what was the largest diocese in England; fewer than four cases per year in any single county.[4] Lollardy, then, retained a nuisance value for the official Church in England, but never remotely threatened wholesale subversion from within.

That, however, could not be said of the Hussites in Bohemia. In the opinion of Malcolm Lambert they went further than any other popular medieval heretical movement in 'shaking the old order'.[5] Successful to a degree, he still regards them, nevertheless, as in the end just another chapter in the story of the failures of medieval heresy. Like the Lollards, their symbolic founder was another university academic, Jan Hus of Prague (*c.* 1372–1415). Indeed, it was partly through reading the works of Wyclif that Hus and his supporters found much of their terminology if not their precise ideas.

Unlike England there was a clear linguistic division within Bohemia which aided the dissenters. For several generations German-speakers had been migrating into Bohemia, settling especially in the towns and cities and establishing a strong position within Charles University in Prague. Among the Czech-speakers there was already a movement of spiritual and pastoral renewal before Hus appeared on the scene; thus he was little more than the symbolic figurehead of a pre-existing reform movement that became associated mainly, but not exclusively, with Czech-speakers. The turning point came in 1415 when, having gone to the Council of Constance to plead the cause of Czech reform, Hus was condemned and burned for heresy. Some 452 Bohemian nobles signed a protest document, a measure of the strength of support inside Bohemia.[6] By 1420 the country was clearly sliding into civil war, with outside intervention by imperial forces attempting to suppress any ecclesiastical and political revolt. The Hussites themselves were divided between moderate and radical wings which fought each other as enthusiastically as they resisted the imperialists. Fighting finally subsided after a compromise was reached at Jihlava in 1436, leaving the Hussites 'the first declared heretics to beat off a Catholic crusade'.[7] By 1485 the moderates had won a major concession from the official Church in being allowed to retain their practice of administering wine from the chalice as well as bread to the laity at the Eucharist.

Hussitism remained a uniquely Bohemian phenomenon, however, and never spread in any significant way beyond the Czech linguistic frontier. While it disrupted political and economic as well as ecclesiastical life within

Bohemia, it had little if any impact beyond that kingdom. Although Luther was later to be called the 'Saxon Hus' he had little knowledge of its ideas until some years after the Reformation was itself under way. Thus there was no direct linkage backwards from the Protestant Reformers of the sixteenth century to the late medieval heresies. Similarities between them were entirely accidental.

All of this, however, is very far from leading to a conclusion that the late medieval Church experienced anything that could be realistically described as 'decline' or 'decay', terms which most modern historians would now regard as quite inappropriate and certainly not accurately reflecting the evidence. The Reformation cannot be explained by reference to a preceding late medieval ecclesiastical deterioration in either institutional or popular terms. The papacy in about 1500, for instance, was in a far less parlous state than it had been in 1000, when it was effectively at the mercy of the Holy Roman Emperors and the local Roman nobility. Popes like Alexander VI (1492–1503) or Julius II (1503–13) may have been worldly and open to the charge of corruption, but the same accusations could have been levelled at quite a number of the previous occupants of the throne of St Peter. Julius II did indeed personally lead papal armies to war, but so had medieval popes before him. On the other hand, Pope Pius II (1458–64) was an internationally renowned scholar, an important figure in the first generations of the Renaissance, and a reforming pope who sent his legate, Cardinal Nicholas of Cusa, on a series of embassies to promote reform.

Moving from the pinnacles of Church government to the more popular levels, the evidence for thriving spiritual life is abundant in the fourteenth and fifteenth centuries. Nowhere is this clearer than in the extraordinary outpouring of mystical writings in these centuries. England alone produced a string of works that are now regarded as classics of Christian mysticism. Julian of Norwich (*c.* 1342–1416), the anchoress who wrote the *Revelation of Divine Love*, the anonymous author of the *Cloud of Unknowing*, Walter Hilton (*c.* 1343–96), the hermit and Augustinian canon, who composed the *Scale of Perfection*, or Margery Kempe (*c.* 1373–1438) who not only gave birth to fourteen children but also suffered from periodic madness interspersed with visions, and who recorded her experiences in the work known as the *Book of Margery Kempe*, are probably the best-known examples. But England was not alone in producing schools of mysticism in the late Middle Ages. Germany could boast the Dominican, Meister Eckhart (*c.* 1260–*c.* 1328), John Tauler (d. 1361), and Henry Suso (*c.* 1295–1366).

Perhaps the most outstanding example of popular lay spirituality in these centuries was the *Devotio Moderna* or Modern Devotion, which laid great stress on the internal spiritual life of the individual, and was often associated with meditation on the life and death of Jesus. Its most famous literary product was probably the *Imitation of Christ* by Thomas à Kempis (*c.* 1380–1471). It also found institutional form in the Brethren of the Common Life. Originally founded by Gerard Groote (1340–84), who had experienced a call to a deeper spirituality in 1374, the Brethren did not consist of a formal Order, and the members, whether clerical or lay, took no vows. But they combined an intense personal spirituality with an active life in the world, especially that of education. Spreading from The Netherlands into the Rhineland and to other parts of Europe, they became famous for their schools which were both free and also centres of the most advanced academic ideas of their day. By 1500 the Brethren had some 26 houses in Germany alone.[8] Clearly a development of that intensely personal spirituality of the central Middle Ages, especially in the concentration on the person of Jesus, the *Devotio Moderna* and the Brethren were also to have an influence on the future, on figures as diverse as the great Renaissance scholar Erasmus (1466–1536), Martin Luther, and the founder of the Jesuits, Ignatius Loyola (1491–1556).[9]

The advent of the Reformation, then, had little to do with the condition of the late medieval Church, which was certainly no more in a state of 'decline' or 'decay' than in any other period of ecclesiastical history. The form that the history of Christianity took in the sixteenth century probably had more to do with what was happening in the world outside the late medieval Church, and the changing attitudes that this engendered in individuals and groups towards the institution. This was true of the intellectual and cultural spheres where a series of profound changes was in part reflected by such people as John Wyclif or movements like the Brethren of the Common Life. The first of these changes was to occur within Scholasticism. The optimistic rationalism of the thirteenth century was to experience a profound challenge in the fourteenth, especially when such catastrophies as the Black Death seemed to question both the order of nature and the human capacity to understand and regulate its environment. God and his creation seemed far less predictable or benign than they had previously, and for a while the smile of reason was replaced on the streets of many cities by the horrific processions of flagellants lacerating their bodies in a desperate attempt to appease the displeasure of God with their extreme offering of penitence.

This new mood of religious uncertainty was nowhere better reflected than in the followers of the Scholastic philosopher William of Ockham (1285–1347). Aquinas, following Aristotle, had argued that all intellectual concepts and arguments start with sensory perceptions: 'There is nothing in the mind that was not first in the senses.'[10] Thus for Aquinas knowledge was a quite natural process, and in his arguments for the proof of God's existence he started with the concepts of natural law, design and purpose in creation to point to an original organizer. This led him on to argue that all particular things had features common to them serving as a medium through which the mind knew individual things. Thus God, humanity and creation were interconnected by the structure of reality itself: 'People knew and spoke of God by analogy with human experience because a real, albeit imperfect, relation existed between God, man and the world of human discourse.'[11]

Ockham came to disagree fundamentally with many of the assumptions behind the theology of Aquinas. He attacked the idea of a common nature or Universals, which he argued existed not in reality but only in human minds, and that creation was only organized in the sense that the human intellect conceived it in that way. Thus knowledge is not mediated but direct and intuitive, and God's existence cannot be proven by reference to a quite arbitrary view of creation; all such things are ultimately a matter of faith, not reason. To see God as part of any scheme was to place limitations on him. God, to be truly God, had to be free to save humanity in any way he chose, which implied an attack on the sacramental system of the Church itself.[12]

The idea that Ockham and later Scholastics themselves represented a 'decline' in medieval philosophy was, in the twentieth century, largely associated with the French scholar, Etienne Gilson (1884–1978). Gilson saw Aquinas as the summit of medieval theology, reconciling reason and revelation. For him, Ockham thus represented a retreat from this high intellectual plateau into the more tangled plains of faith where reason took a back seat. In more recent decades, however, Ockham has been reassessed and seen more as part of a lively and fertile ongoing medieval debate than as a decline into sterility.[13]

Whatever the truth of the matter, what was certain was that beginning in the late fourteenth and early fifteenth centuries, Scholasticism itself had a new intellectual rival in the form of Humanism, a crucial aspect of the phenomenon we know as the Renaissance. Clearly this latter term presents as many problems as 'Reformation'. As we have already seen, the central Middle Ages experienced what historians have come to call the Twelfth-Century Renaissance. What were the similarities or differences between the two? One obvious point of connection was that they both sought inspiration from the remote past, from classical antiquity and its great writings. However, there are also subtle but profound distinctions here. The earlier medieval movement had had to rely on translations into Latin from translations into Arabic taken from the original Greek. Knowledge of the ancients was thus very much at third hand. What is significant about the later movement was the obvious desire to get back behind the translations to the originals. This was true also for works that had survived the fall of Rome in the West, and had been progressively copied for a thousand years. Here the problems could range from copyists' errors to the rather different form of Latin employed by the medieval

Scholastics compared to that of the ancients. Latin in the medieval world had been a living, changing and developing language.

One of the problems also faced by medieval scholars was the almost complete absence of a knowledge of ancient Greek in the West. This too had almost completely died out in the centuries after the collapse of Roman power. Understanding of Greek had to be slowly and painfully relearned over a number of generations. One obvious source of still-existing Greek speakers was the Byzantine Empire. But with what was left of the once-mighty Eastern Roman Empire shrivelled to a husk of its former glory, that was no easy undertaking. However, the abortive reunion negotiations between the Eastern and Western Churches at the Council of Florence in 1438–45 was one opportunity to make scholarly contact, something maintained by the curia for much of the early fifteenth century.[14] Another method was for Western scholars and collectors to physically travel to Constantinople themselves and bring back original Greek manuscripts. This was done in the 1420s, for instance, by the Sicilian Giovanni Aurispa, who returned with two hundred and thirty eight Greek manuscripts, including plays, and philosophical works by Plato.[15] Great patrons like Lorenzo di Medici employed agents who purchased and brought back to Florence for him about 200 codices of Greek manuscripts, some 80 of which were then unknown in the West.[16]

But it was not only works in Greek that were being rediscovered in original manuscripts: Latin masters were also reappearing in the West, most notably Cicero. Francesco Petrarch (1304–74) was something of a pioneer in this field, and he was to be followed by others. Indeed, it has been estimated that about half of all the works by Cicero that we now possess were rediscovered during the first half of the fifteenth century.[17] For the scholars of these first generations of the Renaissance the great motto was *Ad fontes*, 'back to the sources'.

It was not merely the rediscovery of lost manuscripts, however, that characterized this later movement, but what was then subsequently done with them. First of all, as the knowledge of Greek, and of Ciceronian Latin advanced, scholars came to make comparisons between the originals and the translations in Scholastic Latin. It was soon obvious to them that the latter were riddled with textual errors. This resulted in an extensive linguistic exercise to correct and edit texts so that scholars could get as near to the meaning of the originals as possible. Second, the Scholastic method of placing contradictory statements from ancient texts against each other and then using the dialectic method to display an underlying agreement, was seen as inadequate. Doing this for texts sometimes separated by centuries was to ignore the differences produced by historical change. Thus the new scholars began the process of placing sources within their historical contexts. Fifteenth-century men of letters like Lorenzo Valla began to employ the new linguistic and historical techniques to reveal not only inconsistencies and misinterpretations, but also downright forgeries. Starting this process with Roman law, Valla and others moved on to documents more directly associated with the Church, most famously with the so-called Donation of Constantine. This text, purporting to be from the fourth century and showing the Roman Emperor handing authority over to the bishop of Rome was, in reality, a forgery probably executed in the eighth century in papal Rome, as Valla and others demonstrated.

Not surprisingly, by the fifteenth century many of these new scholars had come to despise Scholasticism and through it much of what we would now regard as typical of medieval culture, from painting and sculpture, to architecture and literature. For many of them the West had been sunk in a millennium of darkness since the fall of Rome to the barbarians, and only now was the veil being lifted to let in the light of true civilization. Typical of this way of thinking was Matteo Palmieri (1406–75) who, writing in the 1430s could describe how 'the real guides to distinction in all the arts, the solid foundation of all civilization, have been lost to mankind for 800 years or more'. And that now at last the new Latin 'has begun to shine forth in its ancient purity, its beauty, its majestic rhythm'. God, he wrote, should be thanked that we have been 'born into this new age, so full of hope and promise, which already rejoices in a greater array of nobly-gifted souls than the world has seen in the thousand years that have preceded it'.[18] In all the arts, then, a new beginning should be made, the Middle Ages rejected and the classical world revived as the great source and model of a new culture. Starting in Italy, most notably Florence and the surrounding Tuscan cities, these ideas began to spread out slowly across Europe during the fifteenth century, accompanied by other rediscoveries, such as the *Ten Books of Architecture* by the ancient Roman, Vitruvius. More and more people believed that they were indeed privileged to be present at the birth of a new age, in which innovation was inspired by renovation.

These discoveries were to have further ramifications. For one, the old Scholastic curriculum of the seven Liberal Arts came under assault. The logical or dialectic method was criticized as inadequate for the study of ancient texts, and the whole concept of an educational system designed to produce lawyers, medical doctors, and above all theologians, was seen as too restricting. Grammar, the study of Latin and Greek, should be at the heart of education. But that should lead on to the same eloquent style that the great classical poets or playwrights had demonstrated, so rhetoric and poetry should form part of the new curriculum. History, too, had been demonstrated to be an invaluable tool. And since the end of education should be the production of someone well versed in right values and conduct, ethics should form part of the system. As Leonardo Bruni, the fifteenth-century Florentine wrote in one of his letters: 'Thus one must not only learn from the scholars . . . but must also get instruction from poets, orators and historians, so that one's style may be eloquent, elegant, and never crude in substance . . . For they combine to produce a good man, than which nothing can be thought more useful.'[19]

For behind all this rediscovery of old texts and reconstruction of the educational curriculum lay the idea that a new concept of human nature itself was emerging from this growing acquaintance with the ancient world. 'Man is the measure of all things' was a saying that the Renaissance took over from the ancient Greek philosopher Protagoras (*c.* 485–411 BC). At the heart of the Renaissance was an elevated and exalted view of the dignity and potential of humanity which Renaissance scholars believed they had rediscovered in the classical texts and which the new curriculum, the *Studia Humanitatis* or Humane Studies, was designed to foster. Hence these new 'Humanities' were central to the new Humanists. Petrarch in the fourteenth century believed that he was rediscovering moral qualities in the ancients quite compatible with Christian concepts.[20] In the next century Marsilio Ficino (1433–99), the Florentine Platonist, was to take up the theme, identifying Socrates as a Platonist precursor of Christ,[21] and it was to culminate with Erasmus openly speaking of 'Saint Socrates'. Giovanni Pico della Mirandola (1463–94) was to encapsulate these ideas in his *Oration on the Dignity of Man* in 1486, which argued for the potential of human moral perfection through the cultivation of the arts and humanities.[22]

Such massive optimism was in stark contrast to the mood following the Black Death, and with the claim that human instinct could be a true guide to moral virtue and spiritual perfection, the seemingly arbitrary God of the Ockhamists was refuted.[23] Clearly such views of human nature not only went far beyond the earlier medieval Renaissance, but also were to have a significant influence on the shape of the ideas that we associate with the later Reformation. The two movements had a close, sometimes almost symbiotic relationship, that was to be played out in some unusual and paradoxical ways from the sixteenth century onwards, as we shall discover in the next chapter.

Finally, what of the political contexts within which the Reformation was to make its appearance? As early as 1324 Marsilio of Padua (*c.* 1275–*c.* 1342) had argued in his *Defensor Pacis* for the separation of the secular from the sacerdotal, and had seen the state as the great unifying power in society, to which the Church should naturally be subordinated. These views earned him a papal excommunication. But, in a sense, they proved to be prophetic. As the feudal monarchies of Western Europe began the long and slow process of transforming themselves into nation states during the early modern period, there emerged concepts like absolute monarchy and the confessional state. Although a contentious subject among modern historians, absolutism in essence meant a more direct concentration of power, and the relationships derived from power, into the person of the sovereign. This in its turn slowly began to cut through the highly decentralized nature of feudalism with a more unified and centralized concept of the state. At the same time one aspect of this new consolidation of power was to bring the local churches more closely under the supervision of the crown, eventually leading to confessionalism, the idea that the unity and integrity of the state itself was partly dependent on a unified religious profession by its subjects.

Movements in these directions can be seen quite clearly in the fifteenth century. In 1438 the Pragmatic Sanction of Bourges handed over to the French crown huge swathes of patronage within the French Church; hundreds of leading churchmen now relied upon the favour of the king for their appointment to office. In Castile and Aragon, united by dynastic marriage in 1469, the sovereigns Ferdinand and Isabella took a similar position in relation to everything from bishoprics to the Inquisition following the Synod of Seville in 1478. In essence, well before the outbreak of Reformation, many European sovereigns had already achieved a degree of administrative control over their local churches broadly comparable to that acquired by Henry VIII in England in the 1530s. The only vital difference was that Henry could also dictate the doctrinal beliefs of his Church, while the French and Spanish monarchs could not.

In 1494 the political situation in Europe was transformed when the king of France invaded northern Italy in pursuit of dynastic claims. The threat of Gallic domination of perhaps the most densely populated, urbanized and economically advanced region of Europe was immediately contested by Spain. By 1519 the French royal house of Valois was firmly locked in competition with the Habsburgs for the hegenomy of Europe, resulting in a series of wars which were to last until 1559. From Martin Luther to Ignatius Loyola, from Henry VIII's divorce to the summoning of the Council of Trent, almost all the major personalities and issues of the first half of the sixteenth century were to be affected to some degree by this conflict.

It must be understood, however, that none of the phenomena outlined in this section, whether the Avignon papacy, the Great Schism, heresies or mystical writings, the changes within Scholasticism, the emergence of Humanism or the nation state, either individually or collectively *caused* the Reformation. They are not in themselves an explanation of why Reformation was to happen. But they do form part of the framework or matrix within which it was to occur. To some degree the path it took was shaped by these things, but they were not its originators. They gave Reformation its context, in some senses its voice or vocabulary, but they did not make it happen.

So, what was this phenomenon we call Reformation, and why did it happen? In order to begin to understand that, we must now turn to some of the personalities, ideas and events which helped to shape it.

Personalities and Ideas

Martin Luther was both the last great theologian of the Middle Ages and at the same time the first, and perhaps most significant, of the Reformation era. In a way not dissimilar to that later German genius, Ludwig van Beethoven (1770–1827) in whom was to be found both the culminating point of classical music and the beginnings of Romanticism, Luther straddled two worlds. Born in Saxony in 1483, his father, Hans, was a miner who had prospered and become a partner in a firm that controlled a number of copper mines and foundries. The family money was able to buy the young Martin a superb education, completed in 1505 with the award of a master's degree from the University of Erfurt. During a violent thunderstorm in the year of his final graduation the terrified young man supposedly vowed to enter the religious life if he was spared, which he subsequently did, joining the prestigious Augustinian house in Erfurt.

There over the next decade or so Luther underwent a protracted spiritual crisis. He was acutely aware of his own spiritual and moral unworthiness before God and, with escalating desperation, tried to find a way of reconciling his depraved state, as he saw it, with that of the holy and just God who eventually was to judge him. He threw himself enthusiastically into the traditional medieval ascetic and penitential system, with physically debilitating fasting, and confessions reputedly lasting anything up to six hours at a time. Clearly this was a scrupulosity of conscience that exceeded anything normally experienced by the most pious medieval monk, and out of which grew his rejection of so much in that medieval religious system.

How is this to be understood? Over the centuries many explanations have been offered. In his own day Luther was regarded by many as an heroic figure, who through his own undoubted sufferings refined by his intellect had demonstrated that the whole medieval system from monasticism to papalism was a colossal corruption and fraud foisted on a wickedly-deceived laity by immoral clerics. Thus the system in its entirety should be swept away and a return to the pure and simple faith of the Gospel reinstituted to replace it. For his opponents and detractors, on the other hand, Luther was the spawn of Satan, demonically possessed, and an instrument of the Evil One in his campaign against God's Son and his holy Church. Variations on such extreme positions persisted for centuries and Luther the hero of Protestantism or the villain of Catholicism became institutionalized and reflected in partisan historical writing.

Happily in more recent generations, partly under the influence of the modern spirit of Ecumenism, such a dichotomy of views has diminished significantly. At the same time modern historians have developed a more dispassionate and scientific approach to their sources, and real attempts have been made to get back behind the mythical Luther to the genuine sixteenth-century article. Yet this in its turn can also result in quite violently different, if academically inspired, interpretations. In 1958, for example, the distinguished American psychologist, Erik Erikson, published a book entitled *Young Man Luther* in which he attempted to apply modern psychological insights to the youthful Luther. For this author: 'Luther's theological and religious problems are seen to have been more parentally than culturally induced, the product of a universal spiritual Odyssey of youth rather than of a time-bound religious culture.'[24] For Erikson, in this famous piece of 'psychohistory', Luther's spiritual crises stemmed more from a classic 'identity crisis' derived from his relationship with his father, than from a growing questioning of the medieval monastic experience. Luther's anxieties about his relationship to divinity were but projections of his own deeply flawed relationship with his overbearing father.

Historians, while appreciating any academic tool that can help their reconstructions and interpretations of the past, have been less than happy with the work of Erikson. Unfortunately we really know far too little about Luther's childhood, and far too much about his father that was clearly fabrication, to make authoritative statements about his psychological state. At the same time what we do know would not indicate anything unusual, let alone noteworthy, in young Martin's upbringing or his relationship with his father in the context of the conventions of the time. The danger is to impose, or read backwards, onto a medieval person's views and experiences much later interpretations of what they might mean in that much later, and in many significant ways different cultural environment. Fascinating and provocative as Erikson's young Martin Luther is, there must be grave doubts about its historical accuracy.[25]

New and controversial interpretations of Luther still continue to be offered, nevertheless, if few of them are quite so outstanding as Erikson's. Luther's most recent biographer, Richard Marius, sees his crises in very different terms from Erikson's. For Marius they are the result of the continual conflict within him between seemingly opposing forces; a fear of death and hell on the one hand struggled with a deep faith in the resurrection and saving power of Jesus on the other: 'his titanic wrestling with the dilemma of the desire for faith and the omnipresence of doubt and fear became an augury for the development of the religious consciousness of the West in modern times'.[26] Is Luther, then, the first modern religious man? Whether or not that is so, Marius is equally sure that Luther was an equally titanic negative force: 'I believe that Luther represents a catastrophe in the history of Western civilization' resulting in 'carnage that consumed Europe for well over a century after Luther died' and 'in my view, whatever good Luther did is not matched by the calamities that came because of him'.[27] By contrast, at the other extreme of the most modern evaluations of Luther lies Patrick Collinson. 'In the pages that follow', he writes in his recent short history of the Reformation, 'it will be hard to conceal from the intelligent reader my love of Luther'.[28] Clearly this historian retains something of the highly positive regard in which Luther has always been held by the Protestant school of Reformation history. However distant the echoes of denominational conflict now are, just sometimes the perceptive and trained ear can still catch a note lingering on the air.

However his crises are to be interpreted, and his legacy evaluated, at the time, in the teens of the sixteenth century, Luther was at work trying to resolve his problems in the ways that seemed most appropriate to him as a medieval monk and scholar, through an intense study of the Bible, especially the letters of St Paul, illuminated by the writings of the greatest theologians from the earliest centuries of Christianity to the latest Ockhamists of his own time. Perhaps not surprisingly, after St Paul himself, the next most important authority for Luther was that giant of Latin theology who had himself wrestled with problems of faith and doubt, St Augustine. His relationship with the Ockhamists, and through them the whole Scholastic tradition, was more complex. While coming to appreciate Ockham's stress on the primacy of faith, he was equally repelled by the Pelagian implications of some of his ideas. Above all, Luther came to detest the methodology of Scholasticism as passionately as any Humanist, if for subtly different reasons. He hated what he saw as the cold logic of rationalizing the things of God. Luther was a man of deep passions, and he was most passionate above all about his religion. The cool and detached reasoning of the schoolroom was not for him. His God had to be reached in a way similar to the late medieval mystics, whom he read and admired, deep inside the very heart and core of his being.

As such, one sentence of St Paul perhaps above all others came to be the key that unlocked the door blocking the way to an understanding of a loving God in Luther's soul. Writing of the saving power of the Gospel, St Paul asserted: 'For in it the righteousness of God is revealed through faith for faith; as it is written, "The one who is righteous will live by faith"' (Rom. 1:17). Alone, in a room in a tower in the university city of Wittenberg where he was a professor of theology, Luther struggled with the meaning of St Paul's words. And then, in one of the most sensational moments of spiritual illumination, something seemed to 'click' in Luther's mind and soul. This 'Tower Experience' is one of the greatest moments of religious conversion in Christian history. Staring at him from a passage of scripture he must have read or heard countless times, but leaping out at him now from the page in a new way, was the key to his and all religious doubts and dilemmas: faith.

But by faith Luther did not mean a dispassionate assent to credal formulas or doctrinal decrees. He meant, rather, a total reorientation of the personality, a radical re-forming of the individual, an unconditional turning to God. As another Protestant Reformer, Guillaume Farel, was to write some years later of faith: 'It is an affection, an experience, and a true knowledge that God our father is good, perfect, powerful, and wise, and he in his self-love has chosen us to be his sons, saving and redeeming us by our Saviour Jesus.'[29] Or as Luther himself was to describe this moment of insight so powerfully in his own words: 'At once I felt myself to be reborn and as though I had entered paradise through the opened gates' (Document 20).[30]

Unfortunately we do not know the precise date of this re-formative experience. Historians have argued about it endlessly, and any point between 1513 and 1518 seems possible. What we do know about, however, is the consequences. Being 'justified', or made acceptable to the holy and loving God, was hardly a new idea. But never before Luther had it been so relentlessly promoted as the centrepiece of Christian belief and practice. Quoting Augustine as his authority, Luther went so far as to argue that Justification by Faith *Alone* was the essential ingredient of true Christianity.[31] But from this essential insight flowed a series of equally powerful consequences that 'demolished at a stroke whole wings of the edifice of contemporary piety'.[32]

If Justification was essentially about a person's 'being', what they are in their deepest selves, then their 'doing', the tasks they perform, cannot in any way lead to Justification. For the latter is, in Luther's view, the totally unmerited gift of God. We cannot work ourselves into a right relationship with God; we must trust him to do it for us. Thus it is through the grace of God that justifying faith is gifted to us, not through our 'works'. And so the whole medieval penitential system tottered and collapsed before Luther's onslaught, bringing down monks and confessors in its fall. All the unaided efforts of even the most sincere and conscientious of monks were futile; all that was needed was the gift of faith. But, here following Augustine, this led Luther to believe that only some people would be so undeservedly rewarded, and thus predestination was revived as an essential Christian concept.

But not only monks were targeted. If faith was an unmerited and *direct* gift of God to the individual, then the mediation of everyone else, from priests to saints, was called into question. The individual should need no intermediaries between itself and God apart from Jesus. Where, then, should the Christian look to find this gracious gift? The answer was obvious. It was there in the words of scripture, the great book of life. So alongside Justification by Faith Alone, Luther placed scripture alone; an equally massive shift in the concept of

Christian authority. Tradition, the Church, the papacy, all must give way to this supreme authority. In the pages of scripture the individual reader had all that was needed for the nourishment of the soul. And it thus necessarily followed that those scriptures should be available in the vernacular for all, clergy or laity, to read, study and pray. As for the Christian community, all that was required for the organization of its life, its liturgy and leadership, were to be found in scripture too. Anything that was not found in scripture had no true authority. That in its turn led to other revolutions. Luther could find no scriptural authority for five of the traditional seven sacraments. Only baptism and the Eucharist seemed to have this necessary authority from the Bible; so the other five – confirmation, ordination, marriage, penance and extreme unction – were downgraded from their sacramental status.

If the mediation of priests was no longer essential, then the status of another group, the laity, was consequently raised. Luther came to argue for the concept of the Priesthood of All Believers, in which the mediating role of one Christian to another could be performed as legitimately by the laity as by the clergy. This was not to say that the whole concept of the clergy was abolished, because clearly there was scriptural authority for it. But now those who ministered in the Christian community did so more as representatives of that community than the specially chosen and anointed ministers of divinity.

Thus at the heart of what we call Reformation was, perhaps, not so much a division about how Christians viewed God, as of alternative views of humanity or human nature. Patrick Collinson sums this up very neatly: 'What is man? Was his creation in the image of God carried forward triumphantly in his salvation in Christ . . . Or was he a humble, receptive creature, nobody without the overwhelming grace of God?'[33] What had the Fall in Eden done to human nature? Was its essential goodness instilled by God when he created in his own image lost for ever, and its redemption and salvation to be found totally in the sacrificial acts of his Son? Or was human nature fallen only in the sense of being a flawed but still essentially intact vessel capable of autonomous, if diminished, actions of goodness? Were human beings totally and exclusively reliant upon the grace of God and his gift of Justifying faith for their ultimate destiny; or could they, to some extent, and in however weakened a way, co-operate in the process of their own salvation and make valid contributions to it, good in the sight of the author of all goodness? On the answers to those questions hung the whole future shape of Western Christianity.

Broadly speaking, and with only differences in emphasis or degree, most Protestant Reformers accepted Luther's answer to this question encapsulated in his doctrine of Justification by Faith Alone, and the consequences that flowed from it. One of those who did have a difference of emphasis was Zwingli at Zurich. He gave an even greater emphasis to the total corruption of human nature and, by implication, the similar corruption of the whole of creation derived from the Fall, which led him to adopt some distinctive attitudes. In particular, his consequent reluctance to accept that material things could be truly spiritual led to an emphasis on the divinity rather than the humanity of Jesus, to a view of Christ in the Eucharist as spiritual and not physically located in the bread and wine, and to a deep hostility to art, sculpture and music in churches or the liturgy. In Zurich, Zwingli argued that 'graven images' were explicitly condemned in the Old Testament, most notably in the second commandment, and so had all statues, paintings, stained glass and organs removed from churches, along with the stone altars that implied a physical and sacrificial presence of Christ in the Eucharist. Churches became bare, whitewashed preaching halls where the word of God revealed uniquely in the scriptures could be expounded. Luther certainly did not provide the model for this extreme iconoclasm.

Perhaps not surprisingly, Zwingli and Luther had their most profound disagreement over the issue of the eucharistic presence of Christ. At Marburg in 1529 the two Reformers met, agreed on fourteen points of common belief, but were totally unable to reach a satisfactory compromise over the manner of Christ's presence in the bread and wine. Luther, while rejecting Scholastic distinctions between substance and accidents, retained a belief in a real physical presence of Christ located in the bread and wine. This is sometimes called Consubstantiation, although this term was never actually employed by Luther himself. For Luther, St Paul's words in the New Testament could be interpreted in no other way. Zwingli disagreed, and saw Christ's presence as a spiritual as opposed to a material one, dependent upon the faith of the individual members of the community gathered at the eucharistic table.

John Calvin's contribution to the Protestant Reformation was essentially two-fold, and again opened up differences with Lutheranism. These were his work as a systematic theologian, and as an organizer of the new model of Church and society. His greatest theological work, the *Institutes of the Christian Religion*, was the most substantial and systematized exposition of Reformed Christianity produced in the sixteenth century, and contrasted with the rather piecemeal way in which Luther's ideas appeared. It grew from the six chapters of the first edition in 1536 to 80 chapters divided into four books by the time of the final edition of 1560. Based on the structure of the Apostles' Creed, it was in essence an extended catechism, almost a *summa* of Christian belief. As such, after the Bible itself, the *Institutes* was probably the most important source for Reformed doctrine. Calvin is perhaps most remembered theologically for his particular doctrine of predestination and double predestination; yet they only form one small part of his whole concept of Christianity, and to dwell on them to the exclusion of other elements would be to get them hopelessly out of balance within the total structure. In any case it was Calvin's lieutenant and successor, Theodore Beza (1519–1605) who was probably more responsible than anyone else for hardening later Calvinism in this area.[34]

Calvin's other major contribution was his attempt to organize a model Christian society in Geneva. In this he had undoubtedly been influenced by another early giant of Protestantism, Martin Bucer of Strasbourg, during his exile in that city from 1538 to 1541. The essence of the Calvinist model was found in his *Ecclesiastical Ordinances* of 1542, which the city government of Geneva formally adopted as the centrepiece of its reform. Calvin believed that the New Testament did not give authority for the concept of ministry that had emerged during the course of Church history. Bishops, including, of course, the bishop of Rome, were to be swept away, along with any medieval concept of priesthood. Boldly, Calvin replaced them with a four-fold ministry of clerical pastors, lay elders, doctors to administer the education system, and deacons to care for the charitable needs of the Church. Like Zwingli's Zurich, the churches of Geneva were drastically simplified, and preaching became the mainstay of liturgical worship. The Eucharist was certainly retained, but the daily continuity of its medieval celebration was drastically reduced to a handful of times during the year.

What is perhaps most notorious about this new Church order was the way in which it was intended to mould the lives of Geneva's citizens, principally through a court of morals, the Consistory, conducted by the pastors and elders. People could be questioned before it, and punished by it, for offences ranging from witchcraft and blasphemy, through adultery and absence from sermons, to attendance at dances or card parties. Although Calvin did not believe in either religious or moral toleration in our modern sense, it must be remembered that nobody else did in the sixteenth century either. Many of the offences that the Geneva Consistory has become infamous for punishing would have been no more tolerated in almost all European cities of the time, Protestant or Catholic.

Geneva came to be viewed as a model by many Reformed Protestants across Europe, and it attracted a growing army of visitors, exiles and imitators. In the second half of the sixteenth century it became the great centre of international propaganda for Calvin's ideas, and from it his concepts travelled as far as England, Scotland and France in the west, to Poland and Transylvania in the east. English and Dutch colonists were then to transplant Calvinism from Cape Cod to Cape Town in the seventeenth century.

Events

What launched the process of propelling Luther from being a relatively unknown German monk and university teacher into the figurehead of a movement of potentially revolutionary religious change, was the seemingly interminable papal project of rebuilding Constantine's crumbling basilica of St Peter in Rome. This had been under way for decades when in 1515 the pope issued a bull to grant an indulgence to raise money for the continuing construction. Indulgences had had a lengthy and convoluted history in the Middle Ages since the time of the Crusades. By 1476 they had been extended from the living to those already dead and presumed to be in Purgatory, from whence their families and friends could release them, as well as obtaining remission from the penalties of their own sins to date. Luther, however, was very far from being the first theologian to question the assumptions behind the system of indulgences, and many educated laity were equally unconvinced about the operation of such a system. In 1517 a Dominican friar, Johan Tetzel, was organizing a particularly blatant version of what was increasingly seen as a predominantly commercial operation in Germany. On 31 October of that year Luther issued his Ninety-Five Theses or Statements in Latin criticizing the indulgence system. He may or may not have hammered them into the door of the castle church in Wittenberg; but what he certainly did not intend was the initiation of what became the Protestant Reformation.

What Luther found objectionable in indulgences at this stage was neither the ideas of Purgatory nor of penance in themselves. But they did cut across the whole grain of his thinking about Justification. The notion of what could seem, to less sophisticated minds than Luther's, like salvation being obtained by paying money for a piece of paper, fell far short of his conception of the struggle of faith. Translated into German without his authority, and then rapidly multiplied by printing, these theses were soon being read by many people and were turning Luther into a regional celebrity. Answered in print by prominent Dominican theologians such as Sylvester Prierias (1456–1527), interviewed by the Dominican Cardinal Thomas de Vito Cajetan (1469–1534) at Augsburg, and then challenged to debate at Leipzig in 1519 by another youthful university scholar, Johann Eck (1486–1543), Luther's reputation as a rebel was increasing. In 1520 he produced three more works outlining his ideas: *To the Christian Nobility of the German Nation* was a call to the secular princes of Germany to lead a reform of the Church in their land; *The Babylonian Captivity of the Church* had the clergy as its target audience and outlined a programme of reform; *The Freedom of a Christian* was simpler and appealed to the literate laity outlining his idea of Justification. By now these and other books by Luther were selling by the thousand across Germany, and just beginning to percolate beyond her borders as well (Document 21).

What had initially seemed to Rome to be little more than yet another tiresome round of squabbling between rival religious Orders about obscure theological niceties, was now clearly getting out of hand. In 1520 the papacy turned at last to the traditional threat of coercion in its attempt to silence Luther and stifle the controversy. In the bull *Exsurge Domine* ('Arise, O Lord') Luther was commanded to recant or face excommunication. He was, however, no ordinary medieval theologian to be browbeaten by such threats. He publicly burnt the papal bull. Having already appealed for the calling of an Ecumenical Council without receiving any favourable papal response, he now turned instead to the newly elected twenty-year-old, and so far undeclared, Holy Roman Emperor, the Habsburg Charles V. The resulting imperial Diet held at Worms in 1521 considered Luther's works and listened to his explanations, but his intransigence led to official imperial condemnation in the resulting Edict issued by the Emperor and Diet. Luther found himself outlawed and effectively at the mercy of anyone within the Empire; he could be killed at any moment without any judicial proceedings being taken against the killer. Kidnapped by his own prince, the Elector of Saxony, for his own protection, he was spirited away to the safety of the castle of the Wartburg where he was to remain in hiding from May 1521 to March 1522. Here he grew a beard to disguise himself, and translated the New Testament into German.

Across German-speaking lands events were now moving with great rapidity. In Wittenberg itself Luther's absence resulted in the first outbreaks of religious anarchy, with attacks on statues, an unauthorized translation of the Mass into German celebrated in secular dress, and monks and nuns leaving their cloisters, some now marrying. A number of these more fanatical acts were led by one of Luther's colleagues at the university, Andreas Karlstadt (1480–1541), and Thomas Muntzer (1488–1525), a priest from nearby Zwickau. The latter saw himself especially as an instrument of the Holy Spirit and he and his fellow prophets from Zwickau had to be removed before complete chaos ensued in Wittenberg.

Meanwhile to the south Zwingli had arrived in Zurich in 1518 where he began his influential preaching career. By 1523 he had persuaded the authorities to give him a free hand in a wholesale reform of the city, and within two years of that he had cleansed the churches of their 'graven images' and instituted a simplified German eucharistic service. In the years which followed Berne and Basel also adopted the new Reformation inspired by Zwingli's Zurich. But by 1527 his progress was interrupted by the arrival of the first Anabaptists. Some he had condemned by the secular authorities to death by drowning, to become the first Protestants to be judicially executed by other

Protestants. The rest fled. In 1534 the Anabaptists were to take control of another city, Munster in north-western Germany and, inspired by Apocalyptic visions of a new Jerusalem, began to re-baptize its inhabitants by force and to proclaim all property to be held in common. In June 1535 the city fell to imperial forces in what turned into a bloodbath.

But by that point violence had already reared its head at many points across Germany. Zwingli himself was to die in battle at Kappel in 1531 at the hands of a Catholic Swiss army. But most terrible of all had been the Peasants' War of 1524–5. This could be seen as the culminating conflict of that long series of popular uprisings that had followed the Black Death. But now social and economic grievances found an organizing and legitimizing principle in the new religious ideas of the Reformation. In what was to be the largest popular disturbance seen in Europe before the French Revolution, perhaps as many as 100,000 people were to die before the princes, with the wholehearted approval of Luther, regained control of their lands.

John Calvin, born at Noyon in Picardy in 1509, was more the inheritor than the initiator of Reformation, being a generation younger than Luther, Zwingli or the other dominant personalities of the first phases of the movement. With a Humanist education and trained as a lawyer, but unlike Luther or Zwingli a layman, his suspect religious views forced him to flee his native France in 1534, followed by periods of exile in Basel, Geneva and Strasbourg. It was not to be until 1541 that he was officially invited to return to Geneva to organize its Reformation. Here he was to face years of opposition from some of the wealthy citizens who had removed a prince bishop who taxed them to find that he was replaced by a regime that wished to enquire into and regulate their morals. Resentment grew as Calvin's reputation attracted a mounting tide of foreign refugees. This climaxed in 1553 with the arrival of the Radical, Michael Servetus, in the city. His public rejection of the doctrine of the Trinity made him a very suspect ally for Calvin's other opponents. The trial and execution of Sevetus by burning tended to discredit much of the opposition to Calvin. Until his death in 1564 opposition remained at best muted and grumbling.

By that year Protestantism had made huge advances in Europe, with an estimated 80 per cent of the population of even a city like Vienna practising the new Reformed faith.[35] By 1590 it has been calculated that half of the European land-mass was under the control of either Protestant governments or culture.[36] While this may now appear to have been a spectacular success, at the time Protestants themselves were somewhat mystified that their success had not been total. Why had so many people not responded to their message of what they saw as spiritual liberation? Why did the old and, in their view, demonstrably corrupt faith of the Roman Church survive in the face of their righteous onslaught? Not only that, but by 1690 Catholicism had been able to regain the initiative and win back many of those lands initially lost to what, from Rome's perspective, was but the latest in a long line of heresies. So we must now turn to consider these and related questions, examining how the political and intellectual contexts had initially favoured the Protestant Reforms, and how that initiative had been regained by Catholicism.

Suggested Further Reading

An excellent modern starting point would be Patrick Collinson, *The Reformation* (Weidenfeld and Nicolson, 2003). This is a relatively short book, designed for the general reader and written in a very approachable style. If I would have any reservations about it they would run along the same lines as my reaction to a number of other similar accounts, such as the more substantial *The European Reformations* (Oxford University Press, 1991) by Euan Cameron, in that the main focus is firmly on the Protestant variety of the Reformation. Collinson only devotes one chapter of his twelve to an exclusive discussion of the Catholic Reformation. It is often necessary to read books specifically on the subject of Catholic reform to get a balanced view (see the next chapter). This is just one way in which what I have come to call the 'Protestant assumption' still lies behind much of the historical writing which comes from authors within that confessional tradition.

For those seeking a single volume treatment that does attempt to achieve a balance between the two Reformations then Diarmaid MacCulloch, *Reformation: Europe's House Divided 1490–1700* (Allen Lane, 2003) is well worth reading, although bear in mind that it is over 800 pages long. The author comes from an Anglican background but no longer subscribes to any particular dogmatic stance. It is the product of massive scholarship, but is very clear in style. Structurally the first two-thirds of the book are broadly chronological, while the final third is more thematic. It is a model of how to erect so vast a structure without it collapsing into needless repetition. It has excellent black-and-white illustrations, very useful maps, and a bibliography that is up-to-date and reasonably comprehensive without being unwieldy, and that is arranged thematically.

James D. Tracy's book, *Europe's Reformations 1450–1650* (Rowman and Littlefield Publishers Inc., 1999) is half the length of MacCulloch's and makes an interesting contrast in that it takes an exclusively thematic route. It also follows that tradition of giving significantly more space to the Protestant as opposed to the Catholic Reformers. It has an extensive alphabetical bibliography and many black-and-white illustrations.

For the medieval background as well as Malcolm Lambert's *Medieval Heresies*, Francis Oakley, *The Western Church in the Later Middle Ages* (Cornell, 1979) is another excellent account. For the specifically intellectual background, Steven Ozment, *The Age of Reform 1250–1550: An Intellectual and Religious History of Late Medieval and Reformation Europe* (Yale University Press, 1980) is a brilliant, if rather demanding, read. An attempt to get behind the conventional labelling of Catholic and Protestant is found in John Bossy's book, *Christianity in the West 1400–1700* (Oxford University Press, 1985) which emphasizes the points of similarity as well as difference between the two.

The bibliographies for individual Reformers are numerous, but among the most recent are Richard Marius, *Martin Luther: The Christian Between God and Death* (Harvard University Press, 1999), B. Cottret, *Calvin: A Biography* (William Eerdman, 2000), and G. R. Potter, *Zwingli* (Cambridge University Press, 1976). For the Radical Reformation, Michael Mullett, *Radical Religious Movements in Early Modern Europe* (George Allen and Unwin, 1980) is an excellent place to start.

The Renaissance has spawned a bibliography as vast as that for the Reformation. However, there are a number of excellent short introductions. For nearly twenty years Peter Burke's book, *The Renaissance*, has been an obvious starting point (Macmillan, second edition, 1997). There is also Alison Brown, *The Renaissance* (Longman, 1988) which contains a selection of documents, and Jocelyn Hunt *The Renaissance* (Routledge, 1999) which is the most straightforward of the three, aimed more at the A-level than undergraduate market.

9

Diversity Becomes Division

The glory that you have given me I have given them, so that they may be one, as we are one. (John 17:22)

The news spread through the streets of the city of Regensburg like a fire rushing across dry fields of summer corn. It was all over. The great theological issues that had divided Europe for a generation seemed to have been resolved. Two teams of theologians, including Martin Bucer for the Protestants and Cardinal Contarini from Rome, had just agreed a joint statement on Justification, the very heart of what had seemed to divide them. As word of this was carried across the city, many people ran to the belfrys of the churches and soon joyous peals of celebration were ringing out over its roofs. The year was 1541. Nobody knew it at the time, but it would take another four-and-a-half centuries before Catholic and Lutheran theologians would again issue an agreed statement on Justification.

Regensburg was a false dawn. In the days which followed, agreement turned once more into dispute. Contarini could not give ground on transubstantiation, and Bucer similarly could not admit the necessity of confession to a priest. The theologians parted and returned home. The last realistic hope of settlement faded as they went their separate ways. In the decades which followed, disagreements hardened into permanent divisions. Like the battle-fields of 1914 when the early frenetic activity and rapid shifts of ground slowed down and then froze behind entrenched ramparts, so the first energies of the Reformers ran out into the sands of time, and the religious confessions of Western Christendom settled down to a lengthy war of attrition.

Why did this happen? To what extent were the political divisions and rivalries of Europe mirrored in the subsequent religious ones? How did the Renaissance and Humanism affect religious life? And what were the differences, and indeed similarities, between Catholic and Protestant Europe?

Political Contexts

The history of the Reformation was to be played out against the background of the great Habsburg–Valois contest for hegenomy in Europe. On a number of occasions, and sometimes in crucial ways, this conflict was to help steer the fortunes for good or ill of most of the major religious groupings in early modern Europe, and it was to help turn confessional divisions into useful tools of state building and power.

The origins of this gigantic conflict go back into the fifteenth century when the last Duke of Burgundy, Charles the Bold, was killed at the battle of Nancy in 1477. His extensive inheritance was then divided between the French crown and the Habsburg family. One of the latter's many advantageous dynastic marriages now brought them the wealthy provinces of The Netherlands (approximately modern Holland, Belgium and Luxembourg) and the Franche-Compté on the eastern borders of France. Then a series of unexpected deaths combined the traditional Habsburg lands in the Holy Roman Empire with the Burgundian inheritance, and then added the Spanish kingdoms of Castile and Aragon. By 1519 the heir to this vast collection of territories was Charles, the young Habsburg only just emerging from his teens. Through his Castilian crown he was also the ruler of the rapidly expanding territories in the Americas. Potentially he was the most powerful ruler Europe had seen since at least the time of Charlemagne. For some, the God-given prospect of a universal monarchy for the whole of Western Christendom became more of a realistic option than it had been since the fall of the Roman Empire.

But this was perceived as more of a threat than a promise by the single most populous state in Western Europe, France, now surrounded to north, east and south by Habsburg lands. France herself had only emerged from the Hundred Years War with England in the 1450s, and the crown had spent the succeeding decades reintegrating semi-autonomous dukedoms from Brittany to Orleans back under royal control. In 1515 an equally youthful and ambitious king had ascended her throne, Francis I.

By that date it was clear that the ageing Habsburg Holy Roman Emperor, Maximilian, was in the last phases of his reign. Many now either hoped or feared that, if the imperial title were to be added to his others, Charles would become almost invincible. All the diplomatic efforts and financial resources of France would be mobilized to prevent this. For since the so-called Golden Bull of 1386 the election of new Emperors was in the hands of an electoral college with just seven members: the prince archbishops of Cologne, Mainz and Trier, and the secular rulers of Brandenburg, Bohemia, the Palatinate and Saxony. During the second decade of the sixteenth century these seven men received increasing attention not only from their fellow princes and rulers within the Empire, but also from most European states beyond, from the papacy in the south to the Scandinavian kingdoms in the north.

Into this diplomatic maelstrom sailed Martin Luther with his Ninety-Five Theses in 1517. His prince, Frederick the Wise, Elector of Saxony, was obviously a key player on the European scene. Not only did he possess one precious electoral vote himself, but he also wielded considerable influence within the electoral college and was even rumoured to be a potential candidate for the imperial crown himself. So long as Luther could keep his friendship he would be a protector of enormous value. The arrival of Tetzel selling his indulgence had angered Frederick almost as much as Luther, if for rather different reasons. Frederick had built up a collection of 19,000 relics, one of the finest in Christendom, which themselves were supposedly capable of drastically reducing the time a soul would spend in Purgatory if correctly venerated. For this privilege Frederick charged a fee which was a useful source of revenue for him. Tetzel's commercial operation deprived him of valuable income. Not surprisingly, the Dominican friar was barred from Frederick's territories, and Luther (whom he never personally met) gained an immediate ally. On top of that, Luther was a professor at the University of Wittenberg which Frederick himself had founded. The Elector was not prepared to have his prestige tarnished by the condemnation of one of his academic stars. Princely honour was involved – the more so when his cousin and rival, the ruler of Ducal Saxony, staged the debate between Luther and Eck in his own University of Leipzig in 1519.

Power politics thus converged with theological dispute and dynastic pride. This volatile cocktail was to be crucial to Luther in those early years of his revolt when he was at his most vulnerable. For one thing, in the period leading up to the death of Maximilian and the imperial election in 1519, the Church authorities from the pope downwards hesitated to move too drastically against Luther for fear of antagonizing his prince. Even after the election, Frederick still remained one of the most important and influential princes in Germany.

In the campaign to induce individual electors to vote for them, a campaign which was already well under way in the years before 1519, Habsburg money, often borrowed from the great banking house of the Fuggers, washed across Europe in unprecedented waves. France was unable to match these colossal financial resources, most of which were employed to bribe princes and officials, and so the young Habsburg was elected as Charles V. French diplomacy now shifted gear and was deployed to stir up as much internal opposition to Charles within the Empire as possible.

By the early sixteenth century the Holy Roman Empire was a bewildering patchwork of political units varying enormously in size, and in practice a hugely decentralized structure with many of its component parts increasingly willing to defy any Emperor in defence of their liberties and privileges. It consisted of hundreds of princely states, themselves of a variety of sizes. Some, like the House of Wittelsbach in Bavaria, were hugely ambitious and resented the electoral title possessed by the minor branch of the family in the Palatinate, itself geographically divided into Upper and Lower sections. Dozens of prince bishops similarly ruled a series of small states from their cathedral cities. Hundreds of other towns and cities were dotted across Germany, over 60 of which were Free Imperial Cities, meaning that they had no lord apart from the relatively distant Emperor; in effect they were miniature republics set within a loose monarchical structure. Then there were about 1,000 Free Imperial Knights, who again owed allegiance to no lord but the Emperor, most of them existing in states so small that they would be unnoticeable on a map. Altogether 'Germany' consisted of about 3,000 separate political entities. And to the south the Swiss Confederation of cities and Cantons, and the northern Italian city republics and princes, had for generations enjoyed a level of independence from the Emperor even greater than their German counterparts.

The Empire was thus not only a highly complex structure but also a potentially volatile one. The capacity of Emperors to command obedience from their vassals had diminished significantly since the central Middle Ages, and even otherwise so powerful a figure as Charles V would have to rely more on diplomacy and balancing the princes and other rulers off against one another than on naked force. And from the perspective of those princes, the one thing they did not want to lose was their hard-won freedom of action; they would resist any Emperor who attempted to assert imperial authority from the centre.

This gave Charles V's enemies a potentially potent lever against him within his own realm. Francis I could form alliances with those German states which adopted Lutheranism as the religion of their prince and the Church within his territories. The first prince so to declare openly for the Reformation was Philip of Hesse in 1524. By the time of the imperial Diet at Speyer in 1529 the attempt to resurrect the 1521 Edict outlawing Lutheranism provoked a formal 'protest' from six princes and fourteen cities, giving their movement a name: Protestant. The following year at the Diet of Augsburg Charles made an attempt to produce a religious formula acceptable to both Lutherans and Catholics. The failure of this led the Protestant princes and cities to form a defensive military alliance, the Schmalkaldic League, which Charles was unable or unwilling to move against until the mid–1540s. But it gave his French, and other enemies, a potent weapon against him in the heart of his own German lands.

Charles hesitated to move against his Lutheran princes and cities and so foment civil war across large areas of Germany in part because of the threat from the east in the form of the Turks. In 1526 they had annihilated the old kingdom of Hungary, a traditional buffer state protecting the heartlands of Christendom. Charles needed the military and financial resources of a united Germany now that his eastern flank was so exposed. Hence his continual hesitations at moving to quash the new heretics through the 1520s and 1530s. By 1532 a vast Turkish army was besieging Vienna, and the price of Lutheran aid was concessions to them at the Diet of Regensburg. In 1535 at Tunis and 1541 at Algiers Charles was to take the war into Turkish-held lands to divert their attention from Germany. It was not to be until the 1545 Diet of Regensburg that he felt strong enough to take action, effectively outlawing the Lutheran princes of Saxony and Hesse. This finally provoked war, and the defeat of the Schmalkaldic League at the battle of Muhlberg in 1547.

The imperial triumph was short-lived. By 1550 a renewed Lutheran alliance had been formed, and in 1552 Duke Maurice of Saxony changed sides from the Emperor's alliance to the new Lutheran one; with French help the new allies were able to outmanoeuvre Charles and repair the damage done at Muhlberg. Thus the complexities of imperial politics could work in favour of nascent Lutheranism, and give it precious time in which to expand and consolidate. Charles's vast international obligations could also be an advantage as he had several lengthy periods of absence from Germany, perhaps most crucially from 1521 to 1530, when Luther himself was given the time to escape and hide from imperial wrath.

But this could cut both ways. As Francis I was to discover, support for an alliance with Lutheran princes in Germany had its own domestic costs. He, no more than Charles, could smash his own French Protestants for good external political reasons. By the 1520s Luther's works were appearing in France, and small numbers of literate and noble individuals were being attracted to the new ideas. Always a small minority during his reign, he could not, however, afford to move against them for fear of antagonizing and alienating his Lutheran allies in Germany. Only in 1534, when Placards appeared simultaneously in many French cities criticizing, among other things, the Catholic Mass, did he feel compelled to crack down on his own domestic dissidents. This was the occasion of Calvin's flight into exile. But again, this pause on the king's part proved vital. Protestantism was allowed to establish a significant beach-head in France from which it could break out later in a greater expansion. By the 1540s and 1550s Calvinism had become the cutting edge of advance, and by 1560 perhaps two million people in France, about 10 per cent of the population, were Protestants, including perhaps one-third of the nobility. Driving John Calvin into exile in 1534 had back-fired and brought scores of Geneva-trained pastors back into France as his agents.

If the Habsburg–Valois conflict helped Protestantism at its early, formative stage, it also inhibited Catholic revival. The one instrument that might have had the authority to settle the doctrinal differences in their initial phase, and launch a spiritual revival, was an Ecumenical Council. The popes, however, feared a revival of Conciliarism and thus needed any prospective Council to be firmly under their control, preferably in papal territory. Charles V saw things very differently. For him this was primarily a German problem which could only be settled on German soil. In any case, many Lutherans would be rightly fearful of travelling to Italy, to the very den of the Beast himself, as many of them now saw the pope, given the fate of Jan Hus at Constance in 1415. By 1527 relations between the papacy and Charles V had deteriorated to the extent that an imperial army, including German Lutherans, sacked the city of Rome for a month. Now, with this demonstration of Habsburg power, following hard on the heels of the defeat and capture of Francis I at the battle of Pavia in 1525, the popes shifted their stance.

The first casualty was Henry VIII's campaign for a royal divorce. Queen Catherine of Aragon was Charles's aunt, and he had no intention of allowing her to be put aside by Henry in such an affront to family honour. This left Henry little option but to break with Rome. And so the failure of the royal divorce and all that flowed from it became another consequence of the Habsburg–Valois contest.

By 1530 the pope had crowned Charles Emperor in a public gesture of support. But this in its turn alienated the papacy's former ally, France. No bishop would be allowed to leave the soil of France to attend any Council dominated by Habsburg interests. This resulted in yet further delay in the summoning of a Council which could both heal doctrinal divisions and revivify Christianity in the West. By the time it did finally meet in 1545 it was too late to achieve the former ambition, and even the latter one was further delayed as the Council was unable to complete its business until 1564, interrupted again and again by the political manoeuvrings and military threats of a conflict that was to drag on till 1559.

If politics could promote or frustrate Christianity in early modern Europe, equally Christianity could also be a useful tool in state building during that period. As we have already seen, Luther was eager for the princes to take over the leadership of the Reformation. Partly this was a natural result of the elevation of the laity and demotion of the clergy implied by the Priesthood of All Believers. If the laity was as capable of Church leadership as the clergy then the obvious laymen to take this role were the princes. Biblical authority could also be used to support this: 'Let every person be subject to the governing authorities; for there is no authority except from God, and those authorities that exist have been instituted by God' (Rom. 13:1) was a case in point. On the other hand, certain texts seemed to refute the idea of obedience to secular rulers: 'But Peter and the apostles answered, "We must obey God rather than any human authority"' (Acts 5:29). Be that as it may, the new Lutheran princes often needed little encouragement to take control of their local churches, secularize the monasteries and appoint their own clerics. In an age of widespread, if not universal, church attendance, at the most basic level a Church under state control could be a potent weapon for engendering obedience among its subjects. It could be an equally valuable source of patronage allowing a prince to reward or bribe his supporters with lucrative Church offices. Certainly after the Peasants' War of 1524–5 no prince needed further encouragement; the Reformation must be taken firmly under the wing of the princes and governing élites and shifted from being a catalyst for social protest to a vehicle of political obedience.

What was true of Lutheran princes was also valid for Catholic ones as well. A good example of this were the Dukes of Bavaria, especially Maximilian, Duke from 1598 to 1651. He was a devout Catholic who prayed daily and on occasion wore a hair shirt as an act of penitence. In his state traditional Catholic practices such as pilgrimages and shrines were revived and encouraged, and combined with more contemporary uses such as the employment of the new religious Orders, most notably the Jesuits. Clerical moral and educational standards were raised, and education extended to more members of the laity, sometimes in Jesuit-run schools. Loyalty to the Church thus became associated with loyalty to the devout Wittelsbach Dukes. In the words of Michael Mullett: 'Bavaria provides a German example of the successful fusion of popular culture and Catholic Reformation piety', both now firmly linked with the ruling House.[1] In the early seventeenth century the Bavarian Dukes were to become the linchpin of the Catholic Reformation in southern Germany, and the leaders of Catholic military efforts to contain and then contest Protestantism

At the same time this advance was firmly based on a state where Counter Reformation goals happily coincided with centralization based on the prince. The new educational system, firmly under Church and princely control, was providing the educated officials who would staff the expanding bureaucracies of both institutions. Once again princely patronage could be used to bolster religious confessionalism; Catholic practice became the route to Ducal service and upward social mobility in Bavaria.[2] This principle of the confessional state received its first formal acknowledgement at the religious Peace of Augsburg in 1555. Worn out by futile attempts either to heal the religious divisions of Germany or eradicate them by force, Charles V at last opted for a pragmatic compromise in the evening of his reign. An assumption would be made that the religion of the prince, whether Lutheran or Catholic, and that of his subjects would be identical, to be neatly summed up in the Latin phrase *Cuius regio, eius religio*. Those of his subjects whose consciences would not stretch that far could either go into exile or face a future of adverse political as well as religious discrimination.

National Contexts

Why was the Protestant Reformation so successful in some parts of Europe while in others it struggled to obtain even the most limited of toe-holds? Various explanations have been offered to account for this, which include political, social and economic elements as well as religious. There is, however, no definitive answer to this question. All that the historian can do is offer suggestions based on the available evidence.

What we should not do, however, is make the assumption that kings, princes and other members of the governing élite always acted from cynical motivations or calculations of political advantage in their religious policies. As individuals they could hold religious opinions as sincerely and devoutly as any of their subjects. And in a world where the religion of the ruler had so powerful an influence on that of his state Church and subjects, the confessional preferences of princes clearly had enormous implications that went beyond the specifically religious. To take Luther's own Saxony as an example, his prince, the Elector Frederick, was certainly his *protector*, but he could never realistically be described as a *supporter* of Luther in a confessional sense. However, Frederick's death in 1525 changed this, for his heir, Johann the Steadfast, certainly was a convinced Lutheran.[3] Princes could also shift their allegiance from one form of Protestantism to another, the classic case being the change from Lutheranism to Calvinism by the Elector Palatine in 1559. On the other hand, the personal religious views of certain key princes were so vital to the maintenance of the political equilibrium that any alteration in their convictions could have far-reaching consequences. In 1582 the Catholic prince archbishop of Cologne announced his intention of converting to Lutheranism. As one of the seven imperial electors, that would have tilted the balance in the electoral college in favour of the Protestants. The Duke of Bavaria intervened militarily and from 1583 to 1761 all archbishops of Cologne were to be Wittelsbachs, thus securing the vote for the Catholic interest.[4]

On the other hand, there were also instances in which a princely conversion was led by political rather than religious considerations. Perhaps the most notorious was the conversion of King Henry IV of France from Calvinism to

Catholicism. In actual fact he converted twice, returning to his original Protestant convictions in between. His second conversion in 1593 seems to have been motivated by the fact that as a Protestant he would never have been acceptable to the Catholic majority in France and would thus have extended the fighting in the seemingly interminable civil wars that had plagued the country for over 30 years. His supposed comment that 'Paris is worth a Mass' is often quoted as typical of the cynical approach to the relationship between religion and politics. Unfortunately there is no reliable evidence that he ever uttered such words. However, as Diarmaid MacCulloch has recently commented: 'It shows what many of Europe's politicians and rulers felt about the Reformation and Counter-Reformation after seventy years of fighting.' War-weariness and a desperate desire for peace may well have been the real underlying motivations for conversion.[5] Other French kings and statesmen could also be accused with Henry IV of cynicism, but again their motivations were often extremely complex. As we have already seen, Francis I was willing to make alliances with Lutheran princes while personally remaining a practising Catholic. He no more contemplated conversion to Protestantism than he did to Islam when he made a similar, if somewhat briefer, alliance with the Turkish Sultan.

A century later Cardinal Richelieu, the chief minister of Louis XIII, was equally prepared to ally France with Lutheran Sweden against the Catholic Emperor. Yet we know that personally Richelieu was more than conventionally devout, a sincere Catholic who, as Bishop of Luçon from 1607, had been an energetic reformer of his diocese. In many ways far more sophisticated in his approach to the relationship of religion and politics than either Philip II of Spain or Duke Maximilian of Bavaria, he, unlike them, 'did not make the clear connection between heresy and political sedition'. In him it is possible to see the first glimmerings of more modern conceptions. 'Not only the welfare of the state but also the good of religion itself in the long run required toleration.' Having finally defeated his own Calvinists inside France, he did not force them to convert to Catholicism but tolerated them so long as they remained peaceful. His attitude to his fellow Catholic Habsburgs, however, was one of fear and suspicion; he believed they were using religion as a cloak under which their true ambition of European domination was hidden. Thus they should be countered and balanced by combining other powers, Catholic or Protestant, against them (Document 22).[6] There may have been more than a grain of truth in Richelieu's fears for in the century following 1613 the Habsburgs used the lures of territory, office or titles to win back a string of German princes from Protestantism to Catholicism in what could be interpreted as a cynical exercise on both sides.[7]

But beyond the religious and political preferences of princes, what other forces were shaping national confessions of faith? Why, for instance, did Protestantism never gain more than a relatively insignificant number of sympathizers in Spain? Part of the answer may lie in the historical evolution of the Iberian kingdoms from the Middle Ages onwards. One of the most consistent themes of Spanish history for centuries was the *Reconquista*, the reconquest of Muslim Spain that had begun in the eleventh century and was not to be completed until the fall of Granada in 1492. Intermittent warfare lasting almost five centuries left its mark on Spain, especially on its largest kingdom, Castile. Here the association of national destiny with Catholicism became particularly intense. Non-Catholics were increasingly seen as alien forces to be driven from the soil of Castile, or forced to accept the religion of the victors. For the Castilian nobility, 'purity of blood' became essential; all traces of non-Catholic ancestry were 'air-brushed' from family trees.

So who were the 'aliens' Castilian Catholics so despised and feared? In 1391 the first anti-Jewish disturbances occurred. Over time, significant numbers of Castile's Jewish minority converted to Catholicism. But they remained suspect, the genuineness of their Christianity always doubted. It was to investigate these *conversos* that the Spanish Inquisition was instituted in the fifteenth century, and in 1483 its most infamous Inquisitor General, Torquemada, was appointed. The reign of terror which he unleashed reached its climax in 1492 when Spain's remaining Jews were given the stark choice of baptism or exile. Fifty thousand chose the former, and 200,000 the latter.

But Jews were not alone in being seen as aliens. As the *Reconquista* gathered pace and won more lands back for Catholic Spain, large numbers of Islamic Moors became subjects of the Castilian crown. Again, like the Jews, some converted to become *Moriscos*, similarly distrusted by the Inquisition. Through the sixteenth century escalating persecution and intermittent rebellions finally culminated in 1609 with the expulsion of 300,000 of them from Spain. Thus Spanish history had armed her people with a fear of, and hostility to, what could be perceived as alien religions, and an instrument to deal with them, the Inquisition. Clearly Protestantism could easily be accommodated into this mentality. So on the one hand sixteenth-century Spain, led by its King Philip II, became highly defensive, if not positively inward-looking: the King, for instance, ordered the return of all Spanish students studying at foreign universities for fear of religious 'contamination'. On the other hand, running parallel with this intensely negative attitude to non-Catholics was a much more positive one, that ultimately was more important in preserving Spain as an overwhelmingly Catholic country.

Most scholars would accept that the joint reign of Ferdinand and Isabella (1469–1516) was a milestone in Spanish history. They instituted the wholesale reordering of their kingdoms, the first stages in transforming Spain from a medieval feudal to an absolute monarchy. From the royal council to local urban government, everything received their reforming royal attention. And this included the Church. The crown put itself at the head of a powerful movement of reformation across Spain. One key date was the 1478 Synod of Seville. Here the crown obtained the agreement of the church hierarchy to lead a reform of religion that paralleled and complemented the one in the secular sphere. The crown took over institutions from the Inquisition to the still powerful Crusading Military Orders of Santiago and Calatrava. It secured the agreement of Rome to appoint bishops, and generally promoted clerics of a similarly reforming mentality, pious and well educated. The linchpin of this programme was the appointment of Cardinal Ximenes as archbishop of Toledo and primate of Spain in 1495. A renowned Humanist, he founded the University of Alcala in 1508 initially to improve clerical education. Diarmaid MacCulloch has noted of Ximenes that 'many of his reforms anticipate what the Council of Trent was to decree many decades later', and that generally Spain 'had tackled many of the structural abuses which elsewhere gave Protestant Reformers much ammunition against the old Church'.[8] Thus the process of Catholic renewal and revivification began in Spain more than a generation before Luther issued his Ninety-Five Theses. For the vast majority of sixteenth-century Spaniards, Protestantism not only seemed alien, but also frankly irrelevant to what they proudly perceived to be the finest example in Christendom of a true Church.

Italy produced somewhat more Protestants than Spain, but they still constituted little more than an insignificant minority. The Roman Inquisition, however, was only created in 1542, so it cannot account for the lack of interest in the new religious ideas before that time. One clue to this dearth of Protestants lay in the great urban centres of Italy. By the sixteenth century most of the medieval city republics had acquired their own princes, and the map of northern Italy somewhat resembled that of contemporary Germany, namely a patchwork of states of various sizes, if ultimately on a smaller scale than Germany. The cities of northern Italy had also achieved a greater degree of independent self-government than any other part of the Empire. The victory of the Lombard League over Frederick Barbarossa in the twelfth century had initiated a period of several centuries where the city states of northern Italy became to all intents and purposes sovereign. Emperors, Habsburgs or otherwise, rarely intervened in their affairs. What possible political advantages were there, then, for the princes of northern Italy to use Protestantism as a lever against so distant an Emperor? They had already achieved the most extensive political independence that it was realistically possible to attain.

On top of that, any prestige or lustre that could be added to their dynasties was very much tied to the Roman Church. Families like the Gonzaga in

Mantua or the Medici in Florence had traditionally seen the appointment of a member of their family as a cardinal in terms of ultimate social dignity and status; to have one elected pope would be the final accolade. For many of the noble families too the election of a relative as a cardinal would not only confer prestige and honour, it would also open the flood-gates of patronage as offices and titles could be showered on family members, sometimes making their fortunes in an economic as well as social sense. There were thus few, if any, members of the princely or noble families of Italy who would have any incentive to cut the ties that linked them to the papacy and the curia. And if by the sixteenth century neither of these institutions were quite Italian monopolies, then at least Italians were the majority shareholders. They had no incentive to bankrupt such a system.

This network of allegiances then percolated downwards to the hordes of officials who staffed the papal and princely bureaucracies, to the artists, crafts-men and tradesmen who serviced their lavish courts. Linked to the Catholic Church through further ties, most notably confraternities, few in the Italian population had a desire to disturb such arrangements. Indeed, by 1600 it has been estimated that as many as one-third of all Italian men belonged to reli-gious confraternities which ran hospitals, arranged loans or dowries for poorer members, visited prisoners and taught catechism.[9]

Germany could not have made a greater contrast. Whereas for the Italian élite the papacy and curia were routes to riches and social prestige, for many Germans 'Rome' meant little more than a distant city which taxed them, and over which by the sixteenth century they had little if any influence. Above all, the Protestant Reformation was most successful in the towns and cities of Germany and Switzerland. Of the 60 Free Imperial Cities in Germany some 50 opted for the Protestant Reformation at some point during the course of the sixteenth century. Indeed, of the approximately 200 German towns with populations over 1,000 people, the majority had Protestant movements.[10] As a proportion of their respective numbers, far more German cities than princes accepted the Protestant Reformation. Why?

In Germany, unlike Spain or even to some extent France, the crown, in the person of the Emperor, did not have the same degree of control over the Church as his Spanish or French counterparts. There had consequently been little that could be described as a reform of the clergy, from the bishops down-wards. In addition, there were dozens of prince bishops who taxed their subjects like any other prince. The citizens of Geneva had removed their prince bishop, a member of the Ducal family of Savoy, before Calvin ever arrived in the city. Anticlericalism was thus far more of a feature of life in many German towns than it was in their Italian or Spanish equivalents. In many German towns the Reformation had a popular appeal in a way that it did not elsewhere. In the words of Steven Ozment: 'On the eve of the Reformation we find a piety characterized by criticism of manifest religious abuses, skepticism about long-accepted clerical privileges and revered ecclesiastical practices, and a willingness to experiment with new religious forms.'[11] Ozment argues that the depth of the dissatisfaction with the Church in many German cities had, by the sixteenth century, gone beyond any medieval concepts of clerical reform, and now extended to 'the most basic beliefs and practices' of a church represented by a despised clerical caste.[12] What was required was not just an administrative or pastoral reform, but what he calls a 'religious transvaluation'. Iconoclasm was but the outward expression of people who now believed that they had been fooled by something they had previously taken seriously, mirroring the similar reaction to indulgences.[13]

England, however, revealed a pattern of Reformation quite unlike any continental model. Henry VIII had broken with Rome in the 1530s because of his failure to obtain a papal divorce. But what followed in the remainder of his reign down to 1547 can hardly be called Reformation. The monasteries may have been dissolved, but this was as much for economic and political reasons as religious; monastic revenues doubled the royal income, and the great mitred abbots had been eliminated as parliamentary opponents. But the secular clergy were still not allowed to marry, Mass continued to be said in Latin with traditional vestments, and Protestants continued to be persecuted. Henry's Church was in a sort of ecclesiastical limbo cut off from Catholicism, yet unwilling to make the final commitment to Protestantism.

That was to come in the reign of his son, Edward VI (1547–53). The Book of Common Prayer now translated the Mass into English in 1549, and in its 1552 edition moved in a decidedly Zwinglian direction in its eucharistic theology. Altars, vestments and statues were swept away, as were the traditional ceremonies like the anointing of a newly ordained priest in the Ordinal of 1550. Under the next sovereign Mary I (1553–8), however, the confessional pendulum swung back again in the opposite direction. England was restored to communion with Rome, and a serious attempt was made to restore traditional religious practices. This was to be reversed again in the following reign of Mary's half-sister Elizabeth I (1558–1603), when the Protestant version of Reformation returned, but with a characteristically English compromise of preserving at least a framework of Catholic order with bishops, priests and deacons, but then hollowing out their Catholic reality with such things as the Thirty-Nine Articles of Religion in 1563, or the revised Prayer Book of 1559.

How should the religious history of sixteenth-century England be viewed? Conventionally, the progress of reform in England was seen as not that different from the story in Germany; an unpopular Church and clergy finally giving way to a form of belief long desired (the Lollards) but now made possible by a state at last acceding to popular demand. Mary's reign was the exception or indeed aberration in this inevitable progress. This line of argument was to receive its finest scholarly treatment in *The English Reformation* by A. G. Dickens, first published in 1964.

The problem with such a concept, one still widely believed by many people even today, is that it is a house built on sand. As even a historian as sympathetic to the Protestant Reformation as Patrick Collinson now admits: 'from most parts of England there is little evidence to support this view'.[14] In the last generation a school of 'revisionist' historians has blown a series of holes in the conventional view, to such an extent that many scholars think that it is not only now holed below the waterline but actually sinking, if not already sunk. Interestingly, one sixteenth-century figure presented an analysis of the English Reformation which now seems prophetic. Ignatius Loyola, the founder of the Jesuits, argued that England under Elizabeth was ripe for re-conversion to Catholicism as the Protestant Reformation had been imposed not by the will of the people bur rather by the royal and aristocratic élite.

In 1984 the distinguished biographer of Henry VIII, J. J. Scarisbrick, penned a book that echoed what Loyola had argued more than four centuries earlier: 'On the whole, English men and women did not want the Reform-ation and most of them were slow to accept it when it came.'[15] Scarisbrick's view was that the *evidence* would not support the conventional assumptions: 'We have hitherto been content with the image of a Tudor regime unleashing and then riding the back of the tiger of popular anticlericalism, anti-papalism, patriotism and so on. If that is now suspect, this is because one can no longer find much of a tiger.'[16]

Scarisbrick's assault on the conventional interpretation of the English Reformation was to be expanded and largely confirmed by the detailed research of two other historians: Eamon Duffy and Christopher Haigh. As Duffy was to argue: 'It is my conviction . . . that no substantial gulf existed between the religion of the clergy and the educated élite on the one hand and that of the people at large on the other.' In addition, far from being in decline,

> late medieval Catholicism exerted an enormously strong, diverse, and vigorous hold over the imagination and loyalty of the people up to the very moment of Reformation. Traditional religion had about it no par-ticular marks of exhaustion or decay, and indeed in a whole host of ways . . . was showing itself well able to meet new needs and new conditions.

Duffy concludes that 'there was virtually nothing in the character of religion in late medieval England which could *only* or even *best* have been developed within Protestantism . . . the Reformation was a violent disruption, not the natural fulfilment, of most of what was vigorous in late medieval piety and religious practice'.[17] As such, he rehabilitates the reign of Mary I, not as an aberration but rather the logical and reasonable response to deep-seated traditional religion not yet extinguished by the Protestant Reformation.

Christopher Haigh is in broad agreement with this analysis: 'The Catholic Church in England was not corrupt and worldly as in Germany.'[18] He is at pains to draw a distinction between the Reformation on the Continent inspired by Luther or Calvin, and the version in England: 'they were not the same thing'.[19] For Haigh, the key to the English Reformation was not popular demand but the accidents of power politics at the royal court. He thus separates different 'Reformations'; political reform was not the same as evangelical reform. 'England had blundering Reformations, which most did not understand, which few wanted, and which no one knew had come to stay.'[20] He too criticizes the conventional view for the assumptions it makes. Since Protestantism ultimately won, it must therefore have been popular; so the corollary of that is that late-medieval Catholicism must have decayed. Thus historians end up looking for the wrong types of evidence, and missing the vast amount of evidence that contradicts it. So we end with 'an inaccurate version, for the evidence no longer sustains it'.[21] While there is evidence of contemporary critics of late-medieval Catholicism, what has too often been missed is the mass of evidence for the conformists and even enthusiasts for traditional beliefs and practices. So the history of the English Reformations was one not only of Catholics against Protestants, but of the overarching struggle of the state with its people. Thus 'it is likely that most of those who lived in Tudor England experienced Reformation as obedience rather than conversion'.[22] The result of all of these parallel and overlapping types of Reformation was a Church of England whose members 'were de-catholicized, but un-protestantized'.[23] At the margins it left two small minorities who now viewed their parish churches in very different ways: 'The papists thought Christ had been driven from these buildings, the godly thought Antichrist still ruled there.'[24]

Obviously this brief summary cannot do justice to some very sophisticated and extensive reinterpretations. And not all scholars of the English Reformation accept all of their arguments in every detail. For instance, Haigh argues that rising numbers of ordinations in the years immediately before the Reformation indicate that the clergy and the clerical profession remained popular. In itself this is unconvincing. All modern opinion polls, and the declining numbers voting in General Elections, point to the deep unpopularity of politicians; but this has not prevented record numbers from seeking election as MPs. Rising numbers of candidates do not, in themselves, indicate the wider popularity of the group they seek to enter.[25] On top of that is the fact that both

Scarisbrick and Duffy are Catholics. At the more popular level this has resulted in accusations of bias in their work.[26] But Haigh is definitely *not* a Catholic, so such criticisms cannot justifiably be levelled at him, and by implication, would not be legitimate arguments against the work of those who are. But whatever else the revisionists have accomplished, they have at least demonstrated that the history of the Reformation is not so straightforward as once assumed, and that much scope for reinterpretation still exists.

Catholic Reform

'Reformation' is obviously a loaded word in Church history. For most people, at least in the English-speaking world, the immediate association is with the *Protestant* Reformation. But it must always be remembered that there was a parallel movement of Reformation simultaneously under way within the Catholic Church of the sixteenth century. Did these two proceed completely independently of one another, or did they relate to each other in some way? Did they have common or distinct origins? And if there were relationships between them, why did they separate and go their own ways? And in what ways was the Catholic version of Reformation distinct from the Protestant?

Western Christianity in the sixteenth century exposes in the starkest and most dramatic way the tensions inherent not only in the concept of 'reform' but also in that of tradition. As we have seen now in many different ways and across many different epochs, the fundamentally dynamic Pauline concept of re-formation, of the individual Christian as a new creation (2 Cor. 5:17) has had a fundamental influence on the history of the religion and its institutional-ized realization, the Church. To return to the metaphor first encountered in the Introduction, Christian tradition is like an original musical theme followed by a series of variations. Time and again movements of renewal in Christianity have looked backwards to gain inspiration for their own times and so move forwards again. This was true of the medieval Gregorian papacy and for the ascetic movement and its various monastic manifestations. For Gregory VII and his papal successors, the New Testament and the first Christian centuries were fundamental for their movements of reform. For Luther and other Protestant Reformers in the sixteenth century the New Testament was once again the inspirational well-spring of revival. So why did Protestant and Catholic variations on the original theme go in so fundamentally different directions in the sixteenth century?

Part of the reason lay in often opposed understandings of their common Christian inheritance. Both could point to precursors from the past, and modern historians have often followed this line of argument. James D. Tracy has outlined one of the broad premises of the historical explanation of Protestantism. This view sees the Reformation in its Protestant form 'not as unprecedented, but as the high point in a series of "reformations" that convulsed the Latin or western half of Christendom from the eleventh to the eighteenth centuries', but then adds: 'But if the failure of reform efforts in earlier centuries proved to many that Luther's Reformation was necessary, it proved to others that the Catholic Church must once and for all reform itself.'[27] These statements, however, would seem to raise as many questions as they answer. Are we to see the Protestant Reformers of the sixteenth century as the heirs to the Gregorian papal reform or medieval monastic reform? The problem here surely lies in the explicit repudiation of both papal leadership and monastic forms of Christian life by the sixteenth century Protestant Reformers. Luther and others saw both the papacy and monasticism as part of the problem; they were corruptions of the original message that needed sweeping away. For the mainstream Reformers the medieval Church had taken fundamentally wrong paths that led away from the purity of the Gospel. For several centuries the variations introduced by these medieval institutions had broken with the original theme and introduced a series of discordant developments. For the Radical Reformers the problems were even more fundamental and long-lasting. They looked back to the earliest centuries of Christianity before Constantine as the purest expression of a faith that should separate itself from the corruptions of the world, taking up themes of the 'gathered' Church first heard in the works of Tertullian.

So where should the sixteenth-century Reformers look for their distant cousins? Malcolm Lambert has made the point that in the Middle Ages reform and heresy were twins.[28] As we have already seen, there were obvious features in common between the Waldensians and the Franciscans for instance. Some Reformers therefore turned to the movements of medieval reform that had been for whatever reason excluded from the mainstream of Western Church history. In Elizabethan England the famous compiler of the accounts of Protestant martyrs under Mary I, John Foxe, had turned to the Lollards in order to challenge the Catholic jibe: where were you before Luther? 'The most signal service of Lollardy, it may be, was to provide Tudor and subsequent Protestants with a pre-history of heroes and martyrs before Luther' comments Lambert.[29] Wyclif had already argued for a 'golden age' of the Church which had been brought to an end in the pretensions and corruptions of medieval Rome and the clergy, and Foxe generally took over this concept and made it his own. As Lambert points out, Foxe saw the pre-history of Protestantism 'as a simple and unified whole'.[30]

Were the Protestant Reformers the same in both kind and degree as those dissident reformers of the Middle Ages? When the Swiss Calvinists first encountered the Waldensians in northern Italy they found as many differences as similarities between them and themselves. The Waldensian view of poverty remained deeply medieval, seen as a virtue rather than a social problem. Calvinists took a diametrically opposed view; poverty was a curse and wealth an opportunity to do good. Calvin himself never wavered in his view that the Waldensians taught false doctrines, especially in their view of the positive value of good works which cut right across the essential Reformed doctrine of Justification.[31]

Similar problems arise when we review the relationship between Lutheranism and the Lollards. There were clear differences between the two in eucharistic doctrine; if anything, the Lollards were nearer to Zwingli than Luther. Luther did not share the deep-seated hostility of the Lollards to the apparatus of late medieval spirituality, and could not share their devotion to the letter of James in the New Testament with its emphasis on works alongside faith. Further problems also occur when trying to establish links between Luther and Jan Hus. It seems clear that although Luther was aware of the Hussite movement, he had never read any of Hus's works before 1519, and regarded them as schismatics. By 1521 he was calling Hus a saint, but by then the Reformation was already well under way.[32] So, to borrow terminology from Scholastic theology, Luther's connection to Hus was accidental rather than substantial. Thus there was no linear descent from the medieval dissident reform movements to the Reformers of the sixteenth century, in the sense of the former inspiring the latter. Protestants in the sixteenth century might have retrospectively seen points of similarity, but that had more to do with apologetic rhetoric than historical reality.

The Protestant Reformation was new and unique in the sense not only of its sustained doctrinal assault on the Catholic Church, but also in the sheer depth and intensity of that assault. Never before had a movement of dissent originating among university academics both had so many educated supporters and at the same time combined that with a depth of popular lay support that crossed political and linguistic frontiers. Never before had such a movement gained the support of kings, princes and governing élites. No medieval movement of protest had had the backing of kings. But that *in itself* neither invalidated nor confirmed the truth of its message. It might have represented a genuine rediscovery of aspects of Christianity that had either been lost or forgotten in the mists of time; as we shall discover, Luther's doctrine of Justification did not in itself represent a fundamental break with Christian tradition. It has been argued that it was, indeed, a rediscovery. And the reasons why the two Reformations, Catholic and Protestant, took divergent paths had at least as much to do with the failures, mistakes and misperceptions of the Catholic Church, its leaders and theologians, as it did with Luther's own undoubted intransigence.

Another problem with the quotation from Tacy lies with the use of the word 'failure' when describing medieval movements of reform. We have already seen how the movements of reform within the papacy itself, and in such groups as the Cistercians or the friars, both responded to needs and challenges inside the Church and the secular world, and how they also often encountered opposition from entrenched interests within both the ecclesiastical and temporal worlds. We have also seen how it is really inappropriate to describe late medieval Western Christianity as either in a state of 'decline' or 'decay'. Thus an alternative explanation of medieval reform is not so much as a 'failure' as a continual revivifying stream, reflecting the concept of re-formation at the heart of Christianity itself. We must also remember that all ages of Christianity have thrown up examples of individuals or groups critical of the contemporary Church for backsliding from a previous distant purity. The Montanists in the second century saw their movement as a return to a true, charismatic Christian past, from which the contemporary Church had 'declined' and 'decayed'.[33] We must never forget either Gerd Tellenbach's warning that critics of the present supposedly corrupt state of the Church have always been present in Christian history (see above, p. 139). By the mid-seventeenth century there were Protestant critics of the Reformation who, far from seeing it as a unique event, argued that the Reformation itself now needed reforming. Such a critic was John Milton in his *Areopagitica* of 1655.[34]

So it could be argued that Catholic Reformation in the sixteenth century had its own precursors, its own linear descent from the past, which made it, rather than the Protestant variety, the better exemplar of Tracy's 'high point' of that series of reformations commencing in the eleventh century. Thus the Reformations of the sixteenth century raise again fundamental issues about the meaning of tradition in the Christian understanding of that word. But perhaps the best way of all to view both the Protestant and Catholic Reformations of the sixteenth century is to see them as sharing elements of a common ancient and medieval ancestry. The reasons for the parting of the ways in that century were a complex mixture of factors, from the personalities involved, through the conditions of the contemporary Church, to a range of external, secular forces which played upon the internal ecclesiastical ones.

It is possible, therefore, to construct an alternative linear descent for the Catholic Reformation. If we begin at the same point as Tracy with the reform movements in the eleventh century, then obviously those movements themselves were conscious of their own historical inspiration from earlier centuries, and ultimately back to the Gospel itself. Whether papal or monastic, medieval reformations conceived themselves as contemporary reinterpretations of ideas and concepts emanating either from earlier popes and theories of the Petrine office, or from the Rule of St Benedict and the early Egyptian ascetics, both having a common point of origin in the New Testament. Along the way, orthodox medieval reform assimilated the *Humiliati* and elements of Walden-sianism, and absorbed the enthusiasms of individuals like Francis of Assisi. At the same time the four great Lateran Councils of the Middle Ages, including the most significant of them, the Fourth Lateran Council of 1215, all promoted reform in a variety of ways.

If we move from there into the late medieval world it is easy to dismiss the Councils of the fifteenth century, for instance, as merely a failed movement called Conciliarism snuffed out by Pius II in 1460. When we examine their agendas and decrees, however, a rather different picture emerges. These Councils passed some significant measures of reform. The Council of Basel (1431–9) for example, set out something which began to approach a pro-gramme of reform. It issued regulations of both a financial and disciplinary kind about such things as the election of Church officials and procedures for appeals to ecclesiastical courts. It also tackled questions of clerical discipline including the correct performance of the offices, denounced secular intrusions into sacred music, or the inaudable and indecorous saying of Mass. The Council of Florence (1438–45) fixed the number of sacraments definitively for the first time as seven and, as we discovered in the Introduction, the canon of the New Testament was also finally affirmed as consisting of 27 books. It also emphasized the sacramental and pastoral role of the episcopate in an age when bishops were again becoming noted more for their political ambitions. Finally, a Fifth Lateran Council in 1512–17, on the very eve of the Reforma-tion, issued regulations for clerical studies at universities, and the annual episcopal visitation of monasteries. The modern historian, Michael Mullett, has interpreted these late medieval Councils as part of a long chain of reform leading to Trent, with the great sixteenth-century Council once again picking up and reinforcing many of the reforming measures of the earlier Councils: 'Trent had its precedents in the conciliar reforming proceedings of the fif-teenth century and indeed may be seen as the fulfilment of those late medieval councils.' Trent was thus an 'accelerated continuity' of earlier trends and not just a reaction to the Protestant Reformation.[35]

In addition to institutional reform from the centre there were also numerous late medieval examples of local and personal initiatives. Many of the great religious Orders were undergoing at least piecemeal reform in the closing decades of the fifteenth century, based around a series of Observant movements seeking to recall houses to a closer observance of their Rules. Individuals like the Franciscan Bernadino of Sienna (1380–1444) recaptured much of the original spirit and enthusiasm of St Francis and became one of the greatest preachers of his age. A reformer of morals in many Italian cities, he aimed at nothing less than the regeneration of his times. His impact was so great that the future Pope Pius II said that people listened to him as they might have listened to St Paul himself. Later in the same century the Dominican friar Girolamo Savonarola (1452–98) again earned a reputation as one of the finest preachers of the late Middle Ages. Based in Florence in the 1490s he became an outspoken critic of some of the 'pagan' and fashionable excesses of the Renaissance, organizing his famous bonfire of the vanities. But he was also an outspoken critic of both Church and society and a reformer of decidedly radical tendencies in both. A visionary with an apocalyptic sense, he tried to reform his own Order, but eventually the extreme nature of his preaching earned him the condemnation of Rome, excommunication, and burning for heresy. He has been claimed both as a forerunner of Luther's because of his Pauline and Augustinian inheritance, and of Ignatius Loyola and Philip Neri (1515–95), the founder of the Oratorians, as a reformer and inspiration of the ascetic life.

In addition, figures like Cardinal Ximenes in Spain were far from alone as episcopal reformers and administrators in the generation before the Reformation. English bishops like the scholarly John Fisher of Rochester (1469–1535), famous as a Henrician martyr, but more notable in his lifetime as an educational reformer at his university of Cambridge, of which he was chancellor, his friendship with Erasmus and hence support for Humanism, and his reform of his diocese. At Meaux in France from 1518 its bishop, Guillaume Briçonnet (1472–1534) gathered around himself some of the leading Humanist scholars and reformers in the kingdom and launched a wholesale reformation of his diocese. Luther, indeed, was not alone in the early sixteenth century in experiencing an emotional and intellectual conversion based on a revived understanding of the Pauline and Augustinian notions of Justification and grace. In 1511 Gasparo Contarini, the Venetian nobleman and future cardinal, at last found his own spiritual peace in a remarkably similar way to Luther in his Tower Experience. Not surprisingly he was to be one of the leading ecclesiastics most sympathetic to Luther and his ideas.

So in a variety of ways and places we can find ample evidence for a continual stream of reformation within the late-medieval Catholic Church, of which Martin Luther himself, it could be argued, was at least initially a vital part. But we must also be extremely cautious in seeing this as the same thing as the sixteenth-century Catholic Reformation; it shared many features in common with the later movement, but in some respects there were differences of degree if not kind. Late-medieval Catholic reform lacked certain vital ingredients. It had no organizing principle, no common programme of action, and was the spontaneous and largely unconnected or co-ordinated work of inspired individuals and groups. It had not, in a word, many of the features one would expect to find in something that could be called a 'movement'. All of these things were to be supplied by what was effectively the centrepiece of sixteenth-century Catholic Reform: the Council of Trent.

It is difficult to overestimate the importance of the Council of Trent. For one thing its 25 sessions spread over eighteen years generated more legislation than all the previous Ecumenical Councils put together, from Nicaea in 325 onwards. But while its importance is not doubted by historians, its significance has been interpreted very differently both in the past and into the present. A contemporary Lutheran commentator, Martin Chemnitz (1522–86) sneered at the Council: 'It is truly a Pandora's box, under whose cover every kind of corruption, abuse and superstition has been brought into the Church.'[36] While few, if any, modern historians would use such language today, there is still a tendency among those more sympathetic to the Protestant Reformation to interpret the Council in pejorative terms. Patrick Collinson, for example, describes it thus: 'The only answer that Catholicism could give to Protestantism was to define itself as its negative image, not to heal the breach.'[37] Michael Mullett, on the other hand, sees it very differently: 'Consolidating the legislation of its late-medieval predecessors, Trent equipped the Church with a solid body of defined doctrine and a code of reform that provided the essential inspiration for the Catholic renewal in early modern Europe.'[38] In some respects these interpretations are actually more complementary than confrontational. Given the times in which it met, the Council of Trent could hardly do other than respond to the Protestant Reformation in one of its aspects. But the assertion that it only or mainly defined itself as the negative image of Protestantism is about as useful a comment as saying that the Confession of Augsburg (Lutheran) or the Thirty-Nine Articles (Anglican) defined themselves as the negative image of Catholicism. All Christians in the sixteenth century, at least in part, formed their own self-consciousness in contrast to other groups of Christians.

On the other hand, whether Mullett may or may not be right to see Trent as the consolidation of the past, he is surely correct in seeing it as the organizing principle for the future of Catholicism. Trent transformed Catholic reform into a movement. As such it is undoubtedly the most important Catholic Council between the Fourth Lateran of 1215 and the Second Vatican Council of 1962–5. It was instrumental in creating a distinctive Catholic ethos from which Christians in communion with Rome could continue to draw inspiration and energy for the next four centuries.

What did Trent do that was so important? Its work was essentially twofold: doctrinal and pastoral. Its doctrinal decrees always had one eye fixed on correcting and confronting what the bishops and theologians of the Council saw as the errors of Protestantism; but at the same time the other eye was as equally firmly focused on the Catholic faithful. The doctrinal decrees, therefore, always had a double function: external defence and internal rejuvenation. The decree on Justification, for example, agreed with Luther's analysis that the initiative in obtaining the gift of faith was always from God. On the other hand it reaffirmed the importance of human free will, and by implication of the value of good works. It carefully trod a path between Pelagianism on the one side and determinism on the other. As such it has been called 'a theological masterpiece' in successfully managing such a difficult balancing act (Document 23).[39] But like all the theological decrees of Trent, it was not conceived as just an abstruse piece of intellectual wizardry; it was intended to have practical consequences. With good works now revalued, the host of Catholic confraternities and Orders dedicated to charitable work in the world were both renewed and launched into a period of growth and multiplication.

The same was true for the decrees on the Eucharist. Traditional dogmas such as transubstantiation and the sacrificial nature of the Eucharist were reaffirmed in language appropriate to the age of Humanism. Again this was not only to confound Protestantism, but also to reaffirm the faith and practices of Catholics. Now the Catholic laity went to church not only to 'hear Mass' as passive recipients, but were also encouraged to participate, perhaps most notably in an increasingly frequent reception of the bread and wine of Communion. The particularly devout now increased their reception of Communion from once a year at Easter to several times a year, in some cases even monthly. At the same time new eucharistic devotions from Benediction to the Forty Hours adoration were added to the medieval feast of Corpus Christi. Post-Tridentine Catholicism became much more than ever a eucharistically focused faith.

This was also the case for the decrees of Trent on all the sacraments, their number reaffirmed as seven. In the case of matrimony its statements have been described as representing 'some of its finest work, showing respect for human freedom, especially that of women and young people, and infused with shrewd pastoral awareness of human nature'.[40] Trent reasserted that marriage was not only a sacrament, but also that it was one celebrated by the two consenting parties. It must, therefore, be a matter of free choice on both their parts. Thus while it hardly put an end to arranged marriages in Catholic Europe, the Church was clear that women could not be forced into marriage against their will.

Perhaps the pastoral decrees of Trent were, if anything, to have an even greater impact than the doctrinal ones. While they were mostly aimed at the clergy, their effects were to be felt throughout the Church. First of all, bishops were now ordered to be resident in their dioceses for a minimum of nine months of the year. The days of non-resident bishops drawing revenues from their dioceses but residing at royal courts or distant palaces were numbered.

They were also ordered to hold regular Synods, annually for dioceses, every three years for the provinces of archbishops. As a result, during the eight years immediately following the end of the Council in 1564 we know of at least 100 such Synods being called in Europe.[41] In addition, bishops were to hold regular visitations of their dioceses.

Perhaps most significantly of all, bishops were ordered to establish diocesan seminaries for the training of new clergy. Here was a crucial shift of emphasis from the past. While medieval Councils like the Fourth Lateran had ordered some basic training for the secular clergy, this had always followed ordination rather than preceding it. Trent now began the process of creating what we would now call a professional clergy. In Castile by 1610 some 23 seminaries had been established; in France by 1760 the figure was over 150.[42] Yet poorer dioceses found it extremely difficult to establish and finance such permanent institutions. As late as 1630 fewer than half of all Italian dioceses had been able to acquire a seminary.[43]

Yet, despite regional variations, by the first decades of the seventeenth century across many parts of the Catholic world nothing short of a clerical transformation was under way. Educationally as well as morally the secular clergy were beginning to achieve that ideal envisaged for them as far back as the reign of Gregory VII. At last celibacy was becoming a reality rather than a pious hope for the parish clergy, aided by steadily rising clerical incomes removing the need for wives and sons. What was emerging was the picture of the Catholic parish clergy that has become the one familiar to modern times – often university educated, seminary trained, celibate and increasingly clad in a common uniform of black cassock. And these clergy were now armed with three of the most important by-products of Trent: a new catechism, a new breviary with the daily offices in it, and perhaps above all, a new missal.

The Tridentine missal of 1570 is one of the greatest liturgical texts of Christian history. Before the sixteenth century there was no such thing as a common or standard version of the Mass. Different regions of Christendom had many variants of the basic structure. England had a number of such texts including the Uses of Sarum, York and Hereford. Now with the Tridentine missal, for the first time in history Catholics could attend Mass in any part of the world and expect to find the same (Latin) words and the same ceremonies. For four centuries this standardized text was to hold the Catholic world together and help to create a common sense of identity.

It must be emphasized, however, that the theoretically sweeping reforms of Trent did not become reality overnight. They sometimes met resistance from conservative forces that resented change; and poor regions could not always afford the expenses involved. But gradually, more rapidly in some areas than others, Tridentine Catholicism emerged, sometimes taking a century or more to fully materialize, but in the end resulting in a Church both the same and yet different from its medieval predecessor. Whatever else Trent had done, it had launched Catholicism into an era of renewed self-confidence.

The Pope who had finally summoned the bishops to gather at Trent, Paul III (1534–49) equally heralded a new type of papacy. By the later sixteenth century, popes were noted more for their piety and morality than for their Renaissance paganism. But, like many of their princely counterparts, they were also transforming themselves into absolute monarchs. The vast building programme initiated in the fifteenth century was refashioning the city of Rome into a classical masterpiece of town planning and the fitting hub of a centralized state. The medieval curia was giving way to new instruments of government based around congregations for regulating everything from the Papal States to the foreign missions. The Tridentine missal was a symptom of this new centralization and standardization emanating from Rome. The process of declaring individuals to be saints, already 'Romanized' in the thirteenth century, now became even more bureaucratic during the Catholic Reformation. Even the questionnaires sent to witnesses in the process of canonization were now standardized in Rome. Perhaps no single occasion better symbolizes this centralization of the Church and exaltation of the papacy at the heart of it than the day in 1622 when five figures of the Catholic Reformation, including Ignatius Loyola, Francis Xavier and Teresa of Avila, were all proclaimed saints on the same day at the same ceremony of canonization in front of St Peter's Basilica in Rome – perhaps the day that signified the high-water mark of the Catholic Reformation.

These three saints also had one other thing in common: they had all been members of religious Orders. Alongside the Council of Trent and a renewed papacy the other most important characteristic of the Catholic Reformation was the greatest flowering of new religious Orders since the time of the Cistercians, Franciscans and Dominicans in the twelfth and thirteenth centuries. And of these new Orders perhaps the most important was the Society of Jesus: the Jesuits.

The early history of the Jesuits is intimately bound to the biography of their founder, Ignatius Loyola. Born in 1491 into a minor noble family in the Basque region of northern Spain, the young Loyola became a soldier until in 1521 he was wounded in the leg at the siege of Pamplona during one of the interminable Hapsburg–Valois wars. Badly executed surgery resulted in a prolonged convalescence and a lifelong limp. However, it was during his lengthy recovery in his family castle that he turned to reading. Up to this point his education had been perfunctory, but long days of enforced inactivity encouraged him to turn to books. Here in his father's library he came across some of the great classics of Christian spirituality and mysticism. Reading them proved to be the first great turning point in his life. When he was sufficiently recovered he went first to the great Benedictine abbey of Montserrat near Barcelona. The mountain monastery was a place of legend, associated with the Holy Grail, and the keeper of one of the most famous images of the Virgin Mary. Here Loyola performed a profoundly symbolic act. Effectively reversing the ceremony of knighthood when the new knight received the sword, spurs and other tokens of his elevated state at the conclusion of a vigil before the altar of a church, Loyola left behind his sword and donned the habit of a beggar. For him, military struggle was now to give way to spiritual warfare. He then spent a year, 1522–3, at Manresa, where he had a series of visions and other spiritual experiences that were to be the origin of his greatest literary work, the *Spiritual Exercises*. Excessive fasting, deep melancholia, anxiety about his eventual salvation or damnation, finally culminated in his greatest spiritual experience on the shores of the river Cardona (Document 24).

One phase of his spiritual journey was now over; in 1524 a new one began as he returned to the world to complete his neglected education. After periods at Spanish universities he finally went to Paris in 1528 where he graduated with his MA in 1534. Now well versed in the Bible, the Fathers and the Scholastics, and having met a group of like-minded Iberian friends, he and they arrived in Rome in 1537. In a way similar to Francis of Assisi more than three centuries earlier, after a series of interviews with curial officials, finally in 1540 Pope Paul III approved the Constitutions of the Society of Jesus. This new community had one foot firmly planted in the medieval tradition, with influences ranging from the Rules of older Orders, the Brethren of the Common Life, and the friars of the thirteenth century; the other foot, however, was as equally firmly standing on new concepts derived from Renaissance Humanism, especially the characteristic Jesuit combination of obedience with personal initiative. The individualism of the Renaissance was realized by the removal of the necessity of a choral office or prescribed habit; Jesuits were designed for activity in the world and everything else had to be fitted around that priority. This in its turn was combined with an awareness of the new importance of the papacy. All Jesuits were not only to make the three traditional monastic vows of poverty, chastity and obedience, but also a fourth vow of personal obedience to the pope.

At the core of this new Society (a word in itself of immense significance: this was not a conventional Order) was the formation and work of its members through the means of the *Spiritual Exercises* and education. The *Spiritual Exercises* themselves again had roots firmly planted in Christian mystical tradition including the *Devotio Moderna*; but never before had the Christian spiritual life been so systematized. Finally completed in 1548, many people have been both disappointed and puzzled when first reading them. The reason for this is that the *Exercises* were not designed like most spiritual works to be read, pondered and absorbed by a reader. They are, in effect, a set of instructions or guidance for a Spiritual Director who will use them to lead an individual on a notional four-week pilgrimage through the life and ministry of Jesus; a kind of extended mystical tutorial. They include frequent examinations of conscience punctuated by a series of meditations, each one focusing on one event in the life of Jesus as recorded in the Gospels. Again flexibility and the appropriate application to particular individuals at different stages of their own spiritual journeys are at the heart of the *Exercises*. They were one of the essential elements in the formation and continued vocation of Jesuits, and also one of their main tools in their work of conversion. For the *Exercises* were designed to convert those undertaking them, clerical or lay, to a deeper spiritual understanding. These were not exclusively monastic or even clerical guides, but designed to be used with the laity as well. Many who were at first sceptical about this novel type of religious community, like Cardinal Contarini, became supporters after themselves undergoing the *Exercises*.

The other foundation stone of the Society and its work was education. Like the Dominicans before them the Jesuits saw education as being essential to themselves and their work in the world. All Jesuits had to be university graduates, which partly accounted for their lengthy novitiate. Loyola was acutely conscious of his own educational shortcomings and was determined that in the age of educated and critical laity his Society should be armed with the most advanced education possible. Jesuits were to become possibly the most famous and successful educators of Catholic Europe and beyond in the late sixteenth and seventeenth centuries. Religious renewal meant both a spiritual awakening and also an intellectual disciplining. The first Jesuit college began at Messina in 1548, and by the time Loyola died in 1556 there were already some 39. His original small group of nine founding members had also grown into a Society of about 1,000. In the following decades it was to experience its most spectacular expansion, comparable to that of the Cistercians or friars before it; by 1613 there were 13,000 Jesuits, and by 1640, 22,000. By 1607 they ran 300 colleges, and by the middle of the eighteenth century nearly 700.[44] These colleges were what we would now call secondary schools, and by the early seventeenth century the Jesuits had effectively created a system of secondary education across the Catholic world. Academically rigorous, yet again with clear elements of flexibility and spontaneity, the Jesuits learned much from the Renaissance *studia humanitatis*, but at the same time infused it with religious purpose in a school timetable punctuated by prayers and Masses. So famous had the Jesuits become as educators by the seventeenth century that many Catholic princes and noble families employed them as tutors for their children. For generations the Catholic élite of Europe shared this common inheritance of a Jesuit education. Here was education with a purpose; in schools free of all charges the evangelization of Catholic boys, and the potential conversion of the Protestant boys who also attended free, as well as that of non-Christians in the New World, was the aim. The missionary work in the New World meant for many Jesuits a life of dedication, hardship and extreme danger; by 1675 some 304 had lost their lives in the effort to spread their faith.[45]

The Jesuits, however, were not the only new religious Order created in the sixteenth century. Second only to them in importance were the Capuchins. An offshoot of the Franciscans, they were founded by Matteo di Bassio of Urbino (*c*. 1495–1552), receiving papal approval in 1528. They wore beards, sandals and a distinctive pointed cowl or *capuche*, and represented a strict and austere interpretation of the spirit of St Francis. Essentially preaching hermits, by 1530 they already had about 700 friars. The conversion of their fourth master, Bernardino Ochino, to Protestantism in 1542, however, almost destroyed their credibility. But they survived the shock and by 1550 had grown to about 2,500 friars, and by 1587 to about 6,000.[46] Their work among the poor and the sick was to take a toll of their numbers comparable to the sacrifices of the Jesuits in the mission field; Capuchins were particularly noted for their fearless nursing of plague victims, often resulting in terrible losses from their own ranks.[47]

Other smaller Orders were also founded in the first decades of the sixteenth century, including the Theatines in 1524 by Gaetano di Thienne (1480–1547), an Order committed to working in hospitals, to preaching and to study. The Society of the Servants of the Poor founded in 1531 by Girolamo Miani (b. 1480) at Somascha near Milan, and hence known as Somaschi, had its origins in helping the victims of the Italian wars of the period. The Clerks Regular of St Paul were founded by Antonio Maria Zaccaria (1502–47) in 1530, and began with visiting the prisons and hospitals of Cremona, and went on to give spiritual conferences and exercises. From their main church of St Barnabas in Milan they became known as Barnabites.[48] Among the Orders founded later than the Jesuits perhaps the most important was the Congregation of the Oratory, or Oratorians, founded by Philip Neri (1515–95) and given papal approval in 1575. Neri's life was changed for ever in 1544 when, in a pentecostal experience, he had a vision of a ball of fire descending from heaven and entering his heart. He was ordained in 1551, and his new Congregation, which started in the city of Rome, was a very loose clerical society with no vows, a retention of incomes, and a highly decentralized system of government. Oratorians specialized in attractive liturgy, public devotions and the hearing of confessions, and soon spread to other Italian cities and from there across the Catholic world.

Catholic Reformation religious life was also characterized by another flowering, that of a new kind of female religious Order. What differentiated early modern Orders for women from their medieval forebears was, like so many Orders for men, a new sense of vocation for activity in the world. In the Middle Ages most convents had been pious retreats for the daughters of the aristocracy, and normally enclosed, that is with the minimum of contact with the outside world. Even the female, or Second Orders, of such active male religious as the Franciscans and Dominicans had become enclosed during the course of the thirteenth century. And throughout the Middle Ages monks had consistently outnumbered nuns by a very wide margin. All of this was to change in early modern Catholicism.

Perhaps the most important of these new, active Orders for women, and in some ways the female counterpart of the Jesuits, was the Ursulines. Founded by Angela Merici (1474–1540) and given papal approval in 1544 after her death, their great expansion only began in the late sixteenth century, spreading from Italy into France. Just like the Jesuits the main work of the Ursulines was in education; by the 1670s there were over 300 Ursuline houses in France alone, with some 12,000 sisters.[49] One of the things which might have helped them to avoid enclosure and concentrate instead on worldly work was the relatively lowly social origins of the first recruits to the Order which meant they did not bring lavish dowries to support a community of economically inactive sisters.[50] At the same time the education they provided was different from the Jesuits; it was more practical, designed to produce pious managers of households rather than clerics or princes. And second only to the Ursulines, at least in France, was the smaller Congregation of the Daughters of Charity founded by Vincent de Paul and Louise de Marillac in 1633, which cared for the poor and the sick, especially in hospitals.

Perhaps the most famous single nun of the sixteenth century, however, was Teresa of Avila (1515–82). She initially joined a house of Carmelite nuns, the enclosed female counterpart of a small Order of medieval friars. But during the mid–1550s she became dissatisfied with what she perceived as the lax ascetic life of the Order, especially after a profound experience while praying at a statue of Christ being scourged. In 1562 she began a series of foundations of stricter Carmelite houses for 'Discalced' or barefoot nuns. By the time of her death she had established seventeen such houses for nuns, and fifteen for friars, with the help of her fellow Carmelite, John of the Cross. But she is perhaps most remembered as one of the greatest mystics and spiritual writers in Christian history. Her *Autobiography* as well as *The Way of Perfection* and the *Interior Castle* have long been recognized as classics of Christian mysticism. They describe in detail the full range of prayer, from the most basic right up to the total identification with Christ in the so-called 'mystic marriage'. Her own experience of the latter is vividly described in her autobiography and memorably portrayed, with some artistic licence, in the famous statue of Bernini in the seventeenth century, as an angel piercing her heart with a spear, inviting comparisons with the experience of the *stigmata* of St Francis of Assisi.

Thus during the course of the sixteenth and seventeenth centuries medieval Catholicism had been transformed and refashioned by two Reformations, Protestant and Catholic. What did these two movements share in common, and what divided them? The answers to those questions can be no more than tentative; but they must be sought first by considering the influence of two forces which pre-dated both of them.

The Renaissance and Printing

The Renaissance and the Reformation shared a number of perceptions in common. Among these were a group of concepts such as 'rebirth', the idea that a new illumination was coming into the world after centuries of darkness; and the belief that scholars could only truly understand the ancient ideas that now seemed to have a new contemporary validity if the ancient sources themselves were read in their original languages purified of later changes or corruptions. All of these ideas of the Renaissance Humanists were to be absorbed and applied in the religious context by sixteenth-century Reformers. The Protestant Reformation was partly constructed on the idea that medieval Christianity had introduced unwarranted additions or corruptions into the original message of the faith. This focused on the growth of papal claims and resulting Roman government, doctrinal issues concerning the number and meaning of the sacraments, and the theological method of the Scholastics. Thus for the Protestant Reformers the millennium of the Middle Ages was as much a period of darkness in religion as it had been in culture for the Renaissance Humanists.

The Renaissance motto *ad fontes*, 'back to the sources', was also to find its counterpart in the Reformation. For the Protestants the great original source of Christian authority was scripture. But the version of the Bible bequeathed to the sixteenth century by the Middle Ages, the Latin Vulgate, was largely the result of the work done by St Jerome a millennium earlier. Already in the fifteenth century the Humanists were starting to point to the glaring inaccuracies in this as well as in many other medieval Latin translations and editions. It was Erasmus who proved to be the great intermediary between the Humanists and the Reformation in this as in other ways. In 1516 Erasmus published his edition of the Greek New Testament. It proved to be a revelation. The product of years of labour searching for ancient manuscripts in countless libraries, it was the Christian equivalent of having the works of Plato in their original Greek for the first time rather than being transmitted through inaccurate translations. Luther was to use Erasmus's work in his own attacks on the medieval Church and its theology.

At a number of points in the Gospels Jesus called his followers to repentance. But what exactly was he saying? The Latin Vulgate stressed the importance of action, of 'doing' penance, and thus helped to justify the whole medieval system, from sacramental confession, to fasting, vigils, pilgrimages and all the other 'machinery' of penance. Erasmus's Greek version by contrast emphasized not the doing of penance but the 'being' penitent; a change of heart. This clearly seemed to point not to the medieval system of penance but rather to Luther's concept of Justification by Faith Alone, an inner change of heart that came from the passive acceptance of a gracious and unmerited gift of faith from God directly to the individual. And it must be remembered that Luther's own Tower Experience was a religious revelation at least in part based on a linguistic insight. Humanism had thus helped to give a voice to the Reformation.

The whole purpose of the career of Erasmus had been to show how the ancient texts could illuminate the modern understanding of Christianity. He saw Christianity not so much in terms of the outward, the performance of actions, but the inward, not through rituals but rather through the moral stature achieved by individual Christians. This was the theme of his *Praise of Folly* which saw the 'folly' of the cross, God becoming human to die for humanity, as the heart of Christianity, a radically christological approach. In his *Enchiridion* Erasmus painted a picture of the Christian spiritual struggle influenced by the *Devotio Moderna* and the *Imitation of Christ*, but also partly derived from Ficino's edition of Plato's *Timaeus*, and Pico's *Oration*. Here in Erasmus Humanism and Christianity met and fused. As Erasmus wrote in the introduction to his Greek New Testament: 'What else is the philosophy of Christ, which he himself calls rebirth, other than the institution of well-founded human nature?'[51] As Anthony Levi has commented: 'The renaissance development in moral attitudes was not, on the whole, inspired by the gospels, but it was perfectly compatible with evangelical Christianity.'[52] No wonder, then, that in the years immediately following 1517 many Humanists and their readers saw in Luther a fellow-spirit, a critic of medieval corruptions, and an opponent of Scholasticism.

No wonder also that many of the Reformers borrowed techniques first developed by the Humanists. One of these was rhetoric, the arts of persuasion, and its bedfellow, oratory. In the writings and the speeches of the ancients the Humanists had found invaluable tools to promote persuasive argument that were eagerly adopted by the merchants and bankers who vied with one another for the political control of city states like Florence in the fifteenth century. In the following century the Reformers themselves equally adopted such techniques.

The Reformation was a movement heavily dependent upon both the written and the spoken word to achieve its results. Not only learned treatises and literary works of polemic poured from their pens; theirs was also a cause that relied equally heavily on public disputation and sermons. In many German and Swiss cities the authorities organized public debates between the Reformers and their opponents in order to win over the undecided citizens, just as citizens used public speaking in council chambers to win their own more political battles. Sometimes deliberately 'loaded' to favour the winning side, still the techniques of rhetoric or oratory were essential and familiar tools in presenting persuasive arguments to often sophisticated audiences. The same was true of sermons. From the moment he arrived in Zurich the Humanist-educated Zwingli abandoned medieval conventions in his preaching and adopted the methods of his teachers.[53]

As we have already seen, one of the possible reasons for the survival and successes of the Protestant Reformation was the unprecedented level of political support it received. No medieval movement of dissent had ever achieved the backing of kings and princes in the way the Reformation was to do. Why? We have already explored some of the political and diplomatic pressures behind this, but part of the answer may lie also in the Renaissance concept of the political ruler. Ancient texts, most notably Plato's *Republic*, had advocated the concept of the 'philosopher-king', a ruler wise, learned and moral, as the highest and best form of political leadership. Many fifteenth-century Italian princes had self-consciously tried to emulate this ideal in their own miniature states; a ruler like Federigo di Montefeltro, Duke of Urbino, is an obvious example of this phenomenon. Princes like Federigo sought to be seen as men of both moral and intellectual worth, capable of patronizing the arts with a clear sense of understanding about what they were doing, and who could discuss the content of literature or paintings with writers and artists on the same level as their creators. At the same time they should be rulers who extended their own sense of intellect and morality into the way they ruled their subjects.

By the sixteenth century, educated people were sufficiently conscious of these ideas that they could be translated from the political and cultural spheres to the religious. Erasmus was again a vital bridge. His work *The Education of a Christian Prince* portrayed the ruler in Platonic terms as a philosopher-king capable of judging moral issues. In 1521 Henry VIII carried this into the realms of theology when he did what no medieval king before him had contemplated doing: he wrote a work of theology. His *Defence of the Seven Sacraments* was a royal blast against Luther, showing how a Renaissance prince could shift easily from the intellectual, cultural and moral into the specifically religious. However much he might have depended on Thomas More for some of his material, the king certainly took the credit for the book, something which seemed more than plausible to his contemporaries. Although partly intended to demonstrate the king's learning and enhance his vanity as a scholar, the book demonstrated that it was but a short step from the philosopher-king of the Renaissance to the Godly prince of the Reformation. If kings could judge the cultural products of the Renaissance, they were also now equally well equipped to judge the theological issues of the Reformation.[54]

More generally the Renaissance had also helped to create what might be termed a sympathetic intellectual environment for the Reformation. The Renaissance represented a fundamental challenge to many of the received ideas of the Middle Ages; although its sources were ancient it was still perceived as the 'new learning'. By the sixteenth century it had helped to foster an atmosphere in which the received notions of the past were legitimate targets for critical scrutiny, and where new ideas would themselves receive a sympathetic hearing. Again it was but a short step from the assault on Scholasticism to one more generally on the beliefs and practices of medieval Western Christianity.

The Renaissance imagination was also full of ideal societies or cities. Many fifteenth-century Italian painters produced cityscapes of an idealized nature. The literary products of the Renaissance were no less preoccupied by the concept of the ideal society, perhaps most famously in Thomas More's *Utopia* of 1515. Here, again taking Plato's *Republic* as its point of origin, More also borrowed ideas from Erasmus to create 'a fantasy exploring the consequences of massively restored confidence in the moral potential of human nature' that was at the heart of the Renaissance.[55] This concept was taken up by the Protestant Reformers, perhaps most obviously in Johann Eberlin's 1521 fantasy *Fifteen Confederates* in which he described his own religious and secular ideal of Wolfaria, 'the land where all fares well'. Steven Ozment has described this as 'the most ambitious early statement of a Protestant "Utopia" set forth at the inception of the Reformation'.[56] Once again Renaissance concepts could join forces with the biblical narrative and both Protestants and Catholics could be seen as attempting to realize this ideal, the new Jerusalem or the primitive Church of Acts, combined with classical models, in some of their own earthly communities. It has been suggested that this was what the Humanist-educated Calvin was attempting to do in Geneva: create an ideal Christian society.[57]

On the other hand the New World of the Americas was perhaps more fertile, virgin soil in which to plant experiments along these lines. At either end of the continent there were examples of this. In the north in Massachusetts in the 1620s English 'Puritans' left what they saw as a Church incapable of true Reformation and a society tainted with moral corruption, to found their own ideal religious society in isolation from the old world. To the south in what is now Paraguay the Jesuits were doing something not dissimilar. They retreated into the interior with their newly converted local tribes to escape the European slavers to found a series of 'Reductions'. Here they too could protect their converts from a tainted world and establish an idealized form of Christian society.

Back in the old world a new city was also rising. During the course of the sixteenth and seventeenth centuries the papacy was transforming Rome from its pagan and medieval heritages, 'restoring Rome as the Church's ideal city'.[58] From the great project of rebuilding St Peter's, the papacy had extended its programme to include a model of town planning. New avenues and new churches in the classical style were changing the face of the city, and by the late sixteenth century a new style, the Baroque, was being employed. In the following century its greatest exponents, Borromini and Bernini, would leave an indelible mark on the city, with churches, squares and arcades constructed in this new flamboyant style characterized by its kinetic energy. Even the remains of pagan Rome were being forced to yield to revived Catholicism as its columns and monuments were crowned with Christian crosses.

Alongside the continuities, however, the Reformation also came to mean a discontinuity from its Renaissance forebear. Nowhere was this more obvious than in the contrasting attitudes to human nature. The Platonic optimism of Pico's *Oration on the Dignity of Man*, in which humanity rises to approach moral perfection, gave way to the Augustinian pessimism of a Luther or Calvin. For the Protestant Reformers the Fall in Eden had so corrupted human nature that it was now totally dependent on divine grace for its faith and the text of scripture for its morality. This clash was to be exemplified in its starkest form in the bitter exchanges between Luther and Erasmus in 1524–5. For Erasmus, the problem with Luther's view of Justification was that it allowed no place for human free will; his view of grace and predestination made God seem unjust. Erasmus asserted that free will must be allowed some scope, otherwise if our fate is already decided what use is morality? Luther replied that as only God is truly good, and therefore even if he condemns the whole of humanity to perdition, we have no right to judge but only adore him. Thus 'Luther pounds home his conviction that the human will is utterly helpless on its own . . . His view is summed up in his famous utterance that the will is like an ass, that if ridden by God it goes one way and if by Satan another.'[59] In this Luther had 'broken free of the humanism Erasmus represented'.[60] Two contrasting experiences of what it meant to live the Christian life had led to the breakdown of one vital element linking Renaissance Humanism to the Reformation.

Breakdown was also to occur with regard to the Renaissance and Reformation views of Scholasticism. Both rejected its methodology and conclusions, but often for rather different reasons. For the Humanists the final end of learning was the realization of a truly *moral* person; for the Protestant Reformers the object of education was the production of a *religious* person. Thus the Humanist rejection of dogma was not followed by the Reformers. In the words of Steven Ozment: 'Protestants made the liberal arts a handmaiden to a continuing medieval theological ideal . . . [and] continued the scholastic enterprise of defining true doctrine.'[61] They became 'new' Scholastics, using the tools of Humanism for traditional medieval ends. There were thus as many linkages between Thomas Aquinas and his *Summa* and John Calvin in his version of the Scholastic enterprise, the *Institutes*.

'God's highest and extremest act of grace, whereby the business of the Gospel is driven forward.'[62] The subject of Luther's words of praise was not religious but rather technological: printing. In just three years from 1517 to 1520 it has been estimated that over 300,000 copies of 30 works by Luther were printed and sold.[63] The copying and dissemination of such a quantity of material in such a relatively short space of time would have been quite simply impossible in a society still reliant on laborious hand copying. Thus it has long been recognized by scholars that the Reformation and printing were linked in a number of ways. Perhaps the most extensive study of the impact of printing is the one first published by Elizabeth L. Eisenstein in 1979. Here she has analysed what was perhaps the first truly industrial process, doing many of the things that the later machines of the Industrial Revolution would also do, from mass production to standardization. In a variety of ways this affected the Renaissance as well as the Reformation. For one thing it was essential for making the rediscoveries of ancient manuscripts permanent; once printed in unprecedented quantities at unprecedented speed it was far less likely that literary works would ever be lost again. It also eliminated that other problem of a 'scribal culture': copyists' errors. Now, at last, scholars could have agreed standard texts. It also tended to secularize book production, cutting the final links with the medieval monastic *scriptoria*; if the Church had once had something approaching a monopoly of book production, printing finally ended it. Book production now completed its transition from a religious to a commercial operation.

Invented by Gutenberg of Mainz in the 1450s, the new technology of printing by means of movable metal type swept across Europe in the following decades. By about 1520 it had become the normal method of book production and hand copyists were becoming as endangered a species as handloom weavers were to be in the nineteenth century. Thus printing came to maturity just as the Protestant Reformation was beginning. However, for decades churchmen had already come to appreciate the potential of printing, already called the 'divine art' and used to produce everything from Bibles to Indulgences. Yet in some subtle ways printing was also preparing the ground for the Protestant revolution, like an artillery barrage before the infantry assault. For one thing, cheaper and more plentiful books fed the hunger of lay spirituality. Works of mysticism, volumes of sermons, commentaries on the Bible, decrees of Councils and treatises by theologians were now more readily available to the literate lay audience than ever before. What, then, of the traditional role of the clergy as teachers and commentators when the literate laity could find alternative means of instruction?

What, then, of the Bible itself? It is a mistake to imagine that vernacular Bibles were the invention of the Protestant Reformers. There was clearly a hunger to read the sacred texts on the part of the laity and, along with numerous editions of the Latin Vulgate, printing again fed this with vernacular versions as well. Between 1466 and 1522 there were some 22 editions of the Bible in High or Low German, as well as Italian, Dutch, French, Castilian, Catalan and Czech versions pouring from the presses.[64] Into this tidal wave of Latin and vernacular Bibles plunged Erasmus's Greek New Testament in 1516. On one level, then, the Reformers' demands for vernacular Bibles spoke to a ready and willing audience which, to some extent, was the cause rather than the result of the Protestant claim for the essential authority of the Bible.

At the same time it also helped to further undermine the authority of the Church. One of the problems with scores of unauthorized editions of vernacular Bibles was the wide variation in meaning between translations. The possibility of heretical conclusions being drawn from faulty translations out of its control already worried the Church before the end of the fifteenth century. Attempts at biblical censorship were officially sanctioned by the Fifth Lateran Council in 1515. The Greek New Testament of Erasmus was seen in conservative circles as an implied assault on the Vulgate and through it on Catholic orthodoxy itself. Thus, as Eisenstein argues, even before Luther's Ninety-Five Theses were themselves printed, the Church authorities were seen as reactionary and trying to keep the Bible out of the hands of the laity; that perceived attitude was again compared unfavourably with that of the Protestant Reformers.

Yet printing also had some traps laid for those Reformers themselves. Some Radical Reformers not only made the Bible the central authority in Christianity but also began to adopt what we would call a 'fundamentalist' approach to the text; a literalism that contained its own dangers. For one thing, this approach was clearly opposed to another force at work in Protestant territories, increased biblical scholarship. Printing allowed the knowledge of ancient languages and historical information to grow and be disseminated on an unprecedented scale. Protestant scholars continued the Humanist drive to find more and more accurate texts and readings. This in its turn led not to an agreed edition but rather to a proliferation of scholarly disputes. The London Polyglot Bible of 1657 contained passages in up to ten different ancient languages, revealing numerous possible variant readings, as well as maps and plans and other historical information. This now began to raise the question of whether or not the ordinary literate lay person could actually read the Bible with true understanding. Did the laity need authoritative interpreters after all; had the scholars merely replaced the priests? By the nineteenth and twentieth centuries such problems and paradoxes had grown to the point where scholarly activity seemed to be undermining some of the most basic assumptions of Christian belief. Were biblical scholars becoming in some strange sense 'new Gnostics' possessed of esoteric knowledge largely hidden from the laity? As Eisenstein comments: 'The quibbles of Schoolmen about the nature of angels were no more destructive of piety than learned disputes between biblical scholars.'[65]

But in the sixteenth century these problems still lay in the future. There seemed to be a natural alliance between printing and Protestantism. The latter was not only the first dissenting movement to have the support of kings and princes; it was also the first one to be propagated by printing. One of the possible explanations for the unprecedented success of the Protestant Reformers compared to previous movements of dissenting reform may again lie with printing. We have seen already how medieval heretical movements like the Lollards or Hussites were linguistically constrained, hardly able to move beyond their national frontiers. It was obviously very difficult for medieval dissenting movements to disseminate their ideas. Lower levels of literacy than in the sixteenth century were combined with all the problems surrounding hand copying. The medieval Church found it relatively easy to contain heresy to particular regions. But now with printing the sheer volume of material quickly overcame the Church's ability to either censor or burn it. Protestantism was rapidly internationalized and made permanent, like the Renaissance before it, partly with the help of mass-produced books.

Printing was also to have other effects on what might be termed Protestant culture. Obviously the Reformers' demands for vernacular Bibles to be read by individual Christians produced a bias in favour of extending literacy. Schools and universities were founded across Protestant Europe, with no fewer than 33 new universities established between 1550 and 1700.[66] Protestantism was pushing literacy downwards through the social strata so that artisans and sailors, industrial workers and even peasants were now becoming literate. But this drive also contained its own potential dangers. Since the

Peasants' War of 1524–5 there had been another potential linkage, that between Protestantism and political dissent. John Foxe's martyrs were often quite ordinary people performing acts of both religious and political heroism. Biblical texts themselves, after centuries in which they had been used to promote obedience, could now be interpreted by some radical political groups in a more egalitarian, not to say revolutionary, way. From the Dutch Sea Beggars in revolt against their king in the sixteenth century, to the Levellers in the English Civil Wars of the 1640s and 1650s, movements of political dissent could interpret particular texts in novel ways. 'For freedom Christ has set us free. Stand firm, therefore, and do not submit again to a yoke of slavery' (Gal. 5:1). The words of St Paul could easily be shifted from an exclusively spiritual to a decidedly political meaning.

Bible reading could also have other consequences in Protestant lands. Vernacular Bibles could help to harden linguistic and national frontiers. After the Reformation Western Christians ceased to pray and worship God in a common language. Luther's German Bible or the Authorized English version of 1611 were in themselves significant events in the standardization of national languages. At the same time the encouragement of individuals to read the Bible for themselves could have other unforeseen consequences. Printing had already provided manuals of instruction from everything like music to architecture; in the arts it had helped to foster a more educated and knowledgeable patronage. Already the idea was widely accepted that individuals could effectively teach themselves without the need for properly qualified personal instructors. The sixteenth century was something of an age of intellectual self-help. This principle could now be extended to the Bible. If a single volume could contain all that was needed to sustain faith, then surely individuals in the privacy of their own home could feed themselves spiritually and doctrinally without the need of teachers. This, in its turn, could lead to an inward-looking and increasingly narrow approach to Christianity: 'Open books, in some instances, led to closed minds.'[67]

Protestant Europe was not alone, however, in being affected by printing. The lands of the Catholic Reformation were also subject to its influence. In previous centuries the decrees of Councils or the instructions coming from Rome had flowed plentifully; the problem had been getting them known and enforced. Printing significantly helped to change that. The decrees of Trent were printed and disseminated across the Catholic world more speedily and effectively than ever before. But perhaps the most important single work that affected the spiritual lives of Catholics was the missal of 1570. We have already seen how it standardized the text of the Mass. This would have been impossible to accomplish without printing.

So the Renaissance and the invention of printing both had profound impacts on Western Christianity in the sixteenth century. And while it is relatively easy to identify the differences between the two Reform movements that developed, it is perhaps their similarities that more often get submerged or forgotten.

Similarities

For a number of decades now historians have been pointing to the fact that, whatever their eventual differences, Catholics and Protestants often shared similar motivations and points of origin. Whatever contrasting answers they offered, the initial question was often common to both. In the words of Jean Delumeau, written some 35 years ago, the Catholic and Protestant Reformations were 'two complementary aspects of one and the same process of Christianization' which 'drew on a common past'.[68] More recently James D. Tracy has pointed out that 'The Catholic and Protestant Reformations had many of the same objectives.'[69]

Both shared a desire to improve both the education and morals of the parish clergy. This, it could be argued, had been a goal of all reformers since at least the eleventh century and gave Catholics and Protestants a common heritage. Thus both concentrated heavily on the creation of a graduate clergy. By 1600 the vast majority of Protestant clergy had university degrees; while Catholic priests were proportionally not yet educated to so high a level the number of university graduates was increasing and clearly the new seminaries were equally helping to produce a far better trained secular clergy than the one in the Middle Ages. Both agreed, therefore, that a more 'professional' clergy was desirable. One drawback that was also common to both groups was that as the clergy became better educated it could, especially in more backward rural areas, lead to breakdowns in communication between the pastor and his people. At the same time both wished to improve the morals, and especially the sexual behaviour, of the clergy. Again this was a common inheritance from the medieval reformers who had long been concerned with clerical continence, but had never been able to find universally effective methods of combating it, as much for secular and economic reasons as anything else. In the sixteenth century both Catholics and Protestants asked again how the clergy's sexual morality could be improved. The answers were different, but the question was the same. Protestants generally agreed that biblical precedent accorded with practical reality and advocated a married clergy. Catholics equally emphasized the biblical texts in favour of celibacy and now at last began to make it also a practical reality.

Both Reformations also shared the same goal of Christianizing the laity. Again, education was one of their common instruments, with both building huge numbers of new schools and universities. But in both cases this instruction of the laity overflowed from formal schooling into the more general catechism classes. The sixteenth century was awash with catechisms, again helped by printing; all denominations produced them in abundance. But this education of the laity also extended once again from the academic to the liturgical. Both used sermons and a range of other formal methods. The Eucharist may have been a theological bone of contention, but pastorally both sides saw that it was essential to the spiritual development of the laity and treated the reception of Communion with great reverence. The methods, however, varied. Catholics renewed a sense of lay participation in the Mass, especially through the more frequent reception of Communion. Protestants tended to reduce the frequency of eucharistic celebrations, but with the same objective of increasing the reverence with which it was held. The Calvinist Scottish Kirk celebrated the Eucharist only annually, but insisted on a lengthy period of preparation, reminiscent of the early Church and the elaborate penitential practices leading up to Easter.[70] Both sets of Reformers were also agreed with 'the assertion of the validity of the worldly lay vocation as a Christian way of life'.[71] For Protestants, one of the consequences of this was the abandonment of the monastic way of life; for the Jesuits and others it meant its transformation so that it could accommodate the realities of secular life. Many manuals of spirituality were also produced for the laity by both groups of Reformers, on the Catholic side perhaps the best known being the *Introduction to a Devout Life* by Francis de Sales and published in 1609.[72]

Standing in St Peter's Square in the 1660s any observer would have been only too aware of the vast new colonnades sweeping out from the basilica, recently completed to the designs of Bernini. The two curving arms of the colonnade were not just a Baroque device, they were deliberately intended by their architect to symbolize Christ's arms enfolding the whole of humanity in an embrace. Over the previous century and a half that is what Christianity had begun to do, to shift from a predominantly Eurocentric faith to a world religion. Both Catholics and Protestants believed in mission and conversion. An accident of history had given the Catholic Church a head start in this with the vast colonial empires of Portugal and then Spain becoming the first testing grounds of this fresh expansion. From the Americas to the African coast, from Goa and India to as far as China and Japan, Catholic missionaries fanned out across the globe. Tens of millions of new Christians were to be baptized during the course of the sixteenth and seventeenth centuries in what was to prove to be the biggest expansion of the faith since its first centuries. Perhaps the most famous of these European missionaries was the Jesuit, Francis Xavier, who was instrumental in opening India, China and Japan to Western Christianity in what were arguably the most significant missionary journeys since the time of St Paul.[73] Less well known is the Dominican, Bartolome de Las Casas (1484–1566), one of the first missionaries to advocate what we would now call the human rights of indigenous peoples. He argued in debate before Charles V himself at Valladolid advocating the equality of those many millions that Spanish arms had conquered and Spanish landowners were exploiting. These debates initiated a long process that would eventually culminate in the Declaration of Human Rights by the United Nations in the twentieth century.[74]

Perhaps no two individuals better typified both the differences and the similarities between Protestant and Catholic in the sixteenth century than Martin Luther and Ignatius Loyola. Both shared the experience of religious conversion. Indeed it is notable how many Catholics as well as Protestants underwent profound religious experiences that changed the course of their lives, including Cardinal Contarini, Philip Neri and Charles Borromeo (1538–84) the Archbishop of Milan and a figure himself comparable to Calvin as the shaper of the religious and social life of a city. What was unusual about Loyola, however, was the remarkable similarity between his experience of conversion and that of Luther. At Manresa Loyola suffered from almost crippling depression, 'making him a textbook case of religiously induced psychic crisis, with classic symptoms of deep melancholia, unbearable anxiety over damnation, and suicidal temptations'.[75] The resemblance to Luther is uncanny, down to the problem of penance and the feeling of inadequacy before God. 'Like Luther, he experienced acute scruples over meeting the exacting demands of full contrition that were made of the penitent so as to render the Sacrament of Penance effective.'[76] In both cases the answer to their dilemma was Christocentric; for Luther Justification by Faith Alone, for Loyola the Christ-centred spirituality revealed in his *Spiritual Exercises*. Although they have some structural affinity with the medieval rosary, what was notable about Loyola's meditations was their Christocentric rather than Marian subject matter. And both again shared a common medieval heritage from the mystics to the *Devotio Moderna*, which led both of them to re-examine the form and purpose of medieval monasticism, and to emphasize activity in the world. And at the heart of both their concepts of reform was education.

Behind both Reformations hovered the distant figure of St Augustine. In his recent book, Diarmaid MacCulloch has quoted the words of B. B. Warfield from his 1956 study *Calvin and Augustine*: 'The Reformation, inwardly considered, was just the ultimate triumph of Augustine's doctrine of grace over Augustine's doctrine of the Church.'[77] Today historians would be less confident in the use of the word 'triumph', but the point remains a valid one. Within Augustine's thought there was always a potential disharmony between his anti-Pelagian writings stressing faith, grace and predestination, and his anti-Donatist works with their emphasis on universality and authority in the Church. For a millennium Western Christians had been able to contain these two elements within a common intellectual tradition; if there was a tension it was a fruitful one. But in the sixteenth century diversity at last became division.

The stress on the direct relationship between the individual Christian and God mediated through faith in the saving acts of Jesus could no longer be reconciled with the practices of the institutional Church as Luther and other Reformers experienced them in the early sixteenth century. For them it had drifted too far away from the original purity of the gospel. But division was not the inevitable consequence. As modern Catholic historians now acknowledge, Luther's Tower Experience was actually a rediscovery of the true meaning of the phrase 'justice of God' and as such it was 'fundamentally Catholic . . . Luther routed, as religiously inadequate and not in accord with the Gospel, positions which had been handed down to him from late medieval practice and Ockhamist theology'.[78] Thus it should not be so surprising that Lutheran and Catholic theologians were able to agree on the meaning of Justification at Regensburg in 1541.

The real problem lay in the theological implications and consequences that flowed from Luther's understanding of Justification. The doctrinal assault expanded from the meaning of one technical term and became a broad front of attack on everything, from the number and meaning of the sacraments, the nature of priesthood as it related both to clergy and laity, the authority of the Bible in relation to other authorities, to the function of the Petrine office. Indeed much of the apparatus of Latin Christianity as it had evolved over the previous millennium was now under critical questioning and found wanting. Not only the width but also the speed of the assault was breathtaking. Events in the early years of the Reformation seemed to have a relentless momentum to them. Dozens of books poured from Luther's pen and the printing presses at an unprecedented pace and in previously unheard-of quantities. There never seemed time to pause and reflect on the potential enormity of the consequences of what was unfolding. Rome's only response was to attempt to silence Luther through coercion. His excommunication in 1520 effectively backfired on the papacy; from then onwards Protestant Reformers knew they would never get a sympathetic hearing from Rome and so the only option left to them was defiance and separation. With no voice tuned to the concerns of German Christians in an Italian-dominated curia there was undoubtedly a mutual breakdown in understanding.

The fact that theological controversy then so quickly became intertwined with politics was a further barrier to reconciliation. The Habsburg–Valois contest for hegemony in Europe quickly sucked the nascent Reformation into its own divided loyalties, as it did so many other things in the early sixteenth century, and religious division added one more layer of instability to an already unstable Europe. A conflict on this scale had not been experienced by Latin Christendom before; the Hundred Years War between England and France had involved other states but it was never a dynastic struggle for the control of Europe. Even the medieval Investiture Contest had not had political ramifications as fundamental as the Habsburg–Valois contest. In addition, the process of turning feudal monarchies into centralized ones created a new intensity among the competing factions and parties in the royal courts of countries like England and France, and religious divisions once again became 'politicized'. After his break with Rome the doctrinal shifts observable in Henry VIII's Church were themselves a measure of which party had the king's ear at court at any particular moment. In mid-sixteenth-century France Calvinism and Catholicism similarly became the badges of court factions. And of course all the political, diplomatic and military manoeuvrings that engulfed sixteenth-century Europe impeded the calling of an Ecumenical Council, the one potential instrument that just might have been able to reconcile the doctrinal disputes. By the time it did meet, and then spent eighteen years deliberating, confessional divisions had frozen and the agenda of the Council itself had ceased to be reconciliation.

Diversity became division when and how it did for an unprecedented and bewilderingly complex combination of reasons. The comparison with three-dimensional chess that I made earlier to describe the complexities of the christological debates of the fourth and fifth centuries is equally applicable when trying to unravel the historical puzzle of the Reformation. Why it happened in the way that it did with the consequent but unimagined or unintended fracturing of Western Christianity remains extraordinarily difficult to explain. Humpty Dumpty fell off his wall and all the horses and men of the modern Ecumenical Movement have so far failed to put him back together again. That in itself is but another measure of the complexities and problems inherent in that third great division in the history of Christianity.

Suggested Further Reading

In addition to the general books mentioned in the previous chapter there are a number of excellent but more specialized studies. For the Catholic or Counter Reformation a good, very short introduction (under 50 pages) is Michael Mullett, *The Counter Reformation: And the Catholic Reformation in Early Modern Europe* (Methuen, 1984). Somewhat longer, and primarily designed for students, is *The Catholic and Counter Reformations* (Hodder and Stoughton, 1990) by Keith Randell.

Among the more substantial modern accounts, three stand out. In alphabetical order they are: Robert Bireley, *The Refashioning of Catholicism 1450–1700* (Macmillan,

1999); Michael A. Mullett, *The Catholic Reformation* (Routledge, 1999); R. Po-chia Hsia, *The World of Catholic Renewal 1540–1770* (Cambridge University Press, 1998). They cover much of the same ground but with some differences of emphasis both chronological and thematic. Perhaps the most substantial and well-rounded account is the one by Mullett. Each has extensive bibliographical material.

Among older books on this subject, H. Outram Evenett, *The Spirit of the Counter Reformation* (University of Notre Dame Press, 1968) is a short and brilliant introduction. Jean Delumeau, *Catholicism Between Luther and Voltaire: A New View of the Counter Reformation* (Burns and Oates, 1977; first published in French 1971) was a pioneering study for its day. There is also an excellent collection of pieces on Catholic Reform brought together from different sources by David M. Luebke, *The Counter-Reformation: The Essential Readings* (Blackwell, 1999).

Steven Ozment's book, *The Reformation in the Cities: The Appeal of Protestantism to Sixteenth Century Germany and Switzerland* (Yale University Press, 1975) does much to explain why the Reformers had so much success in the German-speaking lands. For the Reformation in England, among the most controversial modern texts are J. J. Scarisbrick, *The Reformation and the English People* (Basil Blackwell, 1984); Christopher Haigh, *The English Reformations Revisited* (Cambridge University Press, 1987), a collection of essays by a number of historians; the same author's *English Reformations: Religion, Politics and Society under the Tudors* (Clarendon Press, 1993); Eamon Duffy, *The Stripping of the Altars: Traditional Religion in England c1400–c1580* (Yale University Press, 1992). The latter, a substantial book of over 650 pages, has caused controversy both within the academic world and beyond. Written in a forthright, sometimes positively pugnacious style, whatever else it might be, it is certainly a massive work of scholarship. Together these three authors have forced all historians to substantially rethink the Reformation in England. For a rather contrasting approach try Robert Whiting, *The Blind Devotion of the People: Popular Religion and the English Reformation* (Cambridge University Press, 1989).

On the relationship between the Renaissance and the Reformation, Anthony Levi, *Renaissance and Reformation: The Intellectual Genesis* (Yale University Press, 2002) is excellent. It is a long (nearly 500 pages) and often demanding read that confines itself very much to the intellectual sphere. It is not really a comprehensive treatment of what would in that case be a vast subject. For printing, Elizabeth L. Eisenstein, *The Printing Press as an Agent of Change: Communications and Cultural Transformations in Early Modern Europe* (Cambridge University Press, 1979) is again a massive book (nearly 800 pages). It is the result of fifteen years of research and remains a monument of cultural history. But again not an easy read. There is an abridged version.

10

Divine Winds and
Interest Rates

Brother will betray brother to death, and a father his child, and children will rise against parents and have them put to death; and you will be hated by all because of my name. (Mark 13:12–13)

To celebrate their victory over the Spanish Armada in 1588 the English struck a medal. On it were inscribed words from the Old Testament book of Exodus: 'he blew with his wind and they were scattered' (Exod. 15:10). This neatly encapsulated the view that the deliverance from the seemingly overwhelming might of Spain was divinely inspired. A similar 'Protestant Wind' was to blow again a century later and waft William of Orange onto the English throne as William III. But it was not only in England that the outcome of the sea battles of 1588 were viewed in these terms. Spain and her King Philip II also perceived the Armada in religious terms: a great Crusade led by the champions of Catholic orthodoxy to crush the heretics. Its failure caused consternation. How could God abandon his chosen nation and award victory to the heretics? It was thus seen by many Spaniards as a divine punishment for their sins. Portraits of Philip II show him declining rapidly into premature old age after 1588.

Not all contemporaries agreed with the English and Spanish, however, that religious differences were the crucial motive and determining force in early modern warfare. A French monk writing about the same time as the Armada commented ruefully on the civil wars then plaguing his country; for him they were fought 'for honour, for profit, to right some wrong, or just for practice. One could add for religion, except that experience has shown that this most often serves as a pretext'.[1] This rather more cynical opinion was often echoed by the actual behaviour of the soldiers on the battlefield. After his great victory at Breitenfeld in 1631 during the Thirty Years' War the Swedish King,

Gustavus Adolphus, a devout Lutheran and one of the greatest soldiers of his age, surveyed the field; of his imperial enemies 'seven thousand were prisoners in the Swedish camp that night and soldiers in the Swedish army by the morning'.[2] In other words, soldiers who had supposedly been fighting for the imperial and Catholic cause in Germany saw absolutely no problem with changing sides to the supposedly Swedish and Lutheran forces.

From the middle of the sixteenth to the middle of the seventeenth century huge swathes of Western Europe were devastated by a series of wars on a scale never before witnessed. Civil wars in France and rebellion in The Netherlands dragged on for decades with significant demographic, economic and social consequences. Then from 1618 to 1648 Germany became the main stage for what we know as the Thirty Years' War, the mightiest military struggle in Europe before the time of Napoleon. The Habsburg–Valois contest itself became subsumed into these other wars. Collectively this century of conflict has acquired the dubious title of the 'Wars of Religion'.

Modern historians are as divided in their views as the soldiers and statesmen of early modern Europe were about how to assess the place of religion and its significance as a motive for these conflicts. Historians whose main concern is the history of Christianity in the period can tend to ascribe a central role to religious division as the motivating force behind military conflict. Richard Marius, for example, has no doubts; these were 'wars fought over doctrines with no hope of rational solution'.[3] Diarmaid MacCulloch does not go quite so far in seeing religion as effectively the only motivation, but he does believe that it 'was the single greatest motive for the killing'.[4] Robert Bireley takes a further step back when he describes religion as 'a significant, though not always the dominant issue' causing military conflict.[5] James D. Tracy retreats even further when he asserts that 'the wars called "religious" were mainly about politics, but also about religion'.[6] Military historians, on the other hand, tend to take a somewhat more detached attitude and look beyond the religious divisions to the political, social and economic factors also at work in early modern Europe, and while not dismissing the religious element entirely in the causation of war in this period, tend to ascribe to it much more of a supporting than leading role. The opinion of Frank Tallett is typical: 'It is hard to think of any conflict in which religion was the overriding, let alone the sole, motivating factor.'[7]

So what did cause the almost incessant, one might say endemic, warfare in early modern Europe? Was the religious divide *the*, or even *a*, primary motivation? Was it but one of a variety of factors that led to war? Or was it but a convenient excuse for doing what statesmen and soldiers wanted to do anyway: fight each other?

Early Modern Warfare

During the course of the sixteenth century there were only ten years of total peace in Europe; the seventeenth was even worse, with only four years in which fighting was not taking place somewhere on the Continent. One country, Sweden, was continuously at war for 60 consecutive years from 1600 to 1660. Warfare was thus as notable a feature of early modern history as Renaissance or Reformation. This has caused many historians to examine the military history of this period in some detail to try to understand why warfare was so prevalent, and also why it was on a scale unimaginable in the Middle Ages. One of the first modern historians to present a theory to explain this was Michael Roberts who in the 1950s christened the century from 1560 to 1660 a 'military revolution'.[8] Roberts identified changes in tactics such as infantry firing salvos from muskets in linear formations, which in turn required larger armies, changing the scale of their financing and supply, all of which led to a much greater impact on society, the economy and governments in Europe. His theories have subsequently been challenged and modified by other historians, but his work did mark the start of a new interest in the period.

As we have seen, the Religious Peace of Augsburg in 1555 effectively ended the relatively brief warfare between Charles V and the German Lutheran princes allied in the Schmalkaldic League. But from the 1560s the scale and duration of war both increased significantly and mainly centred on The Netherlands where an anti-Habsburg revolt developed into decades of increasingly brutal and destructive fighting, and also in France where a series of no fewer than eight civil wars temporarily crippled her as a great power.

The seventeen provinces of The Netherlands were the most industrialized, urbanized and wealthy of the inheritances of Charles V. Dominated economically by cloth manufacturing and banking, The Netherlands had much in common with northern Italy. Her cloth towns were not that much smaller than many in northern Italy, and her great banking and commercial city of Antwerp was on a scale not dissimilar to Venice. A partly urbanized nobility and a political system that emphasized the privileges and independent spirit of the cities and provinces added to the comparison.

One of the complications of the rising scale of warfare in the sixteenth century was escalating costs. Even the most powerful of rulers found their means stretched to breaking point by the economic drain of war. This in its turn led to an ever-rising burden of taxation. Simultaneously fighting the Turks in the east and the French in the west meant that Charles V was as desperate for funds as any other sovereign. The wealth of The Netherlands was thus an obvious target for imperial taxation, which rose steeply during the 1520s and 1530s. By 1539 growing resentment at financing distant conflicts which seemed almost irrelevant to The Netherlands boiled over, and the great cloth town of Ghent rose in rebellion. Subdued by German mercenaries, her privileges removed and many of her leading citizens executed, the fate of Ghent demonstrated that no mercy was to be expected from the unrelenting demands of the Habsburgs. Taxes and coercion thus left many in The Netherlands open to the ideas of Protestant preachers; a change of religious allegiance seemed to some a means to escape the economic demands of the Habsburgs and provide a route to a restored political liberty.

In 1555 Charles relinquished his titles in The Netherlands and passed them to his son, Philip, soon also to become King of Spain. Conditions between the new ruler and his subjects deteriorated further as Philip began the process of reforming the Church in The Netherlands, increasing the number of bishops and introducing the Inquisition, all to be paid for by his hapless subjects. By the early 1560s streams of Calvinist refugees from the fighting in France began to cross the frontier and brought with them what to some appeared to be an attractive alternative religious option. Matters came to a head in 1566 when about 300 armed nobles presented Philip's Regent, Margaret of Parma, with a list of demands. Their rejection precipitated one of the most violent outbursts of iconoclasm Europe had yet seen, with many works of art in a number of churches destroyed by rampaging mobs. By 1567 large areas of The Netherlands were in open revolt. Local troops loyal to the Habsburgs were inadequate for the task of containing the violence and so the Duke of Alva marched 10,000 crack troops, called Tercios, north from Italy and put down this first revolt with great brutality, executing about 1,000 rebels including leading members of the nobility. In 1568 William of Nassau, Prince of Orange, the greatest of all the aristocrats of The Netherlands, was himself defeated and forced to withdraw back to his German estates.

By 1572 he had returned, however, and taken refuge with the militant and radical 'Sea Beggars' in the northern province of Holland. There now followed years of a terrible war of attrition, years in which Spanish troops massacred garrisons after they had supposedly surrendered with honour, and in which cities like Leiden were only saved from the same fate by having their protecting dykes cut and flooding huge amounts of productive land with sea water to allow the Sea Beggars to sail to its rescue. In 1576 the Spanish captured Antwerp and butchered 8,000 of its citizens. By 1579 the northern seven provinces had formed the Union of Utrecht, a military alliance based on the Swiss model, and in 1581 took the unprecedented political decision to renounce Philip as their sovereign. By this point William of Orange had converted to Calvinism. While hardly commanding the loyalty of more than a minority of people within the seven provinces, Calvinism emerged as the dominant religious force among the rebels.

In 1583 the Duke of Parma, one of the greatest soldiers of the day, took charge of the Habsburg war effort and quickly began to win back lost territory, most spectacularly Antwerp in 1585. The year before, William had been assassinated and it looked as if the rebels were facing defeat. But English intervention with a small army diverted the main thrust of Philip's war, and in 1588 the Armada sailed to destroy the English by linking up with Parma's troops in The Netherlands and transporting them across the Channel. Its failure meant the war would drag on. Only in 1609 was a twelve-year truce signed to halt the fighting and in fact, if not in law, recognize the independent status of the seven provinces.

Meanwhile to the south France had been engulfed in a similar series of destructive wars. For a century from the end of the Hundred Years' War the French monarchy had been trying to impose a centralizing system of government on a country without a common language, legal or taxation system, burdened by rising taxation to pay for its wars, and in which by the 1550s Calvinism was spreading. For some nobles at court the new religion offered the possibility of providing a common ideology for the growing opposition to the policies of the monarchy. In the south and west of the country many landless younger sons adopted it in order to obtain land confiscated from the Catholic Church and its monasteries. Three events in 1559 helped to turn resentment into open revolt. Peace with the Habsburgs opened the prospect of a period in which France could concentrate on her domestic problems; the Calvinists held their first national synod in Paris and began to organize their scattered congregations in more efficient ways; and the young king, Henry II, was accidentally killed at a tournament leaving a widow, Catherine di Medici, as Regent for his four sons and three daughters. The centralizing policies of the crown meant, however, that without a strong king there was no alternative institution to fill the power vacuum.

In 1560, fearful that the Regency was becoming dominated by the intensely Catholic Guise faction, Calvinist nobles attempted to capture the boy king and instal a regime more favourable to themselves. The plot backfired and, following the failure of a religious conference at Poissy to try to reconcile doctrinal and political differences, by 1562 France was plunged into the first of eight civil wars that were to be spread over more than four decades. In 1572 the attempt to bring dynastic and religious peace by marrying the Calvinist prince Henry of Navarre to one of the royal daughters ended with the infamous St Bartholomew's Day Massacre of Huguenots, as the Calvinists were now called. This provoked a political revolution similar to the one in The Netherlands. Church leadership now passed from the Calvinist nobility to the pastors, and a realization that their war was against the crown itself and not just a political faction, led to the creation in the south and west of France of a state within a state. The publication of a series of theoretical works advocating Old Testament concepts of a covenant between king and people followed. A king who now failed to obey the terms of the covenant, it was argued, could legitimately be renounced and removed.

By 1584 the last surviving son of Henry II had ascended the throne as Henry III, all the others having died childless. This left the Calvinist Henry of Navarre as the heir, and the assassination of Henry III in 1589 made him in his turn King as Henry IV. Many Catholics in France were now appalled by this to such an extent that they allied with the old enemy, the Habsburg Philip II, to try to frustrate him. Uncrowned and effectively unrecognized by many of his subjects and without the military resources to capture Paris, Henry IV took the pragmatic decision to convert to Catholicism. By 1598 he had restored peace and in the Edict of Nantes he effectively accepted that the integrity of the state did not depend upon uniformity of belief, by granting religious and political toleration for the Huguenot minority, who were in addition allowed to keep their fortified towns. This position was reaffirmed at the beginning of the following reign of Louis XIII (1610–43) and when the final Huguenot revolt was crushed in the late 1620s Cardinal Richelieu retained toleration for the Calvinist minority in return for their disarmament.

The third major conflict that is normally included under the title 'Wars of Religion' was the Thirty Years' War of 1618–48. This was mainly fought within Germany and at one time or another involved most of the countries of Western Europe. Unprecedented in scale, possibly one million soldiers saw service in this war; it resulted in hundreds of thousands of deaths and devastated many parts of Germany. It began in Bohemia in 1618 when the Calvinist Elector, Frederick of the Palatinate, accepted its crown offered to him by many of its nobles. As this would have given him a second vote in the imperial electoral college and tilted the balance in favour of Protestantism, it was totally unacceptable to the Habsburgs. Defeated in 1620 at the battle of the White Mountain, Frederick was forced out of Bohemia, and the conflict began to spill over into Germany. By 1625 the Danes had entered the war to be humiliatingly defeated by the imperial general, Wallenstein, and simultaneously the Spanish Habsburgs had re-launched their war of conquest in The Netherlands. At the peace of Lubeck in 1629 the fighting seemed to have ended, but the imperial Edict of Restitution sought to restore the abbeys and bishoprics secularized since 1555. This made many German princes, Catholic as well as Protestant, uneasy at the prospect of revived Habsburg power.

In 1630 the conflict resumed when King Gustavus Adolphus of Sweden invaded Germany with the help of French financial subsidies. The sack of Magdeburg in 1631, with another horrendous loss of life, persuaded many otherwise reluctant German Protestant princes into alliance with Sweden, and

Gustavus Adolphus began his famous march across Germany, inflicting total defeats on imperial forces at the battles of Breitenfeld and Lech in 1631, and a third partial defeat at Lutzen in 1632, during which battle the king was killed. Peace was restored at the Treaty of Prague in 1635. But at that point Riche-lieu finally committed France to open warfare once again against the Habs-burgs in alliance with Sweden. In 1643 French forces inflicted a crushing defeat on the Spanish at Rocroi and in 1648 fighting was finally brought to a halt at the Treaty of Westphalia. By 1659 Spain was obliged to abandon her last fortifications along France's eastern frontier at the Treaty of the Pyrenees.

The conduct of war in Europe underwent a profound change in the early modern period, heralded in 1494 when Charles VIII of France invaded northern Italy with a siege train of 40 cannon.[9] In a matter of weeks his guns were demolishing castle walls that had previously withstood sieges lasting months. The new technology based on gunpowder had arrived with a vengeance. The whole concept of fortification had to be re-thought and reconstructed in the sixteenth century. Shorter and much thicker walls, angled bastions protruding from them, and a complex series of ditches and outworks had to be constructed. Hundreds of these new forts and fortified cities were to be built, which now slowed warfare to the speed of sieges and helped to extend the length of time it took to fight them. It could also absorb vast numbers of soldiers in static warfare, many of them as large permanent garrisons.

Field armies too had to alter their tactics and make-up to account for the new technologies. Muskets replaced bows and arrows, and by the late six-teenth century new battle formations were evolving to extract maximum advantage from this. What the British Army was later to call the 'thin red line' had arrived, with infantry now in lines rather than squares, and perfecting volley fire from multiple ranks. It was these complex tactics that were to be employed with such dramatic effect by Gustavus Adolphus in the early 1630s.[10]

All of these technological and tactical innovations led in their turn to a huge increase in the size of armies. At some points during the Thirty Years' War a quarter of a million men were facing each other in combat. This obliged states to find new ways to recruit armies. The military aspect of the feudal system had long since disappeared, so many states now began to employ professional contractors to raise armies for them as a commercial undertaking; the Duke of Saxe-Weimar, for instance, raised 18,000 troops for the king of France.[11] Con-tractors recruited armies with borrowed money lent to them by banks and speculated that they would make a profit from subsequent booty and ransoms. This meant that most 'national' armies were actually nothing of the kind but rather generally composed of mercenaries or soldiers of fortune. We have already seen that the 7,000 imperial troops captured at Breitenfeld happily changed sides and joined the Swedes. By the time of the death of Gustavus Adolphus in 1632 only 12 per cent of his army was actually Swedish.[12]

This huge increase in the scale of fortifications and armies led in its turn to unprecedented logistical problems. Frank Tallett has estimated that an army of 60,000 men required 45 tons of bread, 40,000 gallons of beer, and the meat of 300 cattle every day; it was the equivalent of a large city on the move, vacuuming up everything in its path across a front of several miles and leaving economic ruin in its wake.[13]

All of this had to be paid for. War in the early modern period became economically ruinous. Success or failure in war increasingly depended on a state's ability to finance it. One of the fundamental reasons for the Habsburg's ultimate failure in The Netherlands hinged on their shaky methods of finance. Absolute monarchs like Philip II and his descendants were unrestrained by a representative legislature. As such they borrowed money at a frightening rate and spent it with almost reckless abandon. Philip was to wipe out his debts with aristocratic disdain by declaring periodic bankruptcy, converting expensive short-term loans into cheaper long-term ones. He first did this in 1557, and repeated it in 1560, 1575 and 1596; his successors continued this policy in 1607, 1627, 1647 and 1653. The fatal flaw with this was that as Spain's ability to repay the loan capital, let alone the interest payments, decreased, so her creditworthiness collapsed. As early as the 1520s Charles V was already paying an interest rate of 18 per cent; by the time Philip arrived in Spain in the 1550s this had climbed to a staggering 49 per cent. Spain, at least in its largest component kingdom of Castile, was relatively undeveloped economically; but it did possess one huge financial asset: the precious metals of America. These were now pledged, often many years of supply in advance, to the great banking houses of Europe.

Bankruptcies and crushing interest rates could have disastrous military consequences; the bankruptcy of 1575, for example, left Spanish troops in The Netherlands without pay, which in its turn led to the mutiny in the army in Flanders in 1576. Soldiers unpaid for weeks or even months lost much of the incentive to fight. Again and again the Spanish war effort was paralysed by financial starvation. Despite all the emergency measures, Spain could still not prevent its debts from escalating out of control. When Philip ascended the throne of Spain in 1556 he inherited a debt of six million ducats, already huge by contemporary standards. A century later that debt had ballooned to a totally unpayable 180 million ducats.[14]

Thus it could be argued that what broke Spain as a great power was not divine intervention in her wars in the form of winds, Protestant or otherwise, but interest rates. The arbitrary and irresponsible nature of the royal financing of decades of warfare pushed Spain from the centre to the margins of European power politics. Multiple defaults on her loans led the bankers of Europe to demand ever-higher rates of interest to cover the extreme risk they were taking. Once the mines of South America started to exhaust their supplies of precious metals in the seventeenth century and the treasure fleets began to return half-empty, even if they could evade the Dutch warships, the writing was on the wall. By contrast the bankers of Amsterdam created for the Dutch government the soundest system for financing war in its day. Loans were only raised based on the taxation system's capacity to pay, and then supervised by a representative and responsible political system the members of which were often both the creditors who lent the money and the taxpayers who funded it. They had a vested interest, unlike absolute monarchs, in seeing the system function within manageable limits. Never once defaulting on either interest or capital payments, this reputation for sound finance meant that by 1655 the Dutch government was only paying interest rates of 4 per cent, a fraction of their Spanish opponents.[15]

Motivations for Fighting

What caused such unprecedented numbers of Europeans to fight each other in the early modern period? More specifically, what part did the religious divide play in this? In short, how 'religious' were the 'Wars of Religion'? At first sight the answer seems relatively straightforward; surely all these conflicts were part of the larger struggle to gain or regain confessional allegiance from individuals, cities or states. Certainly it is relatively easy to point to individuals, from kings to commoners, who took their own religious convictions seriously enough to want to fight for them. Philip II of Spain is an obvious example, a king who publicly stated that he had no desire to rule heretics. Religion was a clear personal motivation for fighting his Dutch rebels with such ruinous tenacity, and for launching the Armada against England. And he was not alone. As we have seen, there was a long Castilian tradition of Crusading for the Catholic cause; in 1588 over 200 Castilian nobles enlisted as common soldiers to join the Armada that was, at least in part, perceived as an extension of that Crusading impulse.

From Protestantism too there are many examples of sincere religious conviction among the combatants. Gustavus Adolphus was personally a convinced and pious Lutheran, and his famous march across Germany in 1631–2 has been called a 'Protestant Crusade'. Among the Huguenot leaders in France it is equally possible to find convinced Calvinists; Coligny, the Admiral of France who died in the St Bartholomew's Day Massacre, would be a good example. One of the motivations of the revolt of the 300 Dutch nobles in

1566 was also clearly religious; a deep repugnance, for instance, at the arrival of the Inquisition in a land noted for its relative tolerance. In 1618 the nobles of Bohemia similarly revolted when the Emperor attempted to revoke earlier promises of religious toleration in their kingdom. Specific incidents, such as the outbreak of iconoclasm in The Netherlands in 1566–7, or the St Bartholomew's Day Massacre of Huguenots, outraged Catholic and Protestant feelings respectively. Indeed, there were diplomatic and military linkages between the Protestant rebels in The Netherlands and France. As early as 1567 Huguenots in France, and indeed Protestant sympathizers in England, began sending organized financial aid to people they saw as their religious brethren in The Netherlands. The following year the Huguenot prince of Condé established a powerful fortified base in the port of La Rochelle on the west coast of France, and signed alliances with William of Orange and the Sea Beggars to provide mutual naval assistance. It has been estimated that 25,000 Scots fought during the Thirty Years' War. Since Scotland was at no point directly involved in the war, it must be presumed that one of the motives for so many of her people to go and fight in this war was religious, a fellow-feeling with foreigners based on a shared confessional experience.[16]

Thus there is abundant evidence that many people, from kings downwards, fought for religious reasons. Yet it is extremely difficult, as Frank Tallett argued above, to find cases where religion was the main, let alone the sole motivation for fighting. Religion could be one of a number of motivations, or as the sixteenth-century French monk observed, it could be used as a convenient pretext to mask less noble but more fundamental causes for war.

So for every genuinely religious motivation for fighting, alongside it one can usually find others, often just as fundamental. Philip II, for instance, did not *only* send the Armada in 1588 to convert the English heretics; among his other objectives was stopping the piratical activities of the English privateers raiding his colonies in the Americas or attacking his ships on the high seas, more of an economic than a religious motive. Both William of Orange in 1573 and Henry IV in 1593 changed their religion as much if not more from pragmatic political calculation than personal conviction. Richelieu, a Catholic and a cardinal, subsidized Lutheran Sweden and then in 1635 allied with her to fight Catholic Habsburgs. The methods used to recruit soldiers into armies were a good barometer of the religious pressures, or lack of them, inducing hundreds of thousands of men to fight each other. Normally such methods were confessionally blind. In the late 1620s and early 1630s the imperial general, Wallenstein, openly recruited soldiers of all confessional persuasions into his army. The Dukes of Bavaria, perhaps the most self-consciously Catholic of the German princes and the leaders of the Catholic League of German states during the Thirty Years' War, would, it might be thought, have taken particular care about the religious purity of their armies. Yet we know of one Bavarian regiment in 1644 with soldiers from sixteen different states fighting in it, including fourteen individuals who were Turkish Muslims.[17] There was clearly no system for screening recruits for either their political or religious origins. This comparative lack of concern for confessional considerations is well portrayed by the manuals of three English veterans of the fighting in The Netherlands. All three of them had fought for *both* the Spanish *and* the Dutch rebels at various points in their military careers.[18]

The problem for the modern historian is to disentangle the religious from the other motivations, which sometimes can only be done on an individual, case by case, basis. Religion and politics, for example, were so interwoven in early modern Europe that it is often difficult, if not frankly anachronistic, to try to separate them. Our tidy, modern minds, trained in scientific methods of analysis, do not always give ready access to the thought processes of an early modern person and the reasons for his fighting for whomsoever he did. Were impoverished, landless younger sons of the minor nobility in France fighting for the Huguenots out of deep religious conviction, or to restore their personal fortunes or that of their family from the plundered lands and possessions of Catholic abbeys? Did the Dukes of Bavaria fight for the advancement of the Catholic faith, or to gain territory and the possibility of an eventual Electoral title?

Clearly family and dynastic prestige had already been a reason for warfare long before the Reformation. In 1494 the French invaded Italy in pursuit of the dynastic claims of the House of Valois, and initiated a series of wars that were to rumble on for generations and into which the later divisions of the Reformation were to be subsumed and exploited as we have seen. In 1595 Henry IV led France to war against Spain in alliance with the Dutch rebels and the English; the newly converted Catholic king of France saw that a war against the traditional Habsburg foe would unite all Frenchmen, Catholic as well as Protestant, in a common cause. In 1635 Richelieu finally joined the wars against the Habsburgs as he saw a golden opportunity to smash the old enemy once and for all; religion was only a motivation insofar as he believed that the Habsburgs were themselves cynically using it as a cloak for their own dynastic ambitions. Indeed Spain, the supposed champion of Catholic orthodoxy prepared to fight the supposedly Calvinist Dutch in a protracted and ruinous war, was equally quite ready to step aside and allow the French to tear themselves to pieces in their own civil wars with minimal intervention on the 'Catholic' side. It suited Spain for a mixture of dynastic, political and strategic reasons to allow France to cripple herself. James I of England allowed German Protestants to recruit soldiers in his country in 1624, but that was only *after* the dynastic snub delivered to his Stuart House when the embassy of the Prince of

Wales to the court in Madrid was rebuffed in its aim of contracting a dynastic alliance through the proposed marriage of Prince Charles to the Spanish Infanta. In 1566 the Dutch nobles rebelled at least in part because of what they saw as the threat posed to their traditional political rights and liberties by a tyrannical Habsburg. Likewise, French Huguenots launched their attempt to seize the king in 1560 from a fear that the Guise faction at court threatened their own political liberties. In 1630 Gustavus Adolphus was equally concerned that Wallenstein was about to gobble up the small enclaves of Swedish territory on the north German coast, and so intervened in the Thirty Years' War for political, territorial and strategic reasons at least as much as for religious ones. Religion was thus one thread among many others in the warp and weft of the complex tapestry of early modern Europe.

It could be argued that economics were in fact at least as important as religion in some of the political and military decisions taken by the various powers. It must always be remembered that in conquering additional territory a prince could not only advance the fortunes of his Church by recruiting new members but at the same time also improve his finances by acquiring more subjects to tax. Taxation was also at the heart of the Dutch revolt. As early as 1539 the city of Ghent had already rebelled against Charles V long before religion became a live issue in The Netherlands. Sweden's motivations for fighting in the seventeenth century were also heavily economic. In 1630 Gustavus Adolphus intervened militarily in Germany partly because he feared that imperial advances would cut Sweden off from the European markets that absorbed so much of her exports of timber, copper and iron ore, the staples of Swedish overseas trade. One of the reasons that Sweden fought so many wars in the seventeenth century was that she discovered ways to get others to pay her to do so; war was highly profitable for the Swedish treasury, with large payments in money or kind flowing into its coffers.

If we move from what motivated kings and statesmen to fight, to the concerns of the soldiers they recruited, then economics clearly featured largely in their minds. One of the attractions of war remained unchanged from the Middle Ages: plunder, booty and ransom. These were regarded as legitimate objectives by all the participants in early modern warfare. Farms, villages and even some small towns could be forced to pay a form of protection money called 'Fire Money' as the alternative to payment was arson.[19] It was also regarded as perfectly acceptable to rob either prisoners or corpses after an engagement. Most soldiers also received a money payment or 'bounty' when first recruited; for many, indeed, this was more important than wages which could often be irregular and were normally mean in amount. Some soldiers joined up to avoid the payment of debts; others were recruited from prisons. Thus to assume a religious motivation for fighting among the bulk of the armies that marched their way across Germany from the 1620s to the 1640s would be a mistake. Much baser motives usually drove them. In any case it would certainly be an illusion to imagine that often, at best, semi-literate foot soldiers, were fighting each other in defence of the doctrines of Justification by Faith Alone or Transubstantiation. Confessional allegiance at this level would be more a result of convention or coercion than conviction

By the seventeenth century many merchants were making fortunes from the interminable wars, either by supplying munitions, or as recruiting contractors. In the 1630s we know of hundreds of such contractors at work, ranging enormously in the scale of their operations. Wallenstein was not only a general in imperial service but also perhaps the greatest military contractor of his age. He personally raised 150,000 troops in 40 regiments for the Holy Roman Emperor.[20] But Wallenstein also exemplified the incredibly mixed motives behind warfare in his day. On top of being a general and a contractor he also had clear political ambitions. He was created Duke of Mecklenburg by a grateful ruler with extensive lands in northern Germany, and in addition allowed to purchase about a quarter of all Bohemian land after the defeat of its nobility in 1620 and the sequestration of their estates. He negotiated on his own behalf with Sweden and German princes as well as the Emperor, and was eventually rumoured to be aiming for the imperial title himself. The Habsburgs finally had him murdered in 1634 to put an end to his expanding ambitions.

Thus to describe the wars of the sixteenth and seventeenth centuries as exclusively 'Wars of Religion' may be, to say the least, somewhat misleading, and certainly to oversimplify the highly complex. Looking back, historians can now isolate many reasons for these wars, of which religion was, at best, only one among many. But we must be careful here. To analyse to death the motivations of early modern Europeans from the comfort of a twenty-first-century armchair, and to neatly arrange their motivations for fighting into a series of clearly labelled boxes, rather like butterflies pinned in ranks on a presentation board, may be to misunderstand how they thought. To distinguish one motivation as 'religious', another as 'economic' and a third as 'political' might be to separate the inseparable in early modern European minds. Neither can we, as it were, take religion out of the situation, rather like removing one element from a mathematical equation, and ask what would have happened if the Reformation had not, because it did, and history is about what actually happened, not what might have happened if . . . Early modern people often did things for reasons we now find difficult to appreciate. Trying to comprehend the role of religion in early modern warfare is rather like looking at a cake that has just been baked and trying to isolate the eggs. We know that they must be there somewhere otherwise it would not be a cake, but we can no longer see them, only imagine them. But at least we can taste the result.

The Impact of War

'Compared with the spasmodic nature of the Hundred Years' War, the wars of Italy and The Netherlands were almost unremitting molestations of normal life.'[21] The words of J. R. Hale make the point that warfare in early modern Europe was unprecedented in the degree of destruction and damage it did. Probably not since the time of the barbarian invasions following the fall of the Roman Empire had Western Europe seen such devastation over so much of its territory for such an extended period of time. Frank Tallett sums it up very succinctly when he writes that 'warfare had a more substantial impact upon civilian society . . . than at any previous period'.[22] Across Europe the deaths caused by war, not only in the fighting itself but also from disease and starvation that followed in its wake, killed people in their hundreds of thousands. Germany suffered terribly during the Thirty Years' War, but the uneven geographical spread of that is reflected in the modern estimates for the declines in populations; Lower Saxony's population fell by about 10 per cent in this period, but that of Wurttemburg decreased more dramatically, possibly by as much as 60 per cent.[23] However, by about 1700 most parts of Germany had either recovered or exceeded their pre-1618 population levels. Sweden also experienced a severe demographic impact. With a population of about one million she is estimated to have lost 150,000 men during the Thirty Years' War alone. On top of that individual towns and cities could suffer catastrophic losses during sieges or sacks; Antwerp, Maastricht, Ostend, Paris, La Rochelle and Magdeburg each lost thousands, in some cases tens of thousands, of people in this way.

The remarks of a Spaniard in 1595 expressed the consciousness at the time of the financial and economic burden of warfare: 'Victory will go to whoever possesses the last escudo.'[24] We have already seen how sky-high levels of interest rates crippled the Spanish treasury. The efforts to pay for war affected all states, especially with massively rising tax burdens. Castile was almost brought to its knees economically by tax rises that unrelentingly leapt ahead of wages rises for decades, and were applied to everything from the staples of the Mediterranean diet, meat, wine, oil and vinegar, to luxury items like playing cards. In many European countries titles of nobility and various state offices were up for sale, producing a governing and administrative élite not necessarily best fitted to perform their tasks.

Warfare could also have an impact on the rise and fall of the great powers of Europe. In 1560 the Spanish kingdoms were probably the single most powerful political unit in Western Europe; by 1660 Spain's days as a great power were clearly numbered. Sweden expanded her territories in the sixteenth and seventeenth centuries, acquiring Finland, Estonia, Latvia and enclaves in northern Germany to emerge as the mightiest power of northern Europe. But the demographic and economic costs of acquiring and then defending this Baltic empire proved too great for her limited resources and by the early eighteenth century she was in retreat. Certain powers, however, did sustain longer-term advantages from these wars. France emerged the victor from the century-and-a-half-long struggle with the Habsburgs; Brandenburg was able to lay the foundations of what eventually was to become the predominant power in Germany: Prussia.

And what of Christianity? The results were often paradoxical. On the one hand the wars of the sixteenth and seventeenth centuries possibly forced states to be more tolerant of minorities; the Edict of Nantes is perhaps the classic case. But that toleration of religious minorities was often grudging and extremely limited; Louis XIV was to revoke the Edict of Nantes in 1685 and consequently saw hundreds of thousands of often highly skilled Huguenot craftsmen leave France to settle in other, Protestant lands, much to their economic advantage. After the middle of the seventeenth century religion largely ceased to be a major motivation for war. As Geoffrey Parker has noted: 'The abatement of this major destabilizing influence in European politics was one of the greatest achievements of the Thirty Years' War.'[25] Yet that in itself was also something of a measure of the relative decline of Christianity on all aspects of European life, not just warfare, in the generations that followed the end of that war. The last time a pope excommunicated a European sovereign was Elizabeth I in 1570 with, it could be argued, disastrous consequences for the Catholic minority in England now suspected of treason and armed rebellion as well as religious dissidence. At the peace conferences that led to the Treaty of Westphalia in 1648 the papal legates were effectively ignored by all the other participants, Catholic as well as Protestant. The era in which the papacy could have a decisive influence on both the religious and political affairs of Europe was drawing to a close.

So, how religious were the 'Wars of Religion'? Wars are made by people, not by ideas whether they be religious, economic, political or social. It is how rulers, statesmen and generals choose to use those ideas that give the ideological framework to their decisions. They are the true motivators of warfare. The wars in early modern Europe were so destructive because of the utilization of new technologies and all that flowed from them, not because of the supposed bitterness engendered by divisions within Christianity. The twentieth century was to witness even more devastating wars, but again it was new technologies that allowed the statesmen and generals to wage war on a wholly unprecedented scale; Christianity was by then quite irrelevant as a motivating force.

Suggested Further Reading

There are a number of excellent modern general introductions to warfare in this period which deal mainly with the technical military aspects, but also include considerations of the religious motivations. Truly excellent is Frank Tallett, *War and Society in Early Modern Europe 1495–1715* (Routledge, 1992). It is both comprehensive and compact, well written and with good maps and a bibliography. This can be supplemented by the two relevant volumes in Fontana's History of European War Series: J. R. Hale, *War and Society in Renaissance Europe 1450–1620* (1985) and M. S. Anderson, *War and Society in Europe of the Old Regime 1618–1789* (1988). Geoffrey Parker, *The Military Revolution: Military Innovation and the Rise of the West 1500–1800* (Cambridge University Press, second edition, 1996) covers more ground both geographically and chronologically than is included in this chapter, but Parker is one of the leading scholars on the subject of warfare in this period.

On specific conflicts the following are all good introductions. Geoffrey Parker, *The Dutch Revolt* (Penguin, 1977); Mack P. Holt, *The French Wars of Religion 1562–1629* (Cambridge University Press, 1995); Peter Limm, *The Thirty Years' War* (Longman, 1984).

EPILOGUE

Loss and Gain

I am with you always, to the end of the age. (Matt. 28:20)

The modern age has presented Christianity not only with some profound challenges but also with some equally great opportunities. In the Western world the history of Christianity since the eighteenth century has usually been seen as one of retreat in a number of areas, from the demographic to the cultural. Meanwhile whatever losses have been suffered by the faith in Europe have in many ways been more than compensated for by gains in the wider world.

The Enlightenment of the eighteenth century, which in some respects was a continuation of trends first noticed during the Renaissance, in other ways marked a watershed in the intellectual and cultural history of Europe. For the Renaissance man may have been the measure of all things but the pursuit of knowledge and learning was still undertaken within a Christian framework, and many of the rediscoveries of the fifteenth and sixteenth centuries had behind them the aim of illuminating and advancing Christian truth. Erasmus searched out ancient manuscripts not as an end in itself but in order to produce his Greek New Testament as a service to his faith.

In the eleventh century St Anselm had written of faith seeking understanding. The whole purpose of learning and education had been to come to a greater understanding of a faith which believed that Jesus would send the Spirit to lead his followers into all truth (John 16:13). The pursuit of truth through study and thought was a fundamentally Christian undertaking. The universities of the Middle Ages or the schools and colleges of the sixteenth and seventeenth centuries had advanced literacy and learning in the conviction that the more people who could read and understand the Bible or the writings of the Fathers, the more society itself would be Christianized. Reason was the

God-given means by which humanity could come to a deeper understanding of faith.

When René Descartes (1596–1650) began his philosophical quest with total doubt things began to change. By the eighteenth century Enlightenment thinkers had come to distrust all authorities and traditions and to rely entirely upon human reason. Thus reason itself was seen by some as an autonomous entity at last liberated from the shackles of past tradition or authority, and above all of the authority of the Church. Unaided reason could now be employed to better humanity and lead it out of the superstitious past into an enlightened world of the future. This, combined with the new methodologies of the Scientific Revolution, gave humanity the tools it needed to truly understand and improve the world. Faith was now seen as irrelevant, if not a positive hindrance, to understanding and for the first time in Western history atheism in our understanding of the term gradually became more acceptable. Tradition too changed its meaning from the Christian concept of the use of the past to inspire and revivify the present and future to the idea of the past as a dead weight holding back the future. Progress was now the liberating force. The scientific method, reason and experimentation could be used to conquer knowledge, to understand how everything worked, from astronomy to economies to the natural world itself.

The application of these principles from the eighteenth century onwards led also to a massive technological explosion. New machines with new sources of energy, at first water and steam, then oil and electricity, heralded an Industrial Revolution. Raw materials could be processed and manufactured in quantities and at speeds previously unheard of. Economists then used reason to show how free trade could help to deliver the products of factories to the far corners of the earth and how wealth itself could grow faster than ever before. Populations migrated across Europe and North America from the countryside to the cities, attracted by new prospects of employment and potential fortune. By the time of the 1851 Census for the first time in its history more people in England were living in towns and cities than in the countryside. Cities thus grew in size from tens to hundreds of thousands, and in a few cases to millions.

In the ancient world, in the Middle Ages and in the Renaissance, Christianity had usually found ways of assimilating new learning to the enrichment of the faith. The Enlightenment and modern science seemed to present Christianity with something rather different. Here was a philosophical system that deliberately rejected all things supernatural in its attempt to explain the world. So for some Christians in the nineteenth and twentieth centuries this meant that it must be rejected. To some degree the Evangelical revivals of the eighteenth century were inspired by a revulsion for the rationalistic elements of Natural Theology, which attempted to reconcile the

Enlightenment with Christianity to produce a rational faith devoid of its more miraculous and other irrational elements. Others attempted the traditional route of assimilation, whether in the eighteenth-century school of Natural Theology, or in the nineteenth century with the application of scientific methodology to the study of the Bible as a work primarily of history. Others turned to another movement, Romanticism, itself a reaction against the extreme rationality of the Enlightenment. The Romantics believed that the feelings, intuition and above all the imagination were on an equal footing with the intellect in the pursuit of truth. Nor were natural phenomena seen as just a set of scientific laws to be discovered but things of wonder and mystery that could elevate the human spirit, and in their turn lead from the natural to the supernatural in Christian concepts such as the sacraments. Romanticism lay behind nineteenth-century Christian revivals such as the Oxford Movement in England.[1]

While battles raged in the intellectual sphere Christianity seemed to be losing the war of numbers in the new industrial cities. In the ancient world Christianity had spread most successfully in the urban world; in the Middle Ages the revival of commerce, trade and urban living had been accompanied by new forms of Christian living best exemplified by the friars; during the Reformation it had been the cities that had been in the vanguard of the revival of Christianity. But in the modern world Christian decline in terms of practising adherents was most often at its worst in the cities. Almost all churches failed to keep pace with urban growth. As rootless migrants poured into the new cities, too often there were no churches for them to attend and not enough clergy willing to minister to them. Across swathes of Western Europe Christian practice declined and whole populations became effectively de-Christianized. Christianity had failed to produce modern versions of the thirteenth-century friars to evangelize urban humanity.

At the same time the demands of ever more complex industrial societies required greater numbers of people to attain higher levels of literacy and numeracy. During the nineteenth and twentieth centuries education expanded at all levels, from primary to university, across the Western world. But this was education increasingly detached from its original Christian purpose. As economies expanded, education increasingly became a function of economics; successful economies, it was argued, required increasing levels of education to remain successful. With shrinking numbers, churches increasingly did not have the resources to provide universal education, and more and more the state replaced them as the educator of its people. The churches fought rearguard actions in many European countries to retain some influence over the educational system; the 1944 Education Act in England left some fig-leaves of religious instruction in place, but by the end of the twentieth century even these had largely been torn away to reveal a state education system in all its secular nakedness.

But it was not all a story of retreat and gloom for Western Christianity. From the campaigns to abolish slavery or to introduce the first Factory Acts to regulate the hours and conditions of labour in the new industrial society, Christians have been prominent in many movements of social reform. Within twentieth-century Christianity itself phenomena like the Ecumenical Movement which has been working to repair the divisions of past centuries, or the Second Vatican Council of 1962–5 which again sought to revive Roman Catholicism by a return to the sources of the faith, have shown the vitality of the religion. And while numbers practising Christianity in most parts of Europe have declined dramatically, those who are left often have an intensity and commitment in their lives comparable to those in the earliest centuries of the faith. Nor have science and technology necessarily delivered the brave new world that seemed to be promised in the earlier phases of industrialization. In some cases they have been applied in ways that have brought more misery than enlightenment. The industrialized battlefields of the First World War blew apart the Victorian belief in benign progress. The death camps of the Second revealed the horrors potentially lurking behind modern technology when it was allied to a warped attempt to apply scientific methodology to the concept of racial superiority. Avowedly atheist regimes supposedly promoting modernity have produced their own terrible versions of Inquisition and punishment for heretical beliefs.

To view contemporary Christianity from an exclusively European perspective, however, would be to see only one part of a much larger, and in many ways far more hopeful picture. There is still one advanced Western country, for example, where Christian belief and practice remain at levels not seen in England since the middle of the nineteenth century, and where Christianity and the issues it raises remain much more relevant and central to public life than in Europe, and that country is the United States of America. While large parts of Northern and Western Europe can now be described as post-Christian, in America Christianity is thriving and far from being in retreat. And then if we look further afield beyond the Western world itself, modern Christianity is much more a story of success than failure. In 1900 it is estimated that 80 per cent of all the Christians in the world lived in Europe and North America; today 60 per cent of all the Christians in the world live in Latin America, Asia and Africa, and that percentage is increasing with every passing year.[2] We are living through another major demographic shift in the history of Christianity. In its first centuries most Christians lived around the shores of the eastern Mediterranean. In the Middle Ages, following the Arab conquests in the Middle East and north Africa and Christian expansion into the lands of the barbarians, Christianity was primarily a European religion. Then, starting slowly in the sixteenth century, Christians began to spread their religion across the world. The fruits of that initial effort are seen today, with Christianity expanding rapidly as a global religion. In many parts of Europe there is a crisis of vocation, with few people wishing to be ordained as clergy; in Africa the seminaries are overflowing with clerical recruits. A century ago the term 'African missionary' meant a European or American who went to Africa to convert and minister to 'natives'. Today it is coming to mean African clergy travelling back to Europe to help re-Christianize the continent.

Industrialization, rising wealth, medical advances and a consumer revolution have given most of those people in Western Europe lives of a length and comfort unimaginable to their forebears of only a few generations ago. Yet it has left many with a feeling of dissatisfaction and emptiness at the heart of their beings, a peculiarly modern form of spiritual starvation. There is a growing realization that humanity has a spiritual dimension, and that we are not just rationalizing biological machines, something especially prevalent among the young. As Timothy Radcliffe OP has recently commented on the 1999 European Values Study: 'There is an immense spiritual hunger among the young . . . a growing number of young people define themselves as religious. They are searching for a meaning to their lives. They are often more interested in "spirituality" rather than doctrine, and they are nervous of belonging to any institutional form of religion which might limit their autonomy.'[3]

Interestingly, one of the features of modern Western culture that exemplifies this is the genre of science fiction. A number of recent movies have explored ideas that will be familiar to any reader of this book, but within contexts that at first sight seem remote indeed from institutional Christianity. One component many of them have in common, however, is a questioning of the promises of a scientific and technological world. *The Matrix*, for example, portrays two modes of human existence, one real, the other the construct of a computer program of almost unimaginable complexity. In reality most human beings are 'cultivated' merely for the energy they generate and used to power the machines which have taken over the planet. The brains of these people are connected to the computer program, the matrix, and thus they believe incorrectly that they live in a world as it was just before the machines took over. However, a few people have broken free physically from the machines and their computer, and make it their mission to 'free the minds' of others. Clearly this story has links with the ancient concept of Gnosticism, of an enlightened minority who have unique access to the true source of knowledge. While that obviously had its dangers, equally, as we have seen, it was also argued by many Christian thinkers that there was also a true Christian *gnosis*. Are modern

Christians the ones who have taken the red pill and can now see that much in the contemporary world is nothing more than an illusion?[4]

Gattaca is a movie which explores another set of ideas that have been a perennial dilemma for Christianity, the apparent incompatibility between human free will and divine predestination. This movie portrays a world in which humanity is again divided into two groups. First of all there are those who have been genetically designed to screen out as many human imperfections as possible and to maximize their intellectual and physical potential; these 'Valids' are the natural élite who have been genetically pre-selected for the most prestigious roles in society. Second, in contrast to them are the 'In-Valids'; they are created and born naturally and thus their genetic make-up is random and accidental and their fate normally that of menial and powerless tasks. The story revolves around an 'In-Valid' who has a dream to go into space. But the Gattaca Aerospace Corporation will only select and train those closest to genetic perfection. So he illegally buys a new identity from a physically injured 'Valid'. Is the human will-power of the 'In-Valid' sufficient to overcome the genetic predetermination of the 'Valids'?

Based on the novel of the same name by Carl Sagan, *Contact* is a movie which goes to the heart of the post-Enlightenment dialogue between faith and reason.[5] The main character is a young woman who is a brilliant scientist but who has turned down more economically lucrative opportunities to pursue her dream of making contact with other species from worlds light years from our own. She is also portrayed as a person who will not believe something unless it can be proved by scientific methodology, and is consequently an atheist. When contact is finally made and the distant senders of the electronic messages provide blueprints for a mysterious but gigantic machine designed to travel to their world, she is the one finally selected to make the journey. This she does and spends some hours on a planet light years from earth. Yet, crucially, she is unable to collect any evidence that she has made such a journey or set foot on this new world. Back on earth the machine appears to have propelled her only a very short distance taking a matter of seconds to cover. She is thus forced to ask others for an act of faith in her word for what she has experienced in the total absence of any scientific proof.

Is Christian belief incompatible with modern science? There are, of course, scientists who are militant atheists who argue that science has disproved the claims of Christianity and, for that matter, all other theistic beliefs. But equally there are scientists who see no incompatibility, who believe in God, and in some cases are practising Christians. Even to pose such a question now seems rather quaint and old-fashioned, almost Victorian. What does seem clear is that across much of Western Europe there is a growing spiritual hunger, especially among the young, as reflected in science fiction movies and elsewhere, which is implicitly dissatisfied with the outcomes of post-Enlightenment societies. The problem for the institutional churches is to convert that hunger into a desire for the spiritual nourishment they offer.

In the Roman world a tiny minority of Christians gradually expanded over three centuries into possibly the largest single religion in the Empire. They could not have achieved that without its citizens having an already existent sense of a spiritual dimension and thus offering points of contact for the Christians to attach their ideas to. But nor could Christians have achieved it without finding in Hellenism ideas and concepts that could be legitimately assimilated by Christianity to advance its own understanding of itself and at the same time demonstrate that its faith was the true end of all human enquiry. At the same time Christians had to be perceived as not only similar to, but also different from, the conventional view of religion and philosophy; they had to challenge as well as accommodate the dominant assumptions of their world. In modern Europe the first glimmerings of just such conditions are once again appearing. Will Christianity be able to take advantage of them?

Tertullian's model of the 'gathered Church' has often proven to be a dead-end for Christianity; Jerusalem must embrace Athens. Time and again we have seen Christianity successfully assimilating new learning which has been the well-spring of its own continual rejuvenation. It has grown with the world it has found itself in, not turned against it. If there is truth in the new learning, then it must be good because it reflects the God who is truth himself. If modern Western Christianity retreats into an intellectual bunker it will not grow. Christian tradition, rightly understood, looks to the future with hope, a living faith; mere traditionalism is little more than taking a despairing false comfort in an illusory golden age located somewhere in a past which is dead. The only truly Christian golden age lies always in the future. For Christianity, its history is there to be used to look to that future, not somewhere in which to hide from the uncomfortable realities of the present. Hope is sometimes the most difficult of the theological virtues to embrace. One of the reasons for Christians to engage with their own past is to revivify hope for their future, to listen again to the great theme and its multiplicity of variations, and to draw on those for inspiration to sing their own new song which is actually older than time itself.

APPENDIX

Documents

1. The Earliest Record of the Christian Eucharist

For I received from the Lord what I also handed on to you, that the Lord Jesus on the night when he was betrayed took a loaf of bread, and when he had given thanks, he broke it and said, 'This is my body that is for you. Do this in remembrance of me.' In the same way he took the cup also, after supper, saying, 'This cup is the new covenant in my blood. Do this, as often as you drink it, in remembrance of me.' For as often as you eat this bread and drink the cup, you proclaim the Lord's death until he comes.

St Paul, 1 Corinthians 11:23–6 (mid-50s)

2. The Eucharist in the Second Century

This food is called with us the Eucharist, and of it none is allowed to partake but he that believes that our teachings are true, and has been washed with the washing for the remission of sins and unto regeneration, and who so lives as Christ directed. For we do not receive them as ordinary food or ordinary drink; but as by the word of God, Jesus Christ our Saviour took flesh and blood for our salvation, so also, we are taught, the food blessed by the prayer of the word which we received from him, by which, through its transformation, our blood and flesh is nourished, this food is the flesh and blood of Jesus who was made flesh . . . And on the day which is called the day of the sun there is an assembly of all who live in the towns or in the country; and the memoirs of the Apostles or the writings of the prophets are read, as long as time permits. Then the reader ceases, and the president speaks, admonishing us and exhorting us to imitate these excellent examples. Then we arise all together and offer prayers; and, as we said before, when we have concluded our prayer, bread is brought, and wine and water, and the president in like manner offers up prayers and thanksgivings with all his might; and the people assent with *Amen*; and there is the distribution and partaking by all of the Eucharistic elements; and to them that are not present they are sent by the hand of the deacons. And they that are prosperous and wish to do so give what they will, each after his choice. What is collected is deposited with the president, who gives aid to the orphans and widows and such as are in want by reason of sickness or other cause; and to those also that are in prison, and to strangers from abroad, in fact to all that are in need he is a protector.

Justin Martyr, First Apology (c. 150)

3. Christians Care for the Sick and Dying

Most of our brother-Christians showed unbounded love and loyalty, never sparing themselves and thinking only of one another. Heedless of the danger, they took charge of the sick, attending to their every need and ministering to them in Christ, and with them departed this life serenely happy; for they were infected by others with the disease, drawing on themselves the sickness of their neighbours and cheerfully accepting their pains. Many, in nursing and curing others, transferred their death to themselves and died in their stead, turning the common formula that is normally an empty courtesy into reality: 'Your humble servant bids you good-bye.' The best of our brothers lost their lives in this manner, a number of presbyters, deacons, and laymen winning high commendation, so that death in this form, the result of great piety and strong faith, seems in every way the equal of martyrdom. With willing hands they raised the bodies of the saints to their bosoms; they closed their eyes and mouths, carried them on their shoulders, and laid them out; they clung to them, embraced them, washed them, and wrapped them in grave-clothes. Very soon the same services were done for them, since those left behind were constantly following those gone before. The heathens behaved in the very opposite way. At the first onset of the disease, they pushed the sufferers away and fled from their dearest, throwing them into the roads before they were dead and treating unburied corpses as dirt, hoping thereby to avert the spread and contagion of the fatal disease; but do what they might, they found it difficult to escape.

Easter Letter of Dionysius of Alexandria (c. 260), recorded in Eusebius,
The History of the Church.

4. The Office of the Bishop

Let no one be under any illusion; a man who excludes himself from the sanctuary is depriving himself of the bread of God, for if the prayer of one or two individuals has such efficacy, how much more powerful is that of the bishop together with his whole church. Anyone who absents himself from the congregation convicts himself at once of arrogance and becomes self-excommunicate.

In the same way as the Lord was wholly one with the Father, and never acted independently of Him, either in person or through the Apostles, so you yourselves must never act independently of your bishop and clergy. On no account persuade yourselves that it is right and proper to follow your own private judgement; have a single service of prayer which everybody attends; one united supplication, one mind, one hope, in love and indeed joyfulness, which is Jesus Christ, than whom nothing is better.

Be as submissive to the bishop and to one another as Jesus Christ was to His Father, and as the Apostles were to Christ and the Father; so that there may be complete unity, in the flesh as well as in the spirit.

You will be safe enough so long as you do not let pride go to your head and break away from Jesus Christ and your bishop and the Apostolic institutions. To be inside the sanctuary is to be clean; to be outside it, unclean. In other words, nobody's conscience can be clean if he is acting without the authority of his bishop, clergy, and deacons.

As children of the light of truth, therefore, see that you hold aloof from all disunion and misguided teaching; and where your bishop is, there follow him like sheep. There are plausible wolves in plenty seeking to entrap the runners in God's race with their perilous allurements; but so long as there is solidarity among you, they will find no room for themselves. Make certain, therefore, that you all observe one common Eucharist; for there is but one Body of our Lord Jesus Christ, and but one cup of union with His Blood, and one single altar of sacrifice – even as also there is but one bishop, with his clergy and my own fellow-servitors the deacons. This will ensure that all your doings are in full accord with the will of God.

Make sure that no step affecting the Church is ever taken by anyone without the bishop's sanction. The sole Eucharist you should consider valid is one that is celebrated by the bishop himself, or by some person authorized by him. Where the bishop is to be seen, there let all his people be; just as wherever Jesus Christ is present, we have the Catholic Church.

Ignatius of Antioch, extracts from *Letters to the Ephesians, Magnesians, Trallians, Philadelphians and Smyrneans (c. 107)*

5. The Vision and Dream of Constantine

This God he began to invoke in prayer, beseeching and imploring him to show him who he was, and to stretch out his right hand to assist him in his plans. As he made these prayers and earnest supplications there appeared to the Emperor a most remarkable divine sign. If someone else had reported it, it would perhaps not be easy to accept; but since the victorious Emperor himself told the story to the present writer a long while after, when I was privileged with his acquaintance and company, and confirmed it with oaths, who could hesitate to believe the account, especially when the time which followed provided evidence for the truth of what he said? About the time of the midday sun, when the day was just turning, he said he saw with his own eyes, up in the sky and resting over the sun, a cross-shaped trophy formed from light, and a text attached to it which said, 'By this conquer'. Amazement at the spectacle seized both him and the whole company of soldiers which was then accompanying him on a campaign he was conducting somewhere, and witnessed the miracle.

He was, he said, wondering to himself what the manifestation might mean; then, while he meditated, and thought long and hard, night overtook him. Thereupon, as he slept, the Christ of God appeared to him with the sign which had appeared in the sky, and urged him to make himself a copy of the sign which had appeared in the sky, and to use this as protection against the attacks of the enemy. When the day came he arose and recounted the mysterious communication to his friends. Then he summoned goldsmiths and jewellers, sat down among them, and explained the shape of the sign, and gave them instructions about copying it in gold and precious stones.

Eusebius, *Life of Constantine (330s)*

6. The Statement of Faith of the Council of Nicaea

We believe in one God, the Father Almighty, Maker of all things visible and invisible, and in one Lord Jesus Christ, the Son of God, the only-begotten of the Father, that is of the substance of the Father; God of God, Light of Light, true God of true God; begotten not made, consubstantial (*homoousios*) with the Father; by whom all things were made, both which are in heaven and on earth; who for the sake of us men, and on account of our salvation, descended, became incarnate, and was made man, suffered and arose again on the third day, and ascended into the heavens, and will come again to judge the living and the dead. [We believe] also in the Holy Spirit. But the Holy Catholic and Apostolic Church anathematizes those who say 'There was a time when he was not', and 'He did not exist before he was begotten', and 'He was made of nothing', and assert that 'He is of other substance or essence than the Father'. Or that the Son of God is created, or mutable, or susceptible of change.

Council of Nicaea (325)

7. The Early Life of Antony the Monk

Antony was an Egyptian by race. His parents were well-born and prosperous and since they were Christians, he also was reared in a Christian manner. When he was a child he lived with his parents, cognizant of little else besides them and his home. As he grew and became a boy, and was advancing in years, he could not bear to learn letters, wishing also to stand apart from friendship with other children. All his yearning, as it has been written of Jacob, was for living, an unaffected person, in his home. Of course he accompanied his parents to the Lord's house, and as a child he was not frivolous, nor as a youth did he grow contemptuous; rather, he was obedient to his mother and father, and paying attention to the readings, he carefully took to heart what was profitable in them. And although he lived as a child in relative affluence, he did not pester his parents for food of various and luxurious kinds, nor did he seek the pleasures associated with food, but with merely the things he found before him he was satisfied, and he looked for nothing more.

He was left alone, after his parents' death, with one quite young sister. He was about eighteen or even twenty years old, and he was responsible both for the home and his sister. Six months had not passed since the death of his parents when, going to the Lord's house as usual and gathering his thoughts, he considered while he walked how the apostles, forsaking everything, followed the Saviour, and how in Acts some sold what they possessed and took the proceeds and placed them at the feet of the apostles for distribution among those in need, and what great hope is stored up for such people in heaven. He went into the church pondering these things, and just then it happened that the Gospel was being read, and he heard the Lord saying to the rich man, 'If you would be perfect, go, sell what you possess, and give it to the poor, and you will have treasure in heaven' (Matt. 19:21). It was as if by God's design he held the saints in his recollection, and as if the passage were read on his account. Immediately Antony went out from the Lord's house and gave to the townspeople the possessions he had from his forebears (three hundred fertile and very beautiful *arourae* [207 acres], so that they would not disturb him or his sister in the least. And selling all the rest that was portable, when he collected sufficient money, he donated it to the poor, keeping a few things for his sister.

But when entering the Lord's house once more, he heard in the Gospel the Lord saying, 'Do not be anxious about tomorrow', he could not remain any longer, but going out he gave those remaining possessions also to the needy. Placing his sister in the charge of respected and trusted virgins, and giving her over to the convent for rearing, he devoted himself from then on to the discipline rather than the household, giving heed to himself and patiently training himself. There were not yet any monasteries in Egypt, and no monk knew at all the great desert, but each of those wishing to give attention to his life disciplined himself in isolation, not far from his own village. Now at that time in the neighbouring village there was an old man who had practised from his youth the solitary life. When Antony saw him, he emulated him in goodness. At first he also began by remaining in places proximate to his village. And going forth from there, if he heard of some zealous person anywhere, he searched him out like the wise bee. He did not go back to his own place unless he had seen him, and as though receiving from him certain supplies for travelling the road to virtue, he returned. Spending the beginning stages of his discipline in that place, then, he weighed in his thoughts how he would not look back on things of his parents, nor call his relatives to memory. All the desire and all the energy he possessed concerned the exertion of the discipline. He worked with his hands, though, having heard that he who is idle, 'let him not eat' (2 Thess. 3:10). And he spent what he made partly for bread, and partly on those in need. He prayed constantly, since he learned that it is necessary to pray unceasingly in private. For he paid such close attention to what was read that nothing from Scripture did he fail to take in – rather he grasped everything, and in him the memory took the place of books.

Athanasius, *Life of Antony* (late 350s)

8. The Incarnation

As, then, he who desires to see God Who by nature is invisible and not to be beheld, may yet perceive and know Him through His works, so too let him who does not see Christ with his understanding at least consider Him in His bodily works and test whether they be of man or God. If they be of man, then let him scoff; but if they be of God, let him not mock at things which are not fit subject for scorn, but rather let him recognise the fact and marvel that things divine have been revealed to us by such humble means, that through death deathlessness has been made known to us, and through the Incarnation of the Word the Mind whence all things proceed has been declared, and its Agent and Ordainer, the Word of God Himself. He, indeed, assumed humanity that we might become God. He manifested Himself by means of a body in order that we might perceive the Mind of the unseen Father. He endured shame from men that we might inherit immortality. He Himself was unhurt by this, for he is impassible and incorruptible; but by His own impassibility He kept and healed the suffering men on whose account He thus endured. In short, such and so many are the Saviour's achievements that follow from His Incarnation, that to try to number them is like gazing at the open sea and trying to count the waves. One cannot see all the waves with one's eyes, for when one tries to do so those that are following on baffle one's senses. Even so, when one wants to take in all the achievements of Christ in the body, one cannot do so, even by reckoning them up, for the things that transcend one's thought are always more than those one thinks that one has grasped.

Athanasius, *On the Incarnation* (318–38)

9. The Chalcedonian Definition

Following, then, the holy Fathers, we all with one voice teach that it should be confessed that our Lord Jesus Christ is one and the same Son, the same perfect in Godhead, the same perfect in manhood, truly God and truly man, the Same [consisting] of a rational soul and a body; *homoousios* with the Father as to his Godhead, and the Same *homoousios* with us as to his manhood; in all things like unto us, sin only excepted; begotten of the Father before ages as to his Godhead, and in the last days, the Same, for us and for our salvation, of Mary the Virgin *Theotokos* as to his manhood; One and the same Christ, Son, Lord, Only begotten, made known in two natures [which exist] without confusion, without change, without division, without separation; the difference of the natures having been in no wise taken away by reason of the union, but rather the properties of each being preserved, and [both] concurring into one Person (*prosopon*) and one *hypostasis* – not parted or divided into two persons (*prosopa*), but one and the same Son and Only-begotten, the divine Logos, the Lord Jesus Christ; even as the prophets from of old [have spoken] concerning him, and as the Lord Jesus Christ himself has taught us, and as the Symbol of the Fathers has delivered to us.

Council of Chalcedon, *Statement of Faith* (451)

10. Finding God by Finding Ourselves

Let the reckless and wicked depart and flee from you (Ps. 138:7). You see them and pierce their shadowy existence: even with them everything is beautiful, though they are vile. What injury have they done you? Or in what respect have they diminished the honour of your rule, which from the heavens down to the uttermost limits remains just and intact? Where have those who fled from your face gone? Where can they get beyond the reach of your discovery? (Ps. 138). But they have fled that they should not see you, though you see them, and so in their blindness they stumble over you (Rom. 11:7–11); for you do not desert anything you have made (Wisd. 11:25). The unjust stumble over you and are justly chastised. Endeavouring to withdraw themselves from your gentleness, they stumble on your equity and fall into your anger. They evidently do not know that you are everywhere. No space circumscribes you. You alone are always present even to those who have taken themselves far from you. Let them turn and seek you, for you have not abandoned your creation as they have deserted their creator (Wisd. 5:7). Let them turn, and at once you are there in their heart – in the heart of those who make confession to you and throw themselves upon you and weep on your breast after travelling many rough paths. And you gently wipe away their tears (Rev. 7:17, 21:4) and they weep yet more and rejoice through their tears. For it is you, Lord, not some man of flesh and blood, but you who have made them and now remake and strengthen them. Where was I when I was seeking for you? You were there before me, but I had departed from myself. I could not even find myself, much less you.

St Augustine, *Confessions*, Book V.2 (398–400)

11. The Two Loves

We see then that the two cities were created by two kinds of love: the earthly city was created by self-love reaching the point of contempt for God, the Heavenly City by the love of God carried as far as contempt of self. In fact, the earthly city glories in itself, the heavenly City glories in the Lord. The former looks for glory from men, the latter finds its highest glory in God, the witness of a good conscience. The earthly lifts up its head in its own glory, the Heavenly City says to its God: 'My glory; you lift up my head' (Ps. 3:5). In the former, the lust for domination lords it over its princes as over the nations it subjugates; in the other both those put in authority and those subject to them serve one another in love, the rulers by their counsel, the subjects by obedience. The one city loves its own strength shown in its powerful leaders; the other says to its God, 'I will love you, my Lord, my strength' (Ps. 18:1).

Consequently, in the earthly city its wise men who live by men's standards have pursued the goods of the body or of their own mind, or of both. Or those of them who were able to know God 'did not honour him as God, nor did they give thanks to him, but they dwindled into futility in their thoughts, and their senseless heart was darkened: in asserting their wisdom' – that is, exalting themselves in their wisdom, under the domination of pride – 'they became foolish, and changed the glory of the imperishable God into an image representing a perishable man, or birds or beasts or reptiles' – for in the adoration of idols of this kind they were either leaders or followers of the general public – 'and they worshipped and served created things instead of the Creator, who is blessed for ever' (Rom. 1:21 ff). In the Heavenly City, on the other hand, man's only wisdom is the devotion which rightly worships the true God, and looks for its reward in the fellowship of the saints, not only holy men but also holy angels, 'so that God may be all in all' (1 Cor. 15:28).

St Augustine, *City of God*, XV 28 (412–26)

12. The Theory of the Two Swords

There are, most august Emperor, two powers by which this world is chiefly ruled: the sacred authority of bishops and the royal power. Of these the priestly power is much more important, because it has to render account for the kings of men themselves at the judgement seat of God. For you know, most gracious son, that although you hold the chief place of dignity over the human race, yet you must submit yourself in faith to those who have charge of divine things, and look to them for the means of your salvation. You know that it behoves you, in matters concerning the reception and reverent administration of the sacraments, to be obedient to ecclesiastical authority, instead of seeking to bend it to your will . . . And if the hearts of the faithful ought to be submitted to priests in general . . . how much more ought assent be given to him who presides over the See which the most high God himself desired to be pre-eminent over all priests, and which the pious judgement of the whole Church has honoured ever since?

Pope Gelasius I (492–6), *Letter to the Emperor Anastasius*

13. The Excommunication of Henry IV

Blessed Peter, prince of the apostles, incline to us, we beseech you, your merciful ears; hear me your servant whom you have nurtured from infancy and to this day have delivered from the hands of wicked men who have hated, and do hate, me for my fidelity to you. You are my witness as are, amongst all the saints, my lady the Mother of God and blessed Paul your brother, that your holy Roman church dragged me, unwilling as I was, to be its ruler; that I did not count it a thing to be snatched at to ascend your see; and that I would rather have finished my life in exile than have seized your holy place by worldly guile and for earthly vanity. And so I believe it to have been by your grace and by no works of mine that it was and is your good pleasure for Christian people entrusted personally to you to yield obedience personally to me through your authority committed to me. Likewise, by your grace, power is given me from God of binding and loosing in heaven and upon earth. Therefore, fortified by this confidence and for the honour and defence of your church, on behalf of God Almighty, Father, Son, and Holy Spirit, and by your power and authority, I deny to King Henry, son of the Emperor Henry, who with unheard-of pride has risen up against your church, the government of the whole kingdom of the Germans and of Italy; I absolve all Christians from the bond of any oath that they have made or shall make to him; and I forbid anyone to serve him as king. For it is fitting that, because he has striven to diminish the honour of your church, he himself should forfeit the honour that he seems to possess. Finally, because he has disdained to show the obedience of a true Christian and has not returned to the God whom he forsook by communing with excommunicated men, by – as you are my witness – disdaining my advice which I sent him for his salvation, and by attempting to rend your church and separating himself from it, by your authority I bind him with excommunication. I so bind him with confidence in you, that the nations of the world may know and be convinced that you are Peter, and that upon you as the rock the Son of the living God has built his church, against which the gates of hell shall not prevail.

Letter of Pope Gregory VII (February 1076)

14. Pope Urban II Summons the First Crusade

When these and many other matters were satisfactorily settled, all those present, clergy and people alike, spontaneously gave thanks to God for the words of the Lord Pope Urban and promised him faithfully that his decrees would be kept. But the Pope added at once that another tribulation not less but greater than that already mentioned, even of the worst nature, was besetting Christianity from another part of the world. He said, 'Since, oh sons of God, you have promised Him to keep peace among yourselves and to faithfully sustain the rights of Holy Church more sincerely than before, there still remains for you, newly aroused by God's correction, an urgent task which belongs to both you and God, in which you can show the strength of your good will. For you must hasten to carry aid to your brethren dwelling in the East, who need your help for which they have often entreated. For the Turks, a Persian people, have attacked them, as many of you already know, and have advanced as far into Roman territory as that part of the Mediterranean known as the Arm of St George [the Bosphorus and the Sea of Marmara]. They have seized more and more of the lands of the Christians, have already defeated them in seven times as many battles, killed or captured many people, have destroyed churches, and have devastated the kingdom of God. If you allow them to continue much longer they will conquer God's faithful people much more extensively. Wherefore with earnest prayer I, not I, but God exhorts you as heralds of Christ to repeatedly urge men of all ranks whatsoever, knights as well as foot-soldiers, rich and poor, to hasten to exterminate this vile race from our lands and to aid the Christian inhabitants in time. I address those present; I proclaim it to those absent; moreover Christ commands it. For all those going thither there will be remission of sins if they come to the end of this fettered life while either marching by land or crossing by sea, or in fighting the pagans. This I grant to all who go, through the power vested in me by God. Oh what a disgrace if a race so despicable, degenerate, and enslaved by demons should thus overcome a people endowed with faith in Almighty God and resplendent in the name of Christ! Oh what reproaches will be charged against you by the Lord Himself if you have not helped those who are counted like yourselves of the Christian faith! Let those,' he said, 'who are accustomed to wantonly wage private war against the faithful march upon the infidels in a war which should be begun now and be finished in victory. Let those who have long been robbers now be soldiers of Christ. Let those who once fought against brothers and relatives now rightfully fight against barbarians. Let those who have been hirelings for a few pieces of silver [Matt. 27:3] now attain an eternal reward. Let those who have been exhausting themselves to the detriment of body and soul now labour for a double glory. Yea on the one hand will be the sad and the poor, on the other the joyous and the wealthy; here the enemies of the Lord, there His friends. Let nothing delay those who are going to go. Let them settle their affairs, collect money, and when winter has ended and spring has come, zealously undertake the journey under the guidance of the Lord.'

Fulcher of Chartres, *A History of the Expedition to Jerusalem 1095–1127,*
Book I, iii, 1–8

15. The *Dictatus Papae*

1   The Roman Church is founded by God alone.
2   The Roman Pontiff alone can legitimately take the title of Universal.
3   He alone can depose bishops or reconcile them to the Church.
4   His legate, even if he be of inferior rank, takes precedence of all bishops in council, and can pronounce sentence of deposition against them.
5   The Pope can depose the absent.
6   There shall be no intercourse whatever held with persons excommunicated by the Pope, and none may dwell in the same house with them.
7   To the Pope alone belongs the right of making new law, according to the necessities of the time, of forming new congregations, of raising a canonry to an abbey, of dividing into two a bishopric that is too rich or uniting under one such as are too poor.
8   He alone may wear the imperial insignia.
9   All the princes of the earth shall kiss the feet of the Pope, but of none other.
10   There is a title which one man alone can bear – that of Pope.
11   He has the right of deposing Emperors.

12 He has the right to transfer, when necessary, a bishop from one see to another.

13 He can transfer any priest from any church to any other place he may please.

14 The priest thus appointed by him may rule in another church other than his own; but he may not make war, or receive a superior grade from any bishop.

15 No Council is to be called a General or Ecumenical Council without the Pope's order.

16 No capitulary, no book can be received as canonical without his authority.

17 The sentence of the Pope can be revoked by none.

18 He alone can revoke the sentences pronounced by others.

19 He can be judged by none.

20 None may dare pronounce sentence on one who appeals to the See Apostolic.

21 To it shall be referred all major causes by the whole Church.

22 The Church of Rome never has erred, and never can err, as Scripture warrants.

23 The Roman Pontiff, canonically ordained, at once becomes, by the merits of St Peter, indubitably holy.

24 By his order and with his permission, it is lawful for subjects to accuse princes.

25 He can depose or reconcile bishops without calling a synod.

26 Whoever does not agree in all things with the Roman Church is not to be considered a Catholic.

27 The Pope can loose subjects from the oath of fealty.

Gregory VII, *Registers* (March 1075)

16. Obedience in *The Rule of St Benedict*

The first step of humility is unhesitating obedience, which comes naturally to those who cherish Christ above all. Because of the holy service they have professed, or because of the dread of hell and for the glory of everlasting life, they carry out the superior's order as promptly as if the command came from God himself. The Lord says of men like this: 'No sooner did he hear than he obeyed me' (Ps. 17/18:45); again, he tells teachers: 'Whosoever listens to you, listens to me' (Luke 10:16). Such people as these immediately put aside their own concerns, abandon their own will, and lay down whatever they have in hand, leaving it unfinished. With the ready step of obedience, they follow the voice of authority in their actions. Almost at the same moment, then, as the master gives the instruction the disciple quickly puts it into practice in the fear of God; and both actions together are swiftly completed as one.

It is love that impels them to pursue everlasting life; therefore, they were eager to take the narrow road of which the Lord says: 'Narrow is the road that leads to life' (Matt. 7:14). They no longer live by their own judgement, giving in to their whims and appetites; rather they walk according to another's decisions and directions, choosing to live in monasteries and to have an abbot over them. Men of this resolve unquestionably conform to the saying of the Lord: 'I have come not to do my own will, but the will of him who sent me' (John 6:38).

This very obedience, however, will be acceptable to God and agreeable to men only if compliance with what is commanded is not cringing or sluggish or half-hearted, but free from any grumbling or any reaction of unwillingness. For the obedience shown to superiors is given to God, as he himself said: 'Whoever listens to you, listens to me' (Luke 10:16). Furthermore, the disciples' obedience must be given gladly, for 'God loves a cheerful giver' (2 Cor. 9:7). If a disciple obeys grudgingly and grumbles, not only aloud but also in his heart, then, even though he carries out the order, his action will not be accepted with favour by God, who sees that he is grumbling in his heart. He will have no reward for service of this kind; on the contrary, he will incur punishment for grumbling, unless he changes for the better and makes amends.

The Rule of St Benedict, Chapter 5, 'Obedience' (540s)

17. A Sermon of Bernard of Clairvaux

If then you love the Lord your God with all your heart, with all your soul and with all your strength, and if, transported by fervour in a bound beyond that love of love with which active charity is content, you are set wholly alight by divine love, received in the fullness of the Spirit (and to which the former love serves only as a step), then assuredly you have a knowledge of God. It is true that you do not know him adequately, or as he is, which lies utterly beyond the scope of any creature, but you know him according to your own capacity. Next, you will know your own self as you are when you perceive that there is nothing whatever in you to love, save only in so far as you are God's, since you have poured all your capacity for loving into him. I repeat, you will know yourself as you are when the very experience of the love and affection that you bear yourself reveals to you that there is nothing in you deserving of your love, unless it be on his account without whom you yourself have no existence . . . Give me the man who loves God above all else and with his whole being; who loves himself and his neighbour in the measure in which they both love God; his enemy as one who will perhaps one day love God; his natural parents tenderly as nature prompts; his spiritual parents – namely his teachers – unreservedly as gratitude requires. And in this way he reaches out to the rest of God's creation with an ordered love, looking down on the earth and up to heaven, dealing with this world as though uninvolved and distinguishing with an inward refinement of the soul between what is to be merely employed and what enjoyed, paying passing attention to the transient, and that only as need requires, while embracing all things eternal with a desire that never flags. Give me, I say, a man like that and I dare to proclaim him wise.

St Bernard of Clairvaux, *Sermon 50, On the Song of Songs*, 6 and 8 (1135–53)

18. The *Stigmata* of Francis of Assisi

The whole city of Assisi rushed down as a group and the entire region hurried to see the wonderful works of God which the Lord of majesty gloriously displayed in his holy servant. Each person burst into a song of joy at the urging of a joyful heart, and all of them had their desire fulfilled and blessed the almighty Saviour. Still his sons were mourning, bereft of so great a father, and showed the deep feeling of their hearts in groaning and tears.

They looked at his skin which was black before but now shining white in its beauty, promising the rewards of the blessed resurrection. They saw his face like the face of an angel, as if he were not dead, but alive. All his limbs had become as soft and moveable as in childhood innocence. His muscles were not taut, as they usually are in the dead, his skin was not hard, his limbs were not rigid but could be easily moved back and forth.

All the people saw him glowing with remarkable beauty and his flesh became even whiter than before. It was even more wonderful for them to see in the middle of his hands and feet not just the holes of the nails, but the nails themselves formed by his own flesh, retaining the dark colour of iron, and his right side red with blood. These signs of martyrdom did not provoke horror, but added great beauty and grace, like little black stones in a white pavement.

People considered it a great gift to be allowed to kiss or even to see the sacred marks of Jesus Christ which St Francis bore in his own body.

Thomas of Celano, *The Life of St Francis*, Second Book, Chapter 9 (1228)

19. The *Summa Theologiae*

Article 2: Is there some natural law in us?
It seems that there is not.

1 A man is sufficiently governed by eternal law, for Augustine says in *On Free Will* 1.6 that the eternal law is that by which it is just that all things are perfectly ordered. But nature does not abound in superfluities, just as it is not deficient in what is necessary. Therefore there is no natural law in man.

2 Moreover, by law a man's acts are ordered to the end, as was said above, but the ordering of human acts to the end is not by nature, as happens in irrational creatures, which by natural appetite alone act for the sake of the end; man acts for the sake of the end through reason and will. Therefore, there is no natural law in man.

3 To the degree that one is free he is less subject to the law. But man is freer than the other animals, thanks to free will, which he has beyond the other animals. Therefore since other animals are not subject to natural law, neither should man be subject to any natural law.

On the contrary
On Romans 2:14, 'These having no law are a law unto themselves', the Gloss says that although they do not have the written law, they have the natural law which each understands and is thereby conscious of what is good and what is evil.

Response
It should be said that, as has been urged, law, since it is a rule and measure, can be in something in two ways: in one way, as in the one ruling and measuring, in another way, as in the ruled and measured, since insofar as they participate in something of the rule or measure, they are ruled and measured. Since all things subject to divine providence are ruled and measured by the eternal law, as is clear from what has been said, it is manifest that all things participate in some way in eternal law, insofar as by its impression they have inclinations to their proper acts and ends. Among others, however, the rational creature is subject to divine providence in a more excellent manner, insofar as he comes to be a participant in providence, providing for himself

and others. Hence in him the eternal reason is participated in in such a way that he has a natural inclination to the fitting act and end. Such a participation in eternal law in the rational creature is called natural law. Hence when the Psalmist says in Psalm 4:6, 'Offer sacrifices of righteousness, and hope in the Lord', he adds as if in response to someone asking what the words of justice are, 'Many say: "Who will show us good things?"' Replying to that question says, 'Lift up the light of thy countenance upon us, O Lord', as if the natural light of reason, whereby we discern good and evil, which pertains to natural law, is nothing else than the impression of the divine light in us. Hence it is evident that natural law is nothing other than the participation in eternal law on the part of the rational creature.

St Thomas Aquinas, *Summa Theologiae*, Question 91: The Diversity of Law (1266–73)

20. The Tower Experience

I had been seized upon by a certain wonderful desire to understand Paul in Romans. No lack of seriousness had hitherto stood in my way, but only a single statement in the first chapter: 'The justice of God is revealed in the Gospel.' I had, of course, conceived a hatred of this phrase, 'justice of God', because, in conformity with the custom of all theologians, I had been taught to understand it philosophically as formal or active justice, whereby God is just and punishes sinners and the unjust.

Though as a friar I had led a blameless life, I felt myself to be a sinner before God, with a totally restless conscience, and I could not be confident that I had reconciled God by my satisfactions. Hence I did not love, but rather I hated the just God who punishes sinners. Thus I was angry with God, if not in secret blasphemy, at least in strong grumbling, and I said: It is not enough that wretched sinners and those lost for ever because of original sin should be oppressed according to the law of the Old Covenant with every sort of calamity. No, God also intends to heap affliction upon affliction by the Gospel, while menacingly holding out to us his justice and his anger through the good tidings. And so I was frantic, upset and raving in conscience, and struggled relentlessly with that passage of Paul, filled with an ardent desire to know what Paul meant.

After days and nights of meditation God finally took pity on me and I noted the inner connection of the two passages: 'The justice of God is revealed in the Gospel, as it is written, "The just man lives by faith".' Then I began to understand the justice of God as that by which the just man lives, thanks to the gift of God, that is, by faith; that the justice of God, which is revealed by the Gospel, is to be understood in the passive sense; that God in his mercy justifies us by faith, as it is written: 'The just man lives by faith.' At once I felt myself to be reborn and as though I had entered paradise through the opened gates. Holy Scripture immediately showed me another face. I then went through Scripture, as my memory presented it, and found a corresponding meaning in other passages. For example, the 'work of God' is what God works in us; the 'strength of God' is that whereby he makes us strong; the 'wisdom of God' is that by which he makes us wise. In a similar manner are to be understood the 'power of God', 'salvation of God', 'glory of God'.

Luther's later description of events which took place
somewhere between 1513 and 1518

21. Faith Superior to Works

First, let us consider the inner man to see how a righteous, free, and pious Christian, that is, a spiritual, new, and inner man, becomes what he is. It is evident that no external thing has any influence in producing Christian righteousness or freedom, or in producing unrighteousness or servitude . . .

It does not help the soul if the body is adorned with the sacred robes of priests or dwells in sacred places or is occupied with sacred duties or prays, fasts, abstains from certain kinds of food, or does any work that can be done by the body and in the body. The righteousness and the freedom of the soul require something far different, since the things which have been mentioned could be done by any wicked person. Such works produce nothing but hypocrites . . .

Let us then consider it certain and firmly established that the soul can do without anything except the Word of God and that where the Word of God is missing there is no help at all for the soul. If it has the Word of God it is rich and lacks nothing, since it is the Word of life, truth, light, peace, righteousness, salvation, joy, liberty, wisdom, power, grace, glory, and of every incalculable blessing . . .

The Word of God cannot be received and cherished by any works whatever but only by faith. Therefore it is clear that, as the soul needs only the Word of God for its life and righteousness, so it is justified by faith alone and not any works; for if it could be justified by anything else, it would not need the Word, and consequently it would not need faith.

Martin Luther, The Freedom of a Christian (1520)

22. The Calculations of Cardinal Richelieu

It is more difficult to recognize the illness than to cure it, all the more so because of the very violence of the illness. Moreover, in this case the old maxim of meeting force with force cannot apply, since to do so would put France and Christendom in extreme danger, for reasons which are well known to men of sound judgement and who can apply in matters in statesmanship the same care as doctors who avoid drastic purges during prolonged fevers. The chief difficulty lies in the contradiction presented by the disease, for we are torn between fear of the House of Austria [Habsburgs] and fear of the Protestants. The perfect answer would be to reduce both to such a point that they are no longer to be feared, and it is to this end that efforts must be directed. But at the same time care must be taken to ensure that if the means used do not attain this end, the perfect answer, they should at least serve to ward off the worst effects and provide breathing space in which to muster one's forces and turn events to account without danger . . . As to the Spaniard and the Swede, we must above all take care that in bringing down one we do not raise the other to such a point that he is more to be feared than the former. We must act also with such caution that instead of setting one against the other, we do not become involved in war with one of them. Such a step would allow the other to increase in such strength that even if the king were victorious he would lose more from the easy manner in which the other became more powerful than he would gain from his own victory . . . To carry out this difficult operation, in which the issues are so delicate, we must combine industry with force, and diplomacy with arms.

Cardinal Richelieu, Memorandum (1632)

23. The Council of Trent on Justification

The Synod furthermore declares, that in adults, the beginning of the said Justification is to be derived from the prevenient grace of God, through Jesus Christ, that is to say, from His vocation, whereby, without any merits existing on their parts, they are called; that so they, who by sins were alienated from God, may be disposed through His quickening and assisting grace, to convert themselves to their own justification, by freely assenting to and co-operating with that said grace; in such sort that, that while God touches the heart of man by the illumination of the Holy Spirit, neither is man himself utterly without doing anything while he receives that inspiration, forasmuch as he is also able to reject it; yet he is not able, by his own free will, without the grace of God, to move himself unto justice in His sight. Whence, when it is said in the sacred writings: Turn ye to me, and I will turn to you, we are admonished of our liberty, and when we answer; Convert us, O Lord, to thee, and we shall be converted, we confess that we are prevented by the grace of God.

Council of Trent, *Decree on Justification*, Chapter 5 (1564)

24. The Vision of Ignatius Loyola at the River Cardona

One time he was going out of his devotion to a church a little more than a mile from Manresa; I believe it was called St Paul's. The road ran next to the river. As he went along occupied with his devotions, he sat down for a while with his face toward the river which was running deep. While he was seated there, the eyes of his understanding began to be opened; though he did not see any vision, he understood and knew many things, both spiritual things and matters of faith and of learning, and this was with so great an enlightenment that everything seemed new to him. Though there were many, he cannot set forth the details that he understood then, except that he experienced a great clarity in his understanding. This was such that in the whole course of his life, through sixty-two years, even if he gathered up all the many helps he had had from God and all the many things he knew and added them together, he does not think they would amount to as much as he had received at that one time.

St Ignatius Loyola, *Autobiography* (recounting an event in 1523)

NOTES

Introduction: Making All Things New

1   See Rom. 12:2; Eph. 4:22–4; Col. 3:9–10; 2 Cor. 3:18.

2   See Robert Louis Wilkin, *The Spirit of Early Christian Thought: Seeking the Face of God* (Yale University Press, 2003) pp. 93, 106. See Matt. 3:16; Mark 1:10; John 1:32 for the baptism of Jesus. See Acts 2:1–4 for the Spirit at Pentecost.

3   For accounts of early baptism see Norbert Brox, *A History of the Early Church* (SCM Press, 1994) pp. 93–100; Stuart G. Hall, 'Ministry, Worship and Christian Life' in Ian Hazlett (ed.), *Early Christianity: Origins and Evolution to 600* (SPCK, 1991) pp. 103–4; Wilkin, *Spirit*, pp. 36–42.

4   Ignatius of Antioch, 'Epistle to the Ephesians' in Maxwell Staniforth and Andrew Louth, *Early Christian Writings: The Apostolic Fathers* (Penguin, second edition, 1987) p. 66.

5   Quotations in Henry Chadwick, *The Church in Ancient Society: From Galilee to Gregory the Great* (Oxford University Press, 2001) pp. 25, 213; Philip Rousseau, *The Early Christian Centuries* (Longman, 2002) pp. 42, 317. Fuller descriptions of the early Eucharist can be found in Brox, *History*, pp. 100–6 and Wilkin, *Spirit*, pp. 28–36.

6   G. A. Williamson and Andrew Louth, *Eusebius: The History of the Church from Christ to Constantine* (Penguin, second edition, 1989) Book VI, 43.10, p. 216.

7   Robin Lane Fox, *Pagans and Christians* (Viking, 1986) pp. 341, 351. See also Keith Hopkins, *A World Full of Gods: Pagans, Jews and Christians in the Roman Empire* (Weidenfeld and Nicolson, 1999) pp. 9–45 for the sexually explicit nature of the Roman world.

8   Chadwick, *Church in Ancient Society*, p. 209.

9   Gerard Vallée, *The Shaping of Christianity: The History and Literature of Its Formative Centuries (100–800)* (Paulist Press, 1999) pp. 124–6. See also discussions of Christian morality in Lane Fox, *Pagans and Christians*, pp. 336–74; Rodney Stark, *The Rise of Christianity* (Princeton University Press, 1996) pp. 95–128.

10 For an account of early Christian penance see Brox, *History*, pp. 106–18.

11 For discussions of demography, wealth and literacy see Jane Merdinger, 'The

World of the Roman Empire' in Hazlett, *Early Christianity*, pp. 18–22; Vallée, *Shaping of Christianity*, pp. 13–14; Lane Fox, *Pagans and Christians*, pp. 46–7; Keith Hopkins, 'Christian Number and Its Implications' in the *Journal of Early Christian Studies* 6.2 (1998) pp. 207–9.

12 Cicero, *On the Nature of the Gods* III, 5–9.

13 Lane Fox, *Pagans and Christians*, p. 141. For detailed descriptions of Roman religions see *ibid.*, pp. 64–261; Martin Goodman, *The Roman World 44BC–AD 180* (Routledge, 1997) especially the section on 'Humans and Gods'.

14 Rousseau, *Early Christian Centuries*, p. 35. See also Vallée, *Shaping of Christianity*, p. 73.

15 Chadwick, *Church in Ancient Society*, p. 2. See also Vallée, *Shaping of Christianity*, p. 149.

16 G. L. Archer and G. Chirichigno, *Old Testament Quotations in the New Testament* (Chigago, 1983) p. xi claim over 400 direct quotations.

17 For typology see Jean Daniélou, *The Bible and the Liturgy* (Darton, Longman and Todd, 1960).

18 For a succinct account of Julian, see Vallée, *Shaping of Christianity*, pp. 53–6.

19 Clement of Alexandria, *Stomata* I.5.28.

20 Robert Louis Wilkin, *The Christians as the Romans Saw Them* (Yale University Press, second edition, 2003) p. 199.

21 Tertullian, *De Praescriptione* 7.

22 C. F. D. Moule, *The Birth of the New Testament* (A and C Black, third edition, 1981) p. 57.

23 For a discussion see Wilkin, *Christians as the Romans Saw Them*, pp. 83–93.

24 Chadwick, *Church in Ancient Society*, p. 515. See also Vallée, *Shaping of Christianity*, p. 73; Brox, *History*, pp. 36–8; Hopkins, *World Full of Gods*, pp. 306–7.

25 Rousseau, *Early Christian Centuries*, p. 95.

26 For the novelty of Christian views see Stark, *Rise of Christianity*, pp. 211–12.

27 Lane Fox, *Pagans and Christians*, pp. 378–9.

28 For Dura Europos see Kenneth Painter, 'Archaeology' in Hazlett, *Early Christianity*, p. 285.

29 See for example Vallée, *Shaping of Christianity*, pp. 106–7; Wilkin, *Christians as the Romans Saw Them*, p. 31.

30 Lane Fox, *Pagans and Christians*, pp. 317, 592.

31 See Stark, *Rise of Christianity*, pp. 4–13 for details.

32 Hopkins, 'Christian Number', pp. 187–203.

33 Details in Joseph F. Kelly, *The World of the Early Christians* (The Liturgical Press, 1997) p. 193; Merdinger, 'World of the Roman Empire', p. 25.

34 W. H. C. Frend, *Martyrdom and Persecution in the Early Church: A Study of Conflict from the Maccabees to Donatus* (Basil Blackwell, 1965) p. 390; W. H. C. Frend, *The Rise of Christianity* (Fortress Press, 1984) p. 311.

35 Averil Cameron, *The Later Roman Empire AD 284–430* (Fontana Press, 1993) pp. 1–12.

36 Frend, *Martyrdom*, p. 451; see Lane Fox, *Pagans and Christians*, p. 259.

37 *Ibid.*, p. 585. See especially pp. 572–94.

38 Chadwick, *Church in Ancient Society*, p. 145.

39 Stark, *Rise of Christianity*, p. 37. See also pp. 19, 54 for similar arguments.

40 See *ibid.*, pp. 196–201 for evidence on the weakness of polytheism.

41 Tertullian, *Apology* 50.14.

42 For numbers see Frend, *Martyrdom*, p. 537. For details of state persecutions see pp. 403–13, 423–9, 477–520. For Christians abandoning their faith see Brox, *History*, pp. 39–45; W. H. C. Frend, 'The Failure of Persecutions in the Roman Empire' in M. I. Finley (ed.), *Studies in Ancient Society* (Routledge and Kegan Paul, 1974) pp. 270–1.

43 Lane Fox, *Pagans and Christians*, p. 441; Rousseau, *Early Christian Centuries*, pp. 161–2; Daniel Boyarin, *Dying for God: Martyrdom and the Making of Christianity and Judaism* (Stanford University Press, 1999) p. 101.

44 See Ramsay MacMullen, *Christianizing the Roman Empire (AD 100–400)* (Yale University Press, 1984) pp. 34, 59–61.

45 See Stark, *Rise of Christianity*, especially pp. 17–18, 20, 56. See also Lane Fox, *Pagans and Christians*, pp. 315–16; Rousseau, *Early Christian Centuries*, p. 114; MacMullen, *Christianizing*, p. 40 for similar arguments.

46 See for example Lane Fox, *Pagans and Christians*, pp. 308–11; Kelly, *World of the Early Christians*, pp. 147–52; Rousseau, *Early Christian Centuries*, pp. 96–7; Stark, *Rise of Christianity*, pp. 95–127.

47 Peter Brown, *The World of Late Antiquity AD 150–750* (Thames and Hudson, 1971) p. 66 for quotation. See also Rousseau, *Early Christian Centuries*, pp. 103, 130; Chadwick, *Church in Ancient Society*, p. 255.

48 See Stark, *Rise of Christianity*, pp. 73–91.

49 Staniforth and Louth, *Early Christian Writings*, p. 40.

50 Robert M. Grant, *Irenaeus of Lyons* (Routledge, 1997) pp. 125–5.

51 Chadwick, *Church in Ancient Society*, p. 117.

52 See Vallée, *Shaping of Christianity*, p. 82 for comments on Montanism. Quotations in Frend, *Martyrdom*, p. 502; Rousseau, *Early Christian Centuries*, p. 166. See also Lane Fox, *Pagans and Christians*, pp. 455–9, 494; Chadwick, *Church in Ancient Society*, pp. 149–54.

53 See W. H. C. Frend, '"And I have other sheep" – John 10:16' in Rowan Williams, *The Making of Orthodoxy: Essays in Honour of Henry Chadwick* (Cambridge University Press, 1989) p. 36. See also Philip Rousseau, 'Christian Asceticism and the Early Monks' and Maurice Wiles, 'Orthodoxy and Heresy' in Hazlett, *Early Christianity*, pp. 121, 198–207; Vallée, *Shaping of Christianity*, pp. 77–8.

54 Jaroslav Pelikan, *The Christian Tradition: A History of the Development of Doctrine, Vol. I: The Emergence of the Catholic Tradition (100–600)* (University of Chicago Press, 1971) p. 9; Kelly, *World of the Early Christians*, p. 127.

55 Gerhart B. Ladner, *The Idea of Reform: Its Impact on Christian Thought and Action in the Age of the Fathers* (Harvard University Press, 1959) p. 138.

56 See Kelly, *World of the Early Christians*, p. 128 for a discussion of this text.

57 Arthur G. Patzia, *The Making of the New Testament: Origin, Collection. Text and Canon* (Inter-Varsity Press, 1995) p. 136.

58 Robin Lane Fox, *Alexander the Great* (Allen Lane, 1973) p. 11 for quotation. See also Robin Lane Fox, *The Unauthorized Version: Truth and Fiction in the Bible*

(Viking, 1991) pp. 138–9; Patzia, *Making of the New Testament*, p. 136.

59 For an example of the former see Hopkins, *World Full of Gods*, especially pp. 290–335; for the latter approach see Moule, *Birth of the New Testament*, especially pp. 44–150.

60 See Bruce M. Metzger, *The Canon of the New Testament: Its Origin, Development and Significance* (Clarendon Press, 1987) Appendix I, pp. 289–93.

61 *Ibid.*, p. 257.

62 Williamson and Louth, *Eusebius*, Book III, 25, pp. 88–9; see also the discussion in Metzger, pp. 201–7.

63 See *Ibid.* pp. 209–12 for Athanasius, 223–4 for Armenia and Georgia.

64 Jerome, *Epistle CXXIX*. See Metzger, *Canon*, pp. 251–4 for a discussion of the criteria for canonicity.

65 See *ibid.*, pp. 75–112; and Hans von Campenhausen, *The Formation of the Christian Bible* (A and C Black, 1972) pp. 147–76 for sometimes contrasting views. Campenhausen, for instance, sees Marcion as crucial for the formation of the Canon, while Metzger is not so confident.

66 Metzger, *Canon*, p. 240.

67 Chadwick, *Church in Ancient Society*, pp. 118–23, 338–9; Rowan Williams, 'The Bible' in Hazlett, *Early Christianity*, p. 87; Lane Fox, *Pagans and Christians*, p. 544 for the quotation.

Chapter 1: Imperial Christianity

1 Averil Cameron and Stuart G. Hall (eds), *Eusebius: Life of Constantine* (Clarendon Press, 1999) III. 15. p. 127.

2 See Jaroslav Pelikan, *The Christian Tradition: A History of the Development of Doctrine, Vol. I: The Emergence of the Catholic Tradition (100–600)*, p. 138; Robert Louis Wilkin, *The Spirit of Early Christian Thought: Seeking the Face of God* (Yale University Press, 2003) p. 189; M. I. Finley (ed.), *Studies in Ancient Society* (Routledge and Kegan Paul, 1974), p. 265; Gerhart B. Ladner, *The Idea of Reform: Its Impact on Christian Thought and Action in the Age of the Fathers* (Harvard University Press, 1959), pp. 116–17; Philip Rousseau, *The Early Christian Centuries* (Longman, 2002), p. 206; Gerard Vallée, *The Shaping of Christianity: The History and Literature of Its Formative Centuries (100–800)* (Paulist Press, 1999), p. 173; H. A. Drake, *Constantine and the Bishops: The Politics of Intolerance* (Johns Hopkins University Press, 2000); Origen, *Contra Celsum*, VIII.

3 Drake, *Constantine*, p. 246; Timothy D. Barnes, *Constantine and Eusebius* (Harvard University Press, 1981) pp. 19, 26; Charles Mason Odahl, *Constantine and the Christian Empire* (Routledge, 2004) pp. 65–6.

4 Drake, *Constantine*, pp. 149–53.

5 See T. G. Elliott, *The Christianity of Constantine the Great* (University of Scranton Press, 1996) where this case is argued.

6 See Drake, *Constantine*, pp. 181–3; Barnes, *Constantine and Eusebius*, p. 36; Odahl, *Constantine and the Christian Empire*, pp. 94–5.

7 J. L. Creed (ed.), *De Mortibus Persecutorum* (Clarendon Press, 1984) Chapter 44, p. 63.

8 See Elliott, *Christianity of Constantine*, especially pp. vii, 63–71.

9   See for example Drake, *Constantine*, pp. 180, 183–4 for a discussion of these possibilities.

10 Barnes, *Constantine and Eusebius*, pp. 44–8.

11 See Cameron and Hall, *Eusebius*, p. 38 for a discussion of these points.

12 Drake, *Constantine*, pp. 91, 459–60; Cameron and Hall, *Eusebius*, pp. 43–4, 46.

13 Odahl, *Constantine and the Christian Empire*, p. 188.

14 Drake, *Constantine*, p. 276 for churches as propaganda; Odahl, *Constantine and the Christian Empire*, pp. 147–61, 211–18, 232–44 for Constantine's building programme; R. A. Markus, *The End of Ancient Christianity* (Cambridge University Press, 1990) pp. 139–53 for sacred geography and martyr's tombs.

15 Drake, *Constantine*, p. 213.

16 Cyril, *Catechetical Lectures* 18 n. 23; Augustine, *Letter 49* n. 3.

17 See Barnes, *Constantine and Eusebius*, pp. 201–2; Elliott, *Christianity of Constantine*, pp. 141–5 for details.

18 See Barnes, *Constantine and Eusebius*, p. 204.

19 See Rousseau, *Early Christian Centuries*, pp. 188, 215 for a discussion of this.

20 See Drake, *Constantine*, pp. 238–45 for a discussion of this.

21 Timothy D. Barnes, *Athanasius and Constantius: Theology and Politics in the Constantinian Empire* (Harvard University Press, 1993) p. 2.

22 Averil Cameron, *Christianity and the Rhetoric of Empire: The Development of Christian Discourse* (University of California Press, 1991) p. 170. For a detailed discussion of Athenasius and his opponents see Barnes, *Athanasius and Constantius*. For broadly similar criticisms of him see also Elliott, *Christianity of Constantine* and Drake, *Constantine*.

23 Peter Brown, *Power and Persuasion in Late Antiquity: Towards a Christian Empire* (University of Wisconsin Press, 1992) p. 4.

24 Cameron, *Rhetoric*, p. 4.

25 Peter Brown, *Authority and the Sacred: Aspects of the Christianisation of the Roman World* (Cambridge University Press, 1995) pp. 4–6; Markus, *End of Ancient Christianity*, p. 28.

26 Brown, *Power and Persuasion*, pp. 36–70; *Authority and the Sacred*, pp. 42–3, 47.

27 Cameron, *Rhetoric*, p. 14.

28 Cameron, *Later Roman Empire*, p. 103.

29 See Drake, *Constantine*, pp. 12–14 for Burckhardt; Barnes, *Athanasius and Constantius*, p. 168 for the Germans.

30 Cameron and Hall, *Eusebius*, p. 35; also Odahl, *Constantine and the Christian Empire*, pp. 265–7.

31 Drake, *Constantine*, p. 442.

32 Rousseau, *Early Christian Centuries*, p. 247.

Chapter 2: City and Desert

1   For accounts of these and other conventional views see Marilyn Dunn, *The Emergence of Monasticism: From the Desert Fathers to the Early Middle Ages* (Blackwell, 2000) pp. 1–2; Vincent L. Wimbush and Richard Valantasis, *Asceticism* (Oxford University Press, 1995) p. 50; Derwas J. Chitty, *The Desert a City; An Introduction to the Study of Egyptian and Palestinian Monasticism in the Christian Empire*

(Mowbray, 1977) pp. 6–7; Douglas Burton-Christie, *The Word in the Desert: Scripture and the Quest for Holiness in Early Christian Monasticism* (Oxford University Press, 1993) p. 4.

2   James E. Goehring, *Ascetics, Society and the Desert: Studies in Early Egyptian Monasticism* (Trinity Press International, 1999) pp. 3, 196–7.

3   Peter Brown, *The Body and Society: Men, Women and Sexual Renunciation in Early Christianity* (Columbia University Press, 1988) pp. 53, 62–4 for a discussion of this.

4   David Brakke, *Athanasius and the Politics of Asceticism* (Clarendon Press, 1995) p. 85.

5   See Goehring, *Ascetics*, pp. 14–18 for a discussion of Eusebius.

6   Philip Rousseau, *Basil of Caesarea* (University of California Press, 1994) pp. 15, 17.

7   Samuel Rubenson, *The Letters of St Antony: Monasticism and the Making of a Saint* (Fortress Press, 1995) pp. 89–110 for a description of third- and fourth-century Egypt.

8   Goehring, *Ascetics*, pp. 20–6.

9   Wimbush and Valantasis, *Asceticism*, pp. 80–5.

10   *Paidagogos* 1.13, 102.3. Quoted in Brown, *Body and Society*, p. 127.

11   *Ibid.*, p. 235.

12   See Brakke, *Athanasius*, pp. 149–52.

13   Brown, *Body and Society*, p. 442.

14   *Ibid.*, pp. 224–6; Burton-Christie, *Word in the Desert*, pp. 144–6.

15   *Ibid.*, p. 227. See his discussion of this on pp. 214–33.

16   Brakke, *Athanasius*, pp. 238–9.

17   Brown, *Body and Society*, p. 402.

18   *Ibid.*, pp. 218–23.

19   *Ibid.*, p. 309.

20   *Ibid.*, p. 231.

21   *Ibid.*, pp. 291–9, 351.

22   *Ibid.*, p. 363.

23   *Ibid.*, p. 364.

24   *Ibid.*, pp. 174–5, 407, 231, 421.

25   *Ibid.*, p. 443.

26   Athanasius, edited by Robert C. Gregg, *Life of Antony* (SPCK, 1980) pp. 42–3.

27   Goehring, *Ascetics*, pp. 40–1, 71, 78–90 for a discussion of the physical location of early monasticism.

28   Brown, *Body and Society*, pp. 204–5.

29   Athanasius, *Life of Antony*, p. 83.

30   Brakke, *Athanasius*, pp. 213–14 for comments on this point.

31   Athanasius, *Life of Antony*, p. 81.

32   *Ibid.*, p. 97.

33   Rubenson, *Letters of St Antony*, p. 11.

34   *Ibid.*, p. 187.

35   See Dunn, *Emergence of Monasticism*, pp. 29–30; Goehring, *Ascetics*, p. 26–7.

36   *Ibid.*, p. 31.

37 *Ibid.*, p. 28.
38 Dunn, *Emergence of Monasticism*, pp. 33–4.
39 See Goehring, *Ascetics*, especially pp. 10, 26–32, 47–8, 91, 93, 96, 97–100, 108–9.
40 *Ibid.*, pp. 170–9, 199–200.
41 See Brown, *Body and Society*, pp. 332–3; Wimbush and Valantasis, *Asceticism*, p. 221.
42 Dunn, *Emergence of Monasticism*, p. 19.
43 *Ibid.*, pp. 20–1.
44 Athanasius, *Life of Antony*, p. 10; Wimbush and Valantasis, *Asceticism*, p. 77.
45 Brown, *Body and Society*, pp. 88, 150–1.
46 Goehring, *Ascetics*, pp. 200–8.
47 *Ibid.*, p. 256.
48 *Ibid.*
49 *Ibid.*, p. 210.
50 *Ibid.*, p. 213.
51 Philip Rousseau, *Ascetics, Authority and the Church:In the Age of Jerome and Cassian* (Oxford University Press, 1978) p. 224.
52 See Brown, *Body and Society*, pp. 245, 360–1 for comments on this.
53 Rousseau, *Basil of Caesarea*, Homilies 346, 335, 338 on pp. 178–9, 184, 188.
54 *Ibid.*, pp. 190–222 for comments on his ascetic writings.
55 *Ibid.*, p. 164.
56 Brown, *Body and Society*, p. 254.
57 Brakke, *Athanasius*, pp. 17–18.
58 *Ibid.*, pp. 44–57 for a discussion of this.
59 *Ibid.*, pp. 21–35.
60 *Ibid.*, pp. 182–6.
61 *Ibid.*, p. 109.
62 Dunn, *Emergence of Monasticism*, pp. 62–4, 82–4 for details.
63 Brakke, *Athanasius*, p. 199.

Chapter 3: The Great Debate

1 For a discussion of Pliny's Letter see Robert Louis Wilkin, *The Christians as the Romans Saw Them* (Yale University Press, second edition, 2003) pp. 1–30.
2 Quoted in Aloys Grillmeier, *Christ in Christian Tradition, Vol. I: From the Apostolic Age to Chalcedon (451)* (A R Mowbray, revised edition, 1975) pp. 148, 321; also Gerald O'Collins, *Christology: A Biblical, Historical and Systematic Study of Jesus* (Oxford University Press, 1995) p. 155.
3 See Rowan Williams, *Arius: Heresy and Tradition* (Darton, Longman and Todd, 1987) p. 123 for a short discussion of this point.
4 Quoted in O'Collins, *Christology*, p. 170.
5 Origen, *De Principe* II, 6.6.
6 See Frances Young, *From Nicaea to Chalcedon: A Guide to the Literature and Its Background* (SCM Press, 1983) p. 115.
7 Joseph F. Kelly, *The World of the Early Christians* (The Liturgical Press, 1997), pp. 121, 124 for a discussion of this point.
8 See O'Collins, *Christology*, pp. 178–9 for a discussion of this ambiguity.

9 See Grillmeier, *Christ in Christian Tradition*, pp. 125–9 for its origins and meaning.
10 Quoted in *ibid.*, p. 345.
11 *Ibid.*, pp. 368–9.
12 A detailed discussion of these various labels can be found in O'Collins, *Christology*, pp. 184–5; Young, *From Nicaea to Chalcedon*, pp. 178–82, 195; Williams, *Arius*, pp. 116, 158–9, 234; Grillmeier, *Christ in Christian Tradition*, pp. 218, 341, 367, 418, 421, 446, 482.
13 A Religious of CSMV (trans. and ed.), *St Athanasius On the Incarnation* (A R Mowbray, 1963) p. 26.
14 *Ibid.*, p. 45.
15 Grillmeier, *Christ in Christian Tradition*, p. 311.
16 Apollinarius, *Fragment 7*, quoted in Young, *From Nicaea to Chalcedon*, p. 186.
17 Grillmeier, *Christ in Christian Tradition*, p. 370.
18 Origen, *On First Principles* 2.6.3, quoted in O'Collins, *Christology*, p. 169.
19 Young, *From Nicaea to Chalcedon*, p. 219.
20 Tertullian, quoted in Grillmeier, *Christ in Christian Tradition*, p. 122.
21 For a discussion of the Definition see Grillmeier, *Christ in Christian Tradition*, pp. 543–50.
22 Young, *From Nicaea to Chalcedon*, p. 242.
23 Grillmeier, *Christ in Christian Tradition*, p. 107.
24 O'Collins, *Christology*, p. 13.
25 *Ibid.*, p. 234.
26 Both quoted in Philip Rousseau, *Basil of Caesarea* (University of California Press, 1994) pp. 110–11.
27 *Ibid.*, p. 109.
28 Young, *From Nicaea to Chalcedon*, p. 277.
29 Averil Cameron, *Christianity and the Rhetoric of Empire: The Development of Christian Discourse* (University of California Press, 1991) pp. 59, 226.
30 Williams, *Arius*, p. 237.
31 Young, *From Nicaea to Chalcedon*, p. 246.
32 *Ibid.*, p. 117.
33 *Ibid.*, pp. 64, 207; Williams, *Arius*, pp. 175, 233; Grillmeier, *Christ in Christian Tradition*, p. 444.
34 *Ibid.*, pp. 550, 446.
35 *Ibid.*, p. 555.
36 *Ibid.*, p. 556.
37 Peter Brown, *The Body and Society: Men, Women and Sexual Renunciation in Early Christianity* (Columbia University Press, 1988), p. 429.

Chapter 4: The African Pilgrim

1 Augustine, *Sermon 88.5*, quoted in John Burnaby, *Amor Dei: A Study of the Religion of St Augustine* (Hodder and Stoughton, 1938) p. 70.
2 Augustine, *Letter 231.1* quoted in *ibid.*, p. 170.
3 See Gillian Clark, *Augustine: The Confessions* (Bristol Phoenix Press, 2005) pp. 49–51, 56.
4 *Ibid.*, p. 84.

5 Peter Brown, *Augustine of Hippo: A Biography* (Faber and Faber, revised edition, 2000) pp. 48–9.

6 For a brief and clear analysis of Augustine's theology of evil see Gerald Bonner, *St Augustine of Hippo: Life and Controversies* (Canterbury Press, third edition, 2002) pp. 199–214.

7 Brown, *A Biography*, p. 216.

8 Augustine, *Contra Epistulum Parmeniani* III, iv, 24, quoted in Bonner, *St Augustine of Hippo*, pp. 251–2.

9 Henry Chadwick, *Augustine: A Very Short Introduction* (Oxford University Press, 2001) pp. 85–6.

10 Serge Lancel, *Augustine* (SCM Press, 2002) p. 332.

11 Augustine, *De Gratia Christi* II.28, quoted in *ibid.*, p. 341.

12 Brown, *A Biography*, pp. 367–9 for a brief but very lucid discussion.

13 John Henry Cardinal Newman, *Apologia Pro Vita Sua: Being a History of His Religious Opinions*, ed. Martin J. Svaglic (Oxford University Press, 1967) p. 218.

14 Augustine, *Sermon 169.3*, quoted in Lancel, *Augustine*, p. 341.

15 Augustine, *De Gratia Christi* I, 52, quoted in *ibid.*, p. 341.

16 Augustine, *Sermon 165.3*. Both quotations in Brown, *A Biography*, p. 375.

17 Burnaby, *Amor Dei*, p. 153.

18 See Bonner, *St Augustine of Hippo*, pp. 385–6.

19 See Brown, *A Biography*, pp. 400–10.

20 Lancel, *Augustine*, pp. 342, 425.

21 Bonner, *St Augustine of Hippo*, pp. 10, 139–140.

22 *Ibid.*, p. 273; Burnaby, *Amor Dei*, pp. 211–13.

23 Lancel, *Augustine*, pp. 431–4; Bonner, *St Augustine of Hippo*, pp. 388–9.

24 *Ibid.*, p. 392.

25 *Ibid.*, pp. 386–7.

26 Virgil, *Aeneid* I, 278–9. Dryden's translation.

27 Jerome, *Letter 123.16*, quoted in Brown, *A Biography*, p. 288.

28 Augustine, *Sermon 81. 8*, quoted in Lancel, *Augustine*, p. 392.

29 Augustine, *Sermon 105.11*, quoted in Brown, *A Biography*, p. 293. For the analogy with the olive press see p. 292.

30 Gerard O'Daly, *Augustine's City of God: A Reader's Guide* (Oxford University Press, 1999) Tertullian, *De Corona* 13, quoted on p. 54. See also p. 56.

31 R. A. Markus, *Saeculum: History and Society in the Theology of St Augustine* (Cambridge University Press, 1988) pp. 47–9 for details.

32 See *ibid.*, pp. 116–22.

33 O'Daly, *Augustine's City of God*, pp. 80–5 for a discussion of these points.

34 Markus, *Saeculum*, pp. xv–xvi for a discussion.

35 *Ibid.*, p. 103; see also pp. 83–4.

36 Malcolm Barber, *The Two Cities: Medieval Europe 1050–1320* (Routledge, 1992) pp. 1–2.

Chapter 5: Roads to Canossa

1 Eamon Duffy, *Saints and Sinners: A History of the Popes* (Yale University Press, revised edition, 2001) p. 14.

2   *Ibid.*, p. 60 for figures.
3   *Ibid.*, p. 78; Robert Eno, *The Rise of the Papacy* (Michael Glazier, 1990) pp. 44, 49, 51.
4   Duffy, *Saints and Sinners*, p. 23; Eno, *Rise of the Papacy*, p. 64.
5   *Ibid.*, p. 9.
6   Letters quoted in *ibid.*, pp. 94–5.
7   Walter Ullmann, *A Short History of the Papacy in the Middle Ages* (Methuen, 1972) pp. 20–1.
8   Eno, *Rise of the Papacy*, pp. 102–114; Duffy *Saints and Sinners*, pp. 44–5, 66.
9   Eno, *Rise of the Papacy*, p. 121.
10 *Ibid.*, p. 122.
11 Duffy, *Saints and Sinners*, p. 104.
12 H. E. J. Cowdrey, *Pope Gregory VII 1073–1085* (Clarendon Press, 1998) p. 685.
13 Duffy, *Saints and Sinners*, p. 110.
14 Gerd Tellenbach, *The Church in Western Europe from the Tenth to the Early Twelfth Century* (Cambridge University Press, 1993) pp. 86, 127.
15 *Ibid.*, pp. 76–7.
16 *Ibid.*, pp. 160–1.
17 *Ibid.*, p. 172.
18 Cowdrey, *Pope Gregory*, p. 697.
19 *Ibid.*, p. 537.
20 Quoted in *ibid.*, p. 539.
21 *Ibid.*, p. 508.
22 See *ibid.*, pp. 546–50.
23 *Ibid.*, p. 86.
24 *Ibid.*, p. 153.
25 *Ibid.*, pp. 80–153 for an excellent and detailed account of the events leading up to Canossa.
26 I. S. Robinson, *The Papacy 1073–1198: Continuity and Innovation* (Cambridge University Press, 1990) p. 407.
27 Quoted in *ibid.*, p. 406.
28 See Cowdrey, *Pope Gregory*, pp. 158–67 for his analysis of the meaning of Canossa.
29 Duffy, *Saints and Sinners*, p. 125.
30 *Ibid.*, pp. 127–8.
31 I. S. Robinson, *Authority and Resistance in the Investiture Contest: The Polemical Literature of the Late Eleventh Century* (Manchester University Press, 1978) p. 5.
32 F. Donald Logan, *A History of the Church in the Middle Ages* (Routledge, 2002) p. 112.

Chapter 6: Keepers of the Keys

1   See Helene Tillman, *Pope Innocent III* (North-Holland Publishing Company, 1980) p. 39.
2   I. S. Robinson, *The Papacy 1073–1198: Continuity and Innovation* (Cambridge University Press, 1990) pp. 306–7.
3   Bernard Hamilton, *Religion in the Medieval West* (Edward Arnold, 1986) p. 18.

4 Jane Sayers, *Innocent III: Leader of Europe 1198–1216* (Longman, 1994) p. 101.
5 *Ibid.*, pp. 101–10 for the details of the evolution of Canon law.
6 Walter Ullman, *The Growth of Papal Government in the Middle Ages: A Study in the Ideological Relation of Clerical to Lay Power* (Methuen, third revised edition, 1970) p. 444.
7 John of Salisbury, *Policraticus* IV, 3, quoted in *ibid.*, p. 422.
8 Quoted in Tillman, *Pope Innocent*, p. 51.
9 Sayers, *Innocent III*, p. 124.
10 Robinson, *Papacy*, p. 120.
11 Quoted in *ibid.*, p. 209.
12 *Ibid.*, p. 210.
13 *Ibid.*, pp. 211–18 for a discussion.
14 *Ibid.*, pp. 124–27.
15 For figures see Gerd Tellenbach, *The Church in Western Europe from the Tenth to the Early Twelfth Century* (Cambridge University Press, 1993), p. 67; Robinson, *Papacy*, p. 160.
16 *Ibid.*, pp. 146–78, quote on p. 170. For a detailed discussion of the work of legates see pp. 146–78.
17 Quoted in *ibid.*, p. 90.
18 Sayers, *Innocent III*, p. 87.
19 For a detailed description of the work of the cardinals and the departments of papal government see Robinson, *Papacy*, pp. 33–120.
20 Hamilton, *Religion in the Medieval West*, p. 22.
21 Ullmann, *Growth of Papal Government*, p. 139.
22 Eamon Duffy, *Saints and Sinners: A History of the Popes* (Yale University Press, revised edition, 2001), p. 144.
23 See Sayers, *Innocent III*, p. 135.
24 H. E. J. Cowdrey, *Pope Gregory VII 1073–1085* (Clarendon Press, 1998) p. 126.
25 Sayers, *Innocent III*, p. 55.
26 *Ibid.*, pp. 29–30 for the figures.
27 See Robinson, *Papacy*, p. 119 for the details.
28 See Cowdrey, *Pope Gregory*, pp. 375–398 for the details.
29 Ullmann, *Growth of Papal Government*, p. 249.
30 *Ibid.*, p. xiii.
31 See Sayers, *Innocent III*, pp. 92–3.
32 See Tellenbach, *Church in Western Europe*, p. 185.
33 Robinson, *Papacy*, pp. 367–97 for a detailed discussion of the relationship between the papacy and the Normans.
34 Ullmann, *Growth of Papal Government*, pp. 387–403 for the details.
35 John A. F. Thomson, *The Western Church in the Middle Ages* (Arnold, 1998) p. 96.
36 See Robinson, *Papacy*, pp. 486, 492.
37 Thomson, *Western Church*, p. 104.
38 Tellenbach, *Church in Western Europe*, pp. 218–19.
39 Joseph H. Lynch, *The Medieval Church: A Brief History* (Longman, 1992) p. 178.
40 See Steven Runciman, *The Eastern Schism: A Study of the Papacy and the Eastern Churches During the XIth and XIIth Centuries* (Oxford University Press, 1955).

41 Henry Chadwick, *East and West: The Making of a Rift in the Church: From Apostolic Times Until the Council of Florence* (Oxford University Press, 2003) especially chapters 32 to 35.

42 For details see Robinson, *Papacy*, pp. 325–6.

43 Duffy, *Saints and Sinners*, pp. 138, 136.

44 Jonathan Riley-Smith, *What Were the Crusades?* (Palgrave, second edition, 1992) p. 49.

45 Lynch, *Medieval Church*, p. 149.

46 Cowdrey, *Pope Gregory*, p. 518.

47 Robinson, *Papacy*, p. 205.

48 Quoted in *ibid.*, p. 206.

49 F. Donald Logan, *A History of the Church in the Middle Ages* (Routledge, 2002) pp. 113–14; Tellenbach, *Church in Western Europe*, p. 310.

50 Lynch, *Medieval Church*, p. 146.

51 Cowdrey, *Pope Gregory*, pp. 502–7.

52 *Ibid.*, p. 517.

53 *Ibid.*, p. 518.

54 Quoted in *ibid.*, p. 18.

55 *Ibid.*, pp. 105–6.

56 Brian Tierney, *The Crisis of Church and State 1050–1300* (Prentice-Hall Inc, 1964) pp. 47–8.

57 See Cowdrey, *Pope Gregory*, p. 514.

58 Tillman, *Pope Innocent*, pp. 21–2.

59 Robinson, *Papacy*, p. 403.

60 See *ibid.*, pp. 409–10.

61 *Ibid.*, p. 243.

62 See *ibid.*, pp. 226–7.

63 John C. Moore, *Pope Innocent III (1160/61–1216): To Root Up and to Plant* (Brill, 2003) p. 291.

64 *Ibid.*, p. 285.

Chapter 7: The Enthusiasts

1 Brenda Bolton, *The Medieval Reformation* (Edward Arnold, 1983) p. 39.

2 Giles Constable, *The Reformation of the Twelfth Century* (Cambridge University Press, 1996) p. 19.

3 Ludo J. R. Milis, *Angelic Monks and Earthly Men: Monasticism and its Meaning to Medieval Society* (The Boydell Press, 1992) pp. 11–13.

4 *Ibid.*, p. 127.

5 *Ibid.*, pp. 139–41; Lester K. Little, *Religious Poverty and the Profit Economy in Medieval Europe* (Paul Elek, 1978) p. 68.

6 *Ibid.*, p. 168; C. H. Lawrence, *Medieval Monasticism: Forms of the Religious Life in Western Europe in the Middle Ages* (Longman, third edition, 2001) pp. 69–70.

7 *Ibid.*, p. 66.

8 Milis, *Angelic Monks*, pp. 62–3, 144.

9 *Ibid.*, p. 142; see also Little, *Religious Poverty*, p. 198 for a similar argument.

10 *Ibid.*, p. 64.

11 The term is derived from the dismissal of the people at the conclusion of the Eucharist. In Latin this became *Ite missa est*, 'Go, you are dismissed'.
12 For details of Cluny see Lawrence, *Medieval Monasticism*, pp. 82–106; Little, *Religious Poverty*, pp. 62–4.
13 Bolton, *Medieval Reformation*, pp. 36–7.
14 Little, *Religious Poverty*, p. 70.
15 For details see Lawrence, *Medieval Monasticism*, pp. 149–156; Little, *Religious Poverty*, pp. 70–83.
16 Bolton, *Medieval Reformation*, p. 46.
17 Constable, *The Reformation*, pp. 53–4, 145.
18 *Ibid.*, pp. 77–9.
19 Lawrence, *Medieval Monasticism*, p. 176.
20 See Constable, *The Reformation*, pp. 212–14.
21 David H. Williams, *The Cistercians in the Early Middle Ages* (Gracewing, 1998) p. 81.
22 See Constable, *The Reformation*, pp. 190–4 for a discussion.
23 Williams, *Cistercians*, p. 62.
24 See Constable, *The Reformation*, pp. 118–21 for a discussion.
25 Figures in Williams, *Cistercians*, pp. 12–14; 21.
26 *Ibid.*, pp. 53–4.
27 See Bolton, *Medieval Reformation*, p. 48.
28 Lawrence, *Medieval Monasticism*, p. 183.
29 *Ibid.*, p. 174.
30 See Williams, *Cistercians*, p. 3.
31 *Ibid.*, p. 5.
32 Constable, *The Reformation*, p. 109.
33 Lawrence, *Medieval Monasticism*, p. 181.
34 Williams, *Cistercians*, p. 279.
35 Figures from *ibid.*, pp. 346; 358–9.
36 Figures from *ibid.*, p. 78.
37 See Constable, *The Reformation*, p. 31.
38 Milis, *Angelic Monks*, has twenty revolts 1168–1200; thirty revolts 1200–1300, pp. 33–4; Williams, *Cistercians*, has 123 revolts from 1190 to 1308, p. 59.
39 Lawrence, *Medieval Monasticism*, p. 105.
40 Figures from *ibid.*, p. 160; Little, *Religious Poverty*, p. 85.
41 Constable, *The Reformation*, p. 11 has found at least eight meanings in the Middle Ages.
42 For details see Little, *Religious Poverty*, pp. 99–101.
43 See Lawrence, *Medieval Monasticism*, pp. 160–1 for details.
44 *Ibid.*, p. 164.
45 For details see *ibid.*, pp. 166–8; Little, *Religious Poverty*, pp. 87–9.
46 Little, *Religious Poverty*, p. 99.
47 Figures from Malcolm Barber, *The Two Cities: Medieval Europe 1050–1320* (Routledge, 1992), pp. 22–3.
48 Little, *Religious Poverty*, p. 56.
49 See Milis, *Angelic Monks*, pp. 50–1 for a discussion of this point.

50 For discussions about possible origins see Malcolm Lambert, *Medieval Heresy: Popular Movements from the Gregorian Reform to the Reformation* (Blackwell, second edition, 1992) pp. 6, 7, 27–8, 36–7, 38, 42, 43, 78–9; R. I. Moore *The Origins of European Dissent* (University of Toronto Press, 1994) pp. 44–5, 59, 75–6, 77–8, 194–6, 267–8, 272.

51 Bolton, *Medieval Reformation*, p. 55.

52 See *ibid.*, p. 55; Little, *Religious Poverty*, pp. 125–7; Bernard Hamilton, *The Medieval Inquisition* (Edward Arnold, 1981) p. 23.

53 Lambert, *Medieval Heresy*, p. 62; see also p. 75.

54 *Ibid.*, p. 66.

55 Little, *Religious Poverty*, p. 131.

56 Lambert, *Medieval Heresy*, pp. 81–3.

57 *Ibid.*, p. 102.

58 See Little, *Religious Poverty*, pp. 113–19; Bolton, *Medieval Reformation*, pp. 63–6.

59 *Ibid.*, p. 98.

60 Hamilton, *Medieval Inquisition*, p. 57.

61 See *ibid.*, pp. 41–7 for details.

62 *Ibid.*, p. 58.

63 Moore, *Origins*, p. 222.

64 Hamilton, *Medieval Inquisition*, p. 65.

65 Lambert, *Medieval Heresy*, p. xi.

66 Little, *Religious Poverty*, p. 152.

67 Quoted in Bolton, *Medieval Reformation*, p. 67.

68 C. H. Lawrence, *The Friars: The Impact of the Early Mendicant Movement on Western Society* (Longman, 1994) p. 225.

69 See *ibid.*, p. 157 for a discussion of this point.

70 See *ibid.*, pp. 26–9 for a discussion.

71 *Ibid.*, p. 29.

72 Bolton, *Medieval Reformation*, p. 73.

73 The Liberal Arts were in two groups, the elementary *trivium* (grammar, rhetoric and dialectic) and the more advanced *quadrivium* (music, artithmetic, geometry and astronomy).

74 Steven Ozment, *The Age of Reform 1250–1550: An Intellectual and Religious History of Late Medieval and Reformation Europe* (Yale University Press, 1980) p. 51.

75 Bolton, *Medieval Reformation*, p. 47.

76 Lawrence, *Friars*, p. 82.

77 *Ibid.*, p. 136.

78 *Ibid.*, p. 87.

79 Simon Tugwell OP, *Saint Dominic and the Order of Preachers* (Dominican Publications, 2001) p. 44.

80 Quoted in *ibid.*, p. 45.

81 Quoted in Little, *Religious Poverty*, p. 218.

82 Figures from *ibid.*, p. 185.

83 Quoted in *ibid.*, p. 184.

84 See *ibid.*, pp. 190–2 for details of these works.

85 Quoted in *ibid.*, p. 190.

86 *Ibid.*, p. 190.

87 See for example *ibid.*, p. 196.

88 For a detailed discussion of these points see *ibid.*, pp. 176–83.

Chapter 8: Reformations

1 See Francis Oakley, *The Western Church in the Later Middle Ages* (Cornell University Press, 1979) pp. 38–55.

2 Patrick Collinson, *The Reformation* (Weidenfeld and Nicolson, 2003) p. 94.

3 Malcolm Lambert, *Medieval Heresy: Popular Movements from the Gregorian Reform to the Reformation* (Blackwell, second edition, 1992) p. 266.

4 *Ibid.*, p. 268.

5 *Ibid.*, p. 285.

6 *Ibid.*, p. 308.

7 *Ibid.*, p. 347.

8 Robert Bireley, *The Refashioning of Catholicism 1450–1700: A Reassessment of the Counter Reformation* (Macmillan, 1999) p. 26.

9 Jean Delumeau, *Catholicism Between Luther and Voltaire: A New View of the Counter-Reformation* (Burns and Oates) p. 2.

10 Steven Ozment, *The Age of Reform 1250–1550: An Intellectual and Religious History of Late Medieval and Reformation Europe* (Yale University Press, 1980), p. 49.

11 *Ibid.*, p. 55.

12 For a detailed discussion see *ibid.*, pp. 22–63.

13 For a detailed discussion see *ibid.*, pp. 9–21.

14 Anthony Levi, *Renaissance and Reformation; The Intellectual Genesis* (Yale University Press, 2002) pp. 102–3, 262.

15 Diarmaid MacCulloch, *Reformation: Europe's House Divided 1490–1700* (Allen Lane, 2003) p. 78.

16 Levi, *Renaissance and Reformation*, p. 127.

17 *Ibid.*, p. 99.

18 Palmieri, *Della Vita Civile*, quoted in Denys Hay, *The Renaissance in its Historical Background* (Cambridge University Press, second edition, 1976) p. 12.

19 Quoted in G. R. Elton (ed.), *Renaissance and Reformation 1300–1648* (Macmillan, third edition, 1976) p. 57.

20 Levi, *Renaissance and Reformation*, p. 86.

21 *Ibid.*, p. 117.

22 *Ibid.*, pp. 154–7.

23 *Ibid.*, pp. 124–5.

24 Ozment, *Age of Reform*, p. 223.

25 See *ibid.*, pp. 223–31 for a discussion.

26 Richard Marius, *Martin Luther: The Christian Between God and Death* (Harvard University Press, 1999) p. xiv.

27 *Ibid.*, p. xii.

28 Collinson, *The Reformation*, p. ix.

29 Quoted in Steven Ozment, *The Reformation in the Cities: The Appeal of Protestantism to Sixteenth-Century Germany and Switzerland* (Yale University Press, 1975) p. 70.

30 Quoted in Hubert Jedin and John Dolan (eds), *History of the Church Vol. V:*

Reformation and Counter Reformation by Erwin Iserloh, Joseph Glazik and Hubert Jedin (Burns and Oates, 1980) p. 35.

31 See Michael A. Mullett, *The Catholic Reformation* (Routledge, 1999) p. 43.

32 John Bossy, *Christianity in the West 1400–1700* (Oxford University Press, 1985) p. 94.

33 Collinson, *The Reformation*, p. 49; a more substantial analysis of the main points of Reformation theology can be found in James D. Tracy, *Europe's Reformations 1450–1650* (Rowman and Littlefield Publishers Inc., 1999) pp. 13–29.

34 See Collinson, *The Reformation*, pp. 86–7.

35 Mullett, *The Catholic Reformation*, pp. 185–6.

36 MacCulloch, *Europe's House Divided*, p. 669.

Chapter 9: Diversity Becomes Division

1   Michael A. Mullett, *The Catholic Reformation* (Routledge, 1999) p. 188.

2   For a discussion of this see R. Po-Chia Hsia, *The World of Catholic Renewal 1540–1770* (Cambridge University Press, 1998) pp. 75–6.

3   Anthony Levi, *Renaissance and Reformation; The Intellectual Genesis* (Yale University Press, 2002) p. 303.

4   Diarmaid MacCulloch, *Reformation: Europe's House Divided 1490–1700* (Allen Lane, 2003) p. 452.

5   *Ibid.*, p. 470.

6   Robert Bireley, *The Refashioning of Catholicism 1450–1700: A Reassessment of the Counter Reformation* (Macmillan, 1999) pp. 91–4.

7   Hsia, *World of Catholic Renewal*, p. 77.

8   MacCulloch, *Europe's House Divided*, p. 61.

9   Bireley, *Refashioning of Catholicism*, pp. 115–18.

10 Steven Ozment, *The Reformation in the Cities: The Appeal of Protestantism to Sixteenth-Century Germany and Switzerland* (Yale University Press, 1975) p. 1.

11 *Ibid.*, pp. 42–3.

12 *Ibid.*, p. 44.

13 *Ibid.*, pp. 44–5.

14 Patrick Collinson, *The Reformation* (Weidenfeld and Nicolson, 2003) p. 107.

15 J. J. Scarisbrick, *The Reformation and the English People* (Basil Blackwell, 1984) p. 1.

16 *Ibid.*, p. 1.

17 Eamon Duffy, *The Stripping of the Altars: Traditional Religion in England c1400–c1580* (Yale University Press, 1992) pp. 2, 4.

18 Christopher Haigh, *English Reformations: Religion, Politics and Society under the Tudors* (Clarendon Press, 1993) p. 12.

19 *Ibid.*, p. 13.

20 *Ibid.*, p. 14.

21 *Ibid.*, p. 16.

22 *Ibid.*, p. 21.

23 *Ibid.*, p. 290.

24 *Ibid.*, p. 294.

25 See Christopher Haigh 'Anticlericalism and the English Reformation' in *History*, October, 1983.

26 See the 'Reviews' section of the Amazon website for comments on Duffy's *Stripping of the Altars*.

27 James D. Tracy, *Europe's Reformations 1450–1650* (Rowman and Littlefield Publishers Inc., 1999) pp. 3, 5, 7.

28 Malcolm Lambert, *Medieval Heresy: Popular Movements from the Gregorian Reform to the Reformation* (Blackwell, second edition, 1992) pp. 390–1.

29 *Ibid.*, p. 380.

30 *Ibid.*, p. 380.

31 *Ibid.*, p. 373.

32 *Ibid.*, p. 381.

33 Joseph F. Kelly, *The World of the Early Christians* (The Liturgical Press, 1997) pp. 183–4.

34 See Gerhart B. Ladner, *The Idea of Reform: Its Impact on Christian Thought and Action in the Age of the Fathers* (Harvard University Press, 1959) p. 34.

35 Mullett, *Catholic Reformation*, pp. 7, 1; see especially pp. 1–8 for a discussion.

36 *Analysis of the Council of Trent 1565–73*, quoted in Mullett, *Catholic Reformation*, p. 40.

37 Collinson, *The Reformation*, p. 23.

38 Mullett, *Catholic Reformation*, p. 68.

39 Bireley, *Refashioning of Catholicism*, p. 49.

40 Mullett, *Catholic Reformation*, p. 65.

41 Jean Delumeau, *Catholicism Between Luther and Voltaire: A New View of the Counter-Reformation* (Burns and Oates) p. 31.

42 Mullett, *Catholic Reformation*, pp. 157, 183.

43 MacCulloch, *Europe's House Divided*, p. 414.

44 Figures from Mullett, *Catholic Reformation*, pp. 90–1, 95.

45 Hsia, *World of Catholic Renewal*, pp. 125–6.

46 Figures from Mullett, *Catholic Reformation*, pp. 105–6.

47 See Hsia, *World of Catholic Renewal*, p. 30.

48 See Mullett, *Catholic Reformation*, pp. 70–4 for details.

49 *Ibid.*, p. 107; Bireley, *Refashioning of Catholicism*, pp. 133–4.

50 Hsia, *World of Catholic Renewal*, p. 36.

51 Quoted in Levi, *Renaissance and Reformation*, p. 252.

52 *Ibid.*, p. 364; see also pp. 191–2, 201–2.

53 Euan Cameron, *The European Reformation* (Oxford University Press, 1991) p. 181.

54 For a discussion of these points see John Stephens, *The Italian Renaissance: The Origins of Intellectual and Artistic Change Before the Reformation* (Longman, 1990) chapter 15, pp. 202–24.

55 Levi, *Renaissance and Reformation*, pp. 247–8.

56 Ozment, *Reformation in the Cities*, p. 90. Wolfaria is described on pp. 90–108.

57 Peter Matheson, 'Humanism and Reform' in Anthony Goodman and Angus MacKay (eds) *The Impact of Humanism on Western Europe* (Longman, 1990) pp. 23–42.

58 Mullett, *Catholic Reformation*, p. 113.

59 Richard Marius, *Martin Luther: The Christian Between God and Death* (Harvard University Press, 1999) pp. 458–9.

60 *Ibid.*, p. 468.
61 Steven Ozment, *The Age of Reform 1250–1550: An Intellectual and Religious History of Late Medieval and Reformation Europe* (Yale University Press, 1980) pp. 305, 316.
62 Quoted in Elizabeth L. Eisenstein, *The Printing Press as an Agent of Change: Communications and Cultural Transformations in Early Modern Europe* (Cambridge University Press, 1979) p. 304.
63 *Ibid.*, p. 303.
64 MacCulloch, *Europe's House Divided*, p. 73.
65 Eisenstein, *The Printing Press*, p. 338.
66 Bireley, *Refashioning of Catholicism*, p. 135.
67 Eisenstein, *The Printing Press*, p. 366.
68 Delumeau, *Catholicism*, pp. xi, 1.
69 Tracy, *Europe's Reformations*, p. 270.
70 See MacCulloch, *Europe's House Divided*, p. 602.
71 Bireley, *Refashioning of Catholicism*, p. 176.
72 *Ibid.*, pp. 178–80.
73 See *ibid.*, p. 164.
74 See *ibid.*, pp. 155–7 for a detailed discussion.
75 Mullett, *Catholic Reformation*, p. 80.
76 *Ibid.*, p. 80.
77 Quoted in MacCulloch, *Europe's House Divided*, p. 111.
78 Hubert Jedin and John Dolan (eds), *History of the Church Vol. V: Reformation and Counter Reformation* by Erwin Iserloh, Joseph Glazik and Hubert Jedin (Burns and Oates, 1980) p. 39.

Chapter 10: Divine Winds and Interest Rates

1 Quoted in Frank Tallett, *War and Society in Early Modern Europe 1495–1715* (Routledge, 1992) p. 16.
2 C. V. Wedgwood, *The Thirty Years War* (Jonathan Cape, 1964) p. 301.
3 Richard Marius, *Martin Luther: The Christian Between God and Death* (Harvard University Press, 1999) p. 456.
4 Diarmaid MacCulloch, *Reformation: Europe's House Divided 1490–1700* (Allen Lane, 2003) p. 671.
5 Robert Bireley, *The Refashioning of Catholicism 1450–1700: A Reassessment of the Counter Reformation* (Macmillan, 1999) p. 71.
6 James D. Tracy, *Europe's Reformations 1450–1650* (Rowman and Littlefield Publishers Inc., 1999) p. 146.
7 Tallett, *War and Society*, p. 15.
8 See Geoffrey Parker, *The Military Revolution: Military Innovation and the Rise of the West 1500–1800* (Cambridge University Press, second edition, 1996) pp. 1–2 for a discussion.
9 See *ibid.*, p. 9; J. R. Hale, *War and Society in Renaissance Europe 1450–1620* (Fontana, 1985) p. 48.
10 Parker, *Military Revolution*, pp. 23–4.
11 Tallett, *War and Society*, p. 76.
12 *Ibid.*, p. 89.

13 *Ibid.*, p. 55.
14 Parker, *Military Revolution*, p. 63.
15 *Ibid.*, p. 49.
16 *Ibid.*, p. 49.
17 *Ibid.*, p. 60.
18 *Ibid.*, pp. 50–1.
19 *Ibid.*, p. 65.
20 Tallett, *War and Society*, p. 76.
21 Hale, *War and Society in Renaissance Europe*, p. 179.
22 Tallett, *War and Society*, p. 232.
23 Figures from *ibid.*, p. 161.
24 Quoted in *ibid.*, p. 205.
25 Geoffrey Parker, *The Thirty Years' War* (Routledge and Kegan Paul, 1984) p. 219.

Epilogue: Loss and Gain

1 See George Herring, *What Was the Oxford Movement?* (Continuum, 2002) especially pp. 20–2.
2 Figures from Kenneth L. Woodward, 'Christianity's Newest Converts' in *2002 Britannica Book of the Year* (Encyclopaedia Britannica, 2002) p. 306.
3 Timothy Radcliffe OP, *What is the Point of Being a Christian?* (Continuum, 2005) p. 3.
4 For an interesting collection of essays on the significance of this movie see Glenn Yeffeth (ed.), *Taking the Red Pill: Science, Philosophy and Religion in the Matrix* (Summersdale Publications Ltd, 2003).
5 See Carl Sagan, *Contact: A Novel* (Century Hutchinson, 1986).

INDEX

Aachen, Council of 192
Abelard, Peter 152, 157, 213–14
Abraham 10
Adam 115, 117
Adhemar, Bishop of Le Puy 156
Aelred of Rievaulx 185
agape 14, 98–9
Alaric 118
Albigensian Crusades 203–4
Albigensians 200
Alexander of Alexandria 58
Alexander the Great 32, 33
Alexander VI (pope) 232
Alexis, St 197
Alexius (Byzantine emperor) 169
Alva, Duke of 298
Alypius 108–10
Ambrose, Bishop of Milan 64, 73–4, 108,
    110, 112, 120
America 283–4, 314
Anabaptists 226, 247–8
Anastasius 135
Anglican Church 226
Anonymous of York, the 163
Anselm 213, 214, 311
anti-popes 159
anti-war movements 167–8, 169, 181
Antony of Egypt 68, 207
    Augustine and 109
    charisma 80
    education 76
    letters 76–8
    Life of Antony 74, 75–7, 81, 109, 322–3
Apocalypse 26, 34
apocryphal writings 35
Apollinarius 88, 96, 97, 98, 197
apostasy 27, 56
    re-admittance 56, 81

Apostles' Creed 244
apostolic succession 25, 131, 134, 135, 154,
    173
Aquinas, Thomas 214–15, 216, 233–4
    Summa Theologiae 214, 285, 330–1
Arabic texts 212–13, 234
Aragon 238, 260
    Catherine of 256
architecture
    abbeys 180, 186
    church buildings 54–5
    Cistercian 186
    Dominican 218–19
Arians 62, 76, 77, 90, 95, 98, 133
Aristotle 13, 212, 213, 219, 233
Aristotlean philosophy 13, 214, 219, 230,
    233
Arius 58, 60, 77, 83, 103, 197
art
    in churches 244
    Giotto 202
    'graven images' 244
    portrayals of Jesus 244
    Renaissance painters 283
    Zwingli on 244
asceticism 69, 71, 72, 76, 80, 82–4, 102,
    179, 194
    Athanasius on 82–3
    Stoicism 71
    see also monasticism; sexual renunciation;
        virginity
Athanasius 36, 61–2, 68, 72, 79, 81, 101
    on asceticism 82–4
    christology 93, 95–7
    Life of Antony 74, 75–7, 81, 109, 322–3
    On the Incarnation 95–6, 323–4
    on virginity 83
atheism 8

Augsburg
  Confession of 272
  Diet of 254
  Peace of 257, 297
Augustine of Hippo 57, 106–25, 163, 214,
    291–2
  on Adam 115
  baptism 110
  on the Church 113–14
  The City of God 119–23, 325
  Confessions 110–11, 115, 324
  controversies 111–17
  conversion to Christianity 109–10
  doctrine of grace 112, 115–16, 117, 291
  Donatism and 112–15, 121
  heresy 116
  just wars 168
  Luther and 241, 242
  Manicheaeism 107, 108, 111–12, 113
  monasticism and 109, 122
  Pelagians and 115–17
  Platonism and 108, 112, 122, 214
  on predestination 116–17, 242
  Rule of St Augustine 193, 202, 216
  sack of Rome and 118–19, 121
  on the two loves 119–23, 325
Aurispa, Giovanni 235
authority
  leadership 22–38
  Luther on 242–3
  the New Testament 31–8, 245
  papal 134, 173, 228, 229
  scriptural 242–3, 256–7, 280, 286–7
Averoes 212
Avicenna 212
Avignon papacy 228, 238

banking 195, 253
  see also money-lending
baptism 3–4, 6, 15, 28, 88, 115
  Anabaptists 226, 247–8
  of Jesus Christ 2, 68
  Luther on 243
  re-baptism 31, 56, 226
Barnabas 9
Barnabites 278
Basel, Council of 270
Basil of Caesarea 6, 82, 102
Bassio, Matteo di 278
Bavaria
  Dukes of 304–5
  House of Wittelsbach 254, 257, 258
Baynes, Norman 64
Becket, Thomas 156
begging 178, 179, 197, 203
  Dominicans 211

Franciscans 208
  mendicant friars 179, 212, 216, 217
Beguines 199
Benedict of Aniane 180
  Rule of St Benedict 81, 180, 181, 183,
    184, 185, 186, 191, 193, 202, 269,
    328–9
Benedict XVI (pope) 123
Benedictines 185, 209
Benzo, Bishop of Alba 163
Bernadino of Sienna 270
Bernadone, Francesco *see* Francis of Assisi
Bernard of Caux 204
Bernard of Clairvaux 188–9, 190, 213–14,
    329
Bernard of Pavia 152
Bernard of Toledo 155
Bernini, Gian Lorenzo 280, 284, 290
Beza, Theodore 245
Bible 313
  biblical scholarship 286–7
  censorship 286
  concordance 218
  Erasmus's translation 280–1, 286
  Latin Vulgate 280, 281, 286
  Polyglot Bible 287
  radical interpretations 288
  reading and study 230, 287–8
  vernacular translations 230, 286, 287–8
  see also New Testament
Bireley, Robert 296
bishops 23, 24–5, 31, 38, 63, 64–5, 100
  Calvin on 245
  Cistercians 190
  Council of Trent and 273–4
  election 173, 192
  feudal system and 138
  kings and 164
  lay investiture 142, 173
  marriage 140
  papacy and 160–1
bishops of Rome 129, 133, 134, 135, 136
  see also papacy
Black Death 227, 233, 237, 248
Bogomils 200
Bolton, Brenda 183, 211, 215
Bonaventure 210
Boniface III (pope) 228
Bonner, Gerald 116, 117
Book of Common Prayer 263
Book of Mormon 38
Borromeo, Charles 291
Borromini, Francesco 284
Brethren of the Common Life 233, 276
Briconnet, Guillaume 271
Brown, Peter 72, 74, 104

Bruni, Leonardo 236–7
Bruno of Cologne 191
Bucer, Martin 245, 251
buildings *see* architecture
Bunaby, John 116–17
Burckhardt, Jacob 63–4
Byzantines 165–7
Byzantium 54, 162, 235

Caecilian, Bishop of Carthage 56, 57
Caesaropapism 64
Cajetan, Thomas de Vito 246
Calixtus II (pope) 187
Calvin, John 117, 226, 244–5, 248, 262,
    283, 284
    Ecclesiastical Ordinances 245
    exile 255–6
    Institutes of the Christian Religion 244, 285
Calvinism 255–6, 258, 298
    the Consistory 245
    the Eucharist 245
    Huguenots 299, 300, 303, 304, 309
    predestination 244–5
    St Bartholomew's Day Massacre 299, 303,
    304
    Synods 299
    Waldensians and 267–8
Cameron, Averil 17
Canon law 152–3, 168, 172
    just wars 168
canonization 158, 275
canons 192
    White Canons 193
    see also regular canons
Canons of Chalcedon 175
Canterbury 178
Capuchins 278
cardinals 154, 156–7
    papal elections 157
Carmelites 279–80
Carthage
    Council of 29
    schism at 56–7
Carthusians 191, 192
    Charterhouses 191
    conversi 191
    diet 191
    numbers of foundations 191
    Rule 191
    silence 191
Cassian, John 74, 117
Castile 238, 260
catechism classes 290
Cathars 199–201, 207, 211
    Albigensian Crusades 203–4
    consolamentum 200, 204

dualism 200
    Inquisition and 204, 205–6
    support for 200–1, 205
Catherine of Aragon 256
catholic
    meaning 57
Catholic Reformation 225, 227, 257,
    266–80, 288
    aims of 289–90
    education 289–90
    similarities with Protestant Reformation
    289–93
    see also Trent, Council of
catholicity 57, 113
Catullus 33
Celestine V (pope) 228
celibacy 83, 139–40, 192, 274, 289
    Cathars 200
    lay spirituality 199
    see also sexual renunciation
Chadwick, Henry 4, 167
Chalcedon
    Canons of 175
    Council of 93, 99, 100, 132, 139, 174
Chalcedonian Definition 86, 89, 93, 99,
    102, 103, 104, 133, 324
charisma
    monasticism and 80
charismatic leadership 26–7
Charlemagne 137, 180, 252
Charles the Bold, Duke of Burgundy 252
Charles V (Holy Roman Emperor) 247,
    252–8, 291, 297, 298, 302, 306
Charles VIII (King of France) 301
Charterhouses 191
Chemnitz, Martin 272
Chitty, Derwas 74
Christian charity 6, 21, 320
Christmas crib 207
christology 58, 86–104
    Antiochene 95
    of Apollinarius 88, 96, 97, 98
    of Athanasius 93, 95–7
    birth of Jesus 98–9
    Chalcedonian Definition 86, 89, 93, 99,
    102, 103, 104, 133, 324
    of Cyril of Alexandria 93, 95, 98–9,
    100–1, 103, 104
    divinity of Jesus 83, 87–104
    Hellenism and 90–9, 101
    humanity of Jesus 14, 87–104, 207
    hypostasis 93, 99, 103
    incarnation, doctrine of 71–2, 83
    Jesus as Son of God 87, 90, 91, 94, 95, 96,
    97, 98, 99
    Jesus as Son of Man 87, 95, 97, 98

language, problems of 89–90, 101–2
Logos 11, 72, 91–2, 94–9, 108
logos spermatikos 11, 214
Logos-anthropos 92, 94, 95
Logos-sarx 92, 94, 95, 96
Mary, mother of Jesus and 97–9
Monophysitism 99, 100, 104
of Nestorius 93, 95, 98, 99, 100–1, 103, 104
of Origen 87, 90, 97
ousia 92, 93, 99
physis 93, 99
prosopon/prosopa 93, 98, 99
Stoicism and 91, 93, 96
Tome of Leo 99, 100
Chrysostom, John 73, 101
church architecture *see* architecture
Cicero 8, 10, 107, 108, 235
Ciompi, the 227
circumcision 21
Cistercians 184–91, 192, 193, 201, 269
annual visitation 187
Bernard of Clairvaux 188–9, 190, 329
bishops 190
Carta Caritatis 187
Cathars and 203, 211
churches 186
constitution 187
conversi 184–5, 190, 193
criticisms 190
Definitors 215
feudalism and 189, 190
foundation 184
General Chapter 187, 193, 215
Granges 189
habits 185–6, 193
lay brothers 185
manual labour 185
number of monks 188
organization of Order 187
revolts 190
Rule of St Benedict 184, 185
sign language 186
silence 186
size of Order 187–8
social inclusiveness 185, 188
textiles 189
Waldensians and 198
wilderness 186–7, 190
Clement of Alexandria 12, 25, 31, 36, 37, 71–2, 77, 90, 120, 135
Clement III (anti-pope) 159
Clerks Regular of St Paul 278
Clermont, Council of 169
Cloud of Unknowing 232
Clovis 133

Cluniacs 182–3
Cluny Abbey 175, 182–3, 186, 190
liturgy 183
see also Cistercians
coins 195
Coligny, Gaspard II de 303
Collinson, Patrick 229, 241, 243, 264, 272
Collivaccinus, Peter Benventanus 152
common ownership of property 172
community 1, 2–6, 14
Conciliarism 229, 256, 270
confession
annual 218
hearing 218
public 6
Confession of Augsburg 272
Congregation of the Daughters of Charity 279
Congregation of the Oratory (Oratorians) 271, 278
Constance, Council of 229, 231
Constantine 7, 50–65, 100, 120
Donation of Constantine 236
vision and dream 51, 52, 321
Constantinius 48, 49–50
Constantinople 54
capture of 228
Council of 60, 100, 101, 132, 133, 155, 173
Councils of 60, 100, 101, 132, 133, 155, 173
consubstantiation 244
Contact 316
Contarini, Gasparo, Cardinal 251, 271, 291
conversions 19–20, 53
Councils 31, 59–60, 61, 163, 270
Aachen 192
authority 229
Basel 270
Carthage 29
Chalcedon 93, 99, 100, 132, 139, 174
Clermont 169
Conciliarism and 229, 256, 270
Constance 229, 231
Constantinople 60, 100, 101, 132, 133, 155, 173
Egypt 58
Ephesus 98, 100
Fifth Lateran 270, 286
Florence 38, 235, 270
Fourth Lateran 155, 187, 218, 270, 272, 274
Nicaea 47, 60, 61, 79, 86, 92, 100, 155, 272
papacy and 155–6
Piacenza 169

Pisa 229
Third Lateran 157, 159, 198
Trent *see* Trent, Council of
Counter Reformation 257
Cowdrey, H. E. J. 146, 159, 171
creation 1, 13
credit 195
Creeds
Apostles' Creed 244
Nicene Creed 60, 86, 92, 103, 166–7, 322
crucifixion 13, 71, 72
Crusades 156, 159, 160, 165–71, 197, 228, 261
Albigensian Crusades 203–4
First Crusade 169–70, 184, 200–1, 326–7
Fourth Crusade 159, 170
Richard I and 160
Second Crusade 170
Third Crusades 170
Curia Regis 156
Cynics 10
Cyprian of Carthage 28, 31, 56, 112, 134, 171
Cyril of Alexandria 93, 95, 98–9, 100–1, 103, 104
Cyril of Jerusalem 57

Damian, Peter 140, 156, 172, 197
The Common Life of Canons 192
Dead Sea Scrolls 30, 79
Decian persecution 27, 28, 68
Decius 19
Delumeau, Jean 289
Descartes, René 312
desert 68, 72, 74–8, 80, 183–4, 186–7, 188
Devotio Moderna 232–3, 276, 281, 291
Dickens, A. G. 264
Dictatus Papae 171–2, 327–8
Didache 27, 36
Diego of Osma, Bishop 211
Diets
Augsburg 254
Regensburg 255, 292
Speyer 254
Worms 247
Diocletian 19, 27, 48, 49, 50, 69, 113
Diodore, Bishop of Tarsus 98
Dionysius of Alexandria 21, 320
Diosculus of Alexandria 101
Dissenting communities 226
divorce 5
Docetism 31, 88, 90
Dominic 211, 214
Dominicans 179, 206, 211–12, 214–15, 277
Biblical Concordance 218
charging for goods or labour 219–20

churches 218–19
exempla 218
female Orders 279
financial issues 219–20
General Chapter 215
grades of preachers 217
lay penitents 220
manuals 218
money-lending 219, 220
organization 215–16
prayer 217
preaching 215–16, 217–18
priories 215, 216
purpose 215, 217
Rule of St Augustine 216
Savonarola 271
Scholasticism 214, 218, 219
schools 216
Second Orders 279
study 216, 217
Third Orders 220
visitations 215
Donation of Constantine 236
Donatism 56–7, 81, 120, 198, 230
Augustine and 112–15, 121
Donatus 56
dualism 73, 107
Cathars 200
Gnostics 70, 73
Manicheaens 70, 73, 112, 200
Duffy, Eamon 137, 147–8, 158, 170, 264–5, 266
Durand de Huesca 203

Eberlin, Johann 283
Eck, Johann 246, 253
Eckhart, Meister 232
Ecumenical Councils *see* Councils
Ecumenism 240, 314
Edict of Milan 53
Edict of Nantes 300, 309
education 195–6, 311
catechism classes 290
Catholic Reformation 289–90
Dominican schools 216
Humane Studies 237
Jesuits and 277–8
lay education 289–90
Liberal Arts 213, 216, 236
new curriculum 236–7
Protestant Reformation 289–90
religious instruction in schools 313–14
Renaissance and 212–13, 234–7
seminaries 274, 289
training of clergy 261, 274, 289
Ursulines 279

see also Scholasticism; universities
Edward VI (King of England) 263
Eisenstein, Elizabeth L. 285, 286, 287
ekklesia 3, 28
Eleutherus 25
Elizabeth I (Queen of England) 263, 264
English Reformation 263–6
Enlightenment 311–13
Ephesus, Council of 98, 100
epidemics 21
episkopoi 23–5, 27
Erasmus 237, 271, 280, 311
    on free will 284
    on grace 284
    on Justification 284
    Luther and 281, 284
    on predestination 284
    translation of the Bible 280–1, 286
    works by 280–1, 282
Erikson, Erik 240
Eucharist 4–5, 6, 10, 25, 28, 31, 87–8, 102,
        183, 319–20
    Calvinism and 245, 290
    consubstantiation 244
    Council of Trent and 273
    lay participation 273, 290
    Luther on 243, 244
    real physical presence of Christ 244
    Reformation and 290
    ritual purity and 140
    spiritual presence of Christ 244
    transubstantiation 230
    unleavened bread 167
    Zwingli on 244
Eugenius III (pope) 154, 190
European Values Study 315
Eusebius 12, 36, 48, 51, 52, 64, 118, 119,
        163, 320, 321
Eutyches 99, 100, 197
evil 112
exorcisms 3, 20, 80
exposure of newborns 6

Fall, the 115, 117, 243, 284
Farel, Guillaume 242
Ferdinand (King of Castile and Aragon) 238,
        260–1
feudalism 137–41, 151, 179, 195, 220, 301
    Cistercians and 189, 190
    end of 227, 237, 238
Ficino, Marsilio 237
First World War 314
Fisher, John 271
Flavian of Constantinople 99, 101
Florence, Council of 38, 235, 270
Fontevrault Abbey 184

forgiveness
    authority to forgive 6
    necessity for 6
Foxe, John 267, 288
Francis of Assisi 202, 206–11, 270, 276
    character of 209–10, 211
    death 209
    Innocent III and 202, 208, 209
    problems for biographers 210
    stigmata 209–10, 280, 329–30
    The Canticle of the Sun 209
Francis de Sales 290
Francis I (King of France) 254, 255, 256, 259
Francis Xavier 275, 290
Franciscans 178, 179, 206–11, 216, 267
    Bernadino of Sienna 270–1
    Capuchins 278
    churches 218
    clerical approval 208–9
    female Orders 279
    lay penitents 220
    Little Flowers of St Francis 211
    ordination 210
    papal approval 208
    Second Orders 279
    Spirituals 210–11
    Third Orders 220
Frederick (Elector of Palatine) 300
Frederick I Barbarossa (King of Germany)
        164, 165, 179, 261
Frederick II (Holy Roman Emperor) 170
Frederick the Wise (Elector of Saxony) 247,
        253, 258
Free Imperial Cities 254, 262
Free Imperial Knights 254
free will 284, 316
    see also predestination
Frend, W. H. C. 17, 18
friars 206–20, 269, 276
    begging 208, 211, 212
    Capuchins 278
    itinerant preaching 208, 211
    mendicant friars 179, 212, 216, 217
    see also Dominicans; Franciscans
Fuggers banking house 253

Galerius 48, 49, 50
Gattaca 316
Gebhard of Constance 155
Gelasius I (pope) 135
    theory of the two swords 135, 325
Germany
    Free Imperial Cities 254, 262
    Protestant Reformation 262–3
Gibbon, Edward 17
Gilson, Etienne 234

Giotto 202
Gnosticism 30–1, 37, 79, 80, 81, 315
Gnostics
  dualism 70, 73
'God-fearers' 21
Goehring, James E. 78
Gorze Abbey 182
Gospels 34, 35
  John 34, 35, 91–2, 103, 131
  Luke 34, 37
  Mark 34, 37
  Matthew 34, 73
  Synoptic 34, 35
  Thomas 35, 37
grace 111, 135, 271
  Augustine and 112, 115–16, 117, 291
  Erasmus and 284
  justifying faith and 242
  Luther and 242, 243
  Paul and 112
Gratian of Bologna 152
Great Schism 228–9, 238
Greeks 11–14
  see also Hellenism; philosophy
Gregory I (pope) 134, 135
Gregory IX (pope) 152, 204, 210
Gregory of Nazianzus 36, 87, 90, 93, 97, 103
Gregory of Nyssa 73, 93
Gregory VI (pope) 172
Gregory VII (pope) 129–30, 141–8, 150–75, 266, 274
  absolution of Henry IV 130, 145–8
  Crusades and 166–7
  Dictatus Papae 171–2, 327–8
  excommunication of Henry IV 129, 144, 162, 326
  lay investiture 142, 173
  papal protection 175
  tradition and custom 171
  see also papacy
Gregory VII (pope) 129–30, 141–8, 154
Gregory ('wonder-worker') 20
Grillmeier, Aloys 95, 103
Groote, Gerard 233
Guigues du Pin 191
Gustavus Adolphus (King of Sweden) 295–6, 300, 303, 306
Gutenberg, Johannes 285
Guy of Evreux 217

Habsburg-Valois conflict 252–8, 292–3, 296, 297–9, 304, 305, 309
Haigh, Christopher 264, 265, 266
Hale, J. R. 308
Hamilton, Bernard 157

Harnack, Adolph von 16
Haskins, Charles Homer 212
Helena (mother of Constantine) 48, 54, 55
Hellenism
  Christianity and 11–15, 214, 317
  christology and 90–9, 101
Henry II (King of England) 156
Henry II (King of France) 299
Henry III (Holy Roman Emperor) 140, 142
Henry III (King of France) 300
Henry IV (Holy Roman Emperor) 129–30, 142–8, 159, 164
  absolution 145–8
  Crusades and 166
  excommunication 129, 144, 162, 326
Henry IV (King of France) 258–9, 300, 304, 305
Henry of Navarre 299, 300
Henry VI (Emperor of Germany) 160, 163
Henry VIII (King of England) 238, 256, 263, 264, 282–3, 293
Heraclitus 91
hereditary churches 140
heresy 28–31, 58, 70, 98, 133, 153, 271
  Albigensians 200
  Augustine and 116
  the Inquisition 204–5, 238, 260, 261
  Lollards 230–1, 264, 267, 268, 287
  papal condemnation of 1184 198, 199, 201, 202
  protest movements and 197
  reform and 267
  schism as 114
  Wyclif 230, 231, 233
  see also Cathars; Gnosticism; Waldensians
Hermas 29, 36
hermits 80, 183–4, 186, 191, 193, 278
Herodian 16
Herodotus 33
hierarchy 23–4, 26
Hilary of Poitiers 120
Hildebrand 140, 141, 143
  see also Gregory VII
Hilton, Walter 232
Hippolytus 3, 30, 120
Hirsau Abbey 182
Holy Sepulchre 54
Holy Spirit 23
  Eucharist and 4
  gifts of 25–6
  Pentecost 24, 25
Holy Trinity
  Calvin and 248
  rejection of 226, 248
  Trinitarianism 58
holy war 168–9

Homer 14
homosexuality 5
Honorius I (pope) 133
Hopkins, Keith 16
house churches 15
Hugh of Cluny 146
Hugh of Die 160
Hugh of St Cher 217
Huguenots 299, 300, 303, 304, 309
   see also Calvinism
Humane Studies 237
Humanism 234, 237, 238, 248, 261, 271,
   273, 276, 280, 281
   oratory 281, 282
   the purpose of learning 285
   rhetoric 281–2
   see also Erasmus
Humbert of Romans 217, 218
Humbert of Silva Candida, Cardinal 140,
   167
Humiliati (Humble Ones) 199, 202, 220,
   270
Hundred Years' War 252, 293, 299
Hus, Jan 231, 256, 268
Hussites 230, 231–2, 287
hypostasis 93, 99, 103

iconoclasm 136, 244, 263
Ignatius of Antioch 4, 25, 36, 57, 320–1
Ignatius Loyola 238, 264, 271, 275–6, 291
   Spiritual Exercises 276–7, 291
   vision at the River Cardona 276, 333
   see also Jesuits
Imitation of Christ 233, 281
immortality 4
incarnation, doctrine of 71–2, 83
incest 5, 6
indulgences 168–9, 246, 253, 286
   sale of 246, 253
industrialization 312, 315
Innocent I (pope) 134
Innocent II (pope) 171, 173, 182
Innocent III (pope) 151, 157, 159, 161, 164,
   173–4, 179, 201, 202–4, 206
   Francis of Assisi and 202, 208, 209
Innocent IV (pope) 153
Inquisition 204–5, 238, 261
   Cathars and 204, 205–6
   in Spain 260
Investiture Contest *see* lay investiture
Irenaeus 30, 131
   Against the Heresies 25
Isaac 10
Isabella (Queen of Castile and Aragon) 238,
   260–1
Islam 165–6, 168, 259

converts to Christianity 260
the Spanish *Reconquista* 260
Italy
   Protestantism in 261–2
   seminaries 274
itinerant preaching 178, 179, 197–8
   Dominicans 211
   Franciscans 208

James I (King of England) 305–6
James, letter of 268
James of Vitry 153
Jerome 37, 78, 119, 120
Jesuits 264, 275, 276–8
   education 277–8
   lay vocations 290
   papacy and 276
   in South America 284
   Spiritual Exercises 276–7, 291
   see also Ignatius Loyola
Jesus Christ
   in art 207
   baptism 2, 68
   birth 97–9
   Chalcedonian Definition 86, 89, 93, 99,
      102, 103, 104, 133, 324
   divinity/humanity of *see* christology
   identity of 86–104
   Judaism and 10
   kenosis 92, 98
   as *Logos* 11, 72, 91–2, 94–9, 108
   as *Logos-anthropos* 92, 94, 95
   as *Logos-sarx* 92, 94, 95, 96
   Peter and 24, 130–1, 135, 150, 173, 174
   relationship to God 58, 60
   resurrection 14, 72, 186
   selection of followers 21
   as Son of God 87, 90, 91, 94, 95, 96, 97,
      98, 99
   as Son of Man 87, 95, 97, 98
   washing the disciples' feet 24
Jews 8
   conversion to Christianity 21, 260
   revolts against Rome 11
   in Spain 260
   see also Judaism
Johann the Steadfast, Elector of Saxony 258
John
   the Apocalypse 26, 34
   Gospel of 34, 35, 91–2, 103, 131
John of Antioch 101
John the Baptist 26, 68, 113
John of the Cross 279
John of Lycopolis 80
John of Salisbury 153
Judaism

Christianity and   10–11, 13
  practices   14–15
  see also Jews
Julian the Apostate   15, 64
Julian of Eclanum   116
Julian of Norwich   232
Julius II (pope)   232
just wars   168
Justification by Faith Alone   242, 243, 246,
    251, 268, 271, 281, 291
  Council of Trent and   273, 333
  Erasmus on   284
Justin Martyr   5, 11, 30, 47, 90, 108, 214
  Apology   5, 319–20
  logos spermatikos   11, 214
Justinian (Eastern Roman Emperor)   133,
    152

Karlstadt, Andreas   247
Kempe, Margery   232
Kempis, Thomas à   233
  Imitation of Christ   233, 281
kings
  kingship   163, 174
  papacy and   163–4, 174
kiss of peace   4
koinonia   2–3, 28

Lambert, Malcolm   199, 200–1, 206, 231,
    267
Lancel, Serge   116
Lane Fox, Robin   9, 14, 15, 18
Langton, Stephen   32, 218
language   91–3
  Ancient Greek   235
  imagery, metaphor and analogy   90
  New Testament interpretation   90
  problems of   89–90, 101–2
  translating ancient texts   212–13, 234–7,
    280
Las Casas, Bartolome de   291
Last Supper   4, 24
Lateran Councils   270
  Fifth   270, 286
  Fourth   155, 187, 218, 270, 272, 274
  Third   157, 159, 198
Latin Vulgate   280, 281, 286
Lawrence, C. H.   188, 190, 211, 215, 216
lay investiture   142, 173
  Investiture Contest   148, 163, 293
lay spirituality   194, 196–201, 232–3
  Beguines   199
  Devotio Moderna   232–3, 276, 281, 291
  education   289–90
  Humiliati (Humble Ones)   199, 202, 220,
    270

Luther on   243
  mysticism   232, 238
  Priesthood of All Believers   243, 256
  Waldensians   197–9, 202–3, 208, 209
  women   199, 232
leadership   22–38
  charismatic   26
  hierarchy   23–4, 26
  see also authorities
Lent   3, 83–4
Leo I (pope)   99, 132, 134–5
  Tome of Leo   99, 100, 132
Leo III (Byzantine emperor)   136
Levellers   288
Levi, Anthony   281
Liberal Arts   213, 216, 236
Liberias, Bishop   133
Licinius   52, 53
literacy   287, 311
Little Flowers of St Francis   211
Little, Lester K.   181–2, 183
Liturgy of the Word   4
Livy   33
Logan, F. Donald   148
Logos   11, 72, 91–2, 94–9, 108
logos spermatikos   11, 214
Logos-anthropos   92, 94, 95
Logos-sarx   92, 94, 95, 96
Lollards   230–1, 264, 267, 287
  letter of James and   268
  Lutheranism and   268
  Zwingli and   268
Lombard League   156, 164, 179, 261
Lombard, Peter   213
Lord's Prayer   6
Louis XIII (King of France)   300
Louis XIV (King of France)   309
Luke   32, 33
  Gospel of   34, 37
Luther, Martin   225, 226, 228, 229, 232, 238,
    239–43, 255, 258, 267, 271, 291
  Augustine and   241, 242, 284
  authority of scripture   242–3
  on baptism   243
  biographies   240–1
  Diet of Worms   247
  Erasmus and   281, 284
  on the Eucharist   243, 244
  gift of faith   242
  grace   242, 243
  Justification by Faith Alone   242, 243, 246,
    251, 271, 273, 281, 284, 291
  on lay spirituality   243
  Lollardy and   268
  meeting with Zwingli   244
  Ninety-Five Theses   226, 246, 253, 261

Ockhamists and 241
papal bull 247
Paul and 241, 244
Priesthood of All Believers 243, 256
on the sacraments 243
Scholasticism and 241, 244
spiritual crisis 239
The Freedom of A Christian 246, 332
'Tower Experience' 241–2, 271, 281,
 292, 331
works by 246–7, 255, 285

MacCulloch, Diarmaid 259, 261, 291, 296
Majorinus 56
Manasses of Rheims, Archbishop 160
Mani 70
Manicheaeism 73, 81
 Augustine and 107, 108, 111–12, 113
 dualism 70, 73, 112, 200
Marcian 100
Marcion 37–8, 80
Marcus Aurelius 111
Margaret of Parma 298
Marillac, Louise de 279
Marius, Richard 240–1
Marius Victorinus 108
Mark, Gospel of 34, 37
market economy 195, 196
marriage 5–6, 83, 153
 bishops 140
 clerical 139–40, 289
 Council of Trent and 273
 early marriage 6
 freedom of choice 273
 re-marriage 5–6
 'spiritual marriage' 83
Marsilo of Padua 237
Martel, Charles 136
Martin, Bishop of Tours 84
Martin I (pope) 133
Martin V (pope) 229
martyrdom 2, 4, 18–19, 27, 28, 80, 81, 82
 Donatists 57, 81
 Henrician 271
 monasticism and 68
 Protestant martyrs 267, 288
 relics 55
 Thomas Becket 156
Mary I (Queen of England) 263, 264, 265,
 267
Mary, mother of Jesus 74
 birth of Jesus 98–9
 christology and 97–9
 christotakos 98
 Theotokos 98
Mass *see* Eucharist

materialism 67
Matilda of Tuscany, Countess 129, 144, 146
Matrix, The 315
Matthew 165
 Gospel of 34, 73
Matthias 22
Maurice of Saxony, Duke 255
Maxentius 50
Maximian 48, 50
Maximilian (Duke of Bavaria) 257, 259
Maximilian (Holy Roman Emperor) 252,
 253
Maximilla 26
Medici, Catherine di 299
Melitians 58, 80, 81
Melitius of Lycopolis 58
Melito of Sardis 47
mendicancy *see* begging
mendicant friars *see* friars
Merici, Angela 279
Merovingians 136, 174
Miani, Girolamo 278
Miltiades of Rome 56
Milton, John 269
miracles 20
missal, Tridentine missal of 1570 274–5,
 288
missionaries
 African missionaries 315
 Catholic 290–1
 early Christians 9, 19–20
monasticism 68–84, 239
 Antony and 74–8
 Augustine and 109, 122
 Carthusians 191–2
 celibacy 139
 charisma and 80
 Cistercians 184–91, 193
 Cluniacs 182–3
 Cluny Abbey 175, 182, 183
 coenobitic 78, 191
 the desert 68, 72, 74–8, 80, 183–4, 186–7,
  188
 dissolution of the monasteries in England
  263
 in Egypt 68–71, 74–9
 episcopal authority and 80–1
 feudalism and 138
 geographical location 75
 habits 185–6, 193
 Life of Antony 74, 75–7, 81
 literature 74–5, 81
 manual labour 183, 185
 martyrdom and 68
 new monasticism 180–94, 196, 201
 number of religious houses 154

Pachomian 78–9
the papacy and 153–4, 174–5
Protestant Reformation 290
regular canons 192–3
Rule of St Augustine 193, 202, 216
Rule of St Benedict 81, 180, 181, 183, 184, 185, 186, 191, 193, 202, 269, 328–9
sign language 186
silence 186
in Syria 68, 79, 80
vows 180
Wyclif on 230
young boys 181
money-lending 195
Dominicans and 219, 220
usury 195, 220
see also banking
Monophytism 99, 100, 104
monotheism 10
Montanism 26, 27, 38, 226
Montanus 26
Montefeltro, Fererigo, Duke of Urbino 282
Moonies 18, 20
More, Thomas 283
Utopia 283
Mormons 18, 20
Book of Mormon 38
mosaics 63, 64
Muhlberg, battle of 255
Mullett, Michael 257, 270, 272
Muntzer, Thomas 247
Mystery Cults 14
mysticism 232, 238, 279–80, 291

Nag Hammadi 30, 79
nation states 237–8
Natural Theology 312–13
Neri, Philip 271, 278, 291
Nestorians 104
Nestorius, Patriarch of Constantinople 93, 95, 98, 99, 100–1, 103, 104, 197
Netherlands 252, 300, 302
political revolt in 288, 296, 297–9, 303, 304
the Sea Beggars 288, 298, 304
war financing 303
New Testament
Acts of the Apostles 34, 172
authority of 31–8, 245
Calvin on 245
canon 38, 270
canonicity 35–8
Council of Florence and 38, 270
divine inspiration 35–6
division into chapters 32

John's Gospel 34, 35, 91–2, 103, 131
letter of James 268
letters of Paul 34, 36
Luke's Gospel 34, 37
Mark's Gospel 34, 37
Matthew's Gospel 34, 73
reform and 266, 270
Revelation/Apocalypse 26, 34, 36, 120
vernacular translations 230
Newman, John Henry 61, 111, 115
Nicaea, Council of 47, 60, 61, 79, 86, 92, 100, 155, 272
Nicene Creed 60, 86, 92, 103, 322
et filioque ('and the Son') 166–7
Nicholas of Cusa, Cardinal 232
Noah's Ark 10–11
Nonconformist communities 226
Norbert of Xanten 193
Norman princes 162–3

Ochino, Bernardino 278
Ockhamists 237, 241, 292
see also William of Ockham
O'Collins, Gerald 95
Oldcastle, Sir John 230–1
oracles 9, 26, 49, 109
see also prophetesses
Oratorians 271, 278
oratory 281, 282
Order of Preachers *see* Dominicans
Orders of Mendicant Friars 179
ordination 58
Origen 10, 12, 36, 47, 58, 77, 87, 90, 97, 120
christology 87, 90, 97
On First Principles 90
orthodoxy 28–31, 57, 70, 79, 81, 94, 102, 153
Ossius of Cordoba 56, 60
Otto of Freising 122
Otto I (Holy Roman Emperor) 137
Otto II (Holy Roman Emperor) 138
Otto IV (Holy Roman Emperor) 164
Ottoman Turks 228
Oxford Movement 313
Ozment, Steven 214, 263, 283, 285

Pachomian federation 188
Pachomian monasticism 78–9
Pachomius 68, 78, 79, 80, 81
pagan
meaning 49
Palladius 78
Palmieri, Matteo 236
papacy 130–77
allies 161–3

apostolic succession   25, 131, 134, 135,
   154, 173
authority   134, 173, 228, 229
Avignon papacy   228, 238
bishops and   160–1
bishops of Rome   129, 133, 134, 135, 136
Camera   157
Canon law   152–3, 168, 172
canonization   158
Chancery   157
Conciliarism   229, 256, 270
Consistory   157
Council of Trent and   274–5
Crusades and   156, 159, 160, 165–71
curia   156, 157–8, 159–60, 228, 275
Dictatus Papae   171–2, 327–8
eastern Church and   133–4
Ecumenical Councils and   155–6
empire and   136–7
feudalism and   137–41, 151
finances   164–5
the Great Schism   228–9, 238
Gregorian   129–30, 141–8, 150–75, 192,
   196, 197, 208, 266
Holy Roman Emperors and   129–30,
   136–7, 142–8, 159, 161, 232, 326
Jesuits and   276
kings and   163–4, 174
as law court   153
lay investiture/Investiture Contest   142,
   148, 163, 173, 293
legates   155, 156, 157, 159, 160
Luther and   247
monasticism and   153–4, 174–5
papal absences from Rome   159, 161
papal elections   157
papal government   151–8
'papal monarchy'   151, 170
papal protection   175
papal weaknesses   158–65
the Petrine office   130–5, 269, 292
power   135
reform   137–41, 168, 169, 171–5, 269
revenues   164–5
rival claimants   140
schisms   159, 167, 228–9, 230
'servant of the servants of God'   135, 174
theory of the two swords   135
title of 'pope'   136
tradition and custom   171
'vicar of Christ'   135, 151
vicar of St Peter'   151
Wyclif on   230
Papal States   161
Paris, Matthew   217
Parker, Geoffrey   309

Parma, Duke of   299
Paschal II (pope)   154
Pastoral Letters   29
Pataria, the   197
Patriarchates   132, 166–7
Paul   1, 6, 9, 10, 14, 21, 22, 24, 26, 28–9, 51,
   61, 68, 82, 111, 112, 131–2, 139, 288
   on athletes   71
   before conversion   11
   charisma   26
   community and   3
   on Jesus   87, 92
   on language   89
   letters   34, 36
   Luther and   241, 244
   relics   132, 173
Paul III (pope)   275, 276
Paul of Samosata, Bishop of Antioch   88
Peace of Augsburg   257, 297
Peace of God movement   167–8, 181
Peasants' War 1524–5   248, 257, 288
Pelagians   115–17, 241, 273
Pelagius   115
penance   6, 88, 130, 146, 147, 204, 218, 291
   in Erasmus's translation of the Bible   281
   in the Latin Vulgate   281
Pentecost   3, 24, 25
Pepin   136, 137, 161, 174
Perpetua   28
persecution   27, 28, 49, 57, 113
Peter   15, 130–2, 141, 154, 257
   apostolic succession   25, 131, 134, 135,
      154, 173
   Jesus and   24, 130–1, 135, 150, 173, 174
   relics   132, 173
Peter, Bishop of Alexandria   58
Peter the Venerable   190
Petrarch   237
Petrarch, Francesco   235
Philip the Fair (King of France)   228
Philip of Hesse   254
Philip I (King of France)   169
Philip II (King of France)   160
Phillip II (King of Spain)   259, 260, 295, 298,
   299, 300, 302, 303, 304
Philo   91
'philosopher-kings'   282
philosophy   11–12, 14
   Aristotlean   13, 214, 219, 230, 233
   Cartesian doubt   312
   christology and   90–9
   Cynics   10, 11
   Pythagorean   11
   see also Hellenism; Plato; Platonism;
      Stoicism
Piacenza, Council of   169

Pico della Mirandola, Giovanni
  Oration on the Dignity of Man 237, 281, 284
pilgrimages 54, 55, 169
Pisa, Council of 229
Pius II (pope) 229, 232, 270, 271
Plato 33, 70, 103, 122, 280
  Republic 282, 283
  Timaeus 13, 281
Platonism 10, 12, 13, 77, 91, 103, 214, 237
  Augustine and 108, 112, 122, 214
  divinity 93–4
  evil 112
Pliny the Younger 87
Plotinus 108
Poor Catholics 203
Poor Men of Lyons 198
Porphyry 108
practical Christianity 21
Pragmatic Sanction of Bourges 238
predestination 316
  Augustine of Hippo on 116–17
  Calvin and 244–5
  Erasmus and 284
  Luther and 242
Premonstratensians 193
Prierias, Sylvester 246
Priesthood of All Believers 243, 256
Prim, Bernard 203
printing
  Reformation and 285–9
Prisca 26
prophetesses 80
  see also oracles
Protagoras 237
protest movements 196–7
Protestant Reformation 225, 226, 229, 232,
    238, 239–68
  aims of 289–90
  education 289–90
  in England 263–6
  events 246–9
  in Germany 262–3
  Habsburg-Valois conflict and 252–8,
    292–3, 296, 297–9, 304, 305, 309
  in Italy 261–2
  national contexts 258–66
  princely conversions 258–9, 268
  printing and 285–8
  similarities with Catholic Reformation
    289–93
  in Spain 260–1
  see also Calvin; Luther; Zwingli
Proust, Marcel 111
Pulcheria 100
Puritans 283–4
Pythagorean philosophy 11

Radcliffe, Timothy 315
radical poverty 179, 200
Radical Reformation 226, 267, 286
Rahner, Karl 103
Raymond IV of Toulouse, Count 200–1
Raymond of Pennaforte 152
re-baptism 31, 56
  Anabaptists 226, 247–8
re-marriage 5–6
reason 311–12
'rebirth', concept of 280
recreation 96
Reformation 225, 238–9
  Catholic 225, 227, 257, 266–80, 288
  English Reformation 263–6
  events 246–9
  Habsburg-Valois conflict and 252–8,
    292–3, 296, 297–9, 304, 305, 309
  in Italy 261–2
  national contexts 258–66
  personalities and ideas 239–45
  princely conversions 258–9
  printing and 285–9
  Protestant *see* Protestant Reformation
  Radical 226, 267, 286
  Renaissance and 280–5
  in Spain 260–1
  translations of the Bible 280–1
Regensburg, Diet of 255, 292
regular canons 192–3
  manual labour 193
  number of houses 193
  Premonstratensians 193
  Rule of St Augustine 193
  White Canons 193
relics 55, 132, 173, 253
religious Orders
  Capuchins 278
  Carmelites 279–80
  Clerks Regular of St Paul (Barnabites) 278
  Congregation of the Daughters of Charity
    279
  Congregation of the Oratory (Oratorians)
    271, 278
  female Orders 279–80
  Premonstratensians 193
  regular canons 192–3
  Society of the Servants of the Poor
    (Somaschi) 278
  Theatines 278
  Ursulines 279
  see also Carthusians; Cistercians; Francis-
    cans; friars; Jesuits
Religious Peace of Augsburg 257, 297
Renaissance 212–13, 234–5, 271, 311
  Bible translations 280–1

Humane Studies 237
  new curriculum 236–7
  painters 283
  'philosopher-kings' 282
  printing and 285–9
  Reformation and 280–5
  translating ancient texts 212–13, 234–7,
    280
  see also Humanism
repentance, necessity for 6
resurrection
  doctrine of 71
  of Jesus Christ 14, 72, 186
Revelation 36, 120
rhetoric 281–2
Richard I (King of England) 160
Richelieu, Armand, Cardinal, Duc de 259,
    300, 301, 304, 305, 332
Riley-Smith, Jonathan 170
Robert of Arbrissel 184
Roberts, Michael 297
Robinson, I.S. 145–6, 148, 154, 171, 174–5
Roger II (King of Sicily) 163
Roman Empire 39–40
  Christianity and 1–2, 7–15, 17–18, 47–65
  early marriage 6
  exposure of newborns 6
  gods 8, 9, 17, 18, 48, 49, 119
  Jewish revolts 11
  missionaries 9
  oracles 9, 49
  paganism 49
  persecution of Christians 27, 28, 49
  population 7
  religion in 8–9, 17, 18, 22
  sack of Rome 118–19, 121, 234, 256
  sexual practices 5
  shrines 9
  size 7
Roman law 152, 153, 219, 220
Romanticism 239, 313
Rome
  basilicas 54
  refashioning 275, 284, 290
  sack of 118–19, 121, 234, 256
  St Peter's Basilica 246, 275
Rousseau, Philip 5, 102
Rubenson, Samuel 77, 78
Rudolf of Swabia 145
Rule of St Augustine 193, 202, 216
Rule of St Benedict 81, 180, 181, 183, 184,
    185, 186, 191, 193, 202, 269, 328–9
Runciman, Sir Stephen 167

Sabatier, Paul 210
Sacchoni, Ranier 205

sacraments 280
  Council of Florence and 270
  Luther on 243
sacrifice 14, 49
Sagan, Carl 316
St Bartholomew's Day Massacre 299, 303,
    304
St Peter's Basilica 246, 275
saints *see* canonization
salvation 54–5, 71, 87, 96
  universal 117
San Damiano 207
Savonarola, Girolamo 271
Scarisbrick, J.J. 264, 266
Schmalkaldic League 254, 255, 297
Scholasticism 206, 213, 214, 218, 219
  dialectical method 235, 236
  Eucharist and 244
  later Scholastics 233, 234
  Liberal Arts 213, 216, 236
  Luther and 241, 244
  methodology 213, 235, 236, 241, 244,
    280
  'new' Scholastics 285
  Renaissance and 235, 236–7
  Wyclif and 230
Schwartz, Eduard 61
science 316
science fiction 315–16
scriptural authority 242–3, 256–7, 280,
    286–7
  the New Testament 31–8, 245
Sea Beggars 288, 298, 304
Second Vatican Council 1962–5 272, 314
Second World War 314
seminaries 274, 289
serfdom 138
Servetus, Michael 248
Severus 50
sexual morality 5
  of the clergy 289
sexual renunciation 73, 74, 80, 83, 84
  see also celibacy; virginity
Shenoute 78
shrines
  Roman 9
sign language 186
Simeon 79, 189
Simon Magus 139
simony 139, 142, 192
Simplicianus 108
Society of Jesus *see* Jesuits
Society of the Servants of the Poor (Somaschi)
    278
Socrates 9
Somaschi 278

Spain 260–1
  the Armada 295, 303, 304
  Ferdinand and Isabella 238, 260–1
  impact of war on 308
  the Inquisition 260
  Jews in 260
  Phillip II 259, 260, 295, 298, 299, 300,
    302, 303, 304
  Protestantism in 260, 261
  Reconquista 260
  seminaries 274
  war 295, 298, 302–3
speaking in tongues 23, 26
Speyer, Diet of 254
'spiritual marriage' 83
Stark, Rodney 16, 17, 20
Stephen of Bourbon 218
Stephen of Muret 184
Stephen of Rome 31, 56, 134
stigmata 209–10, 280, 329–30
Stoicism 10, 11, 12, 68
  asceticism 71
  christology and 91, 93, 96
Summa Theologiae 214, 285, 330–1
Suso, Henry 232
Sweden, wars 295–6, 300, 303, 306
Synods 141, 154–5, 157
  Calvinist 299
  Council of Trent and 274
  Pavia 140
  Rome 141, 154, 155
  Seville 238, 261
  Sutri 140, 154
Synoptic Gospels 34, 35

Tacitus 33
Tallett, Frank 296, 302, 304, 308
Tatian 80
Tauler, John 232
Teaching of the Twelve Apostles 27
technology
  industrialization 312, 315
  war and 301–2, 309, 314
Tellenbach, Gerd 138, 139, 269
Teresa of Avila 111, 275, 279–80
Tertullian 12, 18–19, 26, 30, 38, 56, 99, 112,
    120, 226, 267, 317
Tetzel, Johan 246, 253
textiles
  Cistercians and 189
Theatines 278
Theodore of Mopsuestia 79, 88–9, 103
Theodoret 102
Theodosius I 53, 64, 118, 119
Theodosius II 100
Theophilus of Alexandria 101

theory of the two swords 135, 325
Thienne, Gaetano di 278
Third Orders 220
Thirty Years' War 295, 296, 300–1, 304,
    308, 309
Thirty-Nine Articles of Religion 263, 272
Thomas 14
  Gospel of 35, 37
Thomas of Celano 210
Thucyddides 33
Tierney, Brian 173
Tillman, Helene 174
Tome of Leo 99, 100, 132
Torquemada, Tomas de 260
'Tower Experience' of Martin Luther 241–2,
    271, 281, 292, 331
Tracy, James D. 266, 269, 289, 296
trade 195, 312
tradition 29, 39, 102–3
training of clergy 261, 274, 289
Trajan 87
transubstantiation 230
Treaty of Prague 301
Treaty of Westphalia 301, 309
Trent, Council of 229, 261, 270, 272–4, 333
  bishops 273
  doctrinal decrees 272–3
  the Eucharist 273
  goods works, importance of 273
  importance of 272
  Justification by Faith 273, 333
  matrimony 273
  parish clergy 274
  pastoral decrees 273–4
  religious Orders 275
  Synods 274
  training of clergy 274
  Tridentine missal 1570 274–5, 288
  women 273
Tridentine missal 1570 274–5, 288
Trinitarianism 58
Truce of God movement 167, 168, 169, 181
Tugwell, Simon 216
Twelfth-Century Renaissance *see* Renaissance
Tyconius 120

Ugolino, Cardinal 209
Ullmann, Walter 153, 159, 161
Union of Utrecht 298
Unitarians 226
universities 210, 212, 216, 311
  clerical education 261, 289
  Fifth Lateran Council and 270
Urban II (pope) 154–5, 157, 163, 167, 182,
    191
  First Crusade 169–70, 326–7

Urban VI (pope) 228
Ursulines 279
Uses of Sarum, York and Hereford 274
usury 195, 220
    see also money-lending

Valerian 17, 19
Valla, Lorenzo 235–6
vegetarianism 70
vernacular Bibles 230, 286, 287
'vicars of Christ'
    kings as 163
    popes as 135, 151
Vigilius, Bishop 133
Vikings 179
Vincent de Paul 279
Virgil 111, 117
Virgin Mary *see* Mary, mother of Jesus
virginity 68, 73–4, 82
    Athanasius on 83
Vitruvius 236
Vitry, Jacques de 208
vows 168
    monastic 180
Vulgate, the 280, 281, 286

Waldensians 197–9, 202–3, 208, 209, 267,
    270
    Calvinism and 267–8
Waldes, Peter 197, 198
Wallenstein, Albrecht von 300, 304, 307
war 165–6, 259, 295–309
    Augustine on 168
    Battle of Muhlberg 255
    Canon law 168
    demographic impact 308
    early modern warfare 297–303
    family and dynastic prestige 305–6
    financial costs of 302–3
    'Fire Money' 306
    Habsburg-Valois conflict and 252–8,
        292–3, 296, 297–9
    holy war 168–9
    Hundred Years' War 252, 293, 299
    impact of 308–9
    interest rates and 302–3
    just wars 168
    mercenaries 301–2
    motivations for fighting 296, 303–7, 309
    the Netherlands 252, 288, 296, 297–9,
        300, 302, 303, 304
    Peasants' War 1524–5 248, 257, 288

plunder, booty and ransom 306–7
recruitment of soldiers 301, 306
Religious Peace of Augsburg 257, 297
soldiers of fortune 301–2
Spain 295, 298, 302–3
technological and tactical innovations
    301–2, 309, 314
Thirty Years' War 295, 296, 300–1, 304,
    308, 309
'Wars of Religion' 296, 300, 303, 307,
    309
Waugh, Evelyn 111
White Canons 193
William I (King of England) 164
William II (King of the Normans) 163
William of Nassau, Prince of Orange 298
William of Ockham 233, 234, 241
    see also Ockhamists
William of Orange (William III, King of
    England) 295, 298, 304
Williams, David H. 188
Williams, Rowan 103
Wittelsbach, House of 254, 257, 258
women 5
    Beguines 199
    Christianity and 5, 21
    converts 21
    Council of Trent and 273
    lay spirituality 199, 232
    mysticism 232, 279–80
    prophetesses 80
    religious Orders 279–80
    widows 6, 80
wool 189
Worms, Diet of 247
Wyclif (or Wycliffe), John 230, 231, 233,
    267

Xenophon 10
Ximenes, Francisco, Cardinal 261, 271

Young, Frances 98, 101, 102

Zaccaria, Antonio Maria 278
Zosimus (pope) 134
Zwingli, Ulrich (or Hulderich) 226, 243–4,
    247–8, 282
    death of 248
    on the Eucharist 244, 263
    Lollardy and 268
    meeting with Luther 244